INTRODUCTION TO MANAGEMENT ACCOUNTING

HORNGREN

SUNDEM

STRATTON

**SPECIAL EDITION FOR
MICHIGAN STATE UNIVERSITY**

Taken from
Introduction to Management Accounting, Twelfth Edition
by Charles T. Horngren, Gary L. Sundem, and William O. Stratton

PEARSON
Custom
Publishing

PEARSON
Prentice
Hall

Cover Art: *Twisti 1*, by Barry Cronin.

Taken from:

Introduction to Management Accounting, Twelfth Edition
by Charles T. Horngren, Gary L. Sundem, and William O. Stratton
Copyright © 2002 Pearson Education, Inc.
Published by Prentice-Hall, Inc.
Upper Saddle River, New Jersey 07458

This special edition published in cooperation with Pearson Custom Publishing.

Printed in the United States of America

10 9 8 7 6 5 4 3 2 1

ISBN 0-536-74825-X

BA 997934

JA

Please visit our web site at *www.pearsoncustom.com*

PEARSON CUSTOM PUBLISHING
75 Arlington Street, Suite 300, Boston, MA 02116
A Pearson Education Company

BRIEF CONTENTS

All Material Taken from:
Introduction to Management Accounting, Twelfth Edition
by Charles T. Horngren, Gary L. Sundem, and William O. Stratton

1

MANAGERIAL ACCOUNTING & THE BUSINESS ORGANIZATION

Managers at companies work closely with accountants. The accounting system crunches the numbers that these managers need for daily decision making.

www.prenhall.com/horngren

Learning Objectives

When you have finished studying this chapter, you should be able to

1. Describe the major users of accounting information.

2. Explain the cost-benefit and behavioral issues involved in designing an accounting system.

3. Explain the role of budgets and performance reports in planning and control.

4. Discuss the role accountants play in the company's value chain functions.

5. Contrast the functions of controllers and treasurers.

6. Identify current trends in management accounting.

7. Explain a management accountant's ethical responsibilities.

8. **Understand how managerial accounting is used in companies.***

The Internet is hot, hot, hot! One recent study revealed that the Internet economy grew to more than $525 billion in 2000, and now directly supports 2.5 million workers. Businesses are scrambling to establish virtual stores. Educational institutions now offer virtual degrees and certifications And with the click of a mouse, in an instant anyone can find music, e-mail, news articles, and more! Soon we'll be able to access the Internet wherever and whenever we want, for any purpose at all. There's no question that this economy is unlike any we've ever seen. Yet it couldn't exist without the services and products of companies like Cisco Systems.

Cisco is the worldwide leader in networking for the Internet. The company's router products connect people, computers, and computer networks around the globe and help form the infrastructure for the Internet. Cisco shipped its first products in 1986 and has seen its annual revenues explode to over $12 billion in the most recent fiscal year. Last year alone the company acquired 15 smaller firms to fuel its growth and today shows no sign of slowing down. How does Cisco keep track of it all? Accounting systems do the heavy job of "crunching" all the transaction details, yet there are analysts, accountants, and staff operating those systems each day. Managers at all levels rely on the information those systems provide for daily decision making, budgeting, and planning. And since Cisco is a publicly held company, the accounting systems and employees must be prepared to generate financial reports quickly and accurately for use by external decision makers around the globe.

---

* The last learning objective in each chapter is an overall objective It stresses the importance of understanding the material covered throughout the chapter; therefore, it is not identified at a specific point in the text

As you embark on your journey into the world of managerial accounting, you'll discover what it takes for a company like Cisco to be able to manage its financial activities and make decisions with ease. And keep this in mind: Every business that's part of the Internet economy has traveled the same path, and manages the same set of accounting information.

Just as the case at Cisco, managerial accounting can help managers in all types of organizations answer vital questions. Consider questions raised in the following situations:

- Boeing engineers have prepared manufacturing specifications for a new airplane, the 747-X. There are three possible ways to organize the assembly of the plane. Which is the most cost-effective approach?

- A product manager at Kellogg's is designing a new marketing plan for Frosted Flakes. Market research predicts that distributing free samples in the mail will increase annual sales by 4%. How will the cost of the free samples (including the cost of distributing them) compare with the profits from the added sales?

- University National Bank offers free checking to customers who keep a minimum balance of $600 in their account. How much does it cost the bank to provide this free service?

- Kitsap County Special Olympics holds a series of athletic events for disabled youth. How much money must be raised in the group's annual fund drive to support its planned activities?

- Chez Bonaparte is a dinner-only restaurant located in a middle-class neighborhood. The proprietor is considering opening for lunch. To be competitive, the average lunch must be priced about $7, and about 40 patrons can be served. Can the restaurant produce a lunch that meets its quality standards at an average cost of less than $7?

- The Monroe County School District is negotiating with the teachers' union. Among the issues are teachers' salaries, class size, and number of extracurricular activities offered. The union and the district have both made several proposals. How much will each of the various proposals cost? If class size were to increase by one student per class, what would be the added cost, and would these costs differ for elementary, junior high, and high school levels?

In answering these and a wide variety of other questions, managers turn to management accountants for information. In this chapter, we consider the purposes and roles of accounting and accountants in different types of organizations as well as some of the trends and challenges faced by accountants today.

ACCOUNTING AND DECISION MAKING

The basic purpose of accounting information is helping someone make decisions. That someone may be a company president, a production manager, a hospital or school administrator, an investor—the list could go on and on. Regardless of who is making the decision, the understanding of accounting information allows for a more informed, and better, decision.

USERS OF ACCOUNTING INFORMATION

In general, users of accounting information fall into three categories.

1. Internal managers who use the information for short-term planning and controlling routine operations.
2. Internal managers who use the information for making nonroutine decisions (for example, investing in equipment, pricing products and services, choosing which products to emphasize or de-emphasize) and formulating overall policies and long-range plans.
3. External parties, such as investors and government authorities, who use the information for making decisions about the company.

Both internal parties (managers) and external parties use accounting information, but the ways in which they use it differ. The types of accounting information they demand may also differ. Management accounting refers to accounting information developed for managers within an organization. In other words, **management accounting** is the process of identifying, measuring, accumulating, analyzing, preparing, interpreting, and communicating information that helps managers fulfill organizational objectives. In contrast, **financial accounting** refers to accounting information developed for the use of external parties such as stockholders, suppliers, banks, and government regulatory agencies.[1] The major differences between management accounting and financial accounting are listed in Exhibit 1-1. Despite these differences, most organizations prefer a general-purpose accounting system that meets the needs of all three types of users.

What are the needs or uses? Good accounting information helps an organization achieve its goals and objectives by helping to answer three types of questions.

1. *Scorecard questions:* Am I doing well or poorly? **Scorekeeping** is the accumulation and classification of data. This aspect of accounting enables both internal and external parties to evaluate organizational performance.
2. *Attention-directing questions:* Which problems should I look into? **Attention directing** means reporting and interpreting information that helps managers to focus on operating problems, imperfections, inefficiencies, and opportunities. Attention directing is commonly associated with current planning and control, and with the analysis and investigation of recurring routine internal accounting reports.
3. *Problem-solving questions:* Of the several ways of doing a job, which is the best? The **problem-solving** aspect of accounting quantifies the likely results of possible courses of action and often recommends the best course to follow.

The scorecard and attention-directing uses of information are closely related. The same information may serve a scorecard function for a manager and an attention-directing function for the manager's superior. For example, many accounting systems provide performance reports in which actual results of decisions and activities are compared with previously determined plans. By pinpointing where actual results differ from plans, such performance reports can show managers how they are doing and show the managers' superiors where to take action.

In contrast, problem-solving information may be used in long-range planning and in making special, nonrecurring decisions, such as whether to make or buy parts, replace equipment, or add or drop a product. These decisions often require expert advice from specialists such as industrial engineers, budgetary accountants, and statisticians.

---

[1] *For a book-length presentation of the subject, see Charles T Horngren, Gary L Sundem, and John A. Elliott,* Introduction to Financial Accounting *(Upper Saddle River, NJ: Prentice Hall, 2001), the companion to this textbook*

Objective 1
Describe the major users of accounting information.

management accounting The process of identifying, measuring, accumulating, analyzing, preparing, interpreting, and communicating information that helps managers fulfill organizational objectives.

financial accounting The field of accounting that develops information for external decision makers such as stockholders, suppliers, banks, and government regulatory agencies.

scorekeeping The accumulation and classification of data.

attention directing Reporting and interpreting information that helps managers to focus on operating problems, imperfections, inefficiencies, and opportunities.

problem solving The aspect of accounting that quantifies the likely results of possible courses of action and often recommends the best course of action to follow.

Exhibit 1-1

Distinctions Between Management Accounting and Financial Accounting

	Management Accounting	Financial Accounting
Primary users	Organization managers at various levels.	Outside parties such as investors and government agencies but also organization managers.
Freedom of choice	No constraints other than costs in relation to benefits of improved management decisions.	Constrained by generally accepted accounting principles (GAAP).
Behavioral implications	Concern about how measurements and reports will influence managers' daily behavior.	Concern about how to measure and communicate economic phenomena. Behavioral considerations are secondary, although executive compensation based on reported results may have behavioral impacts.
Time focus	Future orientation: formal use of budgets as well as historical records, Example: 20X2 budget versus 20X2 actual performance.	Past orientation: historical evaluation. Example: 20X2 actual performance versus 20X1 actual performance.
Time span	Flexible, varying from hourly to 10 to 15 years.	Less flexible; usually 1 year or 1 quarter.
Reports	Detailed reports: concern about details of parts of the entity, products, departments, territories, etc.	Summary reports: concern primarily with entity as a whole.
Delineation of activities	Field is less sharply defined. Heavier use of economics, decision sciences, and behavioral sciences.	Field is more sharply defined. Lighter use of related disciplines.

ACCOUNTING SYSTEMS

accounting system A formal mechanism for gathering, organizing, and communicating information about an organization's activities.

An **accounting system** is a formal mechanism for gathering, organizing, and communicating information about an organization's activities. Using one accounting system for both financial and management purposes sometimes creates problems. External forces (for example, income tax authorities and regulatory bodies such as the U.S. Securities and Exchange Commission and the California Health Facility Commission) often limit management's choices of accounting methods for external reports. Many organizations develop systems primarily to satisfy legal requirements imposed by external parties. These systems often neglect the needs of internal users.

generally accepted accounting principles (GAAP) Broad concepts or guidelines and detailed practices, including all conventions, rules, and procedures, that together make up accepted accounting practice at a given time.

Consider the annual financial reports by public corporations. These reports must adhere to a set of standards known as **generally accepted accounting principles (GAAP).** GAAP includes broad concepts or guidelines and detailed practices, including all conventions, rules, and procedures, that together make up accepted accounting practice at a given time. However, internal accounting reports need not be restricted by GAAP. For instance, GAAP requires that organizations account for their assets (economic resources) according to their historical cost. For its own management purposes, however, an organization can account for its economic resources on the basis of their current values, as measured by estimates of replacement costs. No outside agency can prohibit such accounting. Managers can create whatever kind of internal accounting system they want—provided they are willing to pay the cost of developing and operating the system.

Of course, satisfying internal demands for information (as well as external demands) means that organizations may have to keep more than one set of records. At least in the United States, there is nothing immoral or unethical about having simultaneous sets of books—but they are expensive. Because external financial reports are required by authorities, many organizations do not choose to invest in a separate system for internal management purposes. Managers are thus forced to use information designed to meet external users' needs instead of information designed for their specific decisions.

EFFECTS OF GOVERNMENT REGULATION

Even when management is willing to pay for a separate internal accounting system, that system may be affected by government regulation. The reason is that government agencies have legal power to order into evidence any internal document that they deem necessary.

Universities and defense contractors, for example, must allocate costs to government contracts in specified ways or risk government's refusal to pay. For example, in a widely publicized case in the early 1990s, Stanford University and several other prominent universities were denied reimbursement for certain costs that the government deemed inappropriate.

The **Foreign Corrupt Practices Act** is a U.S. law forbidding bribery and other corrupt practices. This law also requires that accounting records be maintained in reasonable detail and accuracy, and that an appropriate system of internal accounting controls be maintained. The title is misleading because the act's provisions apply to all publicly held companies, even if they conduct no business outside the United States.

> **Foreign Corrupt Practices Act** U.S. law forbidding bribery and other corrupt practices, and requiring that accounting records be maintained in reasonable detail and accuracy, and that an appropriate system of internal accounting controls be maintained.

The greatest impact of the act on accounting systems stems from the requirement that management must document the adequacy of internal accounting controls. As a result, many companies have greatly increased their internal auditing staffs and have elevated the status of such staffs. Often the internal audit staff reports directly to the president, sometimes even to the board of directors.

Internal auditors help review and evaluate systems to help minimize errors, fraud, and waste. More important, many internal auditing staffs have a primary responsibility for conducting management audits. A **management audit** is a review to determine whether the policies and procedures specified by top management have been implemented. Management audits are not confined to profit-seeking organizations. The General Accounting Office (GAO) of the U.S. government conducts these audits on a massive scale. Most states also have audit agencies that audit departments of state government. Some also audit municipalities and other local government organizations.

> **management audit** A review to determine whether the policies and procedures specified by top management have been implemented.

The overall impact of government regulation is very controversial. Many managers insist that the extra costs of compliance far exceed any possible benefits. One benefit, however, is that operating managers, now more than ever, must become more intimately familiar with their accounting systems. The resulting changes in the systems sometimes provide stronger controls and more informative reports.

The scorekeeping, attention-directing, and problem-solving duties of the accountant are described in this chapter. The accountant's usefulness to management is said to be directly influenced by how good an attention director and problem solver he or she is. We can evaluate this contention by specifically relating the accountant's duties to the duties of operating management. Operating managers may have to be good scorekeepers, but their major duties are to concentrate on the day-to-day problems that need the most attention, to make longer-range plans, and to arrive at special decisions. Accordingly, because managers are concerned mainly with attention directing and problem solving, they will obtain the most benefit from the alert internal accountant who is a useful attention director and problem solver.

MANAGEMENT ACCOUNTING IN SERVICE AND NONPROFIT ORGANIZATIONS

The basic ideas of management accounting were developed in manufacturing organizations. These ideas, however, have evolved so that they apply to all types of organizations including service organizations. Service organizations, for our purposes, are all organizations other than manufacturers, wholesalers, and retailers. That is, they are organizations that do not make or sell tangible goods. Public accounting firms, law firms, management consultants, real estate firms, transportation companies, banks, insurance companies, and hotels are profit-seeking service organizations.

Almost all nonprofit organizations, such as hospitals, schools, libraries, museums, and government agencies, are also service organizations. Managers and accountants in nonprofit organizations have much in common with their counterparts in profit-seeking organizations. There is money to be raised and spent. There are budgets to be prepared and control systems to be designed and implemented. There is an obligation to use resources wisely. If used intelligently, accounting contributes to efficient operations and helps nonprofit organizations achieve their objectives.

The characteristics of both profit-seeking and nonprofit service organizations include the following:

1. *Labor is intensive:* The highest proportion of expenses in schools and law firms are wages, salaries, and payroll-related costs, not the costs relating to the use of machinery, equipment, and physical facilities.

2. *Output is usually difficult to define:* The output of a university might be defined as the number of degrees granted, but many critics would maintain that the real output is "what is contained in the students' brains." Therefore, measuring output is often considered impossible.

3. *Major inputs and outputs cannot be stored:* An empty airline seat cannot be saved for a later flight, and a hotel's available labor force and rooms are either used or unused as each day occurs.

Simplicity is the watchword for installation of systems in service industries and nonprofit organizations. In fact, many professionals such as physicians, professors, or government officials resist even filling out a time card. In fact, simplicity is a fine watchword for the design of any accounting system. Complexity tends to generate costs of gathering and interpreting data that often exceed prospective benefits. Concern for simplicity is sometimes expressed as KISS (which means "keep it simple, stupid," or, better yet, "keep it simple for success").

COST-BENEFIT AND BEHAVIORAL CONSIDERATIONS

In addition to simplicity, managers should keep two other ideas in mind when designing accounting systems: (1) cost-benefit balances and (2) behavioral implications.

cost-benefit balance
Weighing estimated costs against probable benefits, the primary consideration in choosing among accounting systems and methods.

The **cost-benefit balance**—weighing estimated costs against probable benefits—is the primary consideration in choosing among accounting systems and methods. Therefore, we will refer again and again to cost-benefit considerations throughout this book. For now, consider accounting systems to be economic goods—like office supplies or labor—available at various costs. Which system does a manager want to buy? A simple file drawer for amassing receipts and canceled checks? An elaborate budgeting system based on computerized models of the organization and its subunits? Or something in between?

The answer depends on the buyer's perceptions of the expected benefits in relation to the costs. For example, a hospital administrator may consider installing a ConTrol®-computerized system made by Advanced Medical Systems for controlling hospital operations.

Users of such a system need only enter a piece of information once and the system automatically incorporates it into *budgeting, purchasing, and payables records*. Such a system is highly efficient and is subject to few errors, but it costs $300,000. Is the ConTrol® system a good buy? That depends on its expected benefit. If its value to the hospital is greater than $300,000, then it is a good buy. If not, the administrator should consider another accounting system.

Objective 2
Explain the cost-benefit and behavioral issues involved in designing an accounting system.

The value of a loaf of bread may exceed a cost of $0.50 a loaf, but it may not exceed a cost of $5 per loaf. Similarly, a particular accounting system may be a wise investment if its cost is sufficiently small. Like a consumer who switches from bread to potatoes if the cost of bread is too high, managers seek other sources of information if accounting systems are too expensive. In many organizations it may be more economical to gather some kinds of data by one-shot special efforts than by a ponderous system that repetitively gathers rarely used data.

In addition to the costs and benefits of an accounting system, the buyer of such a system should also consider **behavioral implications,** that is, the system's effect on the behavior (decisions) of managers. The system must provide accurate, timely budgets and performance reports in a form useful to managers. If managers do not use accounting reports, the reports create no benefits.

behavioral implications
The accounting system's effect on the behavior (decisions) of managers.

Management accounting reports affect employees' feelings and behavior. Consider a performance report that is used to evaluate the operations under the responsibility of a particular manager. If the report unfairly attributes excessive costs to the operation, the manager may lose confidence in the system and not let it influence future decisions. In contrast, a system that managers believe in and trust can be a major influence on their decisions and actions.

In a nutshell, management accounting can best be understood as a balance between costs and benefits of accounting information coupled with an awareness of the importance of behavioral effects. Even more than financial accounting, management accounting spills over into related disciplines, such as economics, the decision sciences, and the behavioral sciences.

THE MANAGEMENT PROCESS AND ACCOUNTING

Regardless of the type of organization, managers benefit when accounting provides information that helps them plan and control the organization's operations.

THE NATURE OF PLANNING AND CONTROLLING

The management process is a series of activities in a cycle of planning and control. **Decision making**—the purposeful choice from among a set of alternative courses of action designed to achieve some objective—is the core of the management process. Decisions range from the routine (making daily production schedules) to the nonroutine (launching a new product line).

decision making The purposeful choice from among a set of alternative courses of action designed to achieve some objective.

Decisions within an organization are often divided into two types: (1) planning decisions and (2) control decisions. In practice, planning and control are so intertwined that it seems artificial to separate them. In studying management, however, it is useful to concentrate on either the planning phase or the control phase to simplify the analysis.

The left side of Exhibit 1-2 demonstrates the planning and control cycle of current operations for The Chop House restaurant in Colorado Springs. Planning (the top box) refers to setting objectives and outlining how they will be attained. Thus, planning provides the answers to two questions: What is desired? When and how is it to be accomplished? For The Chop House, management desires to improve profitability. This will be accomplished by adding new entrees and improving advertising. In contrast, controlling (the box labeled "Actions" and "Evaluation") refers to implementing plans and using

Objective 3
Explain the role of budgets and performance reports in planning and control.

Exhibit 1-2

The Chop House Restaurant. Accounting Framework for Planning and Control

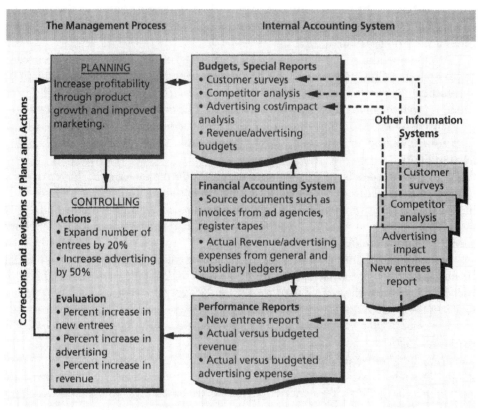

feedback to attain objectives. The Chop House will expand its menu offerings and expand advertising. The effectiveness of these actions will be evaluated based on selected performance measures such as the percent increase in new entrees. Feedback is crucial to the cycle of planning and control. Planning determines action, action generates feedback, and feedback influences further planning and actions. Timely, systematic reports provided by the internal accounting system are the chief source of useful feedback. None of this cycle would be possible without accounting.

MANAGEMENT BY EXCEPTION

budget A quantitative expression of a plan of action, and an aid to coordinating and implementing the plan.

The right side of Exhibit 1-2 shows that accounting formalizes plans by expressing them as budgets. A **budget** is a quantitative expression of a plan of action. The Chop House would express its plan for product growth and improved marketing through revenue and advertising budgets. Budgets are also an aid to coordinating and implementing plans. Budgets are the chief devices for compelling and disciplining management planning. Without budgets, planning may not get the front-and-center focus that it usually deserves.

performance reports Feedback provided by comparing results with plans and by highlighting variances.

The financial accounting system supports both planning and controlling and is a key source for **performance reports.** The accounting system records, measures, and classifies actions to produce performance reports. Accounting formalizes control as performance reports (the last box), which provide feedback by comparing results with plans and by highlighting **variances,** which are deviations from plans. For example, managers of The Chop House restaurant would evaluate the effectiveness of its advertising plan by comparing the percent increase in revenue to the percent increase in advertising. Based on their evaluation, managers at The Chop House would make corrections and revisions to their plans.

variances Deviations from plans.

Exhibit 1-3

Performance Report

	Budgeted Amounts	Actual Amounts	Deviations or Variances	Explanation
Revenue from fees	XXX	XXX	XX	—
Various expenses	XXX	XXX	XX	—
Net income	XXX	XXX	XX	—

Exhibit 1-3 shows a simple performance report for a law firm. Performance reports are used to judge decisions and the productivity of organizational units and managers. By comparing actual results to budgets, performance reports motivate managers to achieve the budgeted objectives.

Performance reports spur investigation of exceptions—items for which actual amounts differ significantly from budgeted amounts. Operations are then made to conform with the plans, or the plans are revised. This is often called **management by exception,** which means concentrating on areas that deviate from the plan and ignoring areas that are presumed to be running smoothly. Thus, the management-by-exception approach frees managers from needless concern with those phases of operations that are adhering to plans. However, well-conceived plans should incorporate enough discretion or flexibility so that the manager may feel free to pursue any unforeseen opportunities. In other words, control should not be a straightjacket. When unfolding events call for actions not specifically authorized in the plan, managers should be able to take these actions.

management by exception
Concentrating on areas that deviate from the plan and ignoring areas that are presumed to be running smoothly.

ILLUSTRATION OF BUDGETS AND PERFORMANCE REPORTS

Suppose the Casaverde Company manufactures and sells electric fans. Consider the department that assembles the fans. Workers assemble the parts and install the motor largely by hand. They then inspect each fan before transferring it to the packaging and shipping department. The present sales forecast has led managers to plan a production schedule of 10,000 fans for the coming month. The assembly department budget in Exhibit 1-4 shows cost classifications.

The operating plan for the department, in the form of a department budget for the coming month, is prepared in conferences attended by the department manager, the manager's supervisor, and an accountant. They scrutinize each of the costs subject to the manager's control. They often use the average amount of the cost for the past few months as a

Exhibit 1-4

Casaverde Company
Assembly Department Budget for the Month Ended March 31, 20X1

Production activity	10,000 fans
Material (detailed by type: metal stampings, motors, and so on)	$ 68,000
Assembly labor (detailed by job classification, number of workers, and so on)	43,000
Other labor (managers, inspectors)	12,000
Utilities, maintenance, and so on	7,500
Supplies (small tools, lubricants, and so on)	2,500
Total	$133,000

Exhibit 1-5

Casaverde Company

Assembly Department Performance Report for the Month Ended March 31, 20X2

	Budget	Actual	Variance
Production activity in units	10,000	9,860	140 U
Material (detailed by type: metal stampings, motors, and so on)	$ 68,000	$ 69,000	$1,000 U
Assembly labor (detailed by job classification, number of workers, and so on)	43,000	44,300	1,300 U
Other labor (managers, inspectors)	12,000	11,200	800 F
Utilities, maintenance, and so on	7,500	7,400	100 F
Supplies (small tools, lubricants, and so on)	2,500	2,600	100 U
Total	$133,000	$134,500	$1,500 U

U = Unfavorable—actual exceeds budget
F = Favorable—actual is less than budget

guide, especially if past performance has been good. However, the budget is a forecast of costs for the projected level of production activity. Hence, conference members must predict each cost in light of trends, price changes, alterations in product mix and characteristics, production methods, and changes in the level of production activity from month to month. Only then can they formulate the budget that becomes the manager's target for the month.

As actual factory costs are incurred, Casaverde's accounting system collects them and classifies them by department. At the end of the month (or weekly, or even daily, for such key items as materials or assembly labor), the accounting department prepares an assembly department performance report. Exhibit 1-5 is a simplified report. In practice, this report may be very detailed and contain explanations of variances from the budget.

Department heads and their superiors use the performance report to help appraise how effectively and efficiently the department is operating. Their focus is on the variances—the deviations from the budget. Casaverde's assembly department performance report (Exhibit 1-5) shows that although the department produced 140 fewer fans than planned, material costs were $1,000 over budget, and assembly labor was $1,300 over budget. By investigating such variances, managers may find better ways of doing things.

Notice that although budgets aid planning and performance reports aid control, it is not accountants but other managers and their subordinates who evaluate accounting reports and actually plan and control operations. Accounting assists the managerial planning and control functions by providing prompt measurements of actions and by systematically pinpointing trouble spots.

PLANNING AND CONTROL FOR PRODUCT LIFE CYCLES AND THE VALUE CHAIN

product life cycle The various stages through which a product passes, from conception and development through introduction into the market through maturation and, finally, withdrawal from the market.

Many management decisions relate to a single good or service, or to a group of related products. To effectively plan for and control production of such goods or services, accountants and other managers must consider the product's life cycle. **Product life cycle** refers to the various stages through which a product passes, from conception and development through introduction into the market through maturation and, finally, withdrawal from the market. At each stage, managers face differing costs and potential returns. Exhibit 1-6 shows a typical product life cycle.

Product life cycles range from a few months (for fashion clothing or faddish toys) to many years (for automobiles or refrigerators). Some products, such as many computer software packages, have long development stages and relatively short market lives. Others, such as Boeing 777 airplanes, have market lives many times longer than their development stage.

Exhibit 1-6
Typical Product Life Cycle

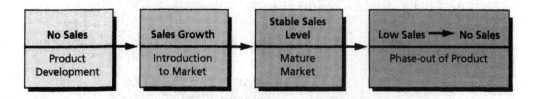

In the planning process, managers must recognize revenues and costs over the entire life cycle—however long or short. Accounting needs to track actual costs and revenues throughout the life cycle, too. Periodic comparisons between planned costs and revenues and actual costs and revenues allow managers to assess the current profitability of a product, determine its current product life-cycle stage, and make any needed changes in strategy.

For example, suppose a pharmaceutical company is developing a new drug to reduce high blood pressure. The budget for the product should plan for costs without revenues in the product development stage. Most of the revenues come in the introduction and mature-market stages, and a pricing strategy should recognize the need for revenues to cover both development and phase-out costs as well as the direct costs of producing the drug. During phase-out, costs of producing the drug must be balanced with both the revenue generated and the need to keep the drug on the market for those who have come to rely on it.

THE VALUE CHAIN

How does a company actually create the goods or services that it sells? Whether we are making donuts in a shopping mall or making $50 million airplanes, all organizations try to create goods or services that are valued by their customers. The **value chain** is the set of business functions that add value to the products or services of an organization. These functions are as follows:

> **value chain** The set of business functions that add value to the products or services of an organization.

- *Research and development*—the generation of, and experimentation with, ideas related to new products, services, or processes.
- *Design of products, services, or processes*—the detailed design and engineering of products.
- *Production*—the coordination and assembly of resources to produce a product or deliver a service.
- *Marketing*—the manner by which individuals or groups learn about the value and features of products or services (for example, advertising).
- *Distribution*—the mechanism by which a company delivers products or services to the customer.
- *Customer service*—the support activities provided to the customer.
- *Support functions*—the support activities provided to other internal business functions (for example, management information systems, accounting)

Exhibit 1-7 shows these business functions. Not all of these functions are of equal importance to the success of a company. Senior management must decide which of these functions enables the company to gain and maintain a competitive edge. For example, Dell Computers (see Chapter 12 for a more detailed company profile) considers the design function a critical success factor. The features designed into Dell's computers create higher quality. In addition, the design of efficient processes used to make and deliver computers lowers costs and speeds up delivery to its customers. Of course, Dell also performs the other value chain functions, but it concentrates on being the best process designer in the computer market.

Exhibit 1-7

The Value Chain of Business Functions

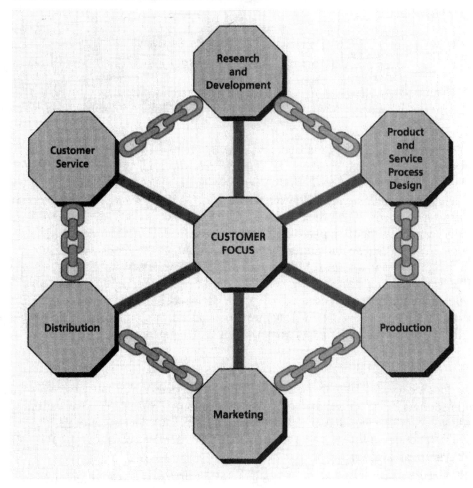

Support activities such as management information systems and accounting are not shown. These activities support all other value chain functions.

Objective 4
Discuss the role accountants play in the company's value chain functions.

Accountants play a key role in all value-chain functions. Providing estimated revenue and cost data during the research and development and design stages (especially the design stage) of the value chain enables managers and engineers to reduce the life-cycle costs of products or services more than in any other value-chain function. Using computer-based planning software, accountants can give managers rapid feedback on ideas for cost reductions long before the company must make a commitment to purchase expensive equipment. Then, during the production stage, accountants help track the effects of continuous improvement programs. Accountants also play a central role in cost planning and control through the use of budgets and performance reporting, as described in the previous section. Marketing decisions have a significant impact on sales but the cost of promotional programs is also significant. Accountants analyze the trade-off between increased costs and revenues. Distributing products or services to customers is a complex function. Should a company sell its products directly to a chain of retail stores, or should it sell to a wholesaler? What transportation system should be used—trucks or trains? What are the costs of each alternative? Finally, accountants provide cost data for customer service activities, such as warranty and repair costs and the costs of goods returned. As you can see, cost management is very important throughout the value chain.

Note that customer focus is at the center of Exhibit 1-7. Successful businesses never lose sight of the importance of maintaining a focus on the needs of its customers. For example, consider the comments of the following business leaders.

> *Customers, by the choices they make, grant companies a future or condemn them to extinction. We will continuously strive to achieve total customer satisfaction. . . . We will seek to truly understand the complexity of our customers' needs, not push our own ideas or technology.*
>
> *Philip Condit, Chairman and Chief Executive Officer, Boeing Company*

> *Improving comparable sales in the competitive U.S. market means selling more food. So, our emphasis is on increasing customer visits. In the U.S., we'll do that by concentrating on our customers: re-energizing and focusing our marketing efforts, being aggressive in providing maximum price value, continuing to improve service in our restaurants and enhancing food taste.*
>
> *Mike Conley, Executive Vice President and Chief Financial Officer, McDonald's Corporation*

The value chain and the concepts of adding value and focusing on the customer are extremely important to companies, and they are becoming more so every day. Accountants must focus on the values created compared to the costs incurred in each link of the value chain. Therefore, we will return to the value chain and use it as a focus for discussion throughout the book.

Starbucks Coffee Company is the leading roaster and retailer of specialty coffee in North America, with annual sales revenue of more than $1.5 billion. For each of the following activities, indicate the value chain function that is being performed.

1. Process engineers investigate methods to reduce the time to roast coffee beans and to better preserve their flavor.
2. A direct-to-your-home mail-order system is established to sell custom coffees.
3. Arabica coffee beans are purchased and transported to company processing plants.
4. Focus groups investigate the feasibility of a new line of Frappuccino drinks.
5. A hot line is established for mail-order customers to call with comments on the quality and speed of delivery.
6. Each company-owned retail store provides information to customers about the processes used to make its coffee products.

ANSWERS

1. Design. Both the design of products and, as here, design of production processes are part of the design function.
2. Distribution. This provides an additional way to deliver products to customers.
3. Production. The purchase price of beans and transportation (or freight-in) costs are part of product costs incurred during the production function.
4. Research and development. These costs (mostly wages) are incurred prior to management's final decision to design and produce a new product.
5. Customer service. These costs include all expenditures made after the product has been delivered to the customer; in this case, Starbucks obtains feedback on the quality and speed of delivery.
6. Marketing. These costs are for activities that enhance the existing or potential customers' awareness and opinion of the product.

ACCOUNTING'S POSITION IN THE ORGANIZATION

To assist other managers in the decision making vital to an organization's success, most companies (and many nonprofit organizations and government agencies) employ a variety of accounting personnel with various types of authority and responsibility.

LINE AND STAFF AUTHORITY

line authority Authority exerted downward over subordinates.

staff authority Authority to advise but not command. It may be exerted downward, laterally, or upward.

The organization chart in Exhibit 1-8 shows how a typical manufacturing company divides responsibilities. Notice the distinction between line and staff authority. **Line authority** is authority exerted downward over subordinates. **Staff authority** is authority to advise but not command. It may be exerted downward, laterally, or upward.

Most organizations specify certain activities as their basic mission. Most missions involve the production and sale of goods or services. All subunits of the organization that are directly responsible for conducting these basic activities are called line departments. The others are called staff departments because their principal task is to support or service the line departments. Thus, staff activities are indirectly related to the basic activities of the organization. Exhibit 1-8 shows a series of factory-service departments that perform staff functions supporting the line functions carried on by the production departments.

Exhibit 1-8

Partial Organization Chart of a Manufacturing Company

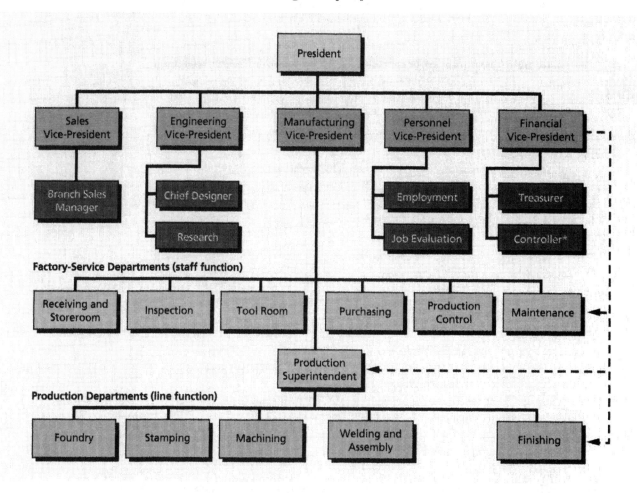

---

* *For detailed organization of a controller's department, see Exhibit 1-9 Dashed line represents staff authority of the finance staff to advise those in manufacturing operations.*

Exhibit 1-9

Organization Chart of a Controller's Department

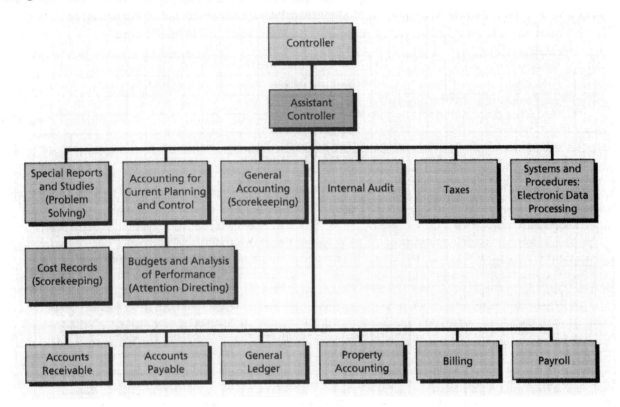

The top accounting officer of an organization is often called the **controller** or, especially in a government organization, a **comptroller**. This executive, like virtually everyone in an accounting function, fills a staff role, whereas sales and production executives and their subordinates fill line roles. The accounting department does not exercise direct authority over line departments. Rather, the accounting department provides other managers with specialized services, including advice and help in budgeting, analyzing variances, pricing, and making special decisions.

Exhibit 1-9 shows how a controller's department may be organized. In particular, note the distinctions among the scorekeeping, attention-directing, and problem-solving roles of various personnel. Unless some internal accountants are given the last two roles as their primary responsibilities, the scorekeeping tasks tend to dominate and the system becomes less responsive to management's decision making.

controller (comptroller)
The top accounting officer of an organization. The term *comptroller* is used primarily in government organizations.

THE CONTROLLER

The controller position varies in stature and duties from company to company. In some firms, the controller is confined to compiling data, primarily for external reporting purposes. In others, such as General Electric, the controller is a key executive who aids managerial planning and control throughout the company's subdivisions. In most firms, controllers have a status somewhere between these two extremes. For example, their opinions on the tax implications of certain management decisions may be carefully weighed, yet their opinions on other aspects of these decisions may not be sought. In many organizations (such as the Marmon Group companies), controllers have a growing role as internal "consultants," helping managers gather relevant information for their decisions.

The Marmon Group, Inc., embodies nearly all of the reasons why management accounting is a vital and growing function in today's leading companies. The Marmon Group, Inc., headquartered in Chicago, is an international association of more than 100 manufacturing, distribution, and service companies with annual revenues in excess of $6 billion. Because operations are spread out in more than 40 different countries with thousands of diverse products and services (such as worker's gloves, water coolers, railroad tank cars, medical products, and credit services for banks), managers at Marmon make extensive use of management accounting information to make important decisions.

What exactly is the role of management accountants at Marmon? According to Jim Smith, Marmon's Director of Cost Management, "The role of the management accountant is changing dramatically in most of our companies." In the past, Marmon's management accountants were basically clerical workers who spent most of their time analyzing monthly cost variances. Now, however, Marmon's management accountants work closely with operating and sales managers, providing cost information in a format that makes sense to those managers. Says Smith, "In the past few years the management accountant has become much more of a financial and business strategy adviser to senior management. Operating and sales managers are demanding meaningful cost information, and management accountants are helping them see how their actions affect costs and the bottom line."

Management accountants have become more important to Marmon, according to Smith, because recessions and foreign competition over the past 10 years have awakened the understanding in most managers that costs must be managed. Knowing what a product truly costs or the cost of servicing a particular customer has become essential to Marmon's profitability.

"To help manage costs," says Smith, "accountants and managers are shying away from using one cost, often the cost used for financial reporting purposes, as the only important cost." Instead, they are now using costs calculated for the decision at hand. "Depending on the decision, any of the cost methods described in *Introduction to Management Accounting* are relevant." According to Smith, this is a very positive change, "since it allows and, in fact, requires the management accountant to understand all of the functions in a business and how each one adds value to the product or service."

Source: Discussions with James Smith.

Although controllers (or comptrollers) have a staff role, they are generally empowered by the firm's president to approve, install, and oversee the organization's accounting system to ensure uniform accounting and reporting methods. In theory, the controller proposes these systems and methods to the president, who approves and orders compliance with them on the part of line personnel (thus preserving the "staff" advisory role of accounting). In practice, however, controllers usually directly specify how production records should be kept or how time records should be completed. The controller holds delegated authority from top-line management over such matters.

In theory, then, controllers have no line authority except over the accounting department. Yet, by reporting and interpreting relevant data, controllers do exert a force or influence that leads management toward logical decisions that are consistent with the organization's objectives.

DISTINCTIONS BETWEEN CONTROLLER AND TREASURER

Objective 5
Contrast the functions of controllers and treasurers.

Many people confuse the offices of controller and treasurer. The Financial Executives Institute, an association of corporate treasurers and controllers, distinguishes their functions as follows:

CONTROLLERSHIP

1. Planning for control
2. Reporting and interpreting

TREASURERSHIP

1. Provision of capital
2. Investor relations

3. Evaluating and consulting
4. Tax administration
5. Government reporting
6. Protection of assets
7. Economic appraisal

3. Short-term financing
4. Banking and custody
5. Credits and collections
6. Investments
7. Risk management (insurance)

Management accounting is the primary means of implementing the first three functions of controllership.

The treasurer is concerned mainly with the company's financial matters, the controller with operating matters. The exact division of accounting and financial duties varies from company to company. In a small organization, the same person might be both treasurer and controller.

SUMMARY PROBLEM FOR YOUR REVIEW

PROBLEM

Using the organization charts in this chapter (Exhibits 1-8 and 1-9), answer the following questions:

1. Which of the following have line authority over the machining manager: maintenance manager, manufacturing vice-president, production superintendent, purchasing agent, scorekeeper, personnel vice-president, president, chief budgetary accountant, chief internal auditor?

2. What is the general role of service departments in an organization? How are they distinguished from operating or production departments?

3. Does the controller have line or staff authority over the cost accountants? Over the accounts receivable clerks?

4. What is probably the major duty (scorekeeping, attention directing, or problem solving) of the following:

Payroll clerk	Cost analyst
Accounts receivable clerk	Head of internal auditing
Cost record clerk	Head of special reports and studies
Head of general accounting	Head of accounting for planning
Head of taxes	and control
Budgetary accountant	Controller

SOLUTION

1. The only executives having line authority over the machining manager are the president, the manufacturing vice-president, and the production superintendent.

2. A typical company's major purpose is to produce and sell goods or services. Unless a department is directly concerned with producing or selling, it is called a service or staff department. Service departments exist only to help the production and sales departments with their major tasks: the efficient production and sale of goods or services.

3. The controller has line authority over all members of his or her own department, all those shown in the controller's organization chart (Exhibit 1-9).

4. The major duty of the first five—through the head of taxes—is typically scorekeeping. Attention directing is probably the major duty of the next three. Problem solving is probably the primary duty of the head of special reports and

studies. The head of accounting for planning and control and the controller should be concerned with all three duties: scorekeeping, attention directing, and problem solving. However, there is a perpetual danger that day-to-day pressures will emphasize scorekeeping. Therefore, accountants and managers should make sure that attention directing and problem solving are also stressed. Otherwise, the major management benefits of an accounting system may be lost.

CAREER OPPORTUNITIES IN MANAGEMENT ACCOUNTING

The many types and levels of accounting personnel found in the typical organization mean that there are broad opportunities awaiting those who master the accounting discipline.

CERTIFIED MANAGEMENT ACCOUNTANT

Certified Public Accountant (CPA) In the United States, an accountant earns this designation by a combination of education, qualifying experience, and the passing of a two-day written national examination.

When accounting is mentioned, most people think first of independent auditors who reassure the public about the reliability of the financial information supplied by company managers. These external auditors are called certified public accountants in the United States and chartered accountants in many other English-speaking nations. In the United States, an accountant earns the designation of **Certified Public Accountant (CPA)** by a combination of education, qualifying experience, and the passing of a two-day written national examination. The major U.S. professional association in the private sector that regulates the quality of outside auditors is the American Institute of Certified Public Accountants (AICPA).

In recent years, increased interest in and demand for management accounting has led to the development of the **Certified Management Accountant (CMA)** designation, the internal accountant's counterpart to the CPA. The **Institute of Management Accountants (IMA)** oversees the CMA program and is the largest U.S. professional organization of accountants whose major interest is management accounting.

Certified Management Accountant (CMA) The management accountant's counterpart to the CPA.

The highlight of the CMA program is a two-day qualifying examination in four parts: (1) economics, finance, and management; (2) financial accounting and reporting; (3) management reporting, analysis, and behavioral issues; and (4) decision analysis and information systems.[2] The CMA designation is recognized as the management accounting equivalent of the CPA.

Institute of Management Accountants (IMA) The largest U.S. professional organization of accountants whose major interest is management accounting.

Recent studies by the IMA have shown that finance and management accounting positions in industry are very closely related. In response, the IMA developed the Certified in Financial Management (CFM) designation. The CFM examination requires three of the same parts as the CMA, with financial accounting and reporting replaced by corporate financial management.

TRAINING FOR TOP MANAGEMENT POSITIONS

In addition to preparing you for a position in an accounting department, studying accounting—and working as a management accountant—can prepare you for the very highest levels of management. Accounting deals with all facets of an organization, no matter how complex, so it provides an excellent opportunity to gain broad knowledge. Accounting must embrace all management functions, including purchasing, manufacturing, wholesaling, retailing, and a variety of marketing and transportation activities. Senior

---

[2]*Information can be obtained from the IMA, 10 Paragon Drive, Montvale, NJ 07645, or log on to www.imanet.org.*

accountants or controllers in a corporation are sometimes picked as production or marketing executives. Why? Because they may have impressed other executives as having acquired general management skills. A number of recent surveys have indicated that more chief executive officers began their careers in an accounting position than in any other area, including marketing, production, and engineering.

For example, former controllers have risen to the top of such mammoth companies as Pepsico and Pfizer. According to *Business Week,* controllers

> *are now getting involved with the operating side of the company, where they give advice and influence production, marketing, and investment decisions as well as corporate planning. Moreover, many controllers who have not made it to the top have won ready access to top management. . . . Probably the main reason the controller is getting the ear of top management these days is that he or she is virtually the only person familiar with all the working parts of the company.*

chapter

2

INTRODUCTION TO COST BEHAVIOR AND COST-VOLUME RELATIONSHIPS

Boeing's 767-400 ER has earned passenger ratings as one of the most preferred airplanes in every class of service. One reason is that 87% of the seats are next to a window or on the aisle. Delivery of the first 767-400 ER to launch customer Delta Airlines was made in 2000.

www.prenhall.com/horngren

Learning Objectives

When you have finished studying this chapter, you should be able to

1. Explain how cost drivers affect cost behavior.

2. Show how changes in cost-driver activity levels affect variable and fixed costs.

3. Calculate break-even sales volume in total dollars and total units.

4. Create a cost-volume-profit graph and understand the assumptions behind it.

5. Calculate sales volume in total dollars and total units to reach a target profit.

6. Differentiate between contribution margin and gross margin.

7. Explain the effects of sales mix on profits (Appendix 2A).

8. Compute cost-volume-profit relationships on an after-tax basis (Appendix 2B).

9. **Understand how cost behavior and cost-volume-profit analysis are used by managers.**

In 1915, William Boeing, a Seattle timberman, assembled his first airplane in a boathouse. Today, the Boeing Company produces more than 50 jetliners each month and has annual revenues of more than $60 billion. The company has two-thirds of the world's market share in airplane sales, but that could change as the competition steps up to meet growing demand. Over the next two decades, the airline industry will need 16,000 new airplanes worth over $1 trillion. How will Boeing maintain its competitive edge and profitability? With increased competition, Boeing knows that profits can be improved more by controlling (reducing) costs than by increasing prices to customers. So, should it build bigger airplanes or more of the existing size but with improvements in features and efficiencies that will lower customers' costs? Which alternative has lower costs for Boeing and its customers? To answer these questions, Boeing had to understand its own costs as well as the costs of its customers. The real question is what do its customers value in return for a price tag of $50+ million per airplane?

A case in point is the Boeing 747-X. Nearly a decade ago, the company began its research and development program for this huge 500-passenger airplane. An important part of its research was the assessment of its customers' costs—both of operating their existing fleet of planes and of the reduced costs of the new 747-X planes. It formed a working group with 19 airline customers (for example, United and American Airlines, and British Airways) to look at their requirements in the 500+-seat market. After four years of research, the company had completed the design of the new airplane and was faced with the final decision to launch. A decision to launch would involve a huge immediate investment in costly plant and equipment resources. To pay for these assets and make a profit, it had to be confident that its customers would demand the new plane.

The key question was whether customers wanted the latest, largest, and most costly airplane or one with the highest value. Despite the years of development activities, Boeing decided not to proceed with the 747-X. According to Philip Condit, Chairman and Chief Executive Officer, "The prospective market for airplanes with over 500 seats was limited. We were at last in a position of balancing the significant cost of the program against the limited size of the market." Most of the company's customers needed more airplanes for the expected increase in the number of nonstop routes. In short, customers said, "We would rather have two new 250-seat airplanes that are more cost efficient than one 500-seat super airplane." So the 747-X program was stopped. Instead, the company is concentrating on upgrading its existing aircraft. For example, Boeing's new model of the existing 747 will offer 16% more seats and up to 10% lower "seat-mile" costs.

Managers need to understand costs. How are the costs and revenues of an airline affected when one more passenger is added at the last moment, or when one more flight is added to the schedule? How should the budget request by the Arizona Department of Motor Vehicles be affected by the predicted increase in the state's population? These questions are really different forms of one common question: What will happen to financial results if a specified level of activity or volume changes?

Although financial results are based on revenues and costs, we will focus primarily on costs in this chapter. After all, as we saw in the case of Boeing, companies usually have more control over their costs than they do over their revenues. In fact, one of the main goals of management accounting is controlling (and reducing) costs. But managers cannot control costs unless they understand **cost behavior**—how costs are related to and affected by the activities of the organization.

cost behavior How costs are related to and affected by the activities of an organization.

ACTIVITIES, COSTS, AND COST DRIVERS

Different types of costs behave in different ways. Consider Boeing Company's costs of an existing plant that makes 737 business jets. The cost of materials such as electrical wire, seats, and aluminum increase as the number of airplanes manufactured increases. But the cost of the plant and salaries of key managers stay the same regardless of the number of airplanes made. Associating cost behavior with units of product produced gives us an overall view of how costs behave, but it does little to help managers control costs on a day-to-day basis.

Objective 1
Explain how cost drivers affect cost behavior.

On a day-to-day basis, managers focus their efforts on managing the activities required to make products or deliver services—not on the products and services themselves. A production manager needs to know how routine activities such as machine maintenance and repairs affect costs. So, because understanding costs is so important for cost control, associating costs with activities is a key. For example, one of the activities performed at Boeing's plant is receiving parts to be installed on the airplane. Receiving managers need to know how their activities affect costs. Costs such as depreciation of the equipment used to move parts from one location in the plant to another do not change when receiving activity increases or decreases. However, costs such as fuel for the same moving equipment do change with activity changes. Actually, we should say that activities such as receiving require resources such as moving equipment and fuel and that these resources cost money.

Exhibit 2-1

Examples of Value Chain Functions, Costs, and Cost Drivers

Value Chain Function and Example Costs	Example Cost Drivers
Research and development	
• Salaries of marketing research personnel, costs of market surveys	Number of new product proposals
• Salaries of product and process engineers	Complexity of proposed products
Design of products, services, and processes	
• Salaries of product and process engineers	Number of engineering hours
• Cost of computer-aided design equipment, cost to develop prototype of product for testing	Number of parts per product
Production	
• Labor wages	Labor hours
• Supervisory salaries	Number of people supervised
• Maintenance wages	Number of mechanic hours
• Depreciation of plant and machinery, supplies	Number of machine hours
• Energy	Kilowatt hours
Marketing	
• Cost of advertisements	Number of advertisements
• Salaries of marketing personnel, travel costs, entertainment costs	Sales dollars
Distribution	
• Wages of shipping personnel	Labor hours
• Transportation costs including depreciation of vehicles and fuel	Weight of items delivered
Customer service	
• Salaries of service personnel	Hours spent servicing products
• Costs of supplies, travel	Number of service calls

But how exactly do accountants relate activities to resource costs in a way that makes cost control possible? Accountants first identify the activities in their organization and determine measures of output for each activity. They then relate each output measure to the resources that are necessary to produce it. Any output measure that causes costs (that is, causes the use of costly resources) is called a **cost driver.** In our receiving example, the cost driver or output measure of receiving activity could be "number of parts received" or "weight of parts received." The receiving manager can easily understand how an increase in the number of parts received or the weight of parts received can increase or "drive" the use (and therefore cost) of fuel and moving equipment.

> **cost driver** Any output measure that causes costs (that is, causes the use of costly resources).

An organization has many cost drivers across its value chain. Exhibit 2-1 lists examples of costs and potential cost drivers for each of the value chain functions. How well the accountant does at identifying the most appropriate cost drivers determines how well managers understand cost behavior and how well costs are controlled.

COMPARISON OF VARIABLE AND FIXED COSTS

A key to understanding cost behavior is distinguishing variable costs from fixed costs. Costs are classified as variable or fixed depending on how much they change as the level of a particular cost driver changes. A **variable cost** is a cost that changes in direct proportion to changes in the cost driver level. In contrast, a **fixed cost** is not immediately affected by changes in the cost-driver level. Suppose units of production is the cost driver of interest. A 10% increase in the units of production would produce a 10% increase in variable costs. However, the fixed costs would remain unchanged.

> **variable cost** A cost that changes in direct proportion to changes in the cost driver level.

> **fixed cost** A cost that is not immediately affected by changes in the cost driver level.

Exhibit 2-2

Variable-Cost Behavior

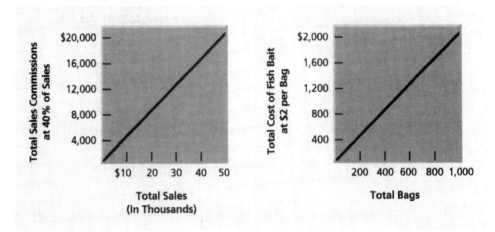

Consider some variable costs. Suppose Watkins Products pays its door-to-door sales personnel a 40% straight commission on sales. The total cost of sales commissions to Watkins is 40% of sales dollars—a variable cost with respect to sales revenues. Or suppose Dan's Bait Shop buys bags of fish bait for $2 each. The total cost of fish bait is $2 times the number of bags purchased—a variable cost with respect to units (number of bags) purchased. Notice that variable costs do not change per unit, but that the total costs change in direct proportion to the cost-driver activity. Exhibit 2-2 shows these relationships between cost and cost-driver activity graphically.

Now consider a fixed cost. Suppose Sony rents a factory to produce picture tubes for color television sets for $500,000 per year. The total cost of $500,000 is not affected by the number of picture tubes produced. The unit cost of rent applicable to each tube, however, does depend on the total number of tubes produced. If 100,000 tubes are produced, the unit cost will be $500,000 ÷ 100,000 = $5. If 50,000 tubes are produced, the unit cost will be $500,000 ÷ 50,000 = $10. Therefore, a fixed cost does not change in total, but it becomes progressively smaller on a per-unit basis as the volume increases.

Note carefully from these examples that the "variable" or "fixed" characteristic of a cost relates to its total dollar amount and not to its per-unit amount. The following table summarizes these relationships.

Objective 2
Show how changes in cost-driver activity levels affect variable and fixed costs.

	If Cost-Driver Activity Level Increases (or Decreases)	
Type of Cost	Total Cost	Cost Per Unit*
Fixed costs	No change	Decrease (or increase)
Variable costs	Increase (or decrease)	No change

* Per unit of activity volume, for example, product units, passenger-miles, sales dollars.

When analyzing costs, two rules of thumb are useful:

1. Think of fixed costs as a total. Total fixed costs remain unchanged regardless of changes in cost-driver activity.

2. Think of variable costs on a per-unit basis. The per-unit variable cost remains unchanged regardless of changes in cost-driver activity.

A key to understanding cost behavior is distinguishing between variable and fixed costs. Test your understanding by answering the following questions.

1. Kilowatt hours used is a cost driver for power cost. Is power cost a variable or a fixed cost?
2. Square feet occupied is a cost driver for occupancy costs such as building depreciation and insurance. Is occupancy cost variable or fixed?

ANSWERS

The best way to determine whether the cost of a resource is fixed or variable is to ask the question, "If the level of the cost driver changes, what will happen to the cost?" If kilowatt hours increases (decreases), then the cost of power will also increase (decrease). Thus, power cost is variable. If the square feet occupied by a particular unit in an organization increases (decreases), the building depreciation and insurance on the building will not change. Thus, building occupancy costs such as depreciation and insurance are fixed costs.

RELEVANT RANGE

Although we have just described fixed costs as unchanging regardless of changes in the given cost driver, this rule of thumb holds true only within reasonable limits. For example, rent costs, which are generally fixed, will rise if increased production requires a larger or additional building—or if the landlord just decides to raise the rent. Conversely, rent costs may go down if decreased production causes the company to move to a smaller plant. The **relevant range** is the limit of cost-driver activity level within which a specific relationship between costs and the cost driver is valid. Even within the relevant range, though, a fixed cost remains fixed only over a given period of time—usually the budget period. Fixed costs may change from budget year to budget year solely because of changes in insurance and property tax rates, executive salary levels, or rent levels. But these items are unlikely to change within a given year.

relevant range The limit of cost-driver activity level within which a specific relationship between costs and the cost driver is valid.

For example, suppose that a General Electric plant has a relevant range of between 40,000 and 85,000 cases of lightbulbs per month and that total monthly fixed costs within the relevant range are $100,000. Within the relevant range, fixed costs will remain the same. If production falls below 40,000 cases, changes in personnel and salaries would slash fixed costs to $60,000. If operations rise above 85,000 cases, increases in personnel and salaries would boost fixed costs to $115,000.

These assumptions—a given period and a given activity range—are shown graphically at the top of Exhibit 2-3. It is highly unusual, however, for monthly operations to be outside the relevant range. Therefore, the three-level refinement at the top of Exhibit 2-3 is usually not graphed. Instead, a single horizontal line is typically extended through the plotted activity levels, as at the bottom of the exhibit. Often a dashed line is used outside the relevant range.

The basic idea of a relevant range also applies to variable costs. That is, outside a relevant range, some variable costs, such as fuel consumed, may behave differently per unit of cost-driver activity. For example, the variable cost of a canning machine at Del Monte might be $5 for every hour it is used, assuming that it will be used between 30 and 50 hours each week. However, if it is used for more than 50 hours a week, the added wear and tear might increase variable costs to $6 for those hours beyond 50.

DIFFERENCES IN CLASSIFYING COSTS

As you may suspect, it is often difficult to classify a cost as exactly variable or exactly fixed. Many complications arise including the possibility of costs behaving in some

Exhibit 2-3

Fixed Costs and Relevant Range

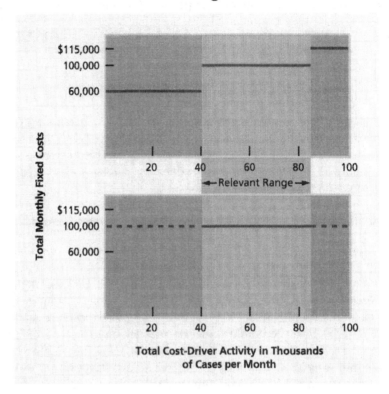

nonlinear way (not producing a straight line graph). For example, as tax preparers learn to process the new year's tax forms, their productivity rises. This means that total costs may actually behave as in Panel A that follows, not as in Panel B.

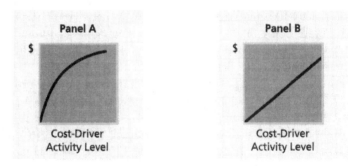

Moreover, costs may simultaneously be affected by more than one cost driver. For example, the costs of shipping labor may be affected by both the weight and the number of units handled. We shall investigate various facets of this problem in succeeding chapters; for now, we shall assume that any cost may be classified as either variable or fixed. We assume also that a given variable cost is associated with only one volume-related cost driver and that relationship is linear.

Classifying costs as fixed or variable depends on the decision situation. More costs are fixed and fewer are variable when decisions involve very short time spans and very small changes in activity level. Suppose a United Airlines plane with several empty seats will depart from its gate in two minutes. A potential passenger is running down a corridor bearing a transferable ticket from a competing airline. Unless the airplane is held for an extra 30 seconds, the passenger will miss the departure and will not switch to United for the planned trip. What are the variable costs to United of delaying the departure and placing one more passenger in an otherwise empty seat? Variable costs (for example, one more meal) are negligible. Virtually all the costs in that decision situation are fixed (for example, maintenance crew salaries). Now in contrast, suppose United's decision is whether to add another flight, acquire another gate, add another city to its routes, or acquire another airplane. Many more costs would be regarded as variable and fewer as fixed. For example, in the case of adding a flight, the salaries of the maintenance crew would now be variable.

This example underscores the importance of how the decision situation affects the analysis of cost behavior. Whether costs are really "fixed" depends heavily on the relevant range, the length of the planning period in question, and the specific decision situation.

COST-VOLUME-PROFIT ANALYSIS

Managers often classify costs as fixed or variable when making decisions that affect the volume of output. The managers want to know how such decisions will affect costs and revenues. They realize that many factors in addition to the volume of output will affect costs. Yet, a useful starting point in their decision process is to specify the relationship between the volume of output and costs and revenues.

The managers of profit-seeking organizations usually study the effects of output volume on revenue (sales), expenses (costs), and net income (net profit). This study is commonly called **cost-volume-profit (CVP) analysis.** The managers of nonprofit organizations also benefit from the study of CVP relationships. Why? No organization has unlimited resources, and knowledge of how costs fluctuate as volume changes helps managers to understand how to control costs. For example, administrators of nonprofit hospitals are constantly concerned about the behavior of costs as the volume of patients fluctuates.

To apply CVP analysis, managers usually resort to some simplifying assumptions. The major simplification is to classify costs as either variable or fixed with respect to a single measure of the volume of output activity. This chapter focuses on such a simplified relationship.

cost-volume-profit (CVP) analysis The study of the effects of output volume on revenue (sales), expenses (costs), and net income (net profit).

CVP SCENARIO

Amy Winston, the manager of food services for Middletown Community College, is trying to decide whether to rent a line of snack vending machines. Although individual snack items have various acquisition costs and selling prices, Winston has decided that an average selling price of 50¢ per unit and an average acquisition cost of 40¢ per unit will suffice for purposes of this analysis. She predicts the following revenue and expense relationships.

	Per Unit	Percentage of Sales
Selling price	$ .50	100%
Variable cost of each item	.40	80
Selling price less variable cost	$ .10	20%
Monthly fixed expenses		
Rent	$1,000	
Wages for replenishing and servicing	4,500	
Other fixed expenses	500	
Total fixed expenses per month	$6,000	

We will now use these data in examining several applications of CVP analysis.

Increased worldwide competition in the automobile industry has made many companies acutely aware of their break-even points. In the early 1990s most auto companies were losing money. With dim prospects for large increases in volume of sales, the companies would be profitable only if they could decrease their break-even points. That is exactly what most companies did.

Break-even points vary greatly for different auto companies. The larger companies have high fixed costs and therefore must achieve higher sales to break even. For example, Chrysler reduced its break-even point from 1.9 million to 1.6 million vehicles from the late 1980s to 1993. Still, the reduction of 16% in the break-even point is less than that achieved by some competitors.

Saab, a Swedish company, has focused on bringing down the number of production hours per car. In the mid-1990s, Saab reduced production hours from 120 hours to 45 hours. This decreased the break-even volume from 125,000 vehicles to 83,000.

The assembly operations for Jaguar, located 100 miles north of London, have had a dual focus: quality and production time. Quality improvements were expected to increase sales, and this appears to be working. Warranty costs in the United States alone are down 60% and sales are up. Production improvements were intended to reduce the break-even volume. During the early 1990s, Jaguar had cut the time required to build a car by 54%. This cut the break-even point from between 50,000 and 60,000 vehicles to 30,000 per year.

In 1993, Volkswagen's variable costs of making a car were actually higher than its average price. As stated by VW's Chairman, Ferdinand Piech, "The more cars we sold, the more money we would lose." But VW lowered its breakeven by redesigning its cars and improving production processes.

It is clear that break-even volumes differ greatly among automobile companies. Rolls-Royce can generate a profit at a sales level of 1,300 vehicles, but Saab, Jaguar, Volkswagen, and Chrysler would go out of business at that volume. Similarly, Chrysler could not survive selling at volumes that are highly profitable to Saab and Jaguar. Each company must compute its own break-even volume based on its own fixed and variable costs. If a company's sales fall below its break-even point, either it must find a way to get more sales or it must restructure its production operations to reduce its break-even point.

Sources: Adapted from Paul A. Eisenstein, "Jaguar Ledgers to Feature Black, Not Red, Ink Next Year," *Washington Times*, September 16, 1994, p. D3; Mary Beth Vander Schaaf, "Saab Counts on V-6 to Boost 9000," *Automotive News*, September 26, 1994, p. 37; "GM's Saab Unit Climbs Back into Black," *Investor's Business Daily*, September 27, 1994, p. A4; James Bennet, "Chrysler Chief's World View: Place to Sell, Not Build, Cars," *New York Times*, September 30, 1994, p. D1; Christopher Jensen, "Jaguar's Renaissance: Ford Helps Its British Acquisition Make Quality Job One," *Plain Dealer*, October 9, 1994, p. 1H; Paul Eisenstein, "VW Can Afford Expansion," *Automotive Industries*, October 1, 1998.

BREAK-EVEN POINT — CONTRIBUTION-MARGIN AND EQUATION TECHNIQUES

break-even point The level of sales at which revenue equals expenses and net income is zero.

The most basic CVP analysis computes the monthly break-even point in number of units and in dollar sales. The **break-even point** is the level of sales at which revenue equals expenses and net income is zero. The business press frequently refers to break-even points. For example, a news story on hotel occupancy rates in San Francisco stated that "seventy percent [occupancy] is considered a break-even for hoteliers." Another news story stated that "the Big Three auto makers have slashed their sales break-even point in North America from 12.2 million cars and trucks to only 9.1 million this year." Finally, an article on Outboard Marine Corporation reported that, as a result of restructuring, the company's "break-even point will be $250 million lower than it was in 1993."

The study of cost-volume-profit relationships is often called break-even analysis. This term is misleading, because finding the break-even point is often just the first step in a planning decision. Managers usually concentrate on how the decision will affect sales, costs, and net income.

One direct use of the break-even point, however, is to assess possible risks. By comparing planned sales with the break-even point, managers can determine a margin of safety:

$$\text{Margin of Safety} = \text{Planned Unit Sales} - \text{Break-Even Unit Sales}$$

The **margin of safety** shows how far sales can fall below the planned level before losses occur.

There are two basic techniques for computing a break-even point: contribution margin and equation.

margin of safety The planned unit sales less the break-even unit sales; it shows how far sales can fall below the planned level before losses occur.

Contribution-Margin Technique. Consider the following commonsense arithmetic approach. Every unit sold generates a **contribution margin** or **marginal income,** which is the unit sales price minus the variable cost per unit. For the vending machine snack items, the contribution margin per unit is $.10:

contribution margin (marginal income) The sales price minus the variable cost per unit.

Unit sales price	$.50
Unit variable cost	.40
Unit contribution margin	$.10

When is the break-even point reached? When enough units have been sold to generate a total contribution margin (total number of units sold × contribution margin per unit) equal to the total fixed costs. Divide the $6,000 in fixed costs by the $.10 unit contribution margin. The number of units that must be sold to break even is $6,000 ÷ $.10 = 60,000 units. The sales revenue at the break-even point is 60,000 units × $.50 per unit, or $30,000.

Objective 3
Calculate break-even sales volume in total dollars and total units.

Think about the contribution margin of the snack items. Each unit purchased and sold generates extra revenue of $.50 and extra cost of $.40. Fixed costs are unaffected. If zero units were sold, a loss equal to the fixed cost of $6,000 would be incurred. Each unit reduces the loss by $.10 until sales reach the break-even point of 60,000 units. After that point, each unit adds (or contributes) $.10 to profit.

The condensed income statement at the break-even point is

	Total	Per Unit	Percentage
Units	60,000		
Sales	$30,000	$.50	100%
Variable costs	24,000	.40	80
Contribution margin*	$ 6,000	$.10	20%
Fixed costs	6,000		
Net income	$ 0		

* Sales less variable costs.

Sometimes the unit price and unit variable costs of a product are not known. This situation is common at companies that sell more than one product because no single price or variable cost applies to all products. For example, a grocery store sells hundreds of products at many different prices. A break-even point in overall units sold by the store would not be meaningful. In such cases, you can use total sales and total variable costs to calculate variable costs as a percentage of each sales dollar.

Consider our vending machine example:

Sales price	100%
Variable expenses as a percentage of dollar sales	80
Contribution-margin percentage	20%

Therefore, 20% of each sales dollar is available for the recovery of fixed expenses and the making of net income: $6,000 ÷ .20 = $30,000 sales are needed to break even. The contribution-margin percentage is based on dollar sales and is often expressed as a ratio (.20 instead of 20%). Using the contribution-margin percentage, you can compute the break-even volume in dollar sales without determining the break-even point in units.

Equation Technique. The equation technique is the most general form of analysis, the one that may be adapted to any conceivable cost-volume-profit situation. You are familiar with a typical income statement. Any income statement can be expressed in equation form, or as a mathematical model, as follows:

$$\text{sales} - \text{variable expenses} - \text{fixed expenses} = \text{net income} \qquad (1)$$

That is,

$$\begin{pmatrix} \text{unit} & \text{number} \\ \text{sales} \times & \text{of} \\ \text{price} & \text{units} \end{pmatrix} - \begin{pmatrix} \text{unit} & \text{number} \\ \text{variable} \times & \text{of} \\ \text{cost} & \text{units} \end{pmatrix} - \begin{matrix} \text{fixed} \\ \text{expenses} \end{matrix} = \begin{matrix} \text{net} \\ \text{income} \end{matrix}$$

At the break-even point net income is zero:

$$\text{sales} - \text{variable expenses} - \text{fixed expenses} = 0$$

Let N = number of units to be sold to break even. Then, for the vending machine example,

$$\$.50N - \$.40N - \$6,000 = 0$$
$$\$.10N = \$6,000$$
$$N = \$6,000 ÷ \$.10$$
$$N = 60,000 \text{ units}$$

Total sales in the equation is a price-times-quantity relationship, which was expressed in our example as $.50N. To find the dollar sales, multiply 60,000 units by $.50, which would yield the break-even dollar sales of $30,000.

You can also solve the equation for sales dollars without computing the unit break-even point by using the relationship of variable costs and profits as a percentage of sales:

$$\text{variable-cost ratio or percentage} = \frac{\text{variable cost per unit}}{\text{sales price per unit}}$$
$$= \frac{\$.40}{\$.50}$$
$$= .80 \text{ or } 80\%$$

Let S = sales in dollars needed to break even. Then

$$S - .80S - \$6,000 = 0$$
$$.20S = \$6,000$$
$$S = \$6,000 ÷ .20$$
$$S = \$30,000$$

Relationship between the Two Techniques. You may have noticed that the contribution-margin technique is merely a shortcut version of the equation technique. Look at the last three lines in the two solutions given for equation 1. They read

Break-Even Volume	
Units	*Dollars*
$\$.10N = \$6,000$	$.20S = \$6,000$
$N = \dfrac{\$6,000}{\$.10}$	$S = \dfrac{\$6,000}{.20}$
$N = 60,000$ units	$S = \$30,000$

From these equations, we can derive the following general shortcut formulas:

$$\text{break-even volume in units} = \frac{\text{fixed expenses}}{\text{contribution margin per unit}} \qquad (2)$$

$$\text{break-even volume in dollars} = \frac{\text{fixed expenses}}{\text{contribution-margin ratio}} \qquad (3)$$

Which should you use, the equation or the contribution-margin technique? Use either. Both yield the same results, so the choice is a matter of personal preference or convenience in a particular case.

Using short-cut formulas (2) and (3), answer the following questions. Remember that the contribution margin per unit equals the sales price per unit minus the variable costs per unit.

1. What would be the effect on the unit and dollar break-even level if fixed costs increase (and there are no other changes)?
2. What would be the effect on the unit and dollar break-even level if variable cost per unit decreases (and there are no other changes)?
3. What would be the effect on the unit and dollar break-even level if sales volume increases (and there are no other changes)?

ANSWERS

1. The break-even level in both units and sales dollars would increase if fixed costs increase.
2. The break-even level in both units and sales dollars would decrease if variable costs decrease.
3. Think before answering this question. The *actual (or even planned)* volume of sales in units has nothing to do with determining the break-even point. This is why unit volume does not appear in either equation (2) or (3).

Break-Even Point — Graphical Techniques. Exhibit 2-4 is a graph of the cost-volume-profit relationship in our vending machine example. Study the graph as you read the procedure for constructing it.

Objective 4
Create a cost-volume-profit graph and understand the assumptions behind it.

1. Draw the axes. The horizontal axis is the sales volume, and the vertical axis is dollars of cost and revenue.
2. Plot sales volume. Select a convenient sales volume, say, 100,000 units, and plot point A for total sales dollars at that volume: $100,000 \times \$.50 = \$50,000$. Draw the revenue (that is, sales) line from point A to the origin, point 0.
3. Plot fixed expenses. Draw the line showing the $6,000 fixed portion of expenses. It should be a horizontal line intersecting the vertical axis at $6,000, point B.

Exhibit 2-4
Cost-Volume-Profit Graph

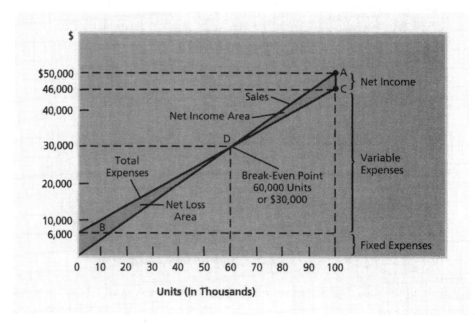

4. Plot variable expenses. Determine the variable portion of expenses at a convenient level of activity: 100,000 units × $.40 = $40,000. Add this to the fixed expenses: $40,000 + $6,000 = $46,000. Plot point C for 100,000 units and $46,000. Then draw a line between this point and point B. This is the total expenses line.

5. Locate the break-even point. The break-even point is where the total expenses line crosses the sales line, 60,000 units or $30,000, namely, where total sales revenues exactly equal total costs, point D.

The break-even point is only one part of this cost-volume-profit graph. The graph also shows the profit or loss at any rate of activity. At any given volume, the vertical distance between the sales line and the total expenses line measures the net income or net loss.

Managers often use break-even graphs because these graphs show potential profits over a wide range of volume more easily than numerical exhibits. Whether graphs or other presentations are used depends largely on management's preference.

Note that the concept of relevant range applies to the entire break-even graph. Almost all break-even graphs show revenue and cost lines extending back to the vertical axis as shown in Exhibit 2-5(A). This approach is misleading because the relationships depicted in such graphs are valid only within the relevant range that underlies the construction of the graph. Exhibit 2-5(B), a modification of the conventional break-even graph, partially demonstrates the multitude of assumptions that must be made in constructing the typical break-even graph. Some of these assumptions follow.

1. Expenses may be classified into variable and fixed categories. Total variable expenses vary directly with activity level. Total fixed expenses do not change with activity level.

2. The behavior of revenues and expenses is accurately portrayed and is linear over the relevant range. The principal differences between the accountant's break-even chart and the economist's are that (1) the accountant's sales line is drawn on the assumption that selling prices do not change with production or sales, and the economist assumes that reduced selling prices are normally associated with

Exhibit 2-5

Conventional and Modified Break-Even Graphs

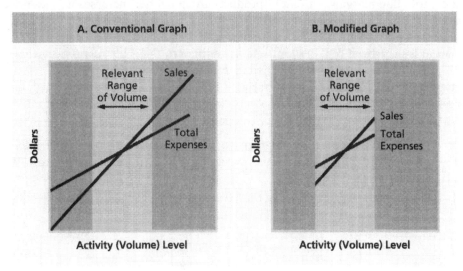

increased sales volume; and (2) the accountant usually assumes a constant variable expense per unit, and the economist assumes that variable expense per unit changes with production levels. Within the relevant range, the accountant's and the economist's sales and expense lines are usually close to one another, although the lines may diverge greatly outside the range.

3. Efficiency and productivity will be unchanged.

4. Sales mix will be constant. The **sales mix** is the relative proportions or combinations of quantities of products that constitute total sales. (See Appendix 2A for more on sales mixes.)

5. The difference in inventory level at the beginning and at the end of a period is insignificant. (The impact of inventory changes on CVP analysis is discussed in Chapter 15.)

sales mix The relative proportions or combinations of quantities of products that constitute total sales.

Changes in Fixed Expenses. Changes in fixed expenses cause changes in the break-even point. For example, if the $1,000 monthly rent of the vending machines were doubled, what would be the monthly break-even point in number of units and dollar sales?

The fixed expenses would increase from $6,000 to $7,000, so

$$\frac{\text{break-even volume}}{\text{in units}} = \frac{\text{fixed expenses}}{\text{contribution margin per unit}} = \frac{\$7,000}{\$.10} = 70,000 \text{ units}$$

$$\frac{\text{break-even volume}}{\text{in dollars}} = \frac{\text{fixed expenses}}{\text{contribution margin ratio}} = \frac{\$7,000}{20} = 35,000$$

Note that a one-sixth increase in fixed expenses altered the break-even point by one-sixth: from 60,000 to 70,000 units and from $30,000 to $35,000. This type of relationship always exists between fixed expenses and the break-even point if everything else remains constant.

Companies frequently lower their break-even points by reducing their total fixed costs. For example, closing or selling factories decreases property taxes, insurance, depreciation, and managers' salaries.

Changes in Contribution Margin per Unit. Changes in variable costs also cause the break-even point to shift. Companies can reduce their break-even points by increasing their contribution margins per unit of product through either increases in sales prices or decreases in unit variable costs, or both.

For example, assume that the fixed rent for the vending machines is still $1,000. (1) If the owner is paid 1¢ of rent per unit sold in addition to the fixed rent, find the monthly break-even point in number of units and in dollar sales. (2) If the selling price falls from 50¢ to 45¢ per unit, and the original variable expenses per unit are unchanged, find the monthly break-even point in number of units and in dollar sales.

Here's what happens to the break-even point:

1. The variable expenses would increase from 40¢ to 41¢, the unit contribution margin would decline from 10¢ to 9¢, and the contribution-margin ratio would become .18 ($.09 ÷ $.50).

   The original fixed expenses of $6,000 would stay the same, but the denominators would change from those previously used. Thus,

$$\text{break-even point in units} = \frac{\$6,000}{\$.09} = 66,667 \text{ units}$$

$$\text{break-even point in dollars} = \frac{\$6,000}{.18} = \$33,333$$

2. If the selling price fell from 50¢ to 45¢, and the original variable expenses were unchanged, the unit contribution would be reduced from 10¢ to 5¢ (that is, 45¢ − 40¢), and the break-even point would soar to 120,000 units ($6,000 ÷ $.05). The break-even point in dollars would also change because the selling price and contribution-margin ratio change. The contribution-margin ratio would be .1111 ($.05 ÷ $.45). The break-even point, in dollars, would be $54,000 (120,000 units × $.45) or, using the formula:

$$\text{break-even point in dollars} = \frac{\$6,000}{.1111} = \$54,000$$

TARGET NET PROFIT AND AN INCREMENTAL APPROACH

Managers can also use CVP analysis to determine the total sales, in units and dollars, needed to reach a target profit. For example, in our snack vending example, suppose Winston considers $480 per month the minimum acceptable net income. How many units will have to be sold to justify the adoption of the vending machine plan? How does this figure "translate" into dollar sales?

The method for computing desired or target sales volume in units to meet the desired or target net income is the same as was used in our earlier break-even computations. Now the targets, however, are expressed in the equations:

Objective 5
Calculate sales volume in total dollars and total units to reach a target profit.

target sales − variable expenses − fixed expenses = target net income   (4)

or

$$\text{target sales volume in units} = \frac{\text{fixed expenses} + \text{target net income}}{\text{contribution margin per unit}}$$

$$= \frac{\$6,000 + \$480}{\$.10} = 64,800 \text{ units}$$

(5)

Another way of getting the same answer is to use your knowledge of the break-even point and adopt an incremental approach. The phrase **incremental effect** is widely used in accounting. It refers to the change in total results (such as revenue, expenses, or income) under a new condition in comparison with some given or known condition.

In this case, the given condition is the 60,000-unit break-even point. All expenses would be recovered at that volume. Therefore the change or increment in net income for every unit beyond 60,000 would be equal to the contribution margin of $.50 − $.40 = $.10. If $480 were the target net profit, $480 ÷ $.10 would show that the target volume must exceed the break-even volume by 4,800 units; it would therefore be 60,000 + 4,800 = 64,800 units.

To find the answer in terms of dollar sales, multiply 64,800 units by $.50 or use the formula:

$$\text{target sales volume in dollars} = \frac{\text{fixed expenses} + \text{target net income}}{\text{contribution-margin ratio}}$$

$$= \frac{\$6,000 + \$480}{.20} = \$32,400 \qquad (6)$$

To solve directly for sales dollars with the alternative incremental approach, we would start at the break-even point in dollar sales of $30,000. Every sales dollar beyond that point contributes $.20 to net profit. Divide $480 by .20. Dollar sales must exceed the break-even volume by $2,400 to produce a net profit of $480. Thus the total dollar sales would be $30,000 + $2,400 = $32,400.

The following table summarizes these computations:

	Break-Even Point	Increment	New Condition
Volume in units	60,000	4,800	64,800
Sales	$30,000	$2,400	$32,400
Variable expenses	24,000	1,920	25,920
Contribution margin	$ 6,000	$ 480	$ 6,480
Fixed expenses	6,000	—	6,000
Net income	$ 0	$ 480	$ 480

MULTIPLE CHANGES IN KEY FACTORS

So far, we have seen only changes in one CVP factor at a time. In the real world, managers often must make decisions about the probable effects of multiple factor changes. For instance, suppose that after the vending machines have been in place a while, Winston is considering locking them from 6:00 P.M. to 6:00 A.M., which she estimates will save $820 in wages monthly. However, the cutback from 24-hour service would hurt volume substantially because many nighttime employees use the machines. Should the machines remain available 24 hours per day? Assume that monthly sales would decline by 10,000 units from current sales. We will perform the analysis assuming two different levels of current sales volume: (1) 62,000 units and (2) 90,000 units. Consider two approaches. One approach is to construct and solve equations for conditions that prevail under each alternative and select the volume level that yields the highest net income.

Regardless of the current volume level, be it 62,000 or 90,000 units, if we accept the prediction that sales will decline by 10,000 units as accurate, the closing from 6:00 P.M. to 6:00 A.M. will decrease net income by $180.

	Decline from 62,000 to 52,000 Units		Decline from 90,000 to 80,000 Units	
Units	62,000	52,000	90,000	80,000
Sales	$31,000	$26,000	$45,000	$40,000
Variable expenses	24,800	20,800	36,000	32,000
Contribution margin	$ 6,200	$ 5,200	$ 9,000	$ 8,000
Fixed expenses	6,000	5,180	6,000	5,180
Net income	$ 200	$ 20	$ 3,000	$ 2,820
Change in net income		($180)		($180)

A second approach—an incremental approach—is quicker and simpler. Simplicity is important to managers because it keeps the analysis from being cluttered by irrelevant and potentially confusing data.

What does the insightful manager see in this situation? First, whether 62,000 or 90,000 units are being sold is irrelevant to the decision at hand. The issue is the decline in volume, which would be 10,000 units in either case. The essence of this decision is whether the prospective savings in fixed costs exceed the prospective loss in total contribution-margin dollars.

Lost total contribution margin, 10,000 units @ .10	$1,000
Savings in fixed expenses	820
Prospective decline in net income	$ 180

Locking the vending machines from 6:00 P.M. to 6:00 A.M. would cause a $180 decrease in monthly net income. Whichever way you analyze it, locking the machines is not a sound financial decision.

CVP ANALYSIS IN THE COMPUTER AGE

As we have seen, cost-volume-profit analysis is based on a mathematical model, the following equation.

$$\text{sales} - \text{variable expenses} - \text{fixed expenses} = \text{net income}$$

The CVP model is widely used as a planning model. Managers in a variety of organizations use a personal computer and a CVP modeling program to study combinations of changes in selling prices, unit variable costs, fixed costs, and desired profits. Many nonprofit organizations also use computerized CVP modeling. For example, some private universities have models that help measure how decisions such as raising tuition, adding programs, and closing dormitories during winter holidays will affect financial results. The computer quickly calculates the results of changes and can display them both numerically and graphically.

Exhibit 2-6 is a sample spreadsheet that shows what the sales level would have to be at three different fixed expense levels and three different variable expense levels to reach three different income levels. The computer calculates the 27 different sales levels rapidly and without error. Managers can insert any numbers they want for fixed expenses (column A), variable expense percentage (column B), target net income (row 3 of columns C, D, and E), or combinations thereof, and the computer will compute the required sales level.

In addition to speed and convenience, computers allow a more sophisticated approach to CVP analysis than the one illustrated in this chapter. The assumptions listed

Exhibit 2-6

Spreadsheet Analysis of CVP Relationships

	A	B	C	D	E
				Sales Required to Earn	
1				Sales Required to Earn	
2	Fixed	Variable		Annual Net Income of	
3	Expenses	Expense %	$ 2,000	$ 4,000	$ 6,000
4					
5	$4,000	0.40	$10,000*	$13,333	$16,667
6	$4,000	0.44	$10,714*	$14,286	$17,857
7	$4,000	0.48	$11,538*	$15,385	$19,231
8	$6,000	0.40	$13,333	$16,667	$20,000
9	$6,000	0.44	$14,286	$17,857	$21,429
10	$6,000	0.48	$15,385	$19,231	$23,077
11	$8,000	0.40	$16,667	$20,000	$23,333
12	$8,000	0.44	$17,857	$21,429	$25,000
13	$8,000	0.48	$19,231	$23,077	$26,923
15					
16	*(A5 + C3)/(1 − B5) = ($4,000 + $2,000)/(1 − $.40) = $10,000				
17	(A6 + C3)/(1 − B6) = ($4,000 + $2,000)/(1 − $.44) = $10,714				
18	(A7 + C3)/(1 − B7) = ($4,000 + $2,000)/(1 − $.48) = $11,538				
19					

on pages 52–53 are necessary to simplify the analysis enough for most managers to construct a CVP model by hand. Computer analysts, however, can construct a model that does not require all the simplifications. Computer models can include multiple cost drivers, nonlinear relationships between costs and cost drivers, varying sales mixes, and analyses that need not be restricted to a relevant range.

Use of computer models is a cost-benefit issue. Sometimes the costs of modeling are exceeded by the value of better decisions made using the models. However, the reliability of these models depends on the accuracy of their underlying assumptions about how revenues and costs will actually be affected. Moreover, in small organizations, simplified CVP models often are accurate enough that more sophisticated modeling is unwarranted.

ADDITIONAL USES OF COST-VOLUME ANALYSIS

BEST COST STRUCTURE

Analyzing cost-volume-profit relationships is an important management responsibility. Managers usually try to find the most profitable cost structure—the combination of variable- and fixed-cost factors. For example, purchasing automated machinery may raise fixed costs but reduce labor cost per unit. Conversely, it may be wise to reduce fixed costs to obtain a more favorable combination. Thus, direct selling by a salaried sales force (a fixed cost) may be replaced by the use of salespeople who are compensated via sales commissions (variable costs).

Generally, companies that spend heavily for advertising are willing to do so because they have high contribution-margin percentages (e.g., airlines, cigarette, and cosmetic companies). Conversely, companies with low contribution-margin percentages usually spend less for advertising and promotion (e.g., manufacturers of industrial equipment). As a result, two companies with the same unit sales volumes at the same unit prices could have different attitudes toward risking an advertising outlay. Assume the following:

	Perfume Company	Janitorial Service Company
Unit sales volume	100,000 bottles	100,000 square feet
Dollar sales at $20 per unit	$2,000,000	$2,000,000
Variable costs	200,000	1,700,000
Contribution margin	$1,800,000	$ 300,000
Contribution-margin percentage	90%	15%

Suppose each company wants to increase sales volume by 10%:

	Perfume Company	Janitorial Service Company
Increase in sales volume, 10,000 × $20	$200,000	$200,000
Increase in contribution margin, 90%, 15%	180,000	30,000

The perfume company would be inclined to increase advertising considerably to boost the contribution margin by $180,000. In contrast, the janitorial service company would be foolhardy to spend large amounts to increase the contribution margin by $30,000.

Note that when the contribution margin as a percentage of sales is low, great increases in volume are necessary before significant increases in net profits can occur. On the other hand, as sales exceed the break-even point, a high contribution-margin percentage increases profits faster than does a small contribution-margin percentage.

OPERATING LEVERAGE

operating leverage A firm's ratio of fixed to variable costs.

In addition to weighing the varied effects of changes in fixed and variable costs, managers need to consider their firm's ratio of fixed to variable costs, called **operating leverage**. In highly leveraged companies—those with high fixed costs and low variable costs—small changes in sales volume result in large changes in net income. Companies with less leverage (that is, lower fixed costs and higher variable costs) are not affected as much by changes in sales volume.

Exhibit 2-7 shows cost behavior relationships at two firms, one highly leveraged and one with low leverage. The firm with higher leverage has fixed costs of $14,000 and variable cost per unit of $.10. The firm with lower leverage has fixed costs of only $2,000 but variable costs of $.25 per unit. Expected sales at both companies are 80,000 units at $.30 per unit. At this sales level, both firms would have net incomes of $2,000. If sales fall short of 80,000 units, profits drop most sharply for the highly leveraged business. If sales exceed 80,000 units, however, profits increase most sharply for the highly leveraged concern.

The highly leveraged alternative is more risky. Why? Because it provides the highest possible net income and the highest possible losses. In other words, net income is highly variable, depending on the actual level of sales. The low-leverage alternative is less risky because variations in sales lead to only small variability in net income. At sales of 90,000 units, net income is $4,000 for the higher-leveraged firm but only $2,500 for the lower-leveraged firm. At sales of 70,000 units, however, the higher-leveraged firm has zero profits, compared to $1,500 for the lower-leveraged firm.

CONTRIBUTION MARGIN AND GROSS MARGIN

variable-cost ratio (variable-cost percentage) All variable costs divided by sales.

Contribution margin may be expressed as a total absolute amount, a unit absolute amount, a ratio, and a percentage. The **variable-cost ratio** or **variable-cost percentage** is defined as all variable costs divided by sales. Thus a contribution-margin ratio of 20% means that the variable-cost ratio is 80%.

Exhibit 2-7

High versus Low Leverage

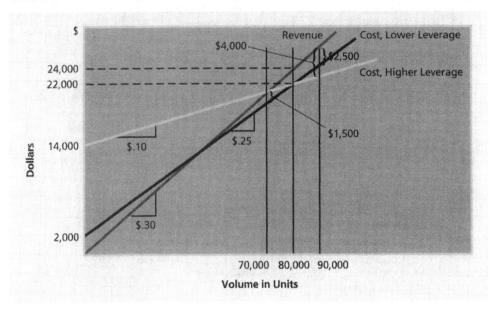

Too often people confuse the terms *contribution margin* and *gross margin*. **Gross margin** (which is also called gross profit) is the excess of sales over the **cost of goods sold** (that is, the cost of the merchandise that is acquired or manufactured and then sold). It is a widely used concept, particularly in the retailing industry.

Compare the gross margin with the contribution margin:

$$\text{gross margin} = \text{sales price} - \text{cost of goods sold}$$

$$\text{contribution margin} = \text{sales price} - \text{all variable expenses}$$

The following comparisons from our vending machine illustration show the similarities and differences between the contribution margin and the gross margin in a retail store:

Sales	$.50
Variable costs: acquisition cost of unit sold	.40
Contribution margin and gross margin are equal	$.10

Thus the original data resulted in no difference between the measure of contribution margin and gross margin. There would be a difference between the two, however, if the firm had to pay additional rent of 1¢ per unit sold:

	Contribution Margin		Gross Margin
Sales		$.50	$.50
Acquisition cost of unit sold	$.40		.40
Variable rent	.01		
Total variable expense		.41	
Contribution margin		$.09	
Gross margin			$.10

gross margin (gross profit) The excess of sales over the total cost of goods sold.

cost of goods sold The cost of the merchandise that is acquired or manufactured and resold.

Objective 6 Differentiate between contribution margin and gross margin.

One way that companies cope with hard economic times is to lower their break-even point. *Business Week* suggested that investors look for such firms "because efficiency gains at companies that have pared fixed costs as well as variable ones should be deep and lasting."

Why is lowering the break-even point important? Because a company that maintains its profitability in times of low sales is poised to take off when the economy improves. Baldwin, the piano maker, actually improved its profits in a time of decreasing sales by successfully cutting costs—especially fixed costs. If it maintains its new cost structure as sales rebound, profits will soar. Lowering fixed costs is especially important because these costs will not necessarily increase as production increases to meet renewed demand for sales.

Tenneco Automotive is one of the world's largest makers of ride-control and exhaust systems, with annual revenues of more than $3 billion (1999). In early 1999, Tenneco announced weak earnings in its automotive aftermarket business. But Chairman and CEO Dana Mead predicted that its profitability would improve and its break-even point would be lower. How? According to Mead, the company is rationalizing manufacturing and distribution capacity (in other words, selling excess and idle plants and equipment), reducing head count, and introducing new high contribution margin products. "The steps we have taken in the aftermarket, which are lowering our break-even point, should position us for the aftermarket rebound," Mead said.

Did Tenneco's strategy work? In April 2000, Tenneco announced that its first-quarter 2000 revenues were up 2% over 1999. According to David Gabriel, senior vice president, "We slashed our break-even point by more than 25% in the last 12 months. The combination of sharper marketing focus, new products, and cost control should continue to drive growth in our North American aftermarket in 2000."

Sources: Adapted from "Lots of Companies Are Lean, But Which Are Mean?" *Business Week*, February 3, 1992, p. 84; News Releases, Tenneco Automotive, Inc., January 5, 1999 and April 27, 2000.

As the preceding tabulation indicates, contribution margin and gross margin are not the same concepts. Contribution margin focuses on sales in relation to all variable costs, whereas gross margin focuses on sales in relation to cost of goods sold. For example, consider MascoTech, a Detroit-based auto parts supplier. A newspaper article reported that MascoTech's "gross profit margin on sales is about 21% today, but for each additional sales dollar the contribution margin is more like 30%."

NONPROFIT APPLICATION

Consider how cost-volume-profit relationships apply to nonprofit organizations. Suppose a city has a $100,000 lump-sum budget appropriation to conduct a counseling program for drug addicts. The variable costs for drug prescriptions are $400 per patient per year. Fixed costs are $60,000 in the relevant range of 50 to 150 patients. If all of the budget appropriation is spent, how many patients can be served in a year?

We can use the break-even equation to solve the problem. Let N be the number of patients.

revenue − variable expenses − fixed expenses = 0 if budget is completely spent

$100,000 lump sum − $400N − $60,000 = 0

$$\$400N = \$100,000 - \$60,000$$

$$N = \$40,000 \div \$400$$

$$N = 100 \text{ patients}$$

Suppose the total budget appropriation for the following year is cut by 10%. Fixed costs will be unaffected, but service will decline.

$$\text{revenue} - \text{variable expenses} - \text{fixed expenses} = 0$$

$$\$90{,}000 - \$400N - \$60{,}000 = 0$$

$$\$400N = \$90{,}000 - \$60{,}000$$

$$N = \$30{,}000 \div \$400$$

$$N = 75 \text{ patients}$$

The percentage reduction in service is more than the 10% reduction in the budget. Unless the city restructures its operations, the service volume must be reduced 25% (from 100 to 75 patients) to stay within budget. Note that lump-sum revenue is a horizontal line on the graph:

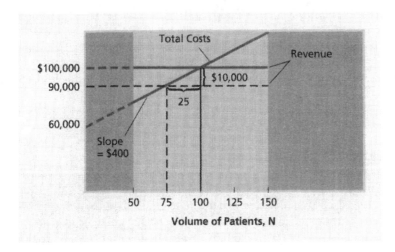

SUMMARY PROBLEM FOR YOUR REVIEW

PROBLEM

The budgeted income statement of Port Williams Gift Shop is summarized as follows.

Net revenue	$800,000
Less: expenses, including $400,000 of fixed expenses	880,000
Net loss	$(80,000)

The manager believes that an increase of $200,000 on advertising outlays will increase sales substantially.

1. At what sales volume will the store break even after spending $200,000 on advertising?
2. What sales volume will result in a net profit of $40,000 after spending the 200,000 on advertising?

SOLUTION

1. Note that all data are expressed in dollars. No unit data are given. Most companies have many products, so the overall break-even analysis deals with dollar sales, not units. The variable expenses are $880,000 − $400,000 = $480,000. The variable-expense ratio is $480,000 ÷ $800,000 = .60. Therefore the contribution-margin ratio is .40. Let S = break-even sales in dollars. Then

$$S - \text{variable expenses} - \text{fixed expenses} = \text{net profit}$$

$$S - .60S - (\$400,000 + \$200,000) = 0$$

$$.40S = \$600,000$$

$$S = \frac{\$600,000}{.40} = \frac{\text{fixed expenses}}{\text{contribution-margin ratio}}$$

$$S = \$1,500,000$$

2.

$$\text{required sales} = \frac{\text{fixed expenses} + \text{target net profit}}{\text{contribution-margin ratio}}$$

$$\text{required sales} = \frac{\$600,000 + \$40,000}{.40} = \frac{\$640,000}{.40}$$

$$\text{required sales} = \$1,600,000$$

Alternatively, we can use an incremental approach and reason that all dollar sales beyond the $1.5 million break-even point will result in a 40% contribution to net profit. Divide $40,000 by .40. Sales must therefore be $100,000 beyond the $1.5 million break-even point to produce a net profit of $40,000.

Highlights to Remember

Explain how cost drivers affect cost behavior. A cost driver is an output measure that causes the use of costly resources. When the level of an activity changes, the level of the cost driver or output measure will also change, causing changes in costs.

Show how changes in cost-driver activity levels affect variable and fixed costs. Different types of costs behave in different ways. If the costs of the resources used changes in proportion to changes in the cost driver level, the resource is a variable-cost resource (its costs are variable). If the cost of the resource used does not change because of cost driver level changes, the resource is a fixed-cost resource (its costs are fixed).

Calculate break-even sales volume in total dollars and total units. CVP analysis (sometimes called break-even analysis) can be approached graphically or with equations. To calculate the break-even point in total units, divide the fixed costs by the unit contribution margin. To calculate the break-even point in total dollars (sales dollars), divide the fixed costs by the contribution-margin ratio.

Create a cost-volume-profit graph and understand the assumptions behind it. A cost-volume-profit graph can be created by drawing revenue and total cost lines as functions of the cost-driver level. Be sure to recognize the limitations of CVP analysis and that it assumes constant efficiency, sales mix, and inventory levels.

Calculate sales volume in total dollars and total units to reach a target profit. Managers use CVP analysis to compute the sales needed to achieve a target profit or to examine the effects on profit of changes in factors such as fixed costs, variable costs, or cost driver volume.

Differentiate between contribution margin and gross margin. The contribution margin—the difference between sales price and variable costs—is an important concept. Do not confuse it with gross margin, the difference between sales price and cost of goods sold.

Understand how cost behavior and CVP analysis are used by managers. Understanding cost behavior patterns and cost-volume-profit (CVP) relationships can help guide a manager's decisions. Because one of the main goals of management accounting is controlling and reducing costs, understanding cost behavior is vital to the manager's decision-making role. CVP analysis is a technique that is used often by management accountants both to gain an understanding of the cost and profit structure in a company and to explain it to other managers.

Appendix 2A: Sales-Mix Analysis

To emphasize fundamental ideas, the cost-volume-profit analysis in this chapter has focused on a single product. Nearly all companies, however, sell more than one product. Sales mix is defined as the relative proportions or combinations of quantities of products that comprise total sales. If the proportions of the mix change, the cost-volume-profit relationships also change.

Objective 7
Explain the effects of sales mix on profits.

Suppose Ramos Company has two products, wallets (W) and key cases (K). The income budget follows.

	Wallets (W)	Key Cases (K)	Total
Sales in units	300,000	75,000	375,000
Sales @ $8 and $5	$2,400,000	$375,000	$2,775,000
Variable expenses @ $7 and $3	2,100,000	225,000	2,325,000
Contribution margins @ $1 and $2	$ 300,000	$150,000	$ 450,000
Fixed expenses			180,000
Net income			$ 270,000

For simplicity, ignore income taxes. What would be the break-even point? The typical answer assumes a constant mix of 4 units of W for every unit of K. Therefore, let K = number of units of product K to break even, and 4K = number of units of product W to break even:

$$\text{sales} - \text{variable expenses} - \text{fixed expenses} = \text{zero net income}$$

$$[\$8(4K) + \$5(K)] - [\$7(4K) + \$3(K)] - \$180,000 = 0$$

$$\$32K + \$5K - \$28K - \$3K - \$180,000 = 0$$

$$\$6K = \$180,000$$

$$K = 30,000$$

$$4K = 120,000 = W$$

The break-even point is 30,000K + 120,000W = 150,000 units.

This is the only break-even point for a sales mix of four wallets for every key case. Clearly, however, there are other break-even points for other sales mixes. For instance, suppose only key cases were sold, fixed expenses being unchanged.

$$\text{break-even point} = \frac{\text{fixed expenses}}{\text{contribution margin per unit}}$$

$$= \frac{\$180,000}{\$2}$$

$$= 90,000 \text{ key cases}$$

If only wallets were sold:

$$\text{break-even point} = \frac{\$180,000}{\$1}$$

$$= 180,000 \text{ wallets}$$

Managers are not interested in the break-even point for its own sake. Instead, they want to know how changes in a planned sales mix will affect net income. When the sales mix changes, the break-even point and the expected net income at various sales levels are altered. For example, suppose overall actual total sales were equal to the budget of 375,000 units. However, only 50,000 key cases were sold.

	Wallets (W)	Key Cases (K)	Total
Sales in units	325,000	50,000	375,000
Sales @ $8 and $5	$2,600,000	$250,000	$2,850,000
Variable expenses @ $7 and $3	2,275,000	150,000	2,425,000
Contribution margins @ $1 and $2	$ 325,000	$100,000	$ 425,000
Fixed expenses			180,000
Net income			$ 245,000

The change in sales mix has resulted in a $245,000 actual net income rather than the $270,000 budgeted net income, an unfavorable difference of $25,000. The budgeted and actual sales in number of units were identical, but the proportion of sales of the product bearing the higher unit contribution margin declined.

Managers usually want to maximize the sales of all their products. Faced with limited resources and time, however, executives prefer to generate the most profitable sales mix achievable. For example, consider a recent annual report of Deere & Co., a manufacturer of farm equipment: "The increase in the ratio of cost of goods sold to net sales resulted from higher production costs [and] a less favorable mix of products sold."

Profitability of a given product helps guide executives who must decide to emphasize or de-emphasize particular products. For example, given limited production facilities or limited time of sales personnel, should we emphasize wallets or key cases? These decisions may be affected by other factors beyond the contribution margin per unit of product. Chapter 5 explores some of these factors, including the importance of the amount of profit per unit of time rather than per unit of product.

Appendix 2B: Impact of Income Taxes

Objective 8
Compute cost-volume-profit relationships on an after-tax basis.

Thus far we have (as so many people would like to) ignored income taxes. In most nations, however, private enterprises are subject to income taxes. Reconsider the vending machine example in this chapter. As part of our CVP analysis, we discussed the sales necessary to achieve a target income before income taxes of $480. If an income tax were levied at 40%, the new result would be

Income before income tax	$480	100%
Income tax	192	40
Net income	$288	60%

Note that

net income = income before income taxes − .40 (income before income taxes)

net income = .60 (income before income taxes)

$$\text{income before income taxes} = \frac{\text{net income}}{.60}$$

or

$$\text{target income before income taxes} = \frac{\text{target after-tax net income}}{1 - \text{tax rate}}$$

$$\text{target income before income taxes} = \frac{\$288}{1 - .40} = \frac{\$288}{.60} = \$480$$

Suppose the target net income after taxes was $288. The only change in the general equation approach would be on the right-hand side of the following equation:

$$\text{target sales} - \text{variable expenses} - \text{fixed expenses} = \frac{\text{target after-tax net income}}{1 - \text{tax rate}}$$

Thus, letting N be the number of units to be sold at $.50 each with a variable cost of $.40 each and total fixed costs of $6,000,

$$\$.50N - \$.40N - \$6,000 = \frac{\$288}{1 - .4}$$

$$\$.10N = \$6,000 + \frac{\$288}{.6}$$

$$\$.06N = \$3,600 + \$288 = 3,888$$

$$N = \$3,888 \div \$.06 = 64,800 \text{ units}$$

Sales of 64,800 units produce an after-tax profit of $288 as shown here and a before-tax profit of $480 as shown in the chapter.

Suppose the target net income after taxes was $480. The volume needed would rise to 68,000 units, as follows:

$$\$.50N - \$.40N - \$6,000 = \frac{\$480}{1 - .4}$$

$$\$.10N = \$6,000 + \frac{\$480}{.6}$$

$$\$.06N = \$3,600 + \$480 = \$4,080$$

$$N = \$4,080 \div \$.06 = 68,000 \text{ units}$$

As a shortcut to computing the effects of volume on the change in after-tax income, use the formula

$$\begin{matrix}\text{change} \\ \text{in net} \\ \text{income}\end{matrix} = \left(\begin{matrix}\text{change in volume} \\ \text{in units}\end{matrix}\right) \times \left(\begin{matrix}\text{contribution margin} \\ \text{per unit}\end{matrix}\right) \times (1 - \text{tax rate})$$

In our example, suppose operations were at a level of 64,800 units and $288 after-tax net income. The manager is wondering how much after-tax net income would increase if sales become 68,000 units.

$$\text{change in net income} = (68,000 - 64,800) \times \$.10 \times (1 - .4)$$

$$= 3,200 \times \$.10 \times .60 = 3,200 \times \$.06$$

$$= \$192$$

In brief, each unit beyond the break-even point adds to after-tax net profit at the unit contribution margin multiplied by (1 − income tax rate).

Throughout our illustration, the break-even point itself does not change. Why? Because there is no income tax at a level of zero profits.

chapter

3

MEASUREMENT OF COST BEHAVIOR

An America West flight on final
approach to San Diego's airport.
America West serves the low
cost–full service market at more than
144 destinations in the United States,
Canada, and Mexico. Understanding
the company's costs is an important
factor in the company's competitive
strategy.

www.prenhall.com/horngren

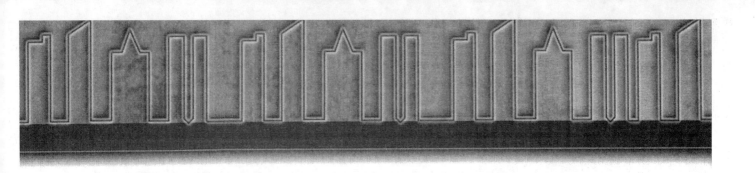

Learning Objectives

When you have finished studying this chapter, you should be able to

1. *Explain step- and mixed-cost behavior.*

2. *Explain management influences on cost behavior.*

3. *Measure and mathematically express cost functions and use them to predict costs.*

4. *Describe the importance of activity analysis for measuring cost functions.*

5. *Measure cost behavior using the account analysis, high-low, visual-fit, and least-squares regression methods.*

6. **Understand the relationship between management decision making and cost behavior.**

With annual revenues of more than $2 billion, America West is the ninth-largest U.S. commercial airline. The company focuses on the low-cost, full-service market with primary operations (hubs) in Phoenix, Las Vegas, and Columbus, Ohio. America West rode a booming economy to increased revenues in the late 1990s. As a result, management decided to expand by introducing service to new destinations including Acapulco, Miami, and Detroit, and by adding more daily flights to existing markets including Las Vegas, Mexico City, and Boston. To accomplish this, the company had to expand its labor force, add new aircraft, and spend more than $40 million on new technology.

Management at America West did not take lightly the decision to invest large amounts of money in aircraft and equipment. They knew that their decision would have a significant influence on costs and thus profits for many years. They also knew that most of the costs would be fixed but the revenues would fluctuate with the economy. When the economy is bad, revenues may not cover these costs.

How does an airline protect itself against losses when the economy turns down? According to Richard Goodmanson, President and Chief Executive Officer of America West, "management has a goal to have from 5% to 10% of the fleet of aircraft leased and thus subject to annual renewal. This enhances the company's ability to decrease capacity (and related costs) in the event of an industry downturn." This example illustrates that understanding how costs behave, as well as how managers' decisions can influence costs, helped the airline improve its cost control.

Chapter 2 demonstrated the importance of understanding the cost structure of an organization and the relationships between an organization's activities and its costs,

measurement of cost behavior Understanding and quantifying how activities of an organization affect levels of costs.

revenues, and profits. This chapter focuses on **measurement of cost behavior,** which means understanding and quantifying how activities of an organization affect levels of costs. Recall that activities use resources and these resources have costs. We measure the relationship between activity and cost using output measures called cost drivers. Understanding relationships between costs and their cost drivers allows managers in all types of organizations—profit-seeking, nonprofit, and government—to

- Evaluate new manufacturing methods or service practices (Chapter 4)
- Make proper short-run marketing decisions (Chapter 5)
- Make short-run production decisions (Chapter 6)
- Plan or budget the effects of future activities (Chapters 7 and 8)
- Design effective management control systems (Chapters 9 and 10)
- Make proper long-run decisions (Chapter 11)
- Design accurate and useful product costing systems (Chapters 12 to 15)

As you can see, understanding cost behavior is fundamental to management accounting. There are numerous real-world cases in which managers have made very poor decisions to drop product lines, close manufacturing plants, or bid too high or too low on jobs because they had erroneous cost behavior information. This chapter, therefore, deserves careful study.

COST DRIVERS AND COST BEHAVIOR

linear-cost behavior Activity that can be graphed with a straight line because costs are assumed to be either fixed or variable.

Accountants and managers often assume that cost behavior is linear over some relevant range of activity levels or cost-driver levels. **Linear-cost behavior** can be graphed with a straight line because each cost is assumed to be either fixed or variable. Recall that the relevant range specifies the limits of cost-driver activity within which a specific relationship between a cost and its cost driver will be valid. Managers usually define the relevant range based on their previous experience with different levels of activity and cost.

Many activities can influence costs. However, in this chapter we focus on those costs for which the volume of a product produced or service provided is the primary driver. These costs are easy to identify with, or trace to, products or services. Examples of volume-driven costs include the costs of printing labor, paper, ink, and binding to produce all the copies of this textbook. The number of copies printed obviously affects the total printing labor, paper, ink, and binding costs. Equally important, we could relatively easily trace the use of these resources to the copies of the text printed. Schedules, payroll records, and other documents show how much of each was used to produce the copies of this text.

Other costs are more affected by activities not directly related to volume and often have multiple cost drivers. Such costs are not easy to identify with or trace to outputs. Examples of costs that are difficult to trace include the wages and salaries of the editorial staff of the publisher of this textbook. These editorial personnel produce many different textbooks, and it would be very difficult to determine exactly what portion of their costs went into a specific book, such as *Introduction to Management Accounting.*

Understanding and measuring costs that are difficult to trace to outputs can be especially challenging. In practice, many organizations use a linear relationship with a single cost driver to describe each cost even though many have multiple causes. This approach is easier and less expensive than using nonlinear relationships or multiple cost drivers. Careful use of linear-cost behavior with a single cost driver often provides cost

Exhibit 3-1

Linear-Cost Behavior

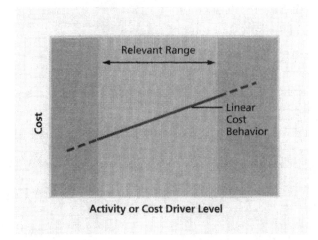

estimates that are accurate enough for most decisions. Linear-cost behavior with a single cost driver may seem at odds with reality and economic theory, but the added benefit of understanding "true" cost behavior may be less than the cost of determining "true" cost behavior.

For ease of communication and understanding, accountants usually describe cost behavior in visual or graphical terms. Exhibit 3-1 shows linear-cost behavior, the relevant range, and an activity or cost driver. Note the similarity to the CVP charts of Chapter 2.

STEP- AND MIXED-COST BEHAVIOR PATTERNS

Chapter 2 described two patterns of cost behavior: variable costs and fixed costs. Recall that a purely variable cost changes in proportion to changes in its cost driver's activity, while a purely fixed cost is not affected by the cost-driver level. In addition to these pure versions of cost, two additional types of costs combine characteristics of both fixed- and variable-cost behavior. These are step costs and mixed costs.

Step Costs. **Step costs** change abruptly at intervals of activity because the resources and their costs are only available in indivisible chunks. If the individual chunks of cost are relatively large and apply to a specific, broad range of activity, the cost is considered a fixed cost over that range of activity. An example is in panel A of Exhibit 3-2, which shows the cost of leasing oil and gas drilling equipment. When oil and gas exploration activity reaches a certain level in a given region, an entire additional rig must be leased. One level of oil and gas rig leasing, however, will support all volumes of exploration activity within a relevant range of drilling. Within each relevant range, this step cost behaves as a fixed cost. The total step cost at a level of activity is the amount of fixed cost appropriate for the range containing that activity level.

In contrast, accountants often describe step costs as variable when the individual chunks of costs are relatively small and apply to a narrow range of activity. Panel B of Exhibit 3-2 shows the wage cost of cashiers at a supermarket. Suppose one cashier can serve an average of 20 shoppers per hour and that within the relevant range of shopping activity, the number of shoppers can range from 40 per hour to 440 per hour. The corresponding number of cashiers would range between two and 22. Because the steps are relatively small, this step cost behaves much like a variable cost and could be used as such for planning with little loss of accuracy.

Objective 1
Explain step- and mixed-cost behavior.

step costs Costs that change abruptly at intervals of activity because the resources and their costs come in indivisible chunks.

Exhibit 3-2

Step-Cost Behavior

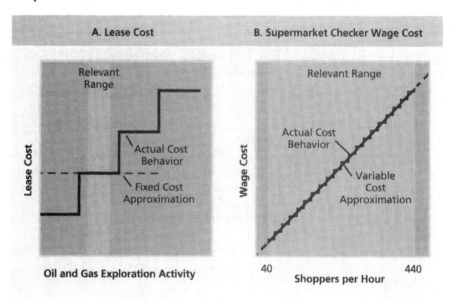

Mixed Costs. **Mixed costs** contain elements of both fixed- and variable-cost behavior. The fixed element is determined for a single planned range of activity level. The variable-cost element of the mixed cost is a purely variable cost that varies proportionately with activity within the single relevant range. In a mixed cost, the variable cost is incurred in addition to the fixed cost: The total mixed cost is the sum of the fixed cost plus the variable cost. You might think of the fixed cost as the cost of having available the capacity necessary to operate at any volume within the relevant range and the variable cost as the additional cost of using that capacity to produce outputs.

Many costs are mixed costs. For example, consider the monthly facilities maintenance department cost of the Parkview Medical Center, shown in Exhibit 3-3. Salaries of the maintenance personnel and costs of equipment are fixed at $10,000 per month. In

> **mixed costs** Costs that contain elements of both fixed- and variable-cost behavior.

Exhibit 3-3

Mixed-Cost Behavior

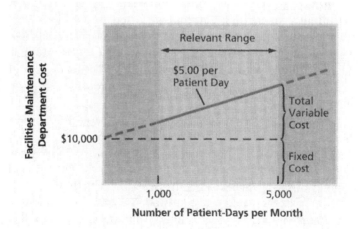

addition, cleaning supplies and repair materials may vary at a rate of $5 per patient-day[1] delivered by the hospital.

The chief administrator at Parkview Medical Center used knowledge of the facilities maintenance department cost behavior to

1. **Plan costs:** In May the hospital expected to service 4,000 patient-days. May's predicted facilities maintenance department costs are $10,000 fixed plus the variable cost of $20,000 (4,000 patient-days times $5 per patient-day) for a total of $30,000.

2. **Provide feedback to managers:** In May the actual facilities maintenance costs were $34,000 in a month when 4,000 patient-days were serviced as planned. The administrator wanted to know why the hospital overspent by $4,000 ($34,000 less the planned $30,000) so that managers could take corrective action.

3. **Make decisions about the most efficient use of resources:** For example, managers might weigh the long-run tradeoffs of increased fixed costs of highly automated floor cleaning equipment against the variable costs of extra hours needed to clean floors manually.

MANAGEMENT INFLUENCE ON COST BEHAVIOR

In addition to measuring and evaluating current cost behavior, managers can influence cost behavior through decisions about such factors as product or service attributes, capacity, technology, and policies to create incentives to control costs.

Objective 2
Explain management influences on cost behavior.

PRODUCT AND SERVICE DECISIONS AND THE VALUE CHAIN

Throughout the value chain, managers influence cost behavior. This influence occurs through their choices of process and product design, quality levels, product features, distribution channels, and so on. Each of these decisions contributes to the organization's performance and should be made in a cost-benefit framework. For example, Hertz, the car rental company, would add a feature to its services only if the cost of the feature (for example, free mileage) could be justified (more than recovered in profit from increased business).

CAPACITY DECISIONS

Strategic decisions about the scale and scope of an organization's activities generally result in fixed levels of capacity costs. **Capacity costs** are the fixed costs of being able to achieve a desired level of production or to provide a desired level of service while maintaining product or service attributes, such as quality. Companies in industries with long-term variations in demand must be careful when making capacity decisions. Fixed capacity costs cannot be recovered when demand falls during an economic downturn. Consider the dilemma facing Ford. In the mid-1980s, Ford was operating at full capacity. To meet demand, workers were on overtime and Ford even contracted with Mazda to produce some of its Probe cars. Ford had to choose either to build new plants and assembly lines or to continue to pay premiums for overtime and outside production. Building new plants would enable Ford to produce cars at lower cost, but the fixed capacity costs could not be reduced if production volumes were to fall. Overtime and outsourcing production to Mazda were expensive, but Ford could eliminate these variable costs during any business downturn when it did not need the extra cars. What did Ford do? According to executives at Ford, "We know in 1986 and 1987 we lost some sales. We could have probably had a higher market share. But we felt it was worth it to keep our costs under

capacity costs The fixed costs of being able to achieve a desired level of production or to provide a desired level of service while maintaining product or service attributes, such as quality.

---

[1] *A patient-day is one patient spending one day in the hospital. One patient spending five days in the hospital is five patient-days of service*

control. . . . Sooner or later there's going to be a downturn and we'll be running down days and short weeks even with the capacity we have." Ford's decision to limit its fixed costs even in the face of higher variable costs helped the company to endure the business downturn in the early 1990s. Ford was better able to reduce its costs as demand for autos fell. Again, in the economic boom of the late 1990s, Ford faced the same strategic decision concerning scale and scope of operations.

COMMITTED FIXED COSTS

committed fixed costs
Costs arising from the possession of facilities, equipment, and a basic organization: large, indivisible chunks of cost that the organization is obligated to incur or usually would not consider avoiding.

Even if, like Ford, a company has chosen to minimize fixed capacity costs, every organization has some costs to which it is committed, perhaps for quite a few years. **Committed fixed costs** usually arise from the possession of facilities, equipment, and a basic organization. These are large, indivisible chunks of cost that the organization is obligated to incur or usually would not consider eliminating. Committed fixed costs include mortgage or lease payments, interest payments on long-term debt, property taxes, insurance, and salaries of key personnel. Only major changes in the philosophy, scale, or scope of operations could change these committed fixed costs in future periods. Recall the example of the facilities maintenance department for the Parkview Medical Center. The capacity of the facilities maintenance department was a management decision, and in this case the decision determined the magnitude of the equipment cost. Suppose Parkview Medical Center were to increase permanently its patient-days per month beyond the relevant range of 5,000 patient-days. Because more capacity would be needed, the committed equipment cost would rise to a new level per month.

DISCRETIONARY FIXED COSTS

discretionary fixed costs
Costs determined by management as part of the periodic planning process in order to meet the organization's goals. They have no obvious relationship with levels of capacity or output activity.

Some costs are fixed at certain levels only because management decided that these levels of cost should be incurred to meet the organization's goals. These **discretionary fixed costs** have no obvious relationship to levels of capacity or output activity but are determined as part of the periodic planning process. Each planning period, management will determine how much to spend on discretionary items such as advertising and promotion costs, public relations, research and development costs, charitable donations, employee training programs, and purchased management consulting services. These costs then become fixed until the next planning period.

Unlike committed fixed costs, managers can alter discretionary fixed costs easily—up or down—even within a budget period, if they decide that different levels of spending are desirable. Conceivably, managers could reduce such discretionary costs almost entirely for a given year in dire times, whereas they could not reduce committed costs. Discretionary fixed costs may be essential to the long-run achievement of the organization's goals, but managers can vary spending levels broadly in the short run.

Consider Marietta Corporation, which is experiencing financial difficulties. Sales for its major products are down, and Marietta's management is considering cutting back on costs temporarily. Marietta's management must determine which of the following fixed costs can be reduced or eliminated and how much money each would save:

Fixed Costs	Planned Amounts
Advertising and promotion	$ 30,000
Depreciation	400,000
Employee training	100,000
Management salaries	800,000
Mortgage payment	250,000
Property taxes	600,000
Research and development	1,500,000
Total	$3,680,000

Can Marietta reduce or eliminate any of these fixed costs? The answer depends on Marietta's long-run outlook. Marietta could reduce costs but also greatly reduce its ability to compete in the future if it cuts carelessly. Rearranging these costs by categories of committed and discretionary costs yields the following analysis:

Fixed Costs	Planned Amounts
Committed	
Depreciation	$ 400,000
Mortgage payment	250,000
Property taxes	600,000
Total committed	$1,250,000
Discretionary (potential savings)	
Advertising and promotion	$ 30,000
Employee training	100,000
Management salaries	800,000
Research and development	1,500,000
Total discretionary	$2,430,000
Total committed and discretionary	$3,680,000

Eliminating all discretionary fixed costs would save Marietta $2,430,000 per year. However, Marietta would be unwise to cut all discretionary costs completely. This would severely impair the company's long-run prospects. Nevertheless, distinguishing committed and discretionary fixed costs would be the company's first step to identifying where costs could be reduced.

Consider the difference between committed and discretionary fixed costs. Committed costs limit management's flexibility, while discretionary costs preserve flexibility Are all fixed costs either committed or discretionary?

ANSWER

No. These are two ends of a spectrum. Most fixed costs have characteristics of both committed and discretionary costs. However, it is helpful to try to classify costs as committed or discretionary, because it forces managers to think about how much influence they might have over the cost if they want to change it.

TECHNOLOGY DECISIONS

One of the most critical decisions that managers make is the type of technology that the organization will use to produce its products or deliver its services. Choice of technology (for example, labor-intensive versus robotic manufacturing, traditional banking services versus automated tellers, or e-commerce versus in-store or mail-order sales) positions the organization to meet its current goals and to respond to changes in the environment (for example, changes in customer needs or actions by competitors). The use of high technology methods rather than labor usually means a much greater fixed-cost component to the total cost. This type of cost behavior creates greater risks for companies with wide variations in demand.

COST-CONTROL INCENTIVES

Finally, the incentives that management creates for employees can affect future costs. Managers use their knowledge of cost behavior to set cost expectations, and employees may receive compensation or other rewards that are tied to meeting these expectations. For example, the administrator of Parkview Medical Center gave the supervisor of the facilities maintenance department a favorable evaluation if the supervisor maintained quality of service and kept department costs below the expected amount for the actual level of patient-days. This feedback motivated the supervisor to watch department costs carefully and to find ways to reduce costs without reducing quality of service.

COST FUNCTIONS

cost measurement
Estimating or predicting costs as a function of appropriate cost drivers.

The decision making, planning, and controlling activities of management accounting require accurate and useful estimates of future fixed and variable costs. The first step in estimating or predicting costs is **cost measurement** or measuring cost behavior as a function of appropriate cost drivers. The second step is to use these cost measures to estimate future costs at expected, future levels of cost-driver activity.

Objective 3
Measure and mathematically express cost functions and use them to predict costs.

cost function An algebraic equation used by managers to describe the relationship between a cost and its cost driver(s).

FORM OF COST FUNCTIONS

To describe the relationship between a cost and its cost driver(s), managers often use an algebraic equation called a **cost function.** When there is only one cost driver, the cost function is similar to the algebraic CVP relationships discussed in Chapter 2. Consider the mixed cost graphed in Exhibit 3-3 on page 88, the facilities maintenance department cost:

$$\text{Monthly facilities maintenance department costs} = \text{Monthly fixed maintenance cost} + \text{Monthly variable maintenance cost}$$

$$= \text{Monthly fixed maintenance cost} + \left(\text{Variable cost per patient-day} \times \text{Number of patient-days in the month} \right)$$

Let

Y = monthly facilities maintenance department cost

F = monthly fixed maintenance cost

V = variable cost per patient-day

X = cost-driver activity in number of patient-days per month

We can rewrite the mixed-cost function as

$$Y = F + VX \text{ or}$$

$$Y = \$10,000 + \$5.00X$$

This mixed-cost function has the familiar form of a straight line—it is called a linear-cost function. When graphing a cost function, F is the intercept, the point on the vertical axis where the cost function begins. In Exhibit 3-3, the intercept is the $10,000 fixed cost per month. V, the variable cost per unit of activity, is the slope of the cost function. In Exhibit 3-3, the cost function slopes upward at the rate of $5 for each additional patient-day.

CRITERIA FOR CHOOSING FUNCTIONS

Managers should apply two principles to obtain accurate and useful cost functions: *plausibility* and *reliability*.

1. The cost function must be plausible or believable. Personal observation of costs and activities, when it is possible, provides the best evidence of a plausible relationship between a cost and its driver. Some cost relationships, by nature, are not directly observable, so the cost analyst must be confident that the proposed relationship is sound. Many costs may move together with a number of cost drivers, but no cause-and-effect relationships may exist. A cause-and-effect relationship (that is, X causes Y) is desirable for cost functions to be accurate and useful.

2. In addition to being plausible, a cost function's estimates of costs at actual levels of activity must reliably conform with actually observed costs. Reliability can be assessed in terms of "goodness of fit"—how well the cost function explains past cost behavior. If the fit is good and conditions do not change, the cost function should be a reliable predictor of future costs.

Note especially that managers use these criteria together in choosing a cost function. Each is a check on the other. Knowledge of operations and how costs are recorded is helpful in choosing a plausible and reliable cost function that links cause and effect. For example, maintenance is often performed when output is low, because that is when machines can be taken out of service. Lower output does not cause increased maintenance costs, however, nor does increased output cause lower maintenance costs. A more plausible explanation is that over a longer period increased output causes higher maintenance costs, but daily or weekly recording of maintenance costs and outputs may make it appear otherwise. Understanding the nature of maintenance costs should lead to a reliable, long-run cost function.

A cost function is a mathematical expression of the components of a particular cost. However, an intuitive understanding of cost functions is just as important as being able to write the mathematical formula. For example, what does it mean when a cost function is linear?

ANSWER

It means that there are two parts to the cost. One part is fixed—that is, it's independent of the cost driver. The other part varies in proportion to the cost driver. That is, if the cost driver increases by $X\%$, this part of the cost also increases by $X\%$.

CHOICE OF COST DRIVERS: ACTIVITY ANALYSIS

How do managers choose reliable and plausible cost functions? Well, you cannot have a good cost function without knowing the right cost drivers, so choosing a cost function starts with choosing cost drivers. Managers use **activity analysis** to identify appropriate cost drivers and their effects on the costs of making a product or providing a service. The final product or service may have a number of cost drivers because a number of separate activities may be involved. The greatest benefit of activity analysis is that it directs management accountants to the appropriate cost drivers for each cost.

Activity analysis is especially important for measuring and predicting costs for which cost drivers are not obvious. **Cost prediction** applies cost measures to expected future activity levels to forecast future costs. Earlier in this chapter we said that a cost is fixed or

activity analysis The process of identifying appropriate cost drivers and their effects on the costs of making a product or providing a service.

cost prediction The application of cost measures to expected future activity levels to forecast future costs.

Objective 4
Describe the
importance of activity
analysis for measuring
cost functions.

variable with respect to a specific cost driver. A cost that appears fixed in relation to one cost driver could in fact be variable in relation to another cost driver. For example, suppose the Jupiter automobile plant uses automated painting equipment. The cost of adjusting this equipment may be fixed with respect to the total number of automobiles produced. That is, there is no clear cost relationship between these support costs and the number of automobiles produced. This same cost may vary greatly, however, with the number of different colors and types of finishes of automobiles produced. Activity analysis examines various potential cost drivers for plausibility and reliability. As always, the expected benefits of improved decision making from using more accurate cost behavior should exceed the expected costs of the cost-driver search.

Identifying the appropriate cost drivers is the most critical aspect of any method for measuring cost behavior. For many years, most organizations used only one cost driver: the amount of labor used. In essence, they assumed that the only activity affecting costs was the use of labor. In the past decade, however, we have learned that previously "hidden" activities greatly influence costs. Often, analysts in both manufacturing and service companies find that activities related to the complexity of performing tasks affect costs more directly than do labor usage or other cost drivers that are related to the volume of output activity.

Consider Northwestern Computers, which makes two products for personal computers: a plug-in music board (Mozart-Plus) and a hard-disk drive (Powerdrive). When most of the work on Northwestern's products was done by hand, most costs, other than the cost of materials, were related to (driven by) labor cost. The use of computer-controlled assembly equipment, however, has increased the costs of support activities and has reduced labor cost. Labor cost is now only 5% of the total costs at Northwestern. Furthermore, activity analysis has shown that most of today's support costs are driven by the number of components added to products (a measure of product complexity), not by labor cost. Mozart-Plus has five component parts, and Powerdrive has nine.

On average, support costs are twice as much as labor costs. Suppose Northwestern wants to predict how much support cost is incurred in producing one Mozart-Plus and how much for one Powerdrive. Using the old cost driver, labor cost, the prediction of support costs would be

	Mozart-Plus	**Powerdrive**
Labor cost	$ 8.50	$130.00
Support cost:		
2 × Direct labor cost	$17.00	$260.00

Using the more appropriate cost driver, the number of components added to products, the predicted support costs are

	Mozart-Plus	**Powerdrive**
Support cost		
at $20 per component		
$20 × 5 components	$100.00	
$20 × 9 components		$180.00
Difference in predicted support cost	$ 83.00	$ 80.00
	higher	lower

By using an appropriate cost driver, Northwestern can predict its support costs much more accurately. Managers will make better decisions with this more accurate information. For example, prices charged for products can be more closely related to the costs of production.

Manufacturing companies were the first organizations to use activity analysis. However, its use has spread to many service industries and nonprofit organizations. A recent article described how the Hospice of Central Kentucky (HCK) undertook an activity analysis to better understand its costs.

HCK is a Medicare/Medicaid–certified program providing medical care to the terminally ill in ten counties in central Kentucky. In addition to seeing to the medical needs of its patients, HCK has social workers, home health aides, volunteers, and chaplains. It also provides an 18-month bereavement program for families of patients.

Many of HCK's costs were directly patient related, and understanding these costs posed no problems. However, support costs were large, and HCK had little information about what caused these costs. Before undertaking an activity analysis, HCK simply assumed that the patient-day was the only cost driver for all support costs. Support costs were computed as $35.53 per patient-day.

Because HCK felt the squeeze of increasing costs and constant reimbursements from HMOs and insurance companies, management at HCK wanted better cost information to make various decisions. To do this, the organization undertook an activity analysis to determine the appropriate cost drivers for support costs. This consisted of two basic tasks: (1) Identify the activities being performed and (2) select a cost driver for each activity.

To identify the activities and the costs related to each activity, HCK formed a cross-functional team. Identifying the activities takes a thorough understanding of all the operations of the hospice, so a team of only finance or accounting professionals would not be knowledgeable enough for this task. The team included the director of operations, the bereavement coordinator, the billing coordinator, a nurse, and a representative of the community service program. Among them they knew all aspects of the hospice's operations.

The team identified 14 activities. The next step was to select a cost driver for each activity. Some of the activities and their related cost drivers are

Activity	Cost Driver
Referral	Number of (indexed) referrals
Admission	Number of admissions
Bereavement	Number of deaths
Accounting/Finance	Number of (indexed) patient days
Billing	Number of billings
Volunteer services	Number of volunteers

Using the cost information from the activity analysis, management was able to learn how much each different activity costs and could recognize that patients that required use of expensive activities were more expensive to treat. Management could then try to reduce the costs of activities that were not worth the amount being spent for them, and they could better negotiate contracts so that HMOs and insurance companies would provide more support for patients that required the most expensive activities.

Source: Adapted from Sidney J. Baxendale and Victoria Dornbusch, "Activity-Based Costing for a Hospice," *Strategic Finance*, March 2000, pp. 65–70.

METHODS OF MEASURING COST FUNCTIONS

After determining the most plausible drivers behind different costs, managers can choose from a broad selection of methods of approximating cost functions. Methods include (1) engineering analysis, (2) account analysis, (3) high-low analysis, (4) visual-fit analysis, and (5) least-squares regression analysis. These methods are not mutually exclusive; managers frequently use two or more together to avoid major errors in measuring cost behavior. The first two methods may rely only on logical analysis, whereas the last three involve analysis of past costs.

ENGINEERING ANALYSIS

The first method, **engineering analysis,** measures cost behavior according to what costs should be, not by what costs have been. It entails a systematic review of materials, supplies, labor, support services, and facilities needed for products and services. Analysts can

engineering analysis The systematic review of materials, supplies, labor, support services, and facilities needed for products and services; measuring cost behavior according to what costs should be, not by what costs have been.

even use engineering analysis successfully for new products and services, as long as the organization has had experience with similar costs. Why? Because measures can be based on information from personnel who are directly involved with the product or service. In addition to actual experience, analysts learn about new costs from experiments with prototypes, accounting and industrial engineering literature, the experience of competitors, and the advice of management consultants. From this information, cost analysts determine what future costs should be. If the cost analysts are experienced and understand the activities of the organization, then their engineering cost predictions may be quite reliable and useful for decision making. The disadvantages of engineering cost analysis are that the efforts are costly and often not timely.

Weyerhauser Company, producer of wood products, used engineering analysis to determine the cost functions for its 14 corporate service departments. These cost functions are used to measure the cost of corporate services used by three main business groups. For example, accounts payable costs for each division are a function of three cost drivers: the number of hours spent on each division, number of documents, and number of invoices. This approach to measuring cost behavior also could be used by nearly any service organization.

At Parkview Medical Center, introduced earlier, an assistant to the hospital administrator interviewed facilities maintenance personnel and observed their activities on several random days for a month. From these data, the assistant confirmed that the most plausible cost driver for facilities maintenance cost is the number of patient-days. The assistant also estimated from current department salaries and equipment charges that monthly fixed costs approximated $10,000 per month. From interviews and supplies usage during the month that the assistant observed, the assistant estimated that variable costs are $5 per patient-day. The assistant gave this information to the hospital administrator but cautioned that the cost measures may be wrong because

1. The month observed may be abnormal.
2. The facilities maintenance personnel may have altered their normal work habits because the assistant was observing them.
3. The facilities maintenance personnel may not have told the complete truth about their activities because of their concerns about the use of the information they revealed.

However, if we assume the observed and estimated information is correct, facilities maintenance cost in any month could be predicted by first forecasting that month's expected patient-days and then entering that figure into the following algebraic, mixed-cost function:

$$Y = \$10,000 \text{ per month} + (\$5 \times \text{patient-days})$$

For example, if the administrator expects 4,000 patient-days next month, facilities maintenance costs are predicted to be

$$Y = \$10,000 + (\$5 \times 4,000 \text{ patient-days}) = \underline{\$30,000}$$

ACCOUNT ANALYSIS

account analysis Selecting a plausible cost driver and classifying each account as a variable cost or as a fixed cost.

In contrast to engineering analysis, users of **account analysis** look to the accounting system for information about cost behavior. The simplest method of account analysis selects a plausible cost driver and classifies each account as a variable or fixed cost with respect to the cost driver. The cost analyst then looks at each cost account balance and estimates either the variable cost per unit of cost-driver activity or the periodic fixed cost.

To illustrate this approach to account analysis, let's return to the facilities maintenance department at Parkview Medical Center and analyze costs for the month of January. Recall that the most plausible driver for these costs is the number of patient-days serviced per month. The table below shows costs recorded in a month with 3,700 patient-days:

Objective 5
Measure cost behavior using the account analysis, high-low, visual-fit, and least-squares regression methods.

Monthly Cost	January Amount
Supervisor's salary and benefits	$ 3,800
Hourly workers' wages and benefits	14,674
Equipment depreciation and rentals	5,873
Equipment repairs	5,604
Cleaning supplies	7,472
Total facilities maintenance cost	$37,423

Next, the analyst determines which costs may be fixed and which may be variable. Assume that the analyst has made the following judgments:

Monthly Cost	January Amount	Fixed	Variable
Supervisor's salary and benefits	$ 3,800	$3,800	
Hourly workers' wages and benefits	14,674		$14,674
Equipment depreciation and rentals	5,873	5,873	
Equipment repairs	5,604		5,604
Cleaning supplies	7,472		7,472
Total facilities maintenance costs	$37,423	$9,673	$27,750

Measuring total facilities maintenance cost behavior, then, requires only simple arithmetic. Add all the fixed costs to get the total fixed cost per month. Divide the total variable costs by the units of cost-driver activity to get the variable cost per unit of cost driver.

Fixed cost per month = $9,673

Variable cost per patient-day = $27,750 ÷ 3,700 patient-days

= $7.50 per patient-day

The algebraic, mixed-cost function, measured by account analysis, is

Y = $9,673 per month + ($7.50 × patient-days)

Account-analysis methods are less expensive to conduct than engineering analyses, but they require recording of relevant cost accounts and cost drivers. In addition, account analysis, like engineering analysis, is subjective because the analyst decides whether each cost is variable or fixed based on his or her own judgment.

SUMMARY PROBLEM FOR YOUR REVIEW

PROBLEM

The Reliable Insurance Company processes a variety of insurance claims for losses, accidents, thefts, and so on. Account analysis using one cost driver has estimated the variable cost of processing each claim at 0.5% (.005) of the dollar value of the claim. This estimate seemed reasonable because higher claims often involve more analysis before settlement. To control processing costs better, however, Reliable Insurance conducted an activity analysis of claims processing. The analysis suggested that there are three main cost drivers and that behavior for automobile accident claims are

0.2% of Reliable Insurance policyholders' property claims

+ 0.6% of other parties' property claims

+ 0.8% of total personal injury claims

Data from two recent automobile accident claims follow:

	Automobile Claim No. 607788	Automobile Claim No. 607991
Policyholder claim	$ 4,500	$23,600
Other party claim	0	3,400
Personal injury claim	12,400	0
Total claim amount	$16,900	$27,000

Required

1. Estimate the cost of processing each claim using data from (a) the single-cost-driver analysis and (b) the three-cost-driver analysis.
2. How would you recommend that Reliable Insurance estimate the cost of processing claims?

SOLUTION

1.

	Automobile Claim No. 607788		Automobile Claim No. 607991	
	Claim Amount	*Processing Cost*	*Claim Amount*	*Processing Cost*
Using single-cost-driver analysis				
Total claim amount	$16,900		$27,000	
Estimated processing cost at 0.5%		$ 84.50		$135.00
Using three-cost-driver analysis				
Policyholder claim	$ 4,500		$23,600	
Estimated processing cost at 0.2%		$ 9.00		$ 47.20
Other party claim	0		3,400	
Estimated processing cost at 0.6%		0		20.40
Personal injury claim	12,400		0	
Estimated processing cost at 0.8%		99.20		0
Total estimated processing cost		$108.20		$ 67.60

2. The three-cost-driver analysis estimates of processing costs are considerably different from those using a single cost driver. If the activity analyses are reliable, then automobile claims that include personal injury losses are more costly to process than property damage claims. If these estimates are relatively inexpensive to keep current and to use, then it seems reasonable to adopt the three-cost-driver approach. Reliable Insurance will have more accurate cost estimates and will be better able to plan its claims processing activities. Reliable

Insurance processes many different types of claims, however. Extending activity analysis to identify multiple cost drivers for all types of claims would result in a complicated system for predicting costs—much more complex (and costly) than simply using the total dollar value of claims. Whether to undertake an activity analysis for all types of policies depends on cost-benefit considerations. Managers can address such considerations by first adopting activity analysis for one type of claim and assessing the usefulness and cost of the more accurate information.

HIGH-LOW, VISUAL-FIT, AND LEAST-SQUARES METHODS

When enough cost data are available, we can use historical data to measure the cost function mathematically. Three popular methods that use such data are the high-low, visual-fit, and least-squares methods. All three of these methods are more objective than the engineering-analysis method because each is based on hard evidence as well as on judgment. They also can be more objective than is account analysis because they use more than one period's cost and activity information. Account analysis and especially engineering analysis will probably remain primary methods of measuring cost behavior because the above three methods require more past cost data. Products, services, technologies, and organizations are changing rapidly in response to increased global competition. In some cases, by the time enough historical data are collected to support these analyses, the data are obsolete—the organization has changed, the production process has changed, or the product has changed. The cost analyst must be careful that the historical data are from a past environment that still closely resembles the future environment for which costs are being predicted. Another concern is that historical data may hide past inefficiencies that could be reduced if they are identified.

Data for Illustration. In discussing the high-low, visual-fit, and least-squares regression methods, we will continue to use the Parkview Medical Center's facilities maintenance department costs. The following table shows monthly data collected on facilities maintenance department costs and on the number of patient-days serviced over the past year:

Facilities Maintenance Department Data

Month	Facilities Maintenance Department Cost (Y)	Number of Patient-Days (X)
January	$37,000	3,700
February	23,000	1,600
March	37,000	4,100
April	47,000	4,900
May	33,000	3,300
June	39,000	4,400
July	32,000	3,500
August	33,000	4,000
September	17,000	1,200
October	18,000	1,300
November	22,000	1,800
December	20,000	1,600

High-Low Method. When sufficient cost data are available, the cost analyst may use historical data to measure the cost function mathematically. The simplest of the three

Exhibit 3-4

High-Low Method

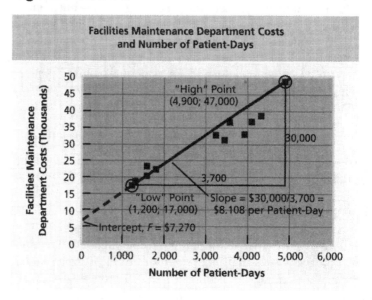

Facilities Maintenance Department Costs and Number of Patient-Days

high-low method A
simple method for
measuring a linear-cost
function from past cost
data, focusing on the
highest-activity and lowest-
activity points and fitting a
line through these two
points.

methods to measure a linear-cost function from past cost data is the **high-low method**
shown in Exhibit 3-4.

The first step in the high-low method is to plot the historical data points on a graph.
This visual display helps the analyst see whether there are obvious errors in the data.
Even though many points are plotted, the focus of the high-low method is normally on
the highest- and lowest-activity points. However, if one of these points is an "outlier"
that seems in error or nonrepresentative of normal operations, we will need to use the
next-highest or next-lowest activity point. For example, you should not use a point from
a period with abnormally low activity caused by a labor strike or fire. Why? Because
that point is not representative of a normal relationship between the cost and the cost
driver.

After selecting the representative high and low points, we can draw a line between
them, extending the line to the vertical (Y) axis of the graph. Note that this extension in
Exhibit 3-4 is a dashed line as a reminder that costs may not be linear outside the range
of activity for which we have data (the relevant range). Also, managers usually are concerned with how costs behave within the relevant range, not with how they behave either
at zero activity or at impossibly high activity levels. Measurements of costs within the
relevant range probably are not reliable measures or predictors of costs outside the relevant range.

The point at which the line intersects the Y-axis is the intercept, F, or estimate of fixed
cost. The slope of the line measures the variable cost, V, per patient-day. The clearest way
to measure the intercept and slope with the high-low method is to use algebra:

Month	Facilities Maintenance Department Cost (Y)	Number of Patient-Days (X)
High: April	$47,000	4,900
Low: September	17,000	1,200
Difference	$30,000	$3,700

Variable cost per patient-day,

$$V = \frac{\text{change in costs}}{\text{change in activity}} = \frac{\$47,000 - \$17,000}{4,900 - 1,200 \text{ patient-days}}$$

$$V = \frac{\$30,000}{3,700} = \underline{\$8.1081} \text{ per patient-day}$$

Fixed cost per month, F = Total mixed cost less total variable cost

at X (high): $F = \$47,000 - (\$8.1081 \times 4,900 \text{ patient-days})$
$= \$47,000 - \$39,730$
$= \underline{\$7,270}$ per month

at X (low): $F = \$17,000 - (\$8.1081 \times 1,200 \text{ patient-days})$
$= \$17,000 - \$9,730$
$= \underline{\$7,270}$ per month

Therefore, the facilities maintenance department cost function, measured by the high-low method, is

$$Y = \$7,270 \text{ per month} + (\$8.1081 \times \text{patient-days})$$

The high-low method is easy to use and illustrates mathematically how a change in a cost driver can change total cost. The cost function that resulted in this case is plausible. Before the widespread availability of computers, managers often used the high-low method to measure a cost function quickly. Today, however, the high-low method is not used as often because of its unreliability and because it makes inefficient use of information, using only two periods' cost experience, regardless of how many relevant data points have been collected.

SUMMARY PROBLEM FOR YOUR REVIEW

PROBLEM

The Reetz Company has its own photocopying department. Reetz's photocopying costs include costs of copy machines, operators, paper, toner, utilities, and so on. We have the following cost and activity data.

Month	Total Photocopying Cost	Number of Copies
1	$25,000	320,000
2	29,000	390,000
3	24,000	300,000
4	23,000	310,000
5	28,000	400,000

1. Use the high-low method to measure the cost behavior of the photocopy department in formula form.
2. What are the benefits and disadvantages of using the high-low method for measuring cost behavior?

SOLUTION

1. The lowest and highest activity levels are in months 3 (300,000 copies) and 5 (400,000 copies).

$$\text{Variable cost per copy} = \frac{\text{change in cost}}{\text{change in activity}} = \frac{\$28,000 - \$24,000}{400,000 - 300,000}$$

$$= \frac{\$4,000}{100,000} = \underline{\$0.04} \text{ per copy}$$

Fixed cost per month = total cost less variable cost

at 400,000 copies: $28,000 - ($0.04 \times 400,000) = $12,000 per month

at 300,000 copies: $24,000 - ($0.04 \times 300,000) = $12,000 per month

Therefore, the photocopy cost function is

Y (total cost) = $12,000 per month + $0.04 × number of copies

2. The benefits of using the high-low method are
   - The method is easy to use.
   - Not many data are needed.

   The disadvantages of using the high-low method are:
   - The choice of the high and low points is subjective.
   - The method does not use all available data.
   - The method may not be reliable.

visual-fit method A method in which the cost analyst visually fits a straight line through a plot of all the available data.

Visual-Fit Method. Because it uses all the available data instead of just two points, the **visual-fit method** is more reliable than is the high-low method. In the visual-fit method, we draw a straight line through a plot of *all* the available data, using judgment to fit the line as close as possible to all the plotted points. If the cost function for the data is linear, it is possible to draw a straight line through the scattered points that comes reasonably close to most of them and thus captures the general tendency of the data. We can extend that line back until it intersects the vertical axis of the graph.

Exhibit 3-5 shows this method applied to the facilities maintenance department cost data for the past 12 months. By measuring where the line intersects the cost axis, we can estimate the monthly fixed cost—in this case, about $10,000 per month. To find the variable cost per patient-day, select any activity level (say, 1,000 patient-days) and find the total cost at that activity level ($17,000). Then divide the variable cost (which is total cost less fixed cost) by the units of activity.

Variable cost per patient-day = ($17,000 − $10,000) ÷ 1,000 patient-days

= $7 per patient-day

The linear-cost function measured by the visual-fit method is

Y = $10,000 per month + ($7 × patient-days)

Although the visual-fit method uses all the data, the placement of the line and the measurement of the fixed and variable costs are subjective. This subjectivity is the main reason that the visual-fit method is now often replaced by least-squares regression analysis.

Exhibit 3-5

Visual-Fit Method

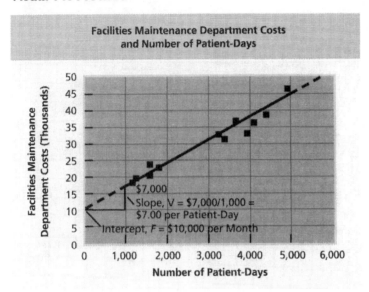

Facilities Maintenance Department Costs and Number of Patient-Days

Least-Squares Regression Method. **Least-squares regression** (or simply **regression analysis**) measures a cost function more objectively (with statistics rather than human eye-sight) than does the visual-fit method. Least-squares regression analysis uses statistics to fit a cost function to all the historical data. Regression analysis that uses one cost driver to measure a cost function is called simple regression. The use of multiple cost drivers for a single cost is called multiple regression. We will discuss only simple regression analysis in this section of the chapter. Appendix 3 presents some statistical properties of regression and shows how to use computer regression software.

Regression analysis measures cost behavior more reliably than other cost measurement methods. In addition, regression analysis yields important statistical information about the reliability of cost estimates, so analysts can assess confidence in the cost measures and select the best cost driver. One such measure of reliability, or goodness of fit, is the **coefficient of determination, R^2** (or R-squared), which measures how much of the fluctuation of a cost is explained by changes in the cost driver. Appendix 3 explains R^2 and discusses how to use it to select the best cost driver.

Exhibit 3-6 shows the linear, mixed-cost function for facilities maintenance costs as measured by simple regression analysis. The fixed-cost measure is $9,329 per month. The variable-cost measure is $6.951 per patient-day. The linear-cost function is

Facilities maintenance department cost = $9,329 per month + $6.951 per patient-day

or

$$Y = \$9,329 + \$6.951 \times \text{patient-days}$$

Compare the cost measures produced by each of the five approaches:

Method	Fixed Cost per Month	Variable Cost per Patient-Day
Engineering analysis	$10,000	$5.000
Account analysis	9,673	7.500
High-low	7,270	8.108
Visual-fit	10,000	7.000
Regression	9,329	6.951

least-squares regression (regression analysis) Measuring a cost function objectively by using statistics to fit a cost function to all the data.

coefficient of determination (R^2) A measurement of how much of the fluctuation of a cost is explained by changes in the cost driver.

Exhibit 3-6

Least-Squares Regression Method

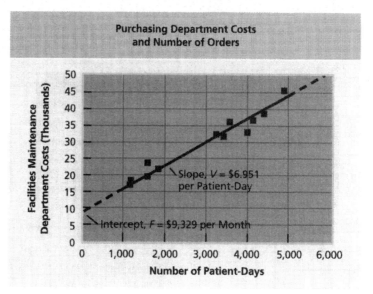

Purchasing Department Costs and Number of Orders

To see the differences in results between methods, we will use account-analysis and regression-analysis measures to predict total facilities maintenance department costs at 1,000 and 5,000 patient-days, the approximate limits of the relevant range:

	Account Analysis	Regression Analysis	Difference
1,000 patient-days:			
Fixed cost	$ 9,673	$ 9,329	$ 344
Variable costs			
$7.500 × 1,000	7,500		
$6.951 × 1,000		6,951	549
Predicted total cost	$17,173	$16,280	$ 893
5,000 patient-days:			
Fixed cost	$ 9,673	$ 9,329	$ 344
Variable costs			
$7.500 × 5,000	37,500		
$6.951 × 5,000		34,755	2,745
Predicted total cost	$47,173	$44,084	$3,089

At lower levels of patient-day activity the difference between cost predictions is small. At higher levels of patient-day activity, however, the account-analysis cost function predicts much higher costs. The difference between the predicted total costs is due primarily to the higher variable cost per patient-day (approximately $0.55 more) measured by account analysis. Because of their grounding in statistical analysis, the regression-cost measures are probably more reliable than are the other methods. Managers would thus have more confidence in cost predictions from the regression-cost function.

4

COST MANAGEMENT SYSTEMS AND ACTIVITY-BASED COSTING

COST MANAGEMENT SYSTEMS AND ACTIVITY-BASED COSTING

AT&T Wireless Services customers can use their cell phones in more than 5,500 locations across the United States and Canada, as well as in Europe, Asia, and Australia. People are able to call you nearly anywhere on Earth by dialing your local wireless number.

www.prenhall.com/horngren

Learning Objectives

When you have finished studying this chapter, you should be able to

1. Describe the purposes of cost management systems.

2. Explain the relationship between cost, cost objective, cost accumulation, and cost allocation.

3. Distinguish between direct, indirect, and unallocated costs.

4. Explain how the financial statements of merchandisers and manufacturers differ because of the types of goods they sell.

5. Understand the main differences between traditional and activity-based costing systems and why ABC systems provide value to managers.

6. Identify the steps involved in the design and implementation of an activity-based costing system.

7. Use activity-based cost information to improve the operations of an organization.

8. **Understand management accounting's role in a company's improvement efforts across the value chain.**

A recent survey asked 1,000 adults for their two choices of a "really good company." The company named the most was AT&T. Chances are, AT&T has reached out and touched you. With 90 million customers, it has annual revenues of more than $53 billion and net income exceeding $6 billion.

There is a communications revolution taking place on a global scale. Today, we communicate using wireless cell phones and computer on-line services in addition to the traditional telephone. How does AT&T, a company that has been synonymous with communications for more than 100 years, ensure that it remains competitive? Certainly AT&T has the people, technology, brand, market presence, and financial resources to get the job done—but it takes more. Like any other company, AT&T's managers, from top executives to local service managers, must understand their customers and their costs. This understanding is a common theme for all successful businesses.

Consider AT&T's Business Communication Services unit (BCS). With annual revenue of more than $16 billion, BCS is responsible for domestic and international voice and data communications services. To keep the unit's competitive edge, management began using a new cost accounting system in the mid-1990s. Accountants and managers designed the new costing system "to help operating managers gain a better understanding of the costs of each kind of service (product)." The old cost system gathered financial data used primarily by top management and accountants. The new cost system measures the key business processes in the BCS and the activities that the unit performs to support its various services.

One example of the results obtained using the new cost system is in the billing center. The BCS team computed the cost of investigating incorrect bills, a cost that was previously unknown. The cost was so high that BCS managers started a cost reduction effort. The result was an annual cost savings of about $500,000. The new cost system was an effective management tool for all operating managers, not just accountants.

COST MANAGEMENT SYSTEMS

Objective 1
Describe the purposes of cost management systems.

cost management system (CMS) Identifies how management's decisions affect costs, by first measuring the resources used in performing the organization's activities and then assessing the effects on costs of changes in those activities.

To support managers' decisions better, accountants go beyond simply determining the cost of products and services. They develop cost management systems. A **cost management system (CMS)** is a collection of tools and techniques that identifies how management's decisions affect costs. To do so, the CMS first measures the costs of resources used in performing the organization's activities and then assesses the effects on costs of changes in those activities. The primary purposes of a cost management system are to provide

1. aggregate measures of inventory value and cost of goods manufactured for external reporting to investors, creditors, and other external stakeholders,
2. cost information for strategic management decisions, and
3. cost information for operational control.

External users of cost information, such as investors and creditors, need aggregate measures of inventory value and the cost of goods sold. They do not need accurate cost information on individual products or services. It is the second and third purposes of a CMS that generate the need for more elaborate tools and techniques. Internal managers need accurate and timely cost information for strategic reasons, such as deciding on the optimal product and customer mix, choosing the value chain functions to be outsourced, and making investment decisions. For these decisions, managers want to know the costs of individual products, services, and customers. The assessment of process improvement efforts and other operational cost control programs also requires accurate and timely feedback on costs.

We have described many CMS tools and techniques throughout this text. An example is the contribution margin technique and cost-volume-profit analysis. This chapter focuses on two other important techniques—activity-based costing and activity-based management. But perhaps the most fundamental tool that supports all cost management systems is the cost accounting system.

COST ACCOUNTING SYSTEMS

cost accounting That part of the cost management system that measures costs for the purposes of management decision making and financial reporting.

All kinds of organizations—manufacturing firms, service companies, and nonprofit organizations—need some form of **cost accounting,** that part of the cost management system that measures costs for the purposes of management decision making and financial reporting. Because it is the most general case, embracing production as well as all other value chain functions, we will focus on cost accounting in a manufacturing setting. Remember, though, that you can apply this framework to any organization.

Managers rely on accountants to design a cost accounting system that measures costs to meet each of the three purposes of a CMS. Consider the following commentaries on the modern role of management accountants.

*We (cost accountants) had to understand what the numbers
mean, relate the numbers to business activity, and recommend alternative courses of action. Finally, we had to evaluate alternatives and
make decisions to maximize business efficiency.*

—South Central Bell

*Because the ABC (Activity-Based Costing) system now mirrors
the manufacturing process, the engineers and production staff
believe the cost data produced by the accounting system. Engineering and production regularly ask accounting to help find the
product design combination that will optimize costs. . . . The
accountants now participate in product design decisions. They help
engineering and production understand how costs behave. . . .
The ABC system makes the professional lives of the accountants
more rewarding.*

—Hewlett-Packard Company

 Cost-management systems have three primary purposes For each of the decisions listed below, indicate the purpose of the CMS being applied.

1. A production manager wants to know the cost of performing a setup for a production run in order to compare to a target cost established as part of a process improvement program.
2. Top management wants to identify the profitability of several product lines to establish the optimum product mix.
3. Financial managers want to know the manufactured cost of inventory to appear on the balance sheet of the annual report.

ANSWERS

The purposes of a CMS are to provide measurements of cost for external financial reporting, internal strategic decisions, and internal operational cost control. The production manager evaluates the operating cost of the setup process to evaluate a process improvement program. This is part of the operational control purpose of the CMS. Identifying the profitability of a com-pany's various products and deciding on an optimal product mix is an example of the strategic purpose of the CMS. Measuring the cost of goods manufactured and determining how much of this cost is reported as inventory on the balance sheet is the external financial reporting purpose of the CMS.

The cost accounting system typically includes two processes.

1. **Cost accumulation:** Collecting costs by some "natural" classification such as materials or labor or by activities performed such as order processing or machine processing.
2. **Cost allocation:** Tracing and reassigning costs to one or more cost objectives such as activities, processes, departments, customers, or products.

Exhibit 4-1 illustrates these processes. First, the system collects the costs of all raw materials. Then it allocates these costs to the departments that use the materials and fur-ther to the specific items made by these departments. The total raw materials cost of a particular product is the sum of the raw materials costs allocated to it in the various departments.

Before describing the types of cost accounting (or simply costing) systems, we need to develop an understanding of the various costs terms that are commonly used in practice.

Objective 2
Explain the relationship between cost, cost objective, cost accumulation, and cost allocation.

cost accumulation
Collecting costs by some natural classification such as materials, labor, or activities performed.

cost allocation Tracing and reassigning costs to one or more cost objectives such as activities, departments, customers, or products.

Exhibit 4-1

Cost Accumulation and Allocation

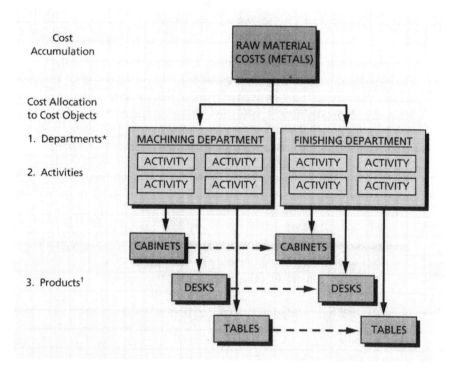

* Purpose: to evaluate performance of manufacturing departments.
† Purpose: to obtain costs of various products for valuing inventory, determining income, and judging product profitability.

DIFFERENT COSTS FOR DIFFERENT DECISIONS

To make intelligent decisions, managers want reliable measurements. Cost accounting systems that do not provide reliable information do not help managers make decisions. In fact, without reliable cost information, many decisions can be downright harmful. For example, an extremely large U.S. grocery chain, A&P, ran into profit difficulties and began retrenching by closing many stores. Management's lack of adequate cost information about individual store operations made the closing program a hit-or-miss affair. A news story reported the following:

> Because of the absence of detailed profit-and-loss statements, and a cost-allocation system that did not reflect true costs, A&P's strategists could not be sure whether an individual store was really unprofitable. For example, distribution costs were shared equally among all the stores in a marketing area without regard to such factors as a store's distance from the warehouse. Says one close observer of the company: "When they wanted to close a store, they had to wing it. They could not make rational decisions, because they did not have a fact basis."

We can classify and report costs in many ways—far too many for us to cover in a single chapter. We have already seen costs classified by their behavior—fixed, variable, step, and mixed. This section concentrates on the big picture of how accounting systems accumulate, classify, and report manufacturing costs.

COST OBJECTIVES

As stated by Jim Smith, former Director of Cost Management for The Marmon Group, "Depending on the decision, any of the cost classifications described in this book are relevant." A **cost** is a sacrifice or giving up of resources for a particular purpose. We generally measure costs by the monetary units (for example, dollars, yen, or euros) that must be paid for goods and services. Systems initially record costs in elementary form (for example, repairs or advertising). Then they group (classify) costs in different ways to help managers make decisions, such as evaluating subordinates and subunits of the organization, expanding or deleting products or territories, and replacing equipment.

To aid decisions, managers want to know the cost of something. We call this "something" a **cost objective** or **cost object,** defined as anything for which decision makers desire a separate measurement of costs. Examples of cost objectives include departments, products, territories, miles driven, bricks laid, patients seen, tax bills sent, checks processed, student hours taught, and library books shelved.

DIRECT, INDIRECT, AND UNALLOCATED COSTS

A major feature of costs in both manufacturing and nonmanufacturing activities is whether the costs have a direct or an indirect relationship to a particular cost objective or whether it is so difficult to determine a relationship that the costs are unallocated. Accountants can identify **direct costs** specifically and exclusively with a given cost objective in an economically feasible way. **Indirect costs** cannot be identified specifically and exclusively with a given cost objective in an economically feasible way. However, we can often identify plausible and reliable output measures (cost drivers) that can be used to allocate these indirect costs among cost objects. An example of an indirect cost is the depreciation on machinery that is used to produce many different products. Systems may allocate this indirect cost to products based on the output measure "machine hours." If making product A requires twice as many machine hours as making product B, then we allocate twice as much machine depreciation expense to A. Finally, there are some costs in many companies for which we can identify no relationship to a cost objective. These are **unallocated costs.** Examples of unallocated costs might include research and development, process design, legal, accounting, information services, and executive salaries. Keep in mind, though, that an unallocated cost for one company may be an indirect or even a direct cost for another. Why? Because businesses vary considerably in their value chains. For some businesses, the design function is a critical part of their success and therefore they are willing to spend the time and effort to deploy sophisticated systems to allocate or even directly trace such costs.

Consider the income statement in Exhibit 4-2. It represents a typical manufacturing company that makes products A, B, and C. Each item in the total column of the income statement represents accumulated totals for all products sold for an entire reporting period. How would we "unbundle" these totals to find the proper amounts for individual products A, B, and C?

First, note that all cost items except administrative salaries and other administrative expenses are either directly traced or allocated to individual products. Consider cost of goods sold. Most companies find that it is fairly easy to trace material costs to individual products. However, other manufacturing costs, even labor, are more difficult to trace and are normally allocated. It is not unusual for the amount of indirect manufacturing costs to be a large component of total company costs. As a result, many companies develop sophisticated cost allocation systems for these indirect costs. The complexity of cost allocation depends on the complexity of the associated production system. Let's assume that the use of machine hours to allocate the indirect manufacturing costs gives a reasonable degree of costing accuracy. Then, managers responsible for products A, B, and C would be satisfied that the cost of goods sold and gross profit amounts shown are fair. This is why most

cost A sacrifice or giving up of resources for a particular purpose, frequently measured by the monetary units that must be paid for goods and services.

cost objective (cost object) Anything for which a separate measurement of costs is desired. Examples include departments, products, activities, and territories.

Objective 3
Distinguish between direct, indirect, and unallocated costs.

direct costs Costs that can be identified specifically and exclusively with a given cost objective in an economically feasible way.

indirect costs Costs that cannot be identified specifically and exclusively with a given cost objective in an economically feasible way.

unallocated costs Costs for which we can identify no relationship to a cost objective.

Exhibit 4-2

Direct, Indirect, and Unallocated Costs in the Income Statement

	Total	Products A	B	C	Cost Type, Costing Method
Sales	$4,700	$2,800	$1,000	$ 900	
Cost of Goods Sold:					
Direct Material	1,200	500	300	400	Direct, Direct Trace
Indirect Manufacturing	1,100	450	300	350	Indirect, Allocation (machine hours)
Cost of Goods Sold	2,300	950	600	750	
Gross Profit	2,400	1,850	400	150	
Selling and Administrative Expenses:					
Commissions	470	280	100	90	Direct, Direct Trace
Distribution to warehouses	300	120	80	100	Indirect, Allocation (weight)
Total Selling and Administrative Expenses	770	400	180	190	
Operating Income (loss)	1,630	$1,450	$ 220	$ (40)	
Unallocated Expenses:					
Administrative Salaries	400				Unallocated
Other Administrative Expenses	600				Unallocated
Total Unallocated Expenses	1,000				
Income Before Tax	$ 630				

companies focus on gross profit as a key measure of individual product profitability. In our example, managers are also satisfied that commission expenses and expenses for distribution to warehouses can be allocated in a fair manner. So, while the managers of product C may not be happy with the reported operating loss of $40, they would feel that it is a reasonable measure of profitability.

We could find no reasonable means to allocate administrative salaries or other administrative expenses. So these expenses remain unallocated. Why not simply allocate the administrative salaries and other administrative expenses to the products by some simple method such as "percent of total revenue generated?" Because managers want allocations to be a fair measure of the costs incurred on their behalf. If we cannot find such a measure, companies often choose not to allocate.

Whenever it is economically feasible, managers prefer to classify costs as direct rather than indirect. In this way, managers have greater confidence in the reported costs of products, services, or other cost objectives. Economically feasible means cost effective, in the sense that managers do not want cost accounting to be too expensive in relation to expected benefits. For example, it may be economically feasible to trace the exact cost of steel and fabric (direct cost) to a specific lot of desk chairs, but it may be economically infeasible to trace the exact cost of rivets or thread (indirect costs) to the chairs.

Other factors also influence whether we consider a cost direct, indirect, or unallocated. The key is the particular cost objective. For example, consider a supervisor's salary in the maintenance department of a telephone company. If the cost objective is the department, the supervisor's salary is a direct cost. In contrast, if the cost objective is a service (the "product" of the company) such as a telephone call, the supervisor's salary is an indirect cost. In general, many more costs are direct when a department is the cost objective than when a service (a telephone call) or a physical product (a razor blade) is the cost objective.

Frequently managers want to know both the costs of running departments and the costs of products, services, activities, or resources. Companies inevitably allocate costs to more than one cost objective. Thus, a particular cost may simultaneously be direct and indirect. As you have just seen, a supervisor's salary can be both direct (with respect to his or her department) and indirect (with respect to the department's individual products or services).

CATEGORIES OF MANUFACTURING COSTS

Any raw material, labor, or other input used by any organization could, in theory, be a direct or indirect cost, depending on the cost objective. In manufacturing operations, which transform materials into other goods through the use of labor and factory facilities, products are frequently the cost objective. Manufacturing operations, though, have their own way of classifying costs. Manufacturing companies classify costs that they wish to allocate to products as either (1) direct material, (2) direct labor, and (3) indirect manufacturing.

1. **Direct-material costs** include the acquisition costs of all materials that a company identifies as a part of the manufactured goods and that it can trace to the manufactured goods in an economically feasible way. Examples are iron castings, lumber, aluminum sheets, and subassemblies. Direct materials often do not include minor items such as tacks or glue because the costs of tracing these items are greater than the possible benefits of having more precise product costs. Such items are usually called supplies or indirect materials, which are classified as a part of indirect manufacturing costs described in this list.

2. **Direct-labor costs** include the wages of all labor that a company can trace specifically and exclusively to the manufactured goods in an economically feasible way. Examples are the wages of machine operators and assemblers. In highly automated factories with a flexible workforce, there may be no direct labor costs. Why? Because workers spend time on numerous products, which makes it economically infeasible to physically trace any labor cost directly to specific products.

3. **Indirect manufacturing costs (or factory overhead)** include all costs associated with the manufacturing process that a company cannot trace to the manufactured goods in an economically feasible way. Other terms used to describe this category are **factory burden** and **manufacturing overhead.** Because each of these terms is used often in practice, we will use them interchangeably throughout this textbook. Many labor costs, such as that of janitors, forklift truck operators, plant guards, and storeroom clerks, are considered to be indirect labor because it is impossible or economically infeasible to trace such activity to specific products. Other examples are power, supplies, indirect labor, supervisory salaries, property taxes, rent, insurance, and depreciation.

direct-material costs The acquisition costs of all materials that are physically identified as a part of the manufactured goods and that may be traced to the manufactured goods in an economically feasible way.

direct-labor costs The wages of all labor that can be traced specifically and exclusively to the manufactured goods in an economically feasible way.

indirect manufacturing costs (factory burden, factory overhead, manufacturing overhead) All costs other than direct material or direct labor that are associated with the manufacturing process.

The application of computer technology has allowed modern cost systems to physically trace many previously indirect overhead costs to products in an economically feasible manner. For example, meters wired to computers can monitor the electricity used to produce each product, and costs of setting up a batch production run can be traced to the items produced in the run. In general, the more overhead costs that we can trace directly to products, the more accurate the product cost.

In addition to direct-material, direct-labor, and indirect manufacturing costs, all manufacturing companies also incur costs associated with the other value chain functions (research and development, design, marketing, distribution, and customer service). Accounting information systems accumulate these costs by departments such as R&D, advertising, and sales. Most firms' financial statements report these costs as selling and administrative expenses. In short, these costs do not become a part of the reported inventory cost of the manufactured products.

PRODUCT COSTS AND PERIOD COSTS

Regardless of the type of cost accounting system used for internal decision making purposes, the resulting costs appear in a company's financial statements for external financial reporting purposes. Costs appear on both the income statement, as cost of goods sold, and the balance sheet, as inventory amounts. When preparing both income statements and balance sheets, accountants frequently distinguish between product costs and period

product costs Costs identified with goods produced or purchased for resale.

period costs Costs that are deducted as expenses during the current period without going through an inventory stage.

costs. **Product costs** are costs identified with goods produced or purchased for resale. Product costs first become part of the inventory on hand. These product costs (inventoriable costs) become expenses (in the form of cost of goods sold) only when the company sells the inventory. In contrast, **period costs** become expenses during the current period without going through an inventory stage.

For example, look at the top half of Exhibit 4-3. A merchandising company (retailer or wholesaler) acquires goods for resale without changing their basic form. The only product cost is the purchase cost of the merchandise. The company holds unsold goods as merchandise inventory and shows their costs as an asset on a balance sheet. As the goods are sold, their costs become expenses in the form of "cost of goods sold."

A merchandising company also has a variety of selling and administrative expenses. These costs are period costs because they are deducted from revenue as expenses without ever being regarded as a part of inventory.

The bottom half of Exhibit 4-3 illustrates product and period costs in a manufacturing company. Note that the company transforms direct materials into salable items with the help of direct labor and indirect manufacturing. All these costs are product costs that are shown as inventory until the goods are sold. As in merchandising accounting, the selling and administrative expenses are period costs, not product costs.

Be sure you are clear on the differences between merchandising accounting and manufacturing accounting for such costs as insurance, depreciation, and wages. In merchandising accounting, all such items are period costs (expenses of the current period). In manufacturing accounting, many of these items are related to production activities and thus, as indirect manufacturing, are product costs (become expenses in the form of cost of goods sold as the inventory is sold).

In both merchandising and manufacturing accounting, selling and general administrative costs are period costs. Thus the inventory cost of a manufactured product excludes sales salaries, sales commissions, advertising, legal, public relations, and the president's salary. Manufacturing overhead is normally regarded as a part of finished-goods inventory cost, whereas selling expenses and general administrative expenses are not.

Confirm your understanding of the classification of manufacturing costs. Classify each of the following as *direct* or *indirect* with respect to traceability to product and as *variable* or *fixed* with respect to whether the costs fluctuates in total as volume of production changes over wide ranges.

1. The cost of components that are assembled into a final product.
2. The cost of supplies consumed when maintenance is performed on machines.
3. The cost of training mechanics who service processing machinery.
4. The cost of machine operators who work on only one product.

ANSWERS

The cost of components used in products is almost always directly traceable and is a variable cost. As volume changes over a wide range, the amount of supplies consumed for maintenance will also change so this cost is variable. However, there usually would not be an economically feasible way to trace these costs to individual products, so these costs would be indirect and allocated (normally the cost driver would be machine hours). Training costs for mechanics would not vary as a function of volume of production assuming that no new products would be made and that no new mechanics would be hired. Training costs are indirect assuming that the training cannot be associated with only one product. The wages of machine operators who work on only one product can be easily traced to the product. These wages would not vary over wide ranges of volume and this would be a fixed cost. We should note that if volume increases rapidly in a short time frame, it is often necessary to work overtime. In this case, the overtime portion of operator wages would be a variable cost.

Exhibit 4-3

Relationships of Product Costs and Period Costs

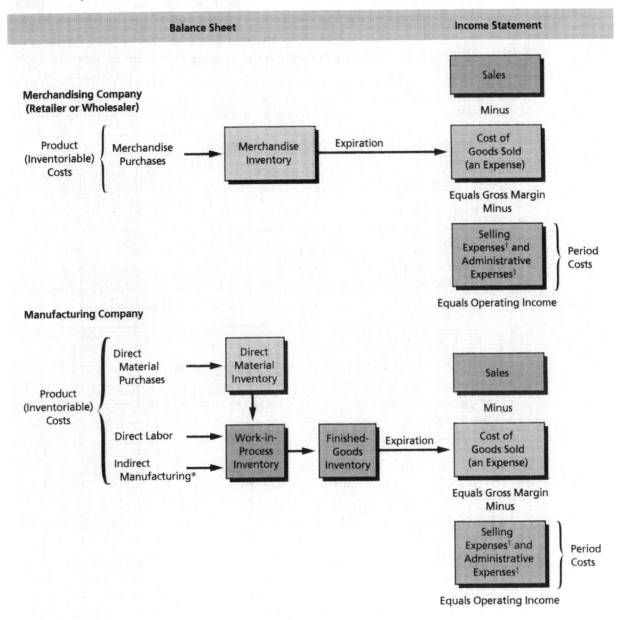

* Examples: indirect labor, factory supplies, insurance, and depreciation on plant

† Examples: insurance on salespersons' cars, depreciation on salespersons' cars, salespersons' salaries.

‡ Examples: insurance on corporate headquarters building, depreciation on office equipment, clerical salaries.

Note particularly that when insurance and depreciation relate to the manufacturing function, they are inventoriable, but when they relate to selling and administration, they are not inventoriable.

BALANCE SHEET PRESENTATION OF COSTS

Examining both halves of Exhibit 4-3 together, you can see that the balance sheets of manufacturers and merchandisers differ with respect to inventories. The merchandiser's inventory account is supplanted in a manufacturing concern by three inventory classes that help managers trace all product costs through the production process to the time of sales. These classes are

Objective 4

Explain how the financial statements of merchandisers and manufacturers differ because of the types of goods they sell.

- Direct-material inventory: Material on hand and awaiting use in the production process.
- Work-in-process inventory: Goods undergoing the production process but not yet fully completed. Costs include appropriate amounts of the three major manufacturing costs (direct material, direct labor, and indirect manufacturing).
- Finished-goods inventory: Goods fully completed but not yet sold.

The only essential difference between the structure of the balance sheet of a manufacturer and that of a retailer or wholesaler would appear in their respective current asset sections:

Current Asset Sections of Balance Sheets

Manufacturer			Retailer or Wholesaler		
Cash		$ 4,000	Cash		$ 4,000
Receivables		25,000	Receivables		25,000
Finished goods	$32,000				
Work in process	22,000				
Direct material	23,000				
Total inventories		77,000	Merchandise inventories		77,000
Other current assets		1,000	Other current assets		1,000
Total current assets		$107,000	Total current assets		$107,000

INCOME STATEMENT PRESENTATION OF COSTS

In income statements, the detailed reporting of selling and administrative expenses is typically the same for manufacturing and merchandising organizations, but the cost of goods sold is different.

MANUFACTURER	RETAILER OR WHOLESALER
Manufacturing cost of goods produced and then sold, usually composed of the three major categories of cost: direct materials, direct labor, and indirect manufacturing.	Merchandise cost of goods sold, usually composed of the purchase cost of items, including freight in, that are acquired and then resold.

Consider the additional details as they are presented in the model income statement of a manufacturing company in Exhibit 4-4. The $40 million cost of goods manufactured includes subdivisions for direct materials, direct labor, and indirect manufacturing. In contrast, a wholesale or retail company would replace the entire cost-of-goods-manufactured section with a single line, cost of goods purchased.

Accountants and managers often use the terms *costs* and *expenses* loosely. Expenses denote all costs deducted from (matched against) revenue in a given period. On the other hand, costs is a much broader term and is used to describe both an asset (the cost of inventory) and an expense (the cost of goods sold). Thus manufacturing costs become an expense on an income statement (in the form of cost of goods sold) via the multistep inventory procedure shown earlier in Exhibit 4-3. In contrast, selling and general administrative costs become expenses immediately as they are incurred.

ACTIVITY-BASED COSTING

In the 1990s, many companies in the United States, struggling to keep up with competitors from Japan, Germany, and other countries, adopted new management philosophies and

Exhibit 4-4

Model Income Statement, Manufacturing Company

Sales (8,000,000 units @ $10)			$80,000,000
Cost of goods manufactured and sold			
Beginning finished-goods inventory		$ –0–	
Cost of goods manufactured			
Direct materials used	$20,000,000		
Direct labor	12,000,000		
Indirect manufacturing	8,000,000	40,000,000	
Cost of goods available for sale		$40,000,000	
Ending finished-goods inventory,			
2,000,000 units @ $4		8,000,000	
Cost of goods sold (an expense)			32,000,000
Gross margin or gross profit			$48,000,000
Less: other expenses			
Selling costs (an expense)		$30,000,000	
General and administrative costs			
(an expense)		8,000,000	38,000,000
Operating income*			$10,000,000

* Also net income in this example because other expenses such as interest and income taxes are ignored here for simplicity

developed new production technologies. In many cases, these changes prompted corresponding changes in cost management systems.

For example, Borg-Warner's Automotive Chain Systems Operation transformed its manufacturing operation to a just-in-time manufacturing system with work cells. This change in the way manufacturing was done at Borg-Warner made the existing cost accounting system obsolete. A new cost accounting system coupled with the new production systems "improved the overall reporting, controls, and efficiency dramatically."[1]

In the past, almost all companies used **traditional costing systems**—those that do not accumulate or report costs of activities or processes. Traditional costing systems work well with fairly simple production and operating systems. In the 1990s, however, many businesses did what Borg-Warner did and changed their operating systems in response to a more complex business environment. This led to a need for new and improved cost accounting systems. The most significant improvement in cost accounting system design has been activity-based costing (ABC). Let's take a look at how ABC differs from traditional costing.

traditional costing systems One that does not accumulate or report costs of activities or processes.

Objective 5
Understand the main differences between traditional and activity-based costing systems and why ABC systems provide value to managers.

ACTIVITY-BASED COSTING AND TRADITIONAL COSTING COMPARED

The primary focus of the changes in operations and accounting has been an increased attention to the cost of the activities undertaken to research, design, produce, sell, and deliver a company's products or services (that is, the entire value chain of business functions). Managers have always focused their attention on operating activities, but, until recently, companies seldom directly measured the costs of these activities. **Activity-based costing (ABC) systems** first accumulate indirect costs for each of the activities of the area being costed (an area can be a plant, department, value chain function, or the entire organization). Then they assign the costs of activities to the products, services, or other cost objects that required that activity. One of the most important differences between traditional and activity-based costing systems is the extent of allocation. Traditional systems generally allocate only

activity-based costing (ABC) systems A system that first accumulates overhead costs for each of the activities of the area being costed, and then assigns the costs of activities to the products, services, or other cost objects that require that activity.

---

[1] A Phillips and Don Collins, "How Borg-Warner Made the Transition from Pile Accounting to JIT," Management Accounting, *October 1990, pp 32–35*

In a recent survey, companies that use ABC were asked to indicate how many managers routinely used the ABC system. The vast majority, 62%, indicated that from 10 to 24 managers used ABC; 23% of the companies reported that between 25 and 99 managers used ABC information. Why do managers use ABC? The most frequent applications are for product and service costing, process and activity analysis, and performance measurement. These are the primary purposes of strategic decision making and operational control that we discussed at the beginning of this chapter.

A specific example of the use of ABC is Blue Cross and Blue Shield of Florida (BCBSF). BCBSF's major customers include local groups (persons in companies with headquarters in Florida), direct pay (individuals), national and corporate accounts (persons in companies with headquarters outside Florida), and government programs (persons 65 years or older with Medicare benefits). During the early 1990s, BCBSF faced increased competition for its healthcare products and services. But its cost management system did not adequately meet the needs of managers.

The primary goal of BCBSF's management was to develop a new cost management system that would help identify opportunities for increased operating control and cost reduction in administrative expenses. Administrative expenses are all the costs of doing business other than claims payments. In 1996 they were $588 million or 20% of total revenue. The company goal was to reduce administrative costs from 20% of revenue to less than 10%. The cost-management-system technique BCBSF used was an ABC system. This new cost accounting system provided more accurate and timely measurements of

1. customer and product profitability—a strategic purpose,
2. activities that provided the most value to managers and customers—an operational control purpose—and
3. costs of nonvalue-added activities–an operational control purpose.

Sources: Mohan Nair, "Activity-Based Costing: Who's Using It and Why?" *Management Accounting Quarterly*, Spring 2000, pp. 29–33; K. Thurston, D. Keleman, and J. MacArthur, "Cost for Pricing at Blue Cross Blue Shield of Florida," *Management Accounting Quarterly*, Spring 2000, pp. 4–13.

production costs to the products. They normally do not allocate the costs of other value chain functions. Activity-based costing systems often expand allocation of costs beyond production to processes such as order processing, design, marketing, and customer service. As a result, ABC systems are more complex but promise more accurate costs to aid decision makers.

Exhibit 4-5 contrasts the traditional costing system with the two major types of ABC systems. In the traditional costing system shown in Panel A, the portion of total indirect resource costs allocated to a product depends on the proportion of total direct-labor-hours (or other volume-based cost driver such as machine hours or units produced) consumed in making the product. Note that traditional systems often use only one cost driver. Also, traditional systems do not attempt to identify, accumulate, or report costs by activities performed. When does a traditional costing system work best? When there is a plausible and reliable relationship between the single cost driver and *all* the indirect resource costs being allocated and when the cost of providing activity-cost information exceeds the benefits of this information. In today's complex business environments, this is rare.

For example, consider a company that makes just two products—(1) plastic casings for pens and (2) plastic casings for cell phones. Pen casings have a very simple design and thus require a very simple production process. The company produces them in very high volumes, using 90% of its direct labor time and machine processing time. Pen casings are made for general use and rarely will require special customer support or engineering work. This means that the indirect costs of customer support and engineering of the pen casings will be very small.

Exhibit 4-5

Comparison of Traditional, Two-Stage ABC, and Multistage ABC Systems

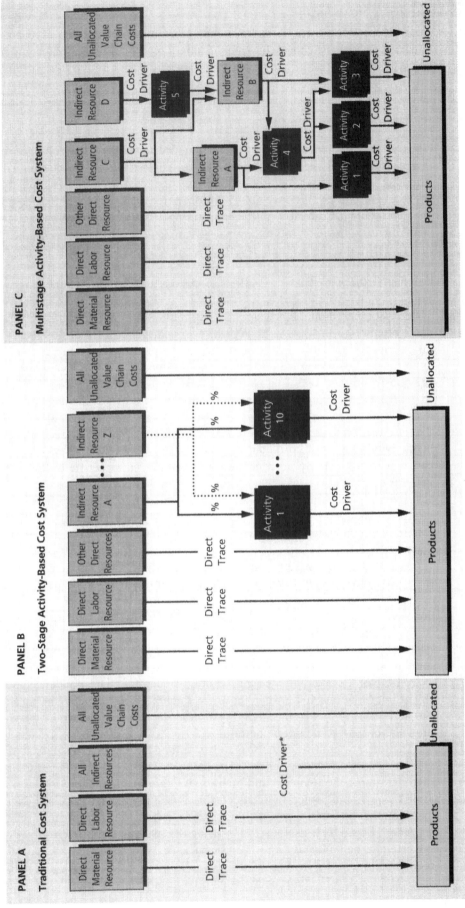

* Direct-labor-hours or other volume-based cost driver such as machine hours or units produced.

On the other hand, cell-phone casings have a much more complex design, and the company produces them in small volumes, accounting for only 10% of its direct labor and machine processing time. Customers (mainly telecommunications companies such as AT&T) who buy cell-phone casings have specific design requirements that cause much engineering work. So, common sense tells us that we *should* allocate most of the costs of engineering to the cell-phone casings. But suppose that we are using the traditional cost system depicted in Panel A of Exhibit 4-5. We would allocate all indirect costs using a volume-based cost driver such as the direct labor time that is spent making the products. Thus, we would allocate only 10% of the engineering costs to the cell-phone casings. This simply does not make sense. A much better cost driver of engineering cost would be "number of customer-generated engineering changes" or "number of distinct parts." If, for example, pen casings have only 5 distinct parts compared to 20 for cell-phone casings, then we would allocate 80% of the engineering activity costs to cell-phone casings rather than only 10% based on the traditional system. In general, the more complex the business environment, the less accurate is a traditional system. Accountants design ABC systems to deal with business complexity.

Just as there are many variations in the design of traditional costing systems, there are also many variations of ABC systems. Exhibit 4-5, Panel B depicts a two-stage ABC system. Compare Panel A to Panel B. During the development of an ABC system, managers often discover ways to trace previously indirect costs to cost objects. For example, an entire production line may be dedicated to produce only one product. This would enable a company to trace directly to the product, costs such as supervision that were previously indirect costs. In a **two-stage ABC system,** there are two stages of allocation to get from the original resource cost to the final product or service cost. The first stage allocates resource costs to activity-cost pools. A **cost pool** is a group of individual costs that is allocated to cost objectives using a single cost driver. The second stage is allocating activity costs to the products or services. In two-stage ABC systems, the first-stage cost drivers are usually percentages. For example, suppose the indirect resource A in Panel B of Exhibit 4-5 was supervisors. We would allocate the cost (salaries) to several activity-cost pools, one for each activity performed by supervisors, based on the percent of effort expended by the supervisors in support of each activity. We would base the second-stage allocation to products or services on the cost driver associated with the particular activity.

Two-stage ABC systems are the simplest ABC systems. They have a financial accounting flavor because the general ledger is at the heart of all the cost data used. It is not necessary to limit the number of stages of allocation to two. In fact, many organizations (such as FedEx, Boeing, and the United States Department of Labor) prefer to design **multistage ABC systems** (shown in Exhibit 4-5, Panel C) with more than two stages of allocations and cost drivers other than percentages. For example, activities two and three in Panel C may be processing customer returns and customer inquiries, respectively. Both of these activities may generate the need for correspondence activity (activity 4). The interrelationship between these three activities is shown by linking activities 2 and 3 to activity 4. In a two-stage ABC system all three activities would be shown but the interrelationship would not be determined.

The focus of multistage ABC is to first understand how a business actually operates by constructing an operations map similar to the one shown in Panel C of Exhibit 4-5. Then determine the financial and operational data needed. There is a distinctive operational flavor to multistage ABC systems because much of the required data comes from operational data sources, not just the general ledger. Many companies such as Pillsbury and AT&T began their use of ABC by using the two-stage approach. However, they later converted to the multistage approach because of its focus on operations and its tendency to enhance operating managers' understanding the business. Managers that use these more complex ABC systems believe that their additional complexity yields more accurate

two-stage ABC system A costing system with two stages of allocation to get from the original cost to the final product or service cost. The first stage allocates resource costs to activity-cost pools. The second stage allocates activity costs to products or services.

cost pool A group of individual costs that is allocated to cost objectives using a single cost driver.

multistage ABC systems Costing systems with more than two stages of allocations and cost drivers other than percentages.

costs and a deeper understanding of operations. A deeper understanding of the business leads to better ideas for process improvement. Process improvements, in turn, lead to more satisfied customers and a competitive edge.

We will illustrate the more general multistage ABC systems. Simple, two-stage ABC systems are simply a special case of the general multistage systems. However, before our detailed illustration of a multistage ABC system, let's explore the central concepts that give multistage ABC systems so much value to managers.

chapter 5

RELEVANT INFORMATION AND DECISION MAKING: MARKETING DECISIONS

The Grand Canyon Railway offers classic train rides to the southern rim of the Grand Canyon. The train departs from the railway's Williams, Arizona, depot for the 65-mile trip.

Learning Objectives

When you have finished studying this chapter, you should be able to

1. Discriminate between relevant and irrelevant information for making decisions.

2. Use the decision process to make business decisions.

3. Decide to accept or reject a special order using the contribution margin technique.

4. Decide to add or delete a product line using relevant information.

5. Compute a measure of product profitability when production is constrained by a scarce resource.

6. Discuss the factors that influence pricing decisions in practice.

7. Compute a target sales price by various approaches, and compare the advantages and disadvantages of these approaches.

8. Use target costing to decide whether to add a new product.

9. Understand how relevant information is used when making marketing decisions.

While you are on vacation, the last thing you want to worry about is transportation. For visitors to Grand Canyon National Park, The Grand Canyon Railway provides a relaxing alternative to driving to the canyon. Why drive when you can sit back and enjoy the scenery across 65 miles of beautiful Arizona countryside from the comfort of a fully reconditioned steam engine? Strolling musicians serenade you, and western characters stage attacks and holdups that offer a glimpse into what train travel might have been like for old-west loggers, miners, and ranchers at the turn of the century. The Grand Canyon Railway thus offers a ride not only to the canyon itself but into the past as well.

Of course, rides into the past aren't exactly cheap. Tracks for the narrow-gauge train as well as the authentic steam engines and passenger cars cost an awful lot to buy new or to recondition. The company spent upwards of $20 million before opening. Recovering that initial investment while earning a profit is not easy. According to the company controller, Kevin Call, "Pricing is really the key in running a successful operation."

The railway offers five different classes of service, and choosing the pricing on each one determines the profit and return on investment the company's going to make. To set prices, management uses the contribution margin technique introduced in Chapter 2. Among the influences on pricing discussed in the chapter, costs and customer demands are the most important to the railway. The prices charged must not only ensure a reasonable profit but also must be attractive to the customer.

Costs are important in the marketing decisions of many types of companies. What price should a Safeway store charge for a pound of hamburger? What should Boeing charge for a 777 airplane? Should a clothing manufacturer accept a special discount order from Wal Mart? Should an appliance manufacturer add a new product, say, an automatic bread maker, to its product line? Or should an existing product be dropped? Marketing managers rely on accounting information to answer these questions and make important decisions on a daily basis. Without accounting information, it would be impossible for a firm to determine a marketing strategy. However, not all accounting information applies to each type of decision. In this chapter, we'll focus on identifying relevant information for marketing decisions. The ability to separate relevant from irrelevant information is often the difference between success and failure in modern business.[1]

THE CONCEPT OF RELEVANCE

Objective 1
Discriminate between relevant and irrelevant information for making decisions.

What information is relevant? That depends on the decision being made. Decision making essentially involves choosing among several courses of action. The available actions are determined by an often time-consuming formal or informal search and screening process, perhaps carried on by a company team that includes engineers, accountants, and operating executives. Accountants have an important role in the decision-making process, not as decision makers but as collectors and reporters of relevant information. (Although many managers want the accountant to recommend the proper decision, the final choice always rests with the operating executive.) The accountant's role in decision making is primarily that of a technical expert on financial analysis who helps managers focus on the relevant information that will lead to the best decision.

RELEVANCE DEFINED

relevant information The predicted future costs and revenues that will differ among alternative courses of action.

Making business decisions requires managers to compare two or more alternative courses of action. Accountants should use two criteria to determine if information is relevant: (1) It must be an expected future revenue or cost, and (2) it must have an element of difference among the alternatives. **Relevant information** is the predicted future costs and revenues that will differ among the alternatives.

Note that relevant information is a prediction of the future, not a summary of the past. Historical (past) data have no direct bearing on a decision. Such data can have an indirect bearing on a decision because they may help in predicting the future. But past figures, in themselves, are irrelevant to the decision itself. Why? Because the decision cannot affect past data. Decisions affect the future. Nothing can alter what has already happened.

Of the expected future data, only those that will differ from alternative to alternative are relevant to the decision. Any item that will remain the same regardless of the alternative selected is irrelevant. For instance, if a department manager's salary will be the same regardless of the products stocked, the salary is irrelevant to the selection of products.

EXAMPLES OF RELEVANCE

The following examples will help you clarify the sharp distinctions needed to discriminate between relevant and irrelevant information.

---

[1] *Throughout this and the next chapter, to concentrate on the fundamental ideas, we shall ignore the time value of money and income taxes (discussed in Chapter 11).*

Suppose you always buy gasoline from either of two nearby gasoline stations. Yesterday you noticed that one station was selling gasoline at $1.50 per gallon. The other was selling it at $1.40. Your automobile needs gasoline, and in making your choice of stations, you assume that these prices have not changed. The relevant costs are $1.50 and $1.40, the expected future costs that will differ between the alternatives. You use your past experience (that is, what you observed yesterday) for predicting today's price. Note that the relevant cost is not what you paid in the past, or what you observed yesterday, but what you expect to pay when you drive in to get gasoline. This cost meets our two criteria: (1) It is the expected future cost, and (2) it differs between the alternatives.

You may also plan to have your car lubricated. The recent price at each station was $12, and this is what you anticipate paying. This expected future cost is irrelevant because it will be the same under either alternative. It does not meet our second criterion.

On a business level, consider the following decision. A manufacturer is thinking of using aluminum instead of copper in making a line of ashtrays. The cost of direct material will decrease from 30¢ to 20¢ per ashtray.

The cost of copper used for this comparison probably came from historical cost records on the amount paid most recently for copper, but the relevant cost in the foregoing analysis is the expected future cost of copper compared with the expected future cost of aluminum.

The direct-labor cost will continue to be 70¢ per unit regardless of the material used. It is irrelevant because our second criterion—an element of difference between the alternatives—is not met.

	Aluminum	Copper	Difference
Direct material	$.20	$.30	$.10
Direct labor	.70	.70	—

Therefore we can safely exclude direct labor from the comparison of alternatives.

Exhibit 5-1 illustrates this simple decision, and it serves to show the appropriate framework for more complex decisions. Box 1(A) represents historical data from the accounting system. Box 1(B) represents other data, such as price indices or industry statistics, gathered from outside the accounting system. Regardless of their source, the data in step 1 help the formulation of predictions in step 2. (Remember that although historical data may act as a guide to predicting, they are irrelevant to the decision itself.)

In step 3 these predictions become inputs to the decision model. A **decision model** is any method used for making a choice. Such models sometimes require elaborate quantitative procedures, such as a petroleum refinery's mathematical method for choosing what products to manufacture for any given day or week. A decision model, however, may also be simple. It may be confined to a single comparison of costs for choosing between two materials. In this example our decision model is to compare the predicted unit costs and select the alternative with the lesser cost.

We will be referring to Exhibit 5-1 frequently because it illustrates the main concept in this chapter. In fact, this decision process applies to all business decisions, no matter how simple or complicated they may be. By using this process you will be able to focus squarely on the relevant information—the predicted future differences between alternatives—in any decision. In the rest of this chapter, we will use this decision process to apply the concept of relevance to several specific marketing decisions.

Objective 2
Use the decision process to make business decisions.

decision model Any method for making a choice, sometimes requiring elaborate quantitative procedures.

ACCURACY AND RELEVANCE

In the best of all possible worlds, information used for decision making would be perfectly relevant and accurate. However, in reality, such information is often too difficult or too costly to obtain. Accountants are thus forced to trade off relevance versus accuracy.

Exhibit 5-1

Decision Process and Role of Information

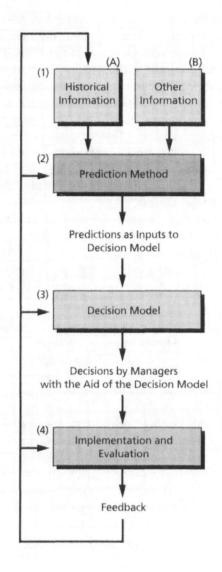

Precise but irrelevant information is worthless for decision making. For example, a university president's salary may be $140,000 per year, to the penny, but may have no bearing on the question of whether to buy or rent data processing equipment. However, imprecise but relevant information can be useful. For example, sales predictions for a new product may be subject to error, but they still are helpful to the decision of whether to manufacture the product. Of course, relevant information must be reasonably accurate but not precisely so.

The degree to which information is relevant or precise often depends on the degree to which it is qualitative or quantitative. Qualitative aspects are those for which measurement in dollars and cents is difficult and imprecise; quantitative aspects are those for which measurement is easy and precise. Accountants, statisticians, and mathematicians try to express as many decision factors as feasible in quantitative terms, because this approach reduces the number of qualitative factors to be judged. Just as we noted that relevance is more crucial than precision in decision making, so a qualitative aspect may easily carry more weight than a measurable (quantitative) financial impact in many decisions. For example, the extreme opposition of a militant union to new labor-saving machinery may cause a manager not to install such machinery even if it would save money. Alternatively, to avoid a long-range dependence on a particular supplier, a company may pass up the opportunity to purchase a component from the supplier at a price below the cost of producing it themselves.

Similarly, managers sometimes introduce new technology (for example, advanced computer systems or automated equipment) even though the expected quantitative results seem unattractive. Managers defend such decisions on the grounds that failure to keep abreast of new technology will surely bring unfavorable financial results sooner or later.

THE SPECIAL SALES ORDER

The first decision for which we examine relevant information is the special sales order.

ILLUSTRATIVE EXAMPLE

In our illustration we'll focus on the Cordell Company. Suppose Cordell makes and sells 1 million units of product, such as some automobile replacement part. The manufacturing cost of goods made is $30,000,000. The unit manufacturing cost of the product is $30,000,000 ÷ 1,000,000, or $30 per unit. Suppose a mail-order house near year-end offered Cordell $26 per unit for a 100,000-unit special order that (1) would not affect Cordell's regular business in any way, (2) would not raise any antitrust issues concerning price discrimination, (3) would not affect total fixed costs, (4) would not require any additional variable selling and administrative expenses, and (5) would use some otherwise idle manufacturing capacity. Should Cordell accept the order? Perhaps we should state the question more sharply: What is the difference in the short-run financial results between not accepting and accepting? As usual, the key question is, What are the differences between alternatives? Exhibit 5-2 presents the income statement (without the special order) of the Cordell Company, using the contribution margin technique.

CORRECT ANALYSIS — FOCUS ON RELEVANT INFORMATION AND COST BEHAVIOR

The correct analysis focuses on determining relevant information and cost behavior. It employs the contribution margin technique. As Exhibit 5-3 shows, this particular order affects only variable manufacturing costs, at a rate of $24 per unit. All other variable costs

Objective 3
Decide to accept or reject a special order using the contribution margin technique.

Exhibit 5-2

Cordell Company
Contribution Form of the Income Statement
For the Year Ended December 31, 20X1 (thousands of dollars)

Contribution Form		
Sales		$40,000
Less: variable expenses		
Manufacturing	$24,000	
Selling and administrative	2,200	26,200
Contribution margin		$13,800
Less: fixed expenses		
Manufacturing	$ 6,000	
Selling and administrative	5,800	11,800
Operating income		$ 2,000

Exhibit 5-3

Cordell Company

Comparative Predicted Income Statements, Contribution Margin Technique for Year Ended December 31, 20X1

	Without Special Order, 1,000,000 Units	Effect of Special Order 100,000 Units		With Special Order, 1,100,000 Units
		Total	Per Unit	
Sales	$40,000,000	$2,600,000	$26	$42,600,000
Less: variable expenses				
Manufacturing	$24,000,000	$2,400,000	$24	$26,400,000
Selling and administrative	2,200,000	—	—	2,200,000
Total variable expenses	$26,200,000	$2,400,000	$24	$28,600,000
Contribution margin	$13,800,000	$ 200,000	$ 2	$14,000,000
Less: fixed expenses				
Manufacturing	$ 6,000,000	—	—	$ 6,000,000
Selling and administrative	5,800,000	—	—	5,800,000
Total fixed expenses	$11,800,000	—	—	$11,800,000
Operating income	$ 2,000,000	$ 200,000	$ 2	$ 2,200,000

and all fixed costs are unaffected and thus irrelevant, so a manager may safely ignore them in making this special-order decision. Note how the contribution margin technique's distinction between variable- and fixed-cost behavior patterns aids the necessary cost analysis. Total short-run income will increase by $200,000 if Cordell accepts the order—despite the fact that the unit selling price of $26 is less than the total unit manufacturing cost of $30. Why did we include fixed costs in Exhibit 5-3? After all, they are irrelevant. They were included because management wants to know the difference in short-run financial results between not accepting and accepting the special order. The analysis could have ended with the contribution margin line but we wanted to show how the difference would effect the "bottom line"—operating income. There will be occasions when irrelevant data will be included in the accountant's presentation of analysis. Why? To suit the preferences of managers who will use the information for decision making.

INCORRECT ANALYSIS — MISUSE OF UNIT COST

Faulty cost analysis sometimes occurs because of misinterpreting unit fixed costs. For instance, Cordell's managers might erroneously use the $30 per-unit total manufacturing cost to make the following prediction for the year:

Incorrect Analysis	Without Special Order 1,000,000 Units	Incorrect Effect of Special Order 100,000 Units	With Special Order 1,100,000 Units
Sales	$40,000,000	$2,600,000	$42,600,000
Less: manufacturing cost			
of goods sold @ $30	30,000,000	3,000,000	33,000,000
Gross margin	10,000,000	(400,000)	9,600,000
Selling and administrative			
expenses	8,000,000	—	8,000,000
Operating income	$ 2,000,000	$ (400,000)	$ 1,600,000

The incorrect prediction of a $3 million increase in costs results from multiplying 100,000 units by $30. Of course, the fallacy in this approach is that it treats a fixed cost (fixed manufacturing cost) as if it were variable. Avoid the assumption that unit costs may be used indiscriminately as a basis for predicting how total costs will behave. Unit costs are useful for predicting variable costs but often misleading when used to predict fixed costs.

CONFUSION OF VARIABLE AND FIXED COSTS

Consider the relationship between total fixed manufacturing costs and a fixed manufacturing cost per unit of product:

$$\text{fixed cost per unit of product} = \frac{\text{total fixed manufacturing costs}}{\text{some selected volume level as the denominator}}$$

$$= \frac{\$6,000,000}{1,000,000 \text{ units}} = \$6 \text{ per unit}$$

As noted in Chapter 2, the typical cost accounting system serves two purposes simultaneously: planning and control and product costing. The total fixed cost for budgetary planning and control purposes can be graphed as a lump sum:

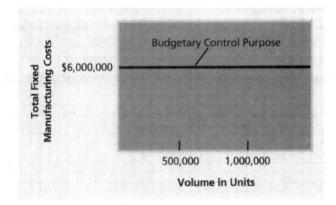

For product-costing purposes, however, using the total unit manufacturing cost implies that these fixed costs have a variable-cost behavior pattern:

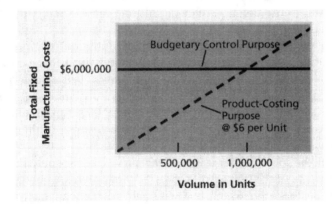

The addition of 100,000 units will not add any total fixed costs as long as total output is within the relevant range. The incorrect analysis, however, includes 100,000 × $6 = $600,000 of fixed cost in the predictions of increases in total costs.

We have presented two key lessons so far in this chapter: relevant information and misuse of unit costs. We cannot stress enough how important it is to clearly understand the definition and concept of relevant information. It is also important to understand why the use of unit fixed costs can lead to an incorrect analysis.

Consider the case where management of a company that makes small appliances is deciding whether to accept or reject a special order for 1,000 units. (Assume there is sufficient capacity available for the order.)

1. Which of the following costs are relevant: (a) parts for the order, (b) supervisor's salary, (c) assembly equipment depreciation, and (d) power to operate the assembly equipment?
2. Suppose the total unit manufacturing cost for the 1,000 units is $100 per unit. We determined this amount by dividing the total cost by 1,000 units. If the customer decided to double the order to 2,000 units, which unit costs listed in question 1 would change? Would the total cost of the order double?

ANSWERS

1. Relevant costs and revenues are predicted future costs and revenues that differ among alternative courses of action. In this case, the cost of parts and power would increase if management accepts the order, and thus they are relevant.
2. Fixed costs per unit will decrease if the customer doubles the order, whereas the variable cost per unit will stay the same. For example, fixed supervisory salaries will be divided by 2,000 units instead of only 1,000 units, and hence per-unit supervisory cost will decrease. The parts cost per unit would stay the same as would the power cost per unit. So, the total unit cost would fall, and the total cost of the order would not double.

In short, we should compute the increase in manufacturing costs by multiplying 1,000,000 units by $24, not by $30. The $30 includes a $6 component that will not affect the total manufacturing costs as volume changes.

ACTIVITY-BASED COSTING, SPECIAL ORDERS, AND RELEVANT COSTS

To identify relevant costs affected by a special order (or by other special decisions), more and more firms are going a step beyond simply identifying fixed and variable costs. As pointed out in Chapters 3 and 4, many different activities are associated with a company's operations. Businesses that have identified all their significant activities and related cost drivers can produce more detailed relevant information to predict the effects of special orders more accurately.

Suppose the Cordell Company examined its $24 million of variable manufacturing costs very closely and identified two significant activities and related cost drivers: $18 million of processing activity that varies directly with units produced at a rate of $18 per unit and $6 million of set-up activity that varies with the number of production setups. Normally, for processing 1,000,000 units, Cordell has 500 setups at a cost of $12,000 per setup, with an average of 2,000 units processed for each setup. Additional sales generally require a proportional increase in the number of setups.

Now suppose the special order is for 100,000 units that vary only slightly in production specifications. Instead of the normal 50 setups, Cordell will need only 5 setups. So processing 100,000 units will take $1,860,000 of additional variable manufacturing cost:

Additional unit-based variable manufacturing cost, 100,000 × $18	$1,800,000
Additional setup-based variable manufacturing cost, 5 × $12,000	60,000
Total additional variable manufacturing cost	$1,860,000

Instead of the original estimate of 100,000 × $24 = $2,400,000 additional variable manufacturing cost, the special order will cost only $1,860,000, or $540,000 less than the original estimate. Therefore, activity-based costing (ABC) allows managers to realize that the special order is $540,000 more profitable than predicted from the simple, unit-based assessment of variable manufacturing cost.

A special order may also be more costly than predicted by a simple fixed- and variable-cost analysis. Suppose the 100,000-unit special order called for a variety of models and colors delivered at various times, so that 100 setups are required. The variable cost of the special order would be $3.0 million.

Additional unit-based variable cost, 100,000 × $18	$1,800,000
Additional setup-based variable cost, 100 × $12,000	1,200,000
Total additional variable cost	$3,000,000

SUMMARY PROBLEM FOR YOUR REVIEW

PROBLEM

1. Return to the basic illustration in Exhibit 5-3. Suppose the Cordell Company received a special order for 100,000 units that had the following terms: Selling price would be $27.00 instead of $26.00, but a manufacturer's agent who had obtained the potential order would have to be paid a flat fee of $80,000 if the order is accepted. Should the special order be accepted?

2. What if the order was for 250,000 units at a selling price of $23.00 and there was no $80,000 agent's fee? Some managers have been known to argue for acceptance of such an order as follows: "Of course, we will lose $1.00 each on the variable manufacturing costs, but we will gain $1.20 per unit by spreading our fixed manufacturing costs over 1.25 million units instead of 1 million units. Consequently, we should take the offer because it represents an advantage of $.20 per unit."

Old fixed manufacturing cost per unit, $6,000,000 ÷ 1,000,000	$6.00
New fixed manufacturing cost per unit, $6,000,000 ÷ 1,250,000	4.80
"Saving" in fixed manufacturing cost per unit	$1.20
Loss on variable manufacturing cost per unit, $23.00 − $24.00	1.00
Net saving per unit in manufacturing cost	$ .20

Explain why this is faulty thinking.

SOLUTION

1. Focus on relevant information—the differences in revenues and costs. In this problem, in addition to the difference in variable costs, there is a difference in fixed costs between the two alternatives.

Additional revenue, 100,000 units @ $27.00 per unit	$2,700,000
Less additional costs	
Variable costs, 100,000 units @ $24 per unit	2,400,000
Fixed costs, agent's fee	80,000
Increase in operating income from special order	$ 220,000

So, from a strictly financial perspective, the special order should be accepted.

2. The faulty thinking comes from attributing a "savings" to the decrease in unit fixed costs. Regardless of how we "unitize" the fixed manufacturing costs or "spread" them over the units produced, the special order will not change the total of $6 million. Remember that we have a negative contribution margin of $1.00 per unit on this special order. Thus, there is no way we can cover any amount of fixed costs! Fixed costs are not relevant to this decision.

DELETION OR ADDITION OF PRODUCTS, SERVICES, OR DEPARTMENTS

Objective 4
Decide to add or delete a product line using relevant information.

Relevant information also plays an important role in decisions about adding or deleting products, services, or departments.

AVOIDABLE AND UNAVOIDABLE COSTS

Often existing businesses will want to expand or contract their operations to improve profitability. How can a manufacturer decide whether to add or to drop products? The same way a retailer decides whether to add or to drop departments: by examining all the relevant cost and revenue information. For example, consider a discount department store that has three major departments: groceries, general merchandise, and drugs. Management is considering dropping the grocery department, which has consistently shown an operating loss. The following table reports the store's present annual operating income (in thousands of dollars).

	Departments			
	Total	Groceries	General Merchandise	Drugs
Sales	$1,900	$1,000	$800	$100
Variable cost of goods sold and expenses*	1,420	800	560	60
Contribution margin	$ 480 (25%)	$ 200 (20%)	$240 (30%)	$ 40 (40%)
Fixed expenses (salaries, depreciation, insurance, property taxes, and so on):				
Avoidable	$ 265	$ 150	$100	$ 15
Unavoidable	180	60	100	20
Total fixed expenses	$ 445	$ 210	$200	$ 35
Operating income	$ 35	$ (10)	$ 40	$ 5

*Examples of variable expenses include paper shopping bags and sales commissions

avoidable costs Costs that will not continue if an ongoing operation is changed or deleted.

unavoidable costs Costs that continue even if an operation is halted.

common costs Those costs of facilities and services that are shared by users.

Notice that the fixed expenses are divided into two categories, avoidable and unavoidable. **Avoidable costs**—costs that will not continue if an ongoing operation is changed or deleted—are relevant. In our example, avoidable costs include department salaries and other costs that could be eliminated by not operating the specific department. **Unavoidable costs**—costs that continue even if an operation is halted—are not relevant in our example because they are not affected by a decision to delete the department. Unavoidable costs include many **common costs,** which are those costs of facilities and services that are shared by users.[2] For example, store depreciation, heating, air

[2] *The concept of avoidable cost is used by government regulators as well as business executives For example, Amtrak divides its costs into avoidable—costs that "would cease if the route were eliminated"—and fixed—costs that would "remain relatively constant if a single route were discontinued" The U S Interstate Commerce Commission then considers the avoidable costs when considering approval of a railroad's request to abandon a route Similarly, the Canadian government looks at the avoidable cost when determining the amount of subsidy to give to the country's passenger rail system The* Montreal Gazette *reported that revenues covered only 35% of the "$7 million in avoidable costs (costs that wouldn't exist if the train disappeared tomorrow—things like staff salaries, food, fuel, and upkeep of train stations) "*

conditioning, and general management expenses are costs of shared resources used by all departments. For our example, assume first that the only alternatives to be considered are dropping or continuing the grocery department, which shows a loss of $10,000. Assume further that the total assets invested would be unaffected by the decision. The vacated space would be idle, and the unavoidable costs would continue. Which alternative would you recommend? An analysis (in thousands of dollars) follows.

Income Statements	Store as a Whole		
	Total Before Change (a)	Effect of Dropping Groceries (b)	Total After Change (a) − (b)
Sales	$1,900	$1,000	$900
Variable expenses	1,420	800	620
Contribution margin	$ 480	$ 200	$280
Avoidable fixed expenses	265	150	115
Profit contribution to common space and other unavoidable costs	$ 215	$ 50	$165
Common space and other unavoidable costs	180	—	180
Operating income	$ 35	$ 50	$ (15)

The preceding analysis shows that matters would be worse, rather than better, if the store drops the groceries department and leaves the vacated facilities idle. In short, as the income statement shows, groceries bring in a contribution margin of $200,000, which is $50,000 more than the $150,000 fixed expenses that would be saved by closing the grocery department. The grocery department showed a loss in the first income statement because of the unavoidable fixed costs charged to it.

Of course, most companies do not like having space left idle, so perhaps the preceding example was a bit too basic. Assume now that the store could use the space made available by the dropping of groceries to expand the general merchandise department. The space would be occupied by merchandise that would increase sales by $500,000, generate a 30% contribution-margin percentage, and have avoidable fixed costs of $70,000. The $80,000 increase in operating income of general merchandise more than offsets the $50,000 decline from eliminating groceries, providing an overall increase in operating income of $65,000 − $35,000 = $30,000.

(In thousands of dollars)	Effects of Changes			
	Total Before Change (a)	Drop Groceries (b)	Expand General Merchandise (c)	Total After Changes (a) − (b) + (c)
Sales	$1,900	$1,000	$500	$1,400
Variable expenses	1,420	800	350	970
Contribution margin	$ 480	$ 200	$150	$ 430
Avoidable fixed expenses	265	150	70	185
Contribution to common space and other unavoidable costs	$ 215	$ 50	$ 80	$ 245
Common space and other unavoidable costs*	180	—	—	180
Operating income	$ 35	$ 50	$ 80	$ 65

*Includes the $60,000 of former grocery fixed costs, which were allocations of unavoidable common costs that will continue regardless of how the space is occupied.

The purpose in deciding whether to add or drop new products, services, or departments is to obtain the greatest contribution possible to pay unavoidable costs. The unavoidable costs will remain the same regardless of any decision, so the key is picking the alternative that will contribute the most toward paying off these costs. The following analysis illustrates this concept for our example.

	Profit Contribution of Given Space (in thousands of dollars)		
	Groceries	Expansion of General Merchandise	Difference
Sales	$1,000	$500	$500 U
Variable expenses	800	350	450 F
Contribution margin	$ 200	$150	$ 50 U
Avoidable fixed expenses	150	70	80 F
Contribution to common space and other unavoidable costs	$ 50	$ 80	$ 30 F

F = Favorable difference resulting from replacing groceries with general merchandise.
U = Unfavorable difference.

In our example, the general merchandise will not achieve the dollar sales volume that groceries will, but the higher contribution margin percentage and the lower wage costs (mostly because of the diminished need for stocking and checkout clerks) combine to produce a more favorable bottom line.

This example illustrates that relevant costs are not always variable. In the special order decision, the relevant costs were the variable costs, which might have led you to believe that you should always ignore fixed costs and focus only on variable costs. However, the key to decision making is not relying on a hard and fast rule about what to ignore and what not to ignore. Rather, you need to analyze all pertinent cost and revenue data to determine what is and what is not relevant. In this case, the relevant costs included the fixed avoidable costs.

When managers face a decision about whether to add or delete a product, service, or department, it is useful to classify the associated fixed costs as avoidable or unavoidable. Indicate whether the following fixed costs are typically avoidable or unavoidable if a company deletes a product. Assume that the company produces many products in a single plant.

1. Depreciation on equipment used to produce the product. The equipment will be sold if the product is discontinued.
2. Salary of the plant manager.
3. Depreciation on the plant building.
4. Advertising costs for the product. Specific ads are placed just for this product.

ANSWER

Items (1) and (4) are avoidable fixed costs. The salary of the plant manager will usually be unchanged if the company discontinues only one product. Thus, it is unavoidable. The same is true for the plant depreciation. Hence, it is also an unavoidable cost.

OPTIMAL USE OF LIMITED RESOURCES

When a plant that makes more than one product is operating at capacity, managers often must decide which orders to accept. The contribution margin technique also applies here, because the product to be emphasized or the order to be accepted is the one that makes the biggest total profit contribution per unit of the limiting factor. A **limiting factor** or **scarce resource** restricts or constrains the production or sale of a product or service. Limiting factors include labor hours and machine hours that limit production (and hence sales) in manufacturing firms, and square feet of floor space or cubic meters of display space that limit sales in department stores.

The contribution margin technique must be used wisely. Managers sometimes mistakenly favor those products with the biggest contribution margin or gross margin per sales dollar, without regard to scarce resources.

Assume that a company has two products: a plain cellular phone and a fancier cellular phone with many special features. Unit data follow:

	Plain Phone	Fancy Phone
Selling price	$80	$120
Variable costs	64	84
Contribution margin	$16	$ 36
Contribution margin ratio	20%	30%

Which product is more profitable? On which should the firm spend its resources? The correct answer is, It depends. If sales are restricted by demand for only a limited number of phones, fancy phones are more profitable. Why? Because sale of a plain phone adds $16 to profit; sale of a fancy phone adds $36. Thus, if the limiting factor is units of sales, the more profitable product is the one with the higher contribution per unit.

Now suppose annual demand for phones of both types is more than the company can produce in the next year. Productive capacity is the limiting factor because only 10,000 hours of capacity are available. If plant workers can make either three plain phones or one fancy phone in one hour, the plain phone is more profitable. Why? Because it contributes more profit per hour of capacity.

	Plain Phone	Fancy Phone
1. Units per hour	3	1
2. Contribution margin per unit	$16	$36
Contribution margin per hour (1) × (2)	$48	$36
Total contribution for 10,000 hours	$480,000	$360,000

As we said earlier, the criterion for maximizing profits when one factor limits sales is to obtain the greatest possible contribution to profit for each unit of the limiting factor. However, the product that is most profitable when one particular factor limits sales may be the least profitable if a different factor restricts sales.

In retail sales, the limiting resource is often floor space. Thus, retail stores must focus either on products taking up less space or on using the space for shorter periods of time — greater **inventory turnover** (number of times the average inventory is sold per year). Consider an example of two department stores. The conventional gross profit percentage (gross profit ÷ selling price) is an insufficient clue to profitability because, as we said, profits depend on the space occupied and the inventory turnover. Discount department stores such as Wal-Mart, Target, and Kmart have succeeded while using lower markups than traditional department stores because they have been able to increase turnover and thus increase the contribution to profit per unit of space. Exhibit 5-4 illustrates the same

limiting factor (scarce resource) The item that restricts or constrains the production or sale of a product or service.

Objective 5
Compute a measure of product profitability when production is constrained by a scarce resource.

inventory turnover The number of times the average inventory is sold per year.

Exhibit 5-4

Effect of Turnover on Profit

	Regular Department Store	Discount Department Store
Retail price	$4.00	$3.50
Cost of merchandise and other variable costs	3.00	3.00
Contribution to profit per unit	$1.00 (25%)	$ .50 (14%)
Units sold per year	10,000	22,000
Total contribution to profit, assuming the same space allotment in both stores	$10,000	$11,000

product, taking up the same amount of space, in each of two stores. The contribution margins per unit and per sales dollar are less in the discount store, but faster turnover makes the same product a more profitable use of space in the discount store. In general, retail companies seek faster inventory turnover. A survey of retail shoe stores showed that those with above-average financial performance had an inventory turnover of 2.6 times per year compared to an industry average of 2.0.

PRICING DECISIONS

One of the major decisions managers face is pricing. Actually, pricing can take many forms. Among the many pricing decisions to be made are

1. Setting the price of a new or refined product
2. Setting the price of products sold under private labels
3. Responding to a new price of a competitor
4. Pricing bids in both sealed and open bidding situations

Pricing decisions are so important, in fact, that we will spend the rest of the chapter discussing the many aspects of pricing. Let us now take a look at some of the basic concepts behind pricing.

THE CONCEPT OF PRICING

perfect competition A market in which a firm can sell as much of a product as it can produce, all at a single market price.

Pricing decisions depend on the characteristics of the market a firm faces. In **perfect competition,** all competing firms sell the same type of product at the same price. Thus, a firm can sell as much of a product as it can produce, all at a single market price. If it charges more, no customer will buy. If it charges less, it sacrifices profits. Therefore, every firm in such a market will charge the market price, and the only decision for managers is how much to produce.

marginal cost The additional cost resulting from producing and selling one additional unit.

Although costs do not directly influence prices in perfect competition, they do affect the production decision. Consider the marginal cost curve in Exhibit 5-5. The **marginal cost** is the additional cost resulting from producing and selling one additional unit. The marginal cost often decreases as production increases up to a point because of efficiencies created by larger amounts. At some point, however, marginal costs begin to rise with increases in production because facilities begin to be overcrowded or overused, resulting in inefficiencies.

marginal revenue The additional revenue resulting from the sale of an additional unit.

Exhibit 5-5 also includes a marginal revenue curve. The **marginal revenue** is the additional revenue resulting from the sale of an additional unit. In perfect competition, the marginal revenue curve is a horizontal line equal to the price per unit at all volumes of sales.

Exhibit 5-5

Marginal Revenue and Cost in Perfect Competition

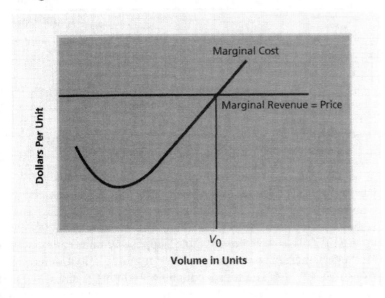

As long as the marginal cost is less than the marginal revenue (price), additional production and sales are profitable. When marginal cost exceeds price, however, the firm loses money on each additional unit. Therefore, the profit-maximizing volume is the quantity at which marginal cost equals price. In Exhibit 5-5, the firm should produce V_0 units. Producing fewer units passes up profitable opportunities, and producing more units reduces profit because each additional unit costs more to produce than it generates in revenue.

In **imperfect competition,** the price a firm charges for a unit will influence the quantity of units it sells. At some point, the firm must reduce prices to generate additional sales. Exhibit 5-6 contains a demand curve (also called the average revenue curve) for

imperfect competition A market in which the price a firm charges for a unit will influence the quantity of units it sells.

Exhibit 5-6

Marginal Revenue and Cost in Imperfect Competition

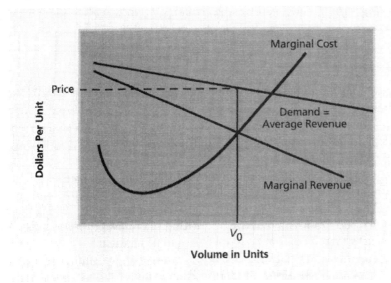

Exhibit 5-7
Profit Maximization in Imperfect Competition

Units Sold	Price per Unit	Total Revenue	Marginal Revenue	Marginal Cost	Profit from Production and Sale of Additional Unit
10	$50	10 × $50 = $500			
11	49	11 × 49 = 539	$539 − $500 = $39	$35	$39 − $35 = $4
12	48	12 × 48 = 576	576 − 539 = 37	36	37 − 36 = 1
13	47	13 × 47 = 611	611 − 576 = 35	37	35 − 37 = (2)

imperfect competition that shows the volume of sales at each possible price. To sell additional units, the firm must reduce the price of all units sold. Therefore, the marginal revenue curve, also shown in Exhibit 5-6, is below the demand curve. That is, the marginal revenue for selling one additional unit is less than the price at which it is sold because the price of all other units falls as well. For example, suppose 10 units can be sold for $50 per unit. However, the firm must drop the price to $49 per unit to sell 11 units, to $48 to sell 12 units, and to $47 to sell 13 units. The fourth column of Exhibit 5-7 shows the marginal revenue for units 11 through 13. Notice that the marginal revenue decreases as volume increases.

price elasticity The effect of price changes on sales volume.

To estimate marginal revenue, managers must predict the effect of price changes on sales volume, which is called **price elasticity.** If small price increases cause large volume declines, demand is highly elastic. If prices have little or no effect on volume, demand is highly inelastic.

For the marginal costs shown in the fifth column of Exhibit 5-7, the optimal production and sales level would be 12 units. The last column of that exhibit illustrates that the 11th unit adds $4 to profit, and the 12th adds $1, but production and sale of the 13th unit would decrease profit by $2. In general, firms should produce and sell units until the marginal revenue equals the marginal cost, represented by volume V_0 in Exhibit 5-6. The optimal price charged will be the amount that creates a demand for V_0 units.

Notice that the marginal cost is relevant for pricing decisions. In managerial accounting, marginal cost is essentially the variable cost. What is the major difference between marginal cost and variable cost? Variable cost is assumed to be constant within a relevant range of volume, whereas marginal cost may change with each unit produced. Within large ranges of production volume, however, changes in marginal cost are often small. Therefore, using variable cost can be a reasonable approximation to marginal cost in many situations.

PRICING AND ACCOUNTING

Objective 6
Discuss the factors that influence pricing decisions in practice.

Accountants seldom compute marginal revenue curves and marginal cost curves. Instead, they use estimates based on judgment to predict the effects of additional production and sales on profits. In addition, they examine selected volumes, not the whole range of possible volumes. Such simplifications are justified because the cost of a more sophisticated analysis would exceed the benefits.

Consider a division of General Electric (GE) that makes microwave ovens. Suppose market researchers estimate that GE can sell 700,000 ovens at $200 per unit and 1,000,000 ovens at $180. The variable cost of production is $130 per unit at production levels of both 700,000 and 1,000,000. Both volumes are also within the relevant range so that changes in volume do not affect fixed costs. Which price should be charged?

GE's accountant would determine the relevant revenues and costs. The additional revenue and additional costs of the 300,000 additional units of sales at the $180 prices are:

Additional revenue: $(1,000,000 \times \$180) - (700,000 \times \$200) =$	$40,000,000
Additional costs: $300,000 \times \$130 =$	39,000,000
Additional profit:	$ 1,000,000

Alternatively, the accountant could compare the total contribution for each alternative:

Contribution at $180: $(\$180 - \$130) \times 1,000,000 =$	$50,000,000
Contribution at $200: $(\$200 - \$130) \times 700,000 \ \ =$	49,000,000
Difference:	$ 1,000,000

Notice that comparing the total contributions is essentially the same as computing the additional revenues and costs—both use the same relevant information. Further, both approaches correctly ignore fixed costs, which are unaffected by this pricing decision.

GENERAL INFLUENCES ON PRICING IN PRACTICE

Several factors interact to shape the market in which managers make pricing decisions. Legal requirements, competitors' actions, and customer demands all influence pricing.

LEGAL REQUIREMENTS

Pricing decisions must be made within constraints imposed by U.S. and international laws. These laws often protect consumers, but they also help protect other companies from predatory and discriminatory pricing.

Predatory pricing involves setting prices so low that they drive competitors out of the market. The predatory pricer then has no significant competition and can raise prices dramatically. For example, Wal-Mart has been accused of predatory pricing—selling at low cost to drive out local competitors. However, in a 4-to-3 vote, the court ruled in favor of Wal-Mart. U.S. courts have generally ruled that pricing is predatory only if companies set prices below their average variable cost and actually lose money in order to drive their competitors out of business.

predatory pricing
Establishing prices so low that competitors are driven out of the market. The predatory pricer then has no significant competition and can raise prices dramatically.

Discriminatory pricing is charging different prices to different customers for the same product or service. For example, a large group of retail druggists and big drugstore chains sued several large drug companies, alleging that their practice of allowing discounts to mail-order drug companies, health maintenance organizations, and other managed-care entities constitutes discriminatory pricing. The discounts were as large as 40%. However, pricing is not discriminatory if it reflects a cost differential incurred in providing the good or service. A tentative settlement to the $600 million class action suit was reached, but it did not require the drug companies to alter their pricing practices.

discriminatory pricing
Charging different prices to different customers for the same product or service.

COMPETITORS' ACTIONS

Competitors usually react to the price changes of their rivals. Many companies will gather information regarding a rival's capacity, technology, and operating policies. In this way, managers make more informed predictions of competitors' reactions to a company's prices. The study of game theory, for which two economists won the 1994 Nobel Prize, focuses on predicting and reacting to competitors' actions.

Tinkering with prices is often most heavily affected by the price setter's expectations of competitors' reactions and of the overall effects on the total industry demand for the good or service in question. For example, an airline might cut prices even if it expects price cuts from its rivals, hoping that total customer demand for the tickets of all airlines will increase sufficiently to offset the reduction in the price per ticket.

Competition is becoming increasingly international. Overcapacity in some countries often causes aggressive pricing policies, particularly for a company's exported goods.

CUSTOMER DEMANDS

More than ever before, managers are recognizing the needs of customers. Pricing is no exception. If customers believe a price is too high, they may turn to other sources for the product or service, substitute a different product, or decide to produce the item themselves.

ROLE OF COSTS IN PRICING DECISIONS

The influence of accounting on pricing is through costs. The exact role costs play in pricing decisions depends on both the market conditions and the company's approach to pricing. Two pricing approaches used by companies are cost-plus pricing and target costing.

COST-PLUS PRICING

markup The amount by which price exceeds cost.

Many managers say that they set prices by "cost-plus" pricing. For example, Grand Canyon Railway sets its prices by computing an average cost and then adding a desired **markup** (that is, the amount by which price exceeds cost) that will generate a target return on investment. The key, however, is the "plus" in cost plus. Instead of being a fixed markup, the "plus" will usually depend on both costs and the demands of customers. For example, the railway has a standard (rack rate) price that does not change during the year, but the company does offer discounts during the slow winter season.

Prices are most directly related to costs in industries where revenue is based on cost reimbursement. Cost-reimbursement contracts generally specify how costs should be measured and what costs are allowable. For example, only coach-class (not first-class) fares are reimbursable for business air travel on government projects, such as defense contracts.

Ultimately, though, the market sets prices. Why? Because the price as set by a cost-plus formula is inevitably adjusted "in light of market conditions." The maximum price a company can charge is the one that does not drive the customer away. The minimum price might be considered to be zero (for example, companies may give out free samples to gain entry into a market). A more practical guide is that, in the short run, the minimum price to be quoted, subject to consideration of long-run effects, should be equal to the costs that may be avoided by not landing the order—often all variable costs of producing, selling, and distributing the good or service. In the long run, the price must be high enough to cover all costs, including fixed costs.

COST BASES FOR COST-PLUS PRICING

Objective 7
Compute a target sales price by various approaches, and compare the advantages and disadvantages of these approaches.

Cost plus is often the basis for target prices. The size of the "plus" depends on target (desired) operating incomes. Target prices can be based on a host of different markups that are in turn based on a host of different definitions of cost. Thus, there are many ways to arrive at the same target price.

Exhibit 5-8 displays the relationships of costs to target selling prices, assuming a target operating income of $1 million. The percentages there represent four popular markup

Exhibit 5-8

Relationships of Costs to Same Target Selling Prices

		Alternative Markup Percentages to Achieve Same Target Sales Prices	
Target sales price	$20.00		
Variable cost:			
(1) Manufacturing	$12.00	($20.00 − $12.00) ÷ $12.00 = 66.67%	
Selling and administrative*	1.10		
(2) Unit variable costs	$13.10	($20.00 − $13.10) ÷ $13.10 = 52.67%	
Fixed costs:			
Manufacturing†	$ 3.00		
Selling and administrative	2.90		
Unit fixed costs	$ 5.90		
(3) Full costs	$19.00	($20.00 − $19.00) ÷ $19.00 = 5.26%	
Target operating income	$ 1.00		

*Selling and administrative costs include costs of value chain functions other than production

†(4) A frequently used formula is based on total manufacturing costs: [$20.00 − ($12.00 + $3.00)] ÷ $15 00 = 33 33%

formulas for pricing: (1) as a percentage of variable manufacturing costs, (2) as a percentage of total variable costs, (3) as a percentage of full costs, and (4) as a percentage to total manufacturing cost.

Note particularly that **full cost** or **fully allocated cost** means the total of all manufacturing costs plus the total of all selling and administrative costs. As noted in earlier chapters, we use "selling and administrative" to include value chain functions other than production. Of course, the percentages differ. For instance, the markup on variable manufacturing costs is 66.67%, and on full costs it is only 5.26%. Regardless of the formula used, the pricing decision maker will be led toward the same target price. For a volume of 1 million units, assume that the target selling price is $20 per unit. If the decision maker is unable to obtain such a price consistently, the company will not achieve its $1 million operating income objective.

We have seen that prices can be based on various types of cost information, from variable manufacturing costs to full costs. Each of these costs can be relevant to the pricing decision. Each approach has advantages and disadvantages.

full cost (fully allocated cost) The total of all manufacturing costs plus the total of all selling and administrative costs.

ADVANTAGES OF CONTRIBUTION MARGIN APPROACH IN COST-PLUS PRICING

Prices based on variable costs represent a contribution approach to pricing. When used intelligently, the contribution margin approach has some advantages over the total-manufacturing-cost and full-cost approaches, because the latter two often fail to highlight different cost behavior patterns.

Obviously, the contribution margin approach offers more detailed information because it displays variable- and fixed-cost behavior patterns separately. Because the contribution margin approach is sensitive to cost-volume-profit relationships, it is a helpful basis for developing pricing formulas. As a result, this approach allows managers to prepare price schedules at different volume levels.

The correct analysis in Exhibit 5-9 shows how changes in volume affect operating income. The contribution margin approach helps managers with pricing decisions by readily displaying the interrelationships among variable costs, fixed costs, and potential changes in selling prices.

In contrast, target pricing with full costing presumes a given volume level. When volume changes, the unit cost used at the original planned volume may mislead managers.

Exhibit 5-9

Analyses of Effects of Changes in Volume on Operating Income

	Correct Analysis			Incorrect Analysis		
Volume in units	900,000	1,000,000	1,100,000	900,000	1,000,000	1,100,000
Sales @ $20.00	$18,000,000	$20,000,000	$22,000,000	$18,000,000	$20,000,000	$22,000,000
Unit variable costs @ $13.10*	11,790,000	13,100,000	14,410,000			
Contribution margin	6,210,000	6,900,000	7,590,000			
Fixed costs†	5,900,000	5,900,000	5,900,000			
Full costs @ $19.00*				17,100,000	19,000,000	20,900,000
Operating income	$ 310,000	$ 1,000,000	$ 1,690,000	$ 900,000	$ 1,000,000	$ 1,100,000

* From Exhibit 5-8.

† Fixed manufacturing costs $3,000,000
  Fixed selling and administrative costs   2,900,000
  Total fixed costs $5,900,000

Managers sometimes erroneously assume that the change in total costs may be computed by multiplying any change in volume by the full unit cost.

The incorrect analysis in Exhibit 5-9 shows how managers may be misled if they use the $19 full cost per unit to predict effects of volume changes on operating income. Suppose a manager uses the $19 figure to predict an operating income of $900,000 if the company sells 900,000 instead of 1,000,000 units. If actual operating income is $310,000 instead, as the correct analysis predicts, that manager may be stunned—and possibly looking for a new job.

The contribution margin approach also offers insight into the short-run versus long-run effects of cutting prices on special orders. For example, assume the same cost behavior patterns as in the Cordell Company example in Exhibit 5-3 (page 186). The 100,000-unit order added $200,000 to operating income at a selling price of $26, which was $14 below the target selling price of $40 and $4 below the total manufacturing cost of $30. Given all the stated assumptions, accepting the order appeared to be the better choice. As you saw earlier, the contribution margin approach generated the most relevant information. Consider the contribution and total-manufacturing-cost approaches.

	Contribution Margin Technique	Total Manufacturing-Cost Approach
Sales, 100,000 units @ $26	$2,600,000	$2,600,000
Variable manufacturing costs @ $24	2,400,000	
Total manufacturing costs @ $30		3,000,000
Apparent change in operating income	$ 200,000	($ 400,000)

Under the total-manufacturing-cost approach, the offer is definitely unattractive because the price of $26 is $4 below total manufacturing costs.

Under the contribution margin approach, the decision maker sees a short-run advantage of $200,000 from accepting the offer. Fixed costs will be unaffected by whatever decision is made and operating income will increase by $200,000. Still, there often are long-run effects to consider. Will acceptance of the offer undermine the long-run price structure? In other words, is the short-run advantage of $200,000 more than offset by highly probable long-run financial disadvantages? The decision maker may think so and may reject the offer. But—and this is important—by doing so the decision maker is, in effect, forgoing $200,000 now to protect certain long-run market advantages. Generally, the decision maker can assess problems of this sort by asking whether the probability of long-run benefits is worth an "investment" equal to the forgone contribution margin ($200,000 in this case). Under full-cost approaches, the decision maker must ordinarily conduct a special study to find the immediate effects. Under the contribution margin approach, the manager has a system that will routinely and more surely provide such information.

ADVANTAGES OF TOTAL-MANUFACTURING-COST AND FULL-COST APPROACHES IN COST-PLUS PRICING

Frequently, managers do not employ a contribution margin approach because they fear that variable costs will be substituted indiscriminately for full costs and will therefore lead to suicidal price cutting. This problem should not arise if the data are used wisely. However, if top managers perceive a pronounced danger of underpricing when variable-cost data are revealed, they may justifiably prefer a total-manufacturing-cost or full-cost approach for guiding pricing decisions.

Actually, total manufacturing costs or full costs are far more widely used in practice than is the contribution margin approach. Why? In addition to the reasons already mentioned, managers have cited the following reasons:

1. In the long run, all costs must be recovered to stay in business. Sooner or later fixed costs do indeed fluctuate as volume changes. Therefore it is prudent to assume that all costs are variable (even if some are fixed in the short run).

2. Computing target prices based on cost plus may indicate what competitors might charge, especially if they have approximately the same level of efficiency as you and also aim at recovering all costs in the long run.

3. Total-manufacturing-cost or full-cost formula pricing meets the cost-benefit test. It is too expensive to conduct individual cost-volume tests for the many products (sometimes thousands) that a company offers.

4. There is much uncertainty about the shape of the demand curves and the correct price-output decisions. Total-manufacturing-cost or full-cost pricing copes with this uncertainty by not encouraging managers to take too much marginal business.

5. Total-manufacturing-cost or full-cost pricing tends to promote price stability. Managers prefer price stability because it eases their professional lives, primarily because planning is more dependable.

6. Total-manufacturing-cost or full-cost pricing provides the most defensible basis for justifying prices to all interested parties including government antitrust investigators.

7. Total-manufacturing-cost or full-cost pricing provides convenient reference (target) points to simplify hundreds or thousands of pricing decisions.

USING MULTIPLE APPROACHES

To say that either a contribution margin approach or a total-manufacturing-cost or full-cost approach provides the "best" guide to pricing decisions is a dangerous oversimplification of one of the most perplexing problems in business. Lack of understanding and judgment can lead to unprofitable pricing regardless of the kind of cost data available or cost accounting system used.

Basically, no single method of pricing is always best. An interview study of executives reported that companies often use both full-cost and variable-cost information in pricing decisions.

The history of accounting reveals that most companies' systems have gathered costs via some form of full-manufacturing-cost system because this is what is required for financial reporting. In recent years, when systems have changed, variable costs and fixed costs were often identified. But managers have regarded this change as an addition to the existing full-manufacturing-cost system. That is, many managers insist on having information regarding both variable costs per unit and the allocated fixed costs per unit before setting selling prices. If the accounting system routinely gathers data regarding both variable and fixed costs, such data can readily be provided. However, most total-manufacturing-cost systems in practice do not organize their data collection to distinguish between variable and fixed costs. As a result, special studies or educated guessing must be used to designate costs as variable or fixed.

Managers are especially reluctant to focus on variable costs and ignore allocated fixed costs when their performance evaluations, and possibly their bonuses, are based on income shown in published financial statements. Why? Because such statements are based on full costing, and thus allocations of fixed costs affect reported income.

FORMATS FOR PRICING

Exhibit 5-8 showed how to compute alternative general markup percentages that would produce the same selling prices if used day after day. In practice, the format and arithmetic of quote sheets, job proposals, or similar records vary considerably.

Exhibit 5-10 is from an actual quote sheet used by the manager of a small job shop that bids on welding machinery orders in a highly competitive industry. The Exhibit 5-10 approach is a tool for informed pricing decisions. Notice that the maximum price is not a matter of cost at all. It is what you think you can obtain. The minimum price is the total variable cost.

Of course, the manager will rarely bid the minimum price. Businesses do need to make a profit. Still, the manager wants to know the effect of a job on the company's total variable costs. Occasionally, a company will bid near that minimum price to establish a presence in new markets or with a new customer.

Note that Exhibit 5-10 classifies costs specifically for the pricing task. Pricing decisions may be made by more than one person. The accountant's responsibility is to prepare an understandable format that involves a minimum of computations. Exhibit 5-10 combines direct labor and variable manufacturing overhead. All fixed costs, whether manufacturing, selling, or administrative, are lumped together and applied to the job using a single fixed-overhead rate per direct-labor-hour. Obviously, if more accuracy is desired, many more detailed cost items and overhead rates could be formulated. To obtain the desired accuracy, many companies are turning to activity-based costing.

Some managers, particularly in construction and in service industries such as auto repair, compile separate categories of costs of (1) direct materials, parts, and supplies and (2) direct labor. These managers then use different markup rates for each category. They use these rates to provide enough revenue to cover both indirect and unallocated costs

Exhibit 5-10
Quote Sheet for Pricing

Direct materials, at cost	$25,000
Direct labor and variable manufacturing overhead,	
600 direct-labor-hours × $30	18,000
Sales commission (varies with job)	2,000
Total variable costs—minimum price*	45,000
Add fixed costs allocated to job, 600 direct-labor-hours × $20	12,000
Total costs	57,000
Add desired markup	30,000
Selling price—maximum price that you think you can obtain*	$87,000

*This sheet shows two prices, maximum and minimum Any amount you can get above the minimum price is a contribution margin

and operating profit. For example, an automobile repair shop might have the following format for each job:

	Billed to Customers
Auto parts ($200 cost plus 40% markup)	$280
Direct labor (Cost is $20 per hour. Bill at 300% to recover	
indirect and unallocated costs and provide for operating profit.	
Billing rate is $20 × 300% = $60 per hour. Total billed for 10 hours	
is $60 × 10 = $600)	600
Total billed to customer	$880

Another example is an Italian printing company in Milan that wants to price its jobs so that each one generates a margin of 28% of revenues—14% to cover selling and administrative expenses and 14% for profit. To achieve this margin, the manager uses a pricing formula of 140% times predicted materials cost plus 25,000 Italian lira (abbreviated Lit) per hour of production time. The latter covers labor and overhead costs of Lit 18,000 per hour. For a product with Lit 400,000 of materials cost and 30 hours of production time, the price would be Lit 1,310,000:

	Cost	Price	Profit
Materials	Lit 400,000	Lit 560,000	Lit 160,000
Labor and overhead	540,000	750,000	210,000
Total	Lit 940,000	Lit 1,310,000	Lit 370,000

The profit of Lit 370,000 is approximately 40% of the cost of Lit 940,000 and 28% of the price of Lit 1,310,000.

Thus there are numerous ways to compute selling prices. However, some general words of caution are appropriate here. Managers are better able to understand their options and the effects of their decisions on profits if they know their costs. That is, it is more informative to pinpoint costs first, before adding markups, than to have a variety of markups already embedded in the "costs" used as guides for setting selling prices. For example, if materials cost $1,000, they should be shown on a price quotation guide at $1,000, not at, say, a marked-up $1,400 because that is what the seller hopes to get.

chapter

6

RELEVANT INFORMATION AND DECISION MAKING: PRODUCTION DECISIONS

When you relax with a bottle of Nantucket Nectars juice, you do not consider the various costs that go into producing, selling, and distributing the bottle. But these costs are very important to the managers at Nantucket Nectars.

www.prenhall.com/horngren

Learning Objectives

When you have finished studying this chapter, you should be able to

1. Use opportunity cost to analyze the income effects of a given alternative.

2. Decide whether to make or to buy certain parts or products.

3. Decide whether a joint product should be processed beyond the split-off point.

4. Identify irrelevant information in disposal of obsolete inventory and equipment replacement decisions.

5. Explain how unit costs can be misleading.

6. Discuss how performance measures can affect decision making.

7. Construct absorption and contribution format income statements and identify which is better for decision making.

8. **Understand the relationship between accounting information and decisions in the production stage of the value chain.**

Starting a beverage business can be a complex maze of decisions. Tom First and Tom Scott should know. After graduating from college, they operated a two-person boat service business off Nantucket Island, provisioning and cleaning yachts during the summer. In 1989, the inspiration for a juice drink made with fresh peaches hit. After a bit of experimentation, the self-proclaimed "juice guys" began bottling and selling their nectar drink from their boat. That first summer, they sold 2,000 bottles at $1.00 each. Today, Nantucket Nectars makes 48 different juice blends and sells millions of cases each year. Sales for 2000 topped $60 million.

Getting to this point, however, has been anything *but* smooth sailing. Their early attempts to sell juice to retailers failed. Profits were nonexistent. They sold half the business to an equity partner for $500,000 to venture into distribution, but ended up losing $1 million the first year. Employees stole caseloads of merchandise from the warehouse. And there have been inevitable product disappointments, such as bayberry tea. But the juice guys are quick learners. They got out of distribution, changed their marketing approach, and stopped the flow of red ink

As the company has grown, it has tackled important production-related decisions. For example, should they build and operate their own bottling facilities? What criteria should be used for developing new products? What's the best approach for tracking and analyzing the growing volume of production, distribution, and sales data?

After examining the cost of building and operating bottling plants, Nantucket Nectars chose to contract with existing beverage co-packers in Rhode Island, Nevada, Florida,

Pennsylvania, and Maryland. This approach gives the company broader distribution options without the capital expenditure and overhead of multiple plants. Its managers scrutinize unit costs associated with new product ideas emerging from the test kitchen to be sure margins are on target. And they meticulously track every detail—from production costs to marketing promotions—through a new computerized Enterprise Resource Planning (ERP) information system from Oracle.

Throughout it all, the juice guys never wavered in their determination to produce a top-quality product and satisfy customers. They readily admit they both failed their first accounting course in college, but they have come to appreciate its relevance in decision making as they've weathered stormy periods and sailed smooth seas.

As with Nantucket Nectars, managers in other companies must make similar production-related decisions. Should Toyota make the tires it mounts on its cars, or should it buy them from suppliers? Should General Mills sell the flour it mills, or should it use the flour to make more breakfast cereal? Should Delta Airlines add routes to use idle airplanes, or should it sell the planes? These decisions all require a good deal of accounting information. But what information will be relevant to each decision? In Chapter 5, we identified relevant information for decisions in the marketing function of the value chain. We now need to determine relevance in the production function. The basic framework for identifying relevant information remains the same for production as it was for marketing. We are still looking only for future costs that differ among alternatives. However, we now expand our analysis by introducing the concepts of opportunity and differential costs.

OPPORTUNITY, OUTLAY, AND DIFFERENTIAL COSTS

differential cost (revenue) The difference in total cost (revenue) between two alternatives.

Management decision making involves the comparison of two or more alternative courses of action. (Of course, if there were only one alternative, no decision would be necessary.) Suppose a manager has only two alternatives to compare. The key to determining the financial difference between the alternatives is to identify the *differential* costs and revenues. **Differential cost (revenue)** is the difference in total cost (revenue) between two alternatives. For example, consider the decision about which of two machines to purchase. Both machines perform the same function. The differential cost is the difference in the price paid for the machines plus the difference in the costs of operating the machines.

incremental cost Another term for differential cost when one alternative includes all the costs of the other plus some additional costs.

If one alternative includes all the costs of the other plus some additional costs, we often use the term **incremental cost** instead of differential cost. For instance, the incremental costs of increasing production from 1,000 automobiles to 1,200 automobiles per week would be the costs of producing the additional 200 automobiles each week. In the reverse situation, the decline in costs caused by reducing production from 1,200 to 1,000 automobiles per week would be called the *differential* or *incremental savings*.

When there are more than two alternative courses of action, managers often compare one particular action against the entire set of alternatives. For example, General Mills might consider introducing a new cereal, Frosted Rice Flakes. There are many alternatives to introducing Frosted Rice Flakes, including introducing other new cereals, expanding production of existing cereals, or producing noncereal products. Computing the differential costs and revenues for Frosted Rice Flakes with every alternative would be cumbersome. Thus, the General Mills managers might use a different approach.

Introducing Frosted Rice Flakes would entail two types of costs: **outlay costs,** which require a future cash disbursement, and opportunity costs. An **opportunity cost** is the maximum available contribution to profit foregone (or passed up) by using limited resources for a particular purpose. Opportunity costs apply to resources that are already owned or for which the company already has a commitment to purchase. The decision regarding Frosted Rice Flakes will not affect whether the company acquires these resources, only how it uses them. The opportunity cost of such resources depends on the potential uses for the resources, not on the amount paid for them. Why? Because the decision about Frosted Rice Flakes will not affect the amount paid. However, the decision to use the resources to produce Frosted Rice Flakes precludes using them for other alternatives. The amount that would have been gained if the resources had been used in their best alternative use (that is, the best use other than using them to produce Frosted Rice Flakes) becomes the opportunity cost of the resources.

Suppose General Mills has a machine for which it paid $100,000. The machine can be used to produce Frosted Rice Flakes or to increase the production of Wheaties. The contribution margin from the additional Wheaties produced would be $60,000. In addition, the machine could be sold for $50,000. The opportunity cost of the machine when analyzing the Frosted Rice Flakes alternative is $60,000, the larger of the $50,000 or $60,000, the two possible gains that could be achieved using the machine in its alternative uses. The $100,000 paid for the machine is irrelevant.

Now suppose that General Mills will sell the Frosted Rice Flakes for $500,000, and the production and marketing costs (outlay costs), excluding the cost of the machine, are $400,000. The net financial benefit from the Frosted Rice Flakes is $40,000.

Revenues		$500,000
Costs:		
Outlay costs	$400,000	
Opportunity costs	60,000	
Total cost		460,000
Net financial benefit		$ 40,000

General Mills will gain $40,000 more financial benefit using the machine to make Frosted Rice Flakes than it would make using it for the next most profitable alternative.

When considering only two alternatives, a manager might use straightforward differential analysis or an opportunity cost analysis. The two approaches are equivalent. To see this, consider Maria Morales, a certified public accountant employed by a large accounting firm for $60,000 per year. She is considering an alternative use of her time, her most valuable resource. The alternative is to have her own independent accounting practice. A straightforward differential analysis follows.

	Alternatives Under Consideration		
	Remain an Employee	*Open an Independent Practice*	**Difference**
Revenues	$60,000	$200,000	$140,000
Outlay costs (operating expenses)		120,000	120,000
Income effects per year	$60,000	$ 80,000	$ 20,000

Maria has revenues of $200,000—quite a bit more than she would have made as an employee of the large firm. However, she also had to pay $120,000 to rent office space, lease equipment, buy advertising, and cover other out-of-pocket expenses. The $80,000 of operating income is $20,000 more than her salary with the firm.

Now if we look in isolation at the alternative of operating an independent practice, essentially comparing it to all alternative uses of Maria's time (which in this case is simply the alternative of working for the large firm), we must consider another cost. Had Maria remained an employee, she would have made $60,000. By starting her own company, Maria will forego this profit. Thus, the $60,000 is an opportunity cost of starting her own business:

		Alternative Chosen: Independent Practice
Revenue		$200,000
Expenses		
Outlay costs (operating expenses)	$120,000	
Opportunity cost of employee salary	60,000	180,000
Income effects per year		$ 20,000

Ponder the two preceding tabulations. Each produces the correct key difference between alternatives, $20,000. The first tabulation does not mention opportunity cost because the economic impacts (in the form of revenues and outlay costs) are individually measured for each of the alternatives (two in this case). We did not exclude either alternative from consideration. The second tabulation mentions opportunity cost because we included the $60,000 annual economic impact of the best excluded alternative as a cost of the chosen alternative. The failure to recognize opportunity cost in the second tabulation will misstate the difference between alternatives.

The major message here is straightforward: Do not overlook opportunity costs. Consider a homeowner who has made the final payment on a home mortgage. While celebrating, the owner says, "It's a wonderful feeling to know that future occupancy is free of any interest cost!" Many owners have similar thoughts. Why? Because no future outlay costs for interest are required. Nevertheless, there is an opportunity cost of continuing to live in the home. After all, an alternative would be to sell the home, place the proceeds in some other investment, and rent an apartment. The owner forgoes the interest in the other investment, so this foregone interest income becomes an opportunity cost of home ownership.

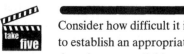

Consider how difficult it is to estimate opportunity costs. There is no sale or purchase to establish an appropriate cost. Further, the opportunity cost depends on the alternatives that are available at a point in time. The same alternatives may not be available at a different time. For example, excess capacity in September does not mean that there will also be excess capacity in October. How might a manager at Mattel, the toy company, estimate the opportunity cost of excess warehouse space in January?

ANSWER

The Mattel manager would know that excess warehouse space is a seasonal phenomenon There is unlikely to be excess space late in the year as Christmas approaches. Therefore, he or she would look for temporary alternatives, ones that use the space for only a few months After identifying alternatives, the manager would estimate the value of each. Because most of the alternatives are ones that are never undertaken, estimating their values is a subjective process. The highest valued alternative would establish the opportunity cost of the space.

Managers often must decide whether to produce a product or service within the firm or purchase it from an outside supplier. They apply relevant cost analysis to a variety of such make-or-buy decisions, including:

Objective 2
Decide whether to make or buy certain parts or products.

- Boeing must decide whether to buy or make many of the tools used in assembling 777 airplanes.
- IBM must decide whether to develop its own operating system for a new computer or to buy it from a software vendor.

BASIC MAKE-OR-BUY AND IDLE FACILITIES

A basic make-or-buy question is whether a company should make its own parts to be used in its products or buy them from vendors. Sometimes the answer to this question is based on qualitative factors. For example, some manufacturers always make parts because they want to control quality. Alternatively, some companies always purchase parts to protect long-run relationships with their suppliers. These companies may deliberately buy from vendors even during slack times to avoid difficulties in obtaining needed parts during boom times, when there may well be shortages of materials and workers, but no shortage of sales orders.

What quantitative factors are relevant to the decision of whether to make or buy? The answer, again, depends on the situation. A key factor is whether there are idle facilities. Many companies make parts only when their facilities cannot be used to better advantage.

Assume that the following costs are reported:

General Electric Company
Cost of Making Part No. 900

	Total Cost for 20,000 Units	Cost per Unit
Direct material	$ 20,000	$ 1
Direct labor	80,000	4
Variable factory overhead	40,000	2
Fixed factory overhead	80,000	4
Total costs	$220,000	$11

Another manufacturer offers to sell General Electric (GE) the same part for $10. Should GE make or buy the part?

Although the $11 unit cost shown seemingly indicates that the company should buy, the answer is rarely so obvious. The essential question is the difference in expected future costs between the alternatives. If the $4 fixed overhead per unit consists of costs that will continue regardless of the decision, the entire $4 becomes irrelevant. Examples of such costs include depreciation, property taxes, insurance, and allocated executive salaries.

Again, are only the variable costs relevant? No. Perhaps $20,000 of the fixed costs will be eliminated if the parts are bought instead of made. For example, a supervisor with a $20,000 salary might be released. In other words, fixed costs that may be avoided in the future are relevant.

For the moment, suppose the capacity now used to make parts will become idle if the parts are purchased and the $20,000 supervisor's salary is the only fixed cost that would be eliminated. The relevant computations follow.

	Make		Buy	
	Total	Per Unit	Total	Per Unit
Purchase cost			$200,000	$10
Direct material	$ 20,000	$1		
Direct labor	80,000	4		
Variable factory overhead	40,000	2		
Fixed factory overhead that can be avoided by not making (supervisor's salary)	20,000*	1*		
Total relevant costs	$160,000	$8	$200,000	$10
Difference in favor of making	$ 40,000	$2		

* Note that unavoidable fixed costs of $80,000 − $20,000 = $60,000 are irrelevant Thus the irrelevant costs per unit are $4 − $1 = $3.

The key to make-or-buy decisions is identifying the additional costs for making (or the costs avoided by buying) a part or subcomponent. Activity analysis, described in Chapter 3, helps identify these costs. Production of a product requires a set of activities. A company with accurate measurements of the costs of its various activities can better estimate the additional costs incurred to produce an item. GE's activities for production of part number 900 were measured by two cost drivers, units of production of $8 per unit and supervision at a $20,000 fixed cost. Sometimes identification and measurement of additional cost drivers, especially nonvolume-related cost drivers, can improve the predictions of the additional cost to produce a part or subcomponent.

MAKE OR BUY AND THE USE OF FACILITIES

Make-or-buy decisions are rarely as simple as the one in our GE example. As we said earlier, the use of facilities is a key to the make-or-buy decision. For simplicity, we assumed that the GE facilities would remain idle if the company chose to buy the product. This means that the opportunity cost of the facilities is zero. Of course, in most cases companies will not leave their facilities idle. Instead, they will often put idle facilities to some other use, and we must consider the financial outcomes of these uses when choosing to make or buy. The value received from the best of these alternative uses is an opportunity cost for the internal production of the parts or subcomponents.

Suppose the released facilities in our example can be used advantageously in some other manufacturing activity (to produce a contribution to profits of, say, $55,000) or can be rented out (say, for $35,000). We now have four alternatives to consider (figures are in thousands):

	Make	Buy and Leave Facilities Idle	Buy and Rent Out Facilities	Buy and Use Facilities for Other Products
Rent revenue	$ —	$ —	$ 35	$ —
Contribution from other products	—	—	—	55
Obtaining of parts	(160)	(200)	(200)	(200)
Net relevant costs	$(160)	$(200)	$(165)	$(145)

The final column indicates that buying the parts and using the vacated facilities for the production of other products would yield the lowest net costs in this case. Using opportunity

Make-or-buy decisions apply to services as well as to products. Companies are increasingly deciding to hire service firms to handle some of their internal operations, an option called outsourcing. According to The Outsourcing Institute, outsourcing is "the strategic use of outside resources to perform activities traditionally handled by internal staff and resources."

Outsourcing has been used for many business functions. The most common items to outsource, ranked by the total percent of outsourcing expenditures, are

Information technology	30%
Human resources	16%
Marketing and sales	14%
Finance	11%
Administration	9%
All others	20%

Although companies can outsource many functions, most of the recent growth in outsourcing has been driven by the Internet. During the 1990s, many companies installed Enterprise Resource Planning (ERP) systems to handle all their computing needs. However, by the beginning of the twenty-first century many companies were realizing that the huge investments necessitated by ERP systems may not be needed. The required services could be purchased over the Internet without investing in the systems' purchase and development costs. The formerly expensive process of communication with the service providers had become essentially free via the Internet. A new group of computing service providers—called Application Service Providers (ASP)—arose to provide outsourcing opportunities for a variety of computing applications.

A prime example of using an ASP is Owens Corning's outsourcing of its travel and expense (T&E) reporting system. By hiring VIN.net International, a specialist in automated expense management, Owens Corning has a state-of-the-art T&E system without a huge up-front investment. The Owens Corning employees can focus on their mission-critical activities, without worrying about a peripheral management function such as T&E management.

The company most identified with outsourcing is Sun Microsystems. Long before most companies seriously considered outsourcing large parts of their operations, Sun outsourced everything except its core technologies. Sun focuses on hardware and software design and outsources nearly everything else. Its employees do not actually produce any of the products that bear the company's name.

The driving forces behind most outsourcing decisions are access to technology and cost savings. As the complexity of data processing and especially networking has grown, companies have found it harder and harder to keep current with the technology. Instead of investing huge sums in personnel and equipment and diverting attention from the value-added activities of their own businesses, many firms have found outsourcing financially attractive. The big stumbling block to outsourcing has been subjective factors, such as control. To make outsourcing attractive, the services must be reliable, be available when needed, and be flexible enough to adapt to changing conditions. Companies that have successful outsourcing arrangements have been careful to include the subjective factors in their decisions.

Outsourcing has become so profitable that 77% of Fortune 500 companies outsource some aspect of their business support services. The total value of outsourcing contracts in the United States is more than $10 billion. An association, The Outsourcing Institute, was formed to provide "objective, independent information on the strategic use of outside resources." The institute regularly sponsors a special advertising section in *Fortune* magazine.

Sources: Adapted from T. Kearney, "Why Outsourcing Is In," *Strategic Finance*, January 2000, pp. 34–38; R. E. Drtina, "The Outsourcing Decision," *Management Accounting*, March, 1994, pp. 56–62; and The Outsourcing Institute, *How and Why to Outsource* (http://www.outsourcing.com/howandwhy/index.htm).

costs, the cost to make the parts is $215,000, which is $15,000 higher than the cost of purchasing them.

Cost to Make Parts or Subcomponents (in thousands)	
Outlay cost	$160
Opportunity cost	55
Total cost	$215

The opportunity cost is the $55,000 that is passed up when the facilities cannot be used to make other products.

In sum, the make-or-buy decision should focus on relevant costs in a particular decision situation. In all cases, companies should relate make-or-buy decisions to the long-run policies for the use of capacity.

To illustrate, suppose a company uses its facilities, on average, 80% of the time. However, because of seasonal changes in the demand for its product, the actual demand for the facilities varies from 60% in the off season to over 100% in the peak season. During the off season, the company may decide to perform special projects for other manufacturers (on a subcontract). There is profit on these projects but not enough to justify expanding the capacity of the facilities. The company will use facilities for these projects only when their opportunity cost is close to zero, that is, when there are no other profitable uses for the facilities. In contrast, during the peak season, the company meets the high volume by purchasing some parts. Again, the cost of purchased parts is higher than the cost to make them in the company's own facilities if there were idle capacity, but purchasing the parts is less costly than buying the facilities to produce them.

SUMMARY PROBLEM FOR YOUR REVIEW

PROBLEM

Exhibit 6-1 contains data for the Block Company for the year just ended. The company makes industrial power drills. Exhibit 6-1 shows the costs of the plastic housing separately from the costs of the electrical and mechanical components.

1. During the year, a prospective customer in an unrelated market offered $82,000 for 1,000 drills. The drills would be in addition to the 100,000 units sold. The regular sales commission rate would have been paid. The president rejected the order because "it was below our costs of $97 per unit." What would operating income have been if the order had been accepted?

Exhibit 6-1

Block Company Cost of Industrial Drills

	A	B	A + B
	*Electrical and Mechanical Components**	*Plastic Housing*	*Industrial Drills*
Sales: 100,000 units, @ $100			$10,000,000
Variable costs			
Direct material	$4,400,000	$ 500,000	$ 4,900,000
Direct labor	400,000	300,000	700,000
Variable factory overhead	100,000	200,000	300,000
Other variable costs	100,000	—	100,000
Sales commissions, @ 10% of sales	1,000,000	—	1,000,000
Total variable costs	$6,000,000	$1,000,000	$ 7,000,000
Contribution margin			$ 3,000,000
Total fixed costs	$2,220,000	$ 480,000	$ 2,700,000
Operating income			$ 300,000

* Not including the costs of plastic housing (column B).

2. A supplier offered to manufacture the year's supply of 100,000 plastic housings for $13.50 each. What would be the effect on operating income if the Block Company purchased rather than made the housings? Assume that $350,000 of the fixed costs assigned to housings would have been avoided if the housings were purchased.

3. The company could have purchased the housings for $13.50 each and used the vacated space for the manufacture of a deluxe version of its drill. Assume that 20,000 deluxe units could have been made (and sold in addition to the 100,000 regular units) at a unit variable cost of $90, exclusive of housings and exclusive of the 10% sales commission. The 20,000 extra plastic housings could also be purchased for $13.50 each. The sales price would have been $130. All the fixed costs pertaining to the plastic housings would have continued, because these costs related primarily to the manufacturing facilities used. What would operating income have been if Block had bought the housings and made and sold the deluxe units?

SOLUTION

1. The costs of filling the special order follow:

Direct material	$49,000
Direct labor	7,000
Variable factory overhead	3,000
Other variable costs	1,000
Sales commission @ 10% of $82,000	8,200
Total variable costs	$68,200
Selling price	82,000
Contribution margin	$13,800

Operating income would have been $300,000 + $13,800, or $313,800, if the order had been accepted. In a sense, the decision to reject the offer implies that the Block Company is willing to invest $13,800 in immediate gains foregone (an opportunity cost) in order to preserve the long-run selling price structure.

2. Assuming that $350,000 of the fixed costs could have been avoided by not making the housings and that the other fixed costs would have continued, the alternatives can be summarized as follows.

	Make	Buy
Purchase cost		$1,350,000
Variable costs	$1,000,000	
Avoidable fixed costs	350,000	
Total relevant costs	$1,350,000	$1,350,000

If the facilities used for plastic housings became idle, the Block Company would be indifferent whether to make or buy. Operating income would be unaffected.

3. The effect of purchasing the plastic housings and using the vacated facilities for the manufacture of a deluxe version of its drill is

Sales would increase by 20,000 units, @ $130		$2,600,000
Variable costs exclusive of parts would increase by		
20,000 units, @ $90	$1,800,000	
Plus: sales commission, 10% of $2,600,000	260,000	$2,060,000
Contribution margin on 20,000 units		$ 540,000
Housings: 120,000 rather than 100,000 would		
be needed		
Buy 120,000 @ $13.50	$1,620,000	
Make 100,000 @ $10 (only the variable costs		
are relevant)	1,000,000	
Excess cost of outside purchase		620,000
Fixed costs, unchanged		—
Disadvantage of making deluxe units		$ 80,000

Operating income would decline to $220,000 ($300,000 − $80,000). The deluxe units bring in a contribution margin of $540,000, but the additional costs of buying rather than making housings is $620,000, leading to a net disadvantage of $80,000.

JOINT PRODUCT COSTS

NATURE OF JOINT PRODUCTS

joint products Two or more manufactured products that (1) have relatively significant sales values and (2) are not separately identifiable as individual products until their split-off point.

split-off point The juncture of manufacturing where the joint products become individually identifiable.

separable costs Any cost beyond the split-off point.

joint costs The costs of manufacturing joint products prior to the split-off point.

When two or more manufactured products (1) have relatively significant sales values and (2) are not separately identifiable as individual products until their split-off point, they are called **joint products.** The **split-off point** is that juncture of manufacturing where the joint products become individually identifiable. Any costs beyond that stage are called **separable costs** because they are not part of the joint process and can be exclusively identified with individual products. The costs of manufacturing joint products prior to the split-off point are called **joint costs.** Examples of joint products include chemicals, lumber, flour, and the products of petroleum refining and meat packing. A meat-packing company cannot kill a sirloin steak; it has to slaughter a steer, which supplies various cuts of dressed meat, hides, and trimmings.

To illustrate joint costs, suppose Dow Chemical Company produces two chemical products, X and Y, as a result of a particular joint process. The joint processing cost is $100,000. This includes raw material costs and the cost of processing to the point where X and Y go their separate ways. Both products are sold to the petroleum industry to be used as ingredients of gasoline. The relationships follow:

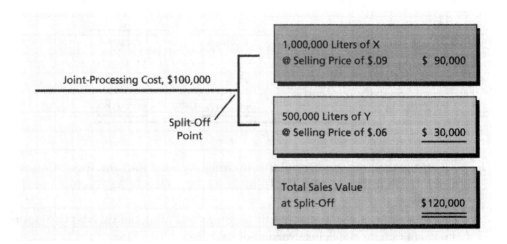

Exhibit 6-2

Illustration of Sell or Process Further

	Sell at Split-Off as Y	Process Further and Sell as YA	Difference
Revenues	$30,000	$80,000	$50,000
Separable costs beyond split-off @ $.08	—	40,000	40,000
Income effects	$30,000	$40,000	$10,000

SELL OR PROCESS FURTHER

Objective 3
Decide whether a joint product should be processed beyond the split-off point.

Managers frequently face decisions of whether to sell joint products at the split-off point or to process some or all products further. Suppose the 500,000 liters of Y can be processed further and sold to the plastics industry as product YA, an ingredient for plastic sheeting. The additional processing cost would be $.08 per liter for manufacturing and distribution, a total of $40,000 for 500,000 liters. The net sales price of YA would be $.16 per liter, a total of $80,000.

Product X cannot be processed further and will be sold at the split-off point, but management is undecided about Product Y. Should Y be sold or should it be processed into YA? To answer this question we need to find the relevant costs involved. Because the joint costs must be incurred to reach the split-off point, they might seem relevant. However, they cannot affect anything beyond the split-off point. Therefore, they do not differ between alternatives and are completely irrelevant to the question of whether to sell or process further. The only approach that will yield valid results is to concentrate on the separable costs and revenue beyond split-off, as shown in Exhibit 6-2.

This analysis shows that it would be $10,000 more profitable to process Y beyond split-off than to sell Y at split-off. Briefly, it is profitable to extend processing or to incur additional distribution costs on a joint product if the additional revenue exceeds the additional expenses.

Exhibit 6-3 illustrates another way to compare the alternatives of (1) selling Y at the split-off point and (2) processing Y beyond split-off. It includes the joint costs, which are the same for each alternative and therefore do not affect the difference.

The allocation of joint costs would not affect the decision, as Exhibit 6-3 demonstrates. The joint costs are not allocated in the exhibit, but no matter how they might be allocated, the total income effects would be unchanged. Additional coverage of joint costs and inventory valuation can be found in Chapter 12.

Exhibit 6-3

Sell or Process Further Analysis—Firm as a Whole

	(1) Alternative One			(2) Alternative Two			(3) Differential Effects
	X	Y	Total	X	YA	Total	
Revenues	$90,000	$30,000	$120,000	$90,000	$80,000	$170,000	$50,000
Joint costs			$100,000			$100,000	—
Separable costs			—		40,000	40,000	40,000
Total costs			$100,000			$140,000	$40,000
Income effects			$ 20,000			$ 30,000	$10,000

IRRELEVANCE OF PAST COSTS

The ability to recognize and thereby ignore irrelevant costs is sometimes just as important to decision makers as identifying relevant costs. How do we know that past costs, although sometimes predictors, are irrelevant in decision making? Consider such past costs as obsolete inventory and the book value of old equipment to see why they are irrelevant to decisions.

OBSOLETE INVENTORY

Objective 4
Identify irrelevant information in disposal of obsolete inventory and equipment replacement decisions.

Suppose General Dynamics has 100 obsolete aircraft parts in its inventory. The original manufacturing cost of these parts was $100,000. General Dynamics can (1) remachine the parts for $30,000 and then sell them for $50,000 or (2) scrap them for $5,000. Which should it do?

This is an unfortunate situation, yet the $100,000 past cost is irrelevant to the decision to remachine or scrap. The only relevant factors are the expected future revenues and costs:

	Remachine	**Scrap**	**Difference**
Expected future revenue	$ 50,000	$ 5,000	$45,000
Expected future costs	30,000	—	30,000
Relevant excess of revenue over costs	$ 20,000	$ 5,000	$15,000
Accumulated historical inventory cost*	100,000	100,000	—
Net overall loss on project	$(80,000)	$(95,000)	$15,000

* Irrelevant because it is unaffected by the decision.

As you can see from the fourth line of the preceding table, we can completely ignore the $100,000 historical cost and still arrive at the $15,000 difference, the key figure in the analysis.

BOOK VALUE OF OLD EQUIPMENT

depreciation The periodic cost of equipment that is spread over (or charged to) the future periods in which the equipment is expected to be used.

Like obsolete parts, the book value of equipment is not a relevant consideration in deciding whether to replace the equipment. Why? Because it is a past cost, not a future cost. When equipment is purchased, its cost is spread over (or charged to) the future periods in which the equipment is expected to be used. This periodic cost is called **depreciation.** The equipment's **book value** (or **net book value**) is the original cost less accumulated depreciation. Accumulated depreciation is the sum of all depreciation charged to past periods. For example, suppose a $10,000 machine with a 10-year life span has depreciation of $1,000 per year. At the end of six years, accumulated depreciation is 6 × $1,000 = $6,000, and the book value is $10,000 − $6,000 = $4,000.

book value (net book value) The original cost of equipment less accumulated depreciation, which is the summation of depreciation charged to past periods.

Consider the following data for a decision whether to replace an old machine:

	Old Machine	**Replacement Machine**
Original cost	$10,000	$8,000
Useful life in years	10	4
Current age in years	6	0
Useful life remaining in years	4	4
Accumulated depreciation	$ 6,000	0
Book value	$ 4,000	Not acquired yet
Disposal value (in cash) now	$ 2,500	Not acquired yet
Disposal value in 4 years	0	0
Annual cash operating costs (maintenance, power, repairs, coolants, and so on)	$ 5,000	$3,000

We have been asked to prepare a comparative analysis of the two alternatives. Before proceeding, consider some important concepts. The most widely misunderstood facet of replacement decision making is the role of the book value of the old equipment in the decision. The book value, in this context, is sometimes called a **sunk cost,** which is really just another term for historical or past cost, a cost that has already been incurred and, therefore, is irrelevant to the decision-making process. At one time or another, we all try to soothe the wounded pride arising from having made a bad purchase decision by using an item instead of replacing it. It is a serious mistake to think, however, that a current or future action can influence the long-run impact of a past outlay. All past costs are down the drain. Nothing can change what has already happened.

sunk cost A cost that has already been incurred and, therefore, is irrelevant to the decision-making process.

The irrelevance of past costs for decisions does not mean that knowledge of past costs is useless. Often managers use past costs to help predict future costs. In addition, past costs affect future payments for income taxes (as explained in Chapter 11). However, the past cost itself is not relevant. The only relevant cost is the predicted future cost.

In deciding whether to replace or keep existing equipment, we must consider the relevance of four commonly encountered items:[1]

- *Book value of old equipment:* Irrelevant, because it is a past (historical) cost. Therefore, depreciation on old equipment is irrelevant.
- *Disposal value of old equipment:* Relevant (ordinarily), because it is an expected future inflow that usually differs among alternatives.
- *Gain or loss on disposal:* This is the difference between book value and disposal value. It is therefore a meaningless combination of irrelevant and relevant items. The combination form, loss (or gain) on disposal, blurs the distinction between the irrelevant book value and the relevant disposal value. Consequently, it is best to think of each separately.
- *Cost of new equipment:* Relevant, because it is an expected future outflow that will differ among alternatives. Therefore, depreciation on new equipment is relevant.

Exhibit 6-4 shows the relevance of these items in our example. Book value of old equipment is irrelevant regardless of the decision-making technique used. The "difference" column in Exhibit 6-4 shows that the $4,000 book value of the old equipment does not differ between alternatives. It should be completely ignored for decision-making purposes. The difference is merely one of timing. The amount written off is still $4,000, regardless of any available alternative. The $4,000 appears on the income statement either as a $4,000 deduction from the $2,500 cash proceeds received to obtain a $1,500 loss on disposal in the first year or as $1,000 of depreciation in each of 4 years. But how it appears is irrelevant to the replacement decision. In contrast, the $2,000 annual depreciation on the new equipment is relevant because the total $8,000 depreciation is a future cost that may be avoided by not replacing. The three relevant items—operating costs, disposal value, and acquisition cost—give replacement a net advantage of $2,500.

EXAMINATION OF ALTERNATIVES OVER THE LONG RUN

Exhibit 6-4 is the first example that looks beyond one year. Examining the alternatives over the equipment's entire life ensures that peculiar nonrecurring items (such as loss on disposal) will not obstruct the long-run view vital to many managerial decisions.[2]

---

[1] *For simplicity, we ignore income tax considerations and the effects of the interest value of money in this chapter. Book value is irrelevant even if income taxes are considered, however, because the relevant item is then the tax cash flow, not the book value The book value is essential information for predicting the amount and timing of future tax cash flows, but, by itself, the book value is irrelevant For elaboration, see Chapter 11*

[2] *A more complete analysis that includes the timing of revenues and costs appears in Chapter 11.*

Exhibit 6-4

Cost Comparison—Replacement of Equipment Including Relevant and Irrelevant Items

| | Four Years Together | | |
	Keep	*Replace*	*Difference*
Cash operating costs	$20,000	$12,000	$ 8,000
Old equipment (book value)			
Periodic write-off as depreciation	4,000	—	
or			—
Lump-sum write-off		4,000*	
Disposal value	—	−2,500*	2,500
New machine			
Acquisition cost	—	8,000 †	−8,000
Total costs	$24,000	$21,500	$ 2,500

The advantage of replacement is $2,500 for the four years together.

* In a formal income statement, these two items would be combined as "loss on disposal" of $4,000 − $2,500 = $1,500.

† In a formal income statement, written off as straight-line depreciation of $8,000 ÷ 4 = $2,000 for each of four years.

Exhibit 6-5 concentrates on relevant items only: the cash operating costs, the disposal value of the old equipment, and the depreciation on the new equipment. To demonstrate that the amount of the old equipment's book value will not affect the answer, suppose the book value of the old equipment is $500,000 rather than $4,000. Your final answer will not change. The cumulative advantage of replacement is still $2,500. (If you are in doubt, rework this example, using $500,000 as the book value.)

It is sometimes difficult to accept the proposition that past or sunk costs are irrelevant to decisions. Consider the ticket you have to a major football game in December. After getting the ticket you learn that the game will be on television, and you really prefer to watch the game in the comfort of your warm home. Does your decision about attending the game or watching it on TV depend on whether you were given the ticket for free or paid $80 for it?

ANSWER

The amount paid, whether it be $0, $80, or $1,000, should make no difference to the decision. You have the ticket, and you have paid for it. That cannot be changed. If you really prefer to watch the game on TV, it may have been a bad decision to pay $80 for a ticket. But you cannot erase that bad decision. All you can do is choose the future action that has most value to you. You should not suffer through a less pleasant experience just because you paid $80 for the ticket.

Exhibit 6-5

Cost Comparison—Replacement of Equipment, Relevant Items Only

| | Four Years Together | | |
	Keep	*Replace*	*Difference*
Cash operating costs	$20,000	$12,000	$ 8,000
Disposal value of old machine	—	−2,500	2,500
New machine, acquisition cost	—	8,000	−8,000
Total relevant costs	$20,000	$17,500	$ 2,500

It is easy to agree that—in theory—sunk costs should be ignored when making decisions. But in practice sunk costs often influence important decisions, especially when a decision maker doesn't want to admit that a previous decision to invest funds was a bad decision.

Consider two examples from the *St. Louis Post Dispatch*: (1) Larry O. Welch, the air force chief of staff, was quoted as saying that "the B-2 already is into production; cancel it and the $17 billion front end investment is lost." (2) Les Aspin, chairman of the House Armed Services Committee, was quoted as stating that "with $17 billion already invested in it, the B-2 is too costly to cancel."

The $17 billion already invested in the B-2 is a sunk cost. It is "lost" regardless of whether production of the B-2 is canceled or not. And whether B-2 production is too costly to continue depends only on the future costs necessary to complete production compared to the value of the completed B-2s. The $17 billion was relevant when the original decision to begin development of the B-2 was made, but now that the money has been spent, it is no longer relevant. No decision can affect it.

Why would intelligent leaders consider the $17 billion relevant to the decision on continuing production of the B-2? Probably because it is difficult to admit that

no benefit would be derived from the $17 billion investment. Those who favor canceling production of the B-2 would consider the outcome of the original investment decision to be unfavorable. With perfect hindsight, they believe the investment should not have been made. It is human nature to find unpleasant the task of admitting that $17 billion was wasted. Yet, it is more important to avoid throwing good money after bad—that is, if the value of the B-2 is not at least equal to the future investment in it, production should be terminated, regardless of the amount spent to date.

Failure to ignore sunk costs is not unique to the U.S. government. In reference to Russia's store of bomb-grade plutonium, the country's Minister of Atomic Energy stated, "We have spent too much money making this material to just mix it with radioactive wastes and bury it." Burying the plutonium may or may not be the best decision, but the amount already spent is not relevant to the decision.

Sources: Adapted from J. Berg, J. Dickhaut, and C. Kanodia, "The Role of Private Information in the Sunk Cost Phenomenon," unpublished paper, November 12, 1991; M. Wald and M. Gordon, "Russia Treasures Plutonium, But U.S. Wants to Destroy It," *New York Times*, August 19, 1994, p. A1.

IRRELEVANCE OF FUTURE COSTS THAT WILL NOT DIFFER

In addition to past costs, some future costs may be irrelevant because they will be the same under all feasible alternatives. These, too, may be safely ignored for a particular decision. The salaries of many members of top management are examples of expected future costs that will be unaffected by the decision at hand.

Other irrelevant future costs include fixed costs that will be unchanged by such considerations as whether machine X or machine Y is selected. However, it is not merely a case of saying that fixed costs are irrelevant and variable costs are relevant. Variable costs can be irrelevant, and fixed costs can be relevant. For instance, sales commissions might be paid on an order regardless of whether the order was filled from plant G or plant H. Variable costs are irrelevant whenever they do not differ among the alternatives at hand, and fixed costs are relevant whenever they differ between the alternatives at hand.

BEWARE OF UNIT COSTS

The pricing illustration in Chapter 5 showed that unit costs should be analyzed with care in decision making. There are two major ways to go wrong: (1) the inclusion of irrelevant costs, such as the $3 allocation of unavoidable fixed costs in the General Electric make-or-buy example (p. 231) that would result in a unit cost of $11 instead of the relevant

Objective 5
Explain how unit costs can be misleading.

unit cost of $8, and (2) comparisons of unit costs not computed on the same volume basis, as the following example demonstrates. Machinery sales personnel, for example, often brag about the low unit costs of using the new machines. Sometimes they neglect to point out that the unit costs are based on outputs far in excess of the volume of activity of their prospective customer. Assume that a new $100,000 machine with a five-year lifespan can produce 100,000 units a year at a variable cost of $1 per unit, as opposed to a variable cost per unit of $1.50 with an old machine. A sales representative claims that the new machine will reduce cost by $.30 per unit. Is the new machine a worthwhile acquisition?

The new machine is attractive at first glance. If the customer's expected volume is 100,000 units, unit-cost comparisons are valid, provided that new depreciation is also considered. Assume that the disposal value of the old equipment is zero. Because depreciation is an allocation of historical cost, the depreciation on the old machine is irrelevant. In contrast, the depreciation on the new machine is relevant because the new machine entails a future cost that can be avoided by not acquiring it.

	Old Machine	New Machine
Units	100,000	100,000
Variable costs	$150,000	$100,000
Straight-line depreciation	—	20,000
Total relevant costs	$150,000	$120,000
Unit relevant costs	$ 1.50	$ 1.20

Apparently, the sales representative is correct. However, if the customer's expected volume is only 30,000 units per year, the unit costs change in favor of the old machine.

	Old Machine	New Machine
Units	30,000	30,000
Variable costs	$45,000	$30,000
Straight-line depreciation	—	20,000
Total relevant costs	$45,000	$50,000
Unit relevant costs	$ 1.50	$1.6667

Generally, be wary of unit fixed costs. Use total costs rather than unit costs. Then, if desired, the totals may be unitized.

7

THE MASTER BUDGET

chapter

7

THE MASTER BUDGET

This entrance to a Ritz-Carlton hotel projects its image of quality. High quality is expensive, and Ritz-Carlton managers must assess the planned expenditures for quality-enhancing features versus the added revenues these features will bring.

www.prenhall.com/horngren

Learning Objectives

When you have finished studying this chapter, you should be able to

1. Explain the major features and advantages of a master budget.

2. Follow the principal steps in preparing a master budget.

3. Prepare the operating budget and the supporting schedules.

4. Prepare the financial budget.

5. Understand the difficulties of sales forecasting.

6. Anticipate possible human relations problems caused by budgets.

7. Use a spreadsheet to develop a budget (Appendix 7).

8. **Understand the importance of budgeting to managers.**

If you have ever traveled, you will know that there is a big difference between staying in a cheap motel and staying in a five-star, world-class hotel. You can think of the difference as that of riding in an old Ford Pinto versus riding in a Rolls-Royce. The first takes care of your basic needs, but the second surrounds you in comfort and luxury, catering to your every whim. The experience of staying in a luxurious hotel can simply take your breath away. No one knows that better than the managers of the Ritz Carlton chain of hotels. After all, the word *ritzy*, which means glamorous and luxurious, is actually derived from the name of the Ritz Hotel. Thanks to fierce competition in the industry, though, Ritz-Carlton managers have their share of challenges in running successful hotels.

What does it take to run a world-class hotel successfully? Good location, exquisite food, luxury, personalized service, and quality are essential ingredients. But you might be surprised to learn that, at the Ritz-Carlton hotels, the budgeting process is also a key to success. According to Ralph Vick, General Manager of the Phoenix Ritz-Carlton, "Budgets are crucial to the ultimate financial success of our hotels." Why are budgets so important? Mainly because they serve as a road map toward achieving goals. Budgets are a manager's tool to understand, plan, and control operations, and Ritz-Carlton wants to give its managers the best tools possible. As a result, the company takes the budgeting process very seriously.

At the Ritz-Carlton hotels, all employees, from the hotel manager, to the controller, to the newest housekeeper, are involved in the budgeting process. Working in teams, they set budget targets for the expenses they can control. These target figures help not only in planning, but also in controlling and evaluating employee performance. Actual results are compared with previously budgeted target figures, and workers are evaluated based on the differences. Even nonfinancial measures of performance are important. Ritz-Carlton managers use nonfinancial measures of quality and customer satisfaction in addition to financial reports to evaluate and reward employees.

Planning is the key to good management. This statement is certainly true for Ritz-Carlton, and it is also true for other types of business organizations—small family-owned companies, large corporations, government agencies, and nonprofit organizations—as well as for individuals. For example, most successful students who earn good grades, finance their education, and finish their degrees on time do so because they plan their time, their work, and their recreation. These students are budgeting their scarce resources to make the best use of their time, money, and energy. Similarly, business owners and managers need to budget their resources—which includes everything from raw materials to human resources to facilities—to make the best and most profitable use of what they have to work with. Budgeting can cover such diverse issues as how much time to spend sanding a piece of wood to how much money the company will allot to research and development in the coming year. Company budgets always aim to squeeze the most out of available resources.

In this chapter we will look at the uses and benefits of budgets and consider the construction of the master budget.

BUDGETS AND THE ORGANIZATION

Most people associate the word *budget* with limitations on spending. For example, governments often approve spending budgets for their various agencies. Then they expect the agencies to keep their expenditures within the limits prescribed by the budget. In contrast, most business organizations use budgets to focus attention on company operations and finances, not just to limit spending. Budgets highlight potential problems and advantages early, allowing managers to take steps to avoid these problems or use the advantages wisely.

A budget is a tool that helps managers in both their planning and control functions. Interestingly, budgets help managers with their control function not only by looking forward but also by looking backward. Budgets, of course, deal with what managers plan for the future. However, they also can be used to evaluate what happened in the past. Budgets can be used as a benchmark that allows managers to compare actual performance with estimated or desired performance. Keeping score is an American tradition, whether on the football field or in the boardroom, and budgets provide the standards for evaluating and "scoring" the company "players."

Recent surveys show just how valuable budgets can be. Study after study has shown the budget to be the most widely used and highest rated tool for cost reduction and control. Advocates of budgeting go so far as to claim that the process of budgeting forces a manager to become a better administrator and puts planning in the forefront of the manager's mind. Actually, many seemingly healthy businesses have died because managers failed to draw up, monitor, and adjust budgets to changing conditions.

ADVANTAGES OF BUDGETS

A budget is a formal business plan. All managers do some kind of planning. Sometimes plans are unwritten. Such plans might work in a small organization, but as an organization grows, informal, seat-of-the-pants planning is not enough. A more formal plan—a budgetary system—becomes a necessity.

Skeptical managers have claimed, "I face too many uncertainties and complications to make budgeting worthwhile for me." Be wary of such claims. Planning and budgeting are especially important in uncertain environments. A budget allows systematic rather than chaotic reaction to change. For example, the Natural Resources Group of W.R. Grace & Co. greatly reduced its planned expansion in reaction to a worldwide abundance of oil and gas. A top executive, quoted in the company's annual report, stated that "management used the business planning process to adjust to changes in operating conditions."

Three major benefits of budgeting are as follows.

1. Budgeting compels managers to think ahead by formalizing their responsibilities for planning.
2. Budgeting provides definite expectations that are the best framework for judging subsequent performance.
3. Budgeting aids managers in coordinating their efforts, so that the plans of an organization's subunits meet the objectives of the organization as a whole.

Let's look more closely at each of these benefits.

FORMALIZATION OF PLANNING

Budgeting forces managers to think ahead—to anticipate and prepare for changing conditions. The budgeting process makes planning an explicit management responsibility. Too often, managers operate on a day-to-day basis, extinguishing one business brush fire after another. They simply have "no time" for any tough-minded thinking beyond the next day's problems. Planning takes a back seat to or is actually obliterated by daily pressures.

The trouble with the day-to-day approach to managing an organization is that objectives are never crystallized. Managers react to current events rather than planning for the future. To prepare a budget, a manager should set goals and objectives and establish policies to aid their achievement. The objectives are the destination points, and budgets are the road maps guiding us to those destinations. Without goals and objectives, company operations lack direction, problems are not foreseen, and results are difficult to interpret afterward.

FRAMEWORK FOR JUDGING PERFORMANCE

Budgeted goals and performance are generally a better basis for judging actual results than is past performance. The news that a company had sales of $100 million this year, as compared with $80 million the previous year, may or may not indicate that the company has been effective and has met company objectives. Perhaps sales should have been $110 million this year. The major drawback of using historical results for judging current performance is that inefficiencies may be concealed in the past performance. Changes in economic conditions, technology, personnel, competition, and so forth also limit the usefulness of comparisons with the past.

Level 3 Communications has focused its business strategy on providing "a broadband, continuously upgradeable, international IP infrastructure for Web-centric companies." The company's loss from continuing operations increased from $487 million in 1999 to $1,455 million in 2000. Suppose the budgeted loss for 2000 was $1,800 million. Evaluate performance for 2000.

ANSWER

Comparing Level 3's performance in 2000 to that in 1999 makes it appear that performance slipped because the loss was $968 larger in 2000 than it was in 1999. However, the loss was $345 less than budgeted, showing that the company did better than expected. During this period Level 3 was implementing a major shift in strategy to recognize the new Internet economy. The company stated that it is "well ahead of our original plans to position ourselves as the leading provider of broadband infrastructure services." Comparing actual results to plans gives a better picture of how well Level 3 is meeting its plans than would a comparison to past results.

COMMUNICATION AND COORDINATION

Budgets tell employees what is expected of them. Nobody likes to drift along, not knowing what the boss expects or hopes to achieve. A good budget process communicates both from the top down and from the bottom up. Top management makes clear the goals and objectives of the organization in its budgetary directives. Employees and lower-level managers then inform higher-level managers how they plan to achieve the goals and objectives.

Budgets also help managers coordinate objectives. For example, a budget forces purchasing personnel to integrate their plans with production requirements, while production managers use the sales budget and delivery schedule to help them anticipate and plan for the employees and physical facilities they will need. Similarly, financial officers use the sales budget, purchasing requirements, and so forth to anticipate the company's need for cash. Thus the budgetary process forces managers to visualize the relationship of their department's activities to those of other departments and the company as a whole.

TYPES OF BUDGETS

There are several different types of budgets used by businesses. The most forward-looking budget is the **strategic plan,** which sets the overall goals and objectives of the organization. Some business analysts won't classify the strategic plan as an actual budget, though, because it does not deal with a specific time frame, and it does not produce forecasted financial statements. In any case, the strategic plan leads to **long-range planning,** which produces forecasted financial statements for five- to ten-year periods. The financial statements are estimates of what management would like to see in the company's future financial statements. Decisions made during long-range planning include addition or deletion of product lines, design and location of new plants, acquisitions of buildings and equipment, and other long-term commitments. Long-range plans are coordinated with **capital budgets,** which detail the planned expenditures for facilities, equipment, new products, and other long-term investments.

Long-range plans and budgets give the company direction and goals for the future, while short-term plans and budgets guide day-to-day operations. Managers who pay attention only to short-term budgets will quickly lose sight of long-term goals. Similarly, managers who pay attention only to the long-term budget could wind up mismanaging day-to-day operations. There has to be a happy medium that allows managers to pay attention to their short-term budgets while still keeping an eye on long-term plans. Enter the master budget. The **master budget** is an extensive analysis of the first year of the long-range plan. A master budget summarizes the planned activities of all subunits of an organization—sales, production, distribution, and finance. The master budget quantifies targets for sales, cost-driver activity, purchases, production, net income, cash position, and any other objective that management specifies. It expresses these amounts in the form of forecasted financial statements and supporting operating schedules. These supporting schedules provide the information that is too highly detailed to appear in the actual financial statements. Thus, the master budget is a periodic business plan that includes a coordinated set of detailed operating schedules and financial statements. It includes forecasts of sales, expenses, cash receipts and disbursements, and balance sheets. Master budgets (also called pro forma statements, another term for forecasted financial statements) might consist of 12 monthly budgets for the year or perhaps monthly budgets for only the first quarter and quarterly budgets for the three remaining quarters. In the process of preparing the master budget, managers make many important decisions about how to best deploy the organization's resources.

Continuous budgets or rolling budgets are a very common form of master budgets that simply add a month in the future as the month just ended is dropped. Budgeting thus becomes an ongoing instead of periodic process. Continuous budgets force managers to always think about the next 12 months, not just the remaining months in a fixed budgeting cycle. As they add a new twelfth month to a continuous budget, managers may update the other 11 months as well. Then they can compare actual monthly results with both the original plan and the most recently revised plan.

COMPONENTS OF MASTER BUDGET

The terms used to describe specific budget schedules vary from organization to organization. However, most master budgets have common elements. The usual master budget for a nonmanufacturing company has the following components:

A. Operating budget
1. Sales budget (and other cost-driver budgets as necessary)
2. Purchases budget
3. Cost-of-goods-sold budget
4. Operating expenses budget
5. Budgeted income statement

B. Financial budget
1. Capital budget
2. Cash budget
3. Budgeted balance sheet

Exhibit 7-1 shows the relationships among the various parts of a master budget for a nonmanufacturing company. In addition to these categories, manufacturing companies that maintain inventories prepare ending inventory budgets and additional budgets for each type of resource activity (such as labor, materials, and factory overhead).

The two major parts of a master budget are the operating budget and the financial budget. The **operating budget** focuses on the income statement and its supporting schedules. Although sometimes called the profit plan, an operating budget may show a budgeted loss, or may even be used to budget expenses in an organization or agency with no sales revenues. In contrast, the **financial budget** focuses on the effects that the operating budget and other plans (such as capital budgets and repayments of debt) will have on cash.

In addition to the master budget, there are countless forms of special budgets and related reports. For example, a report might detail goals and objectives for improvements in quality or customer satisfaction during the budget period.

operating budget (profit plan) A major part of a master budget that focuses on the income statement and its supporting schedules.

financial budget The part of a master budget that focuses on the effects that the operating budget and other plans (such as capital budgets and repayments of debt) will have on cash.

PREPARING THE MASTER BUDGET

Let's return to Exhibit 7-1 and trace the preparation of the master budget components. Follow each step carefully and completely. Although the process may seem largely mechanical, remember that the master-budgeting process generates key decisions regarding all aspects of the company's value chain. Therefore, the first draft of the budget leads to decisions that prompt subsequent drafts before a final budget is chosen.

THE COOKING HUT

To illustrate the budgeting process we will use as an example the Cooking Hut Company (CHC), a local retailer of a wide variety of kitchen and dining room items such as coffeemakers, silverware, and table linens. The company rents a retail store in a midsize community near Denver. CHC's management prepares a continuous budget to aid

Exhibit 7-1

Preparation of Master Budget for Nonmanufacturing Company

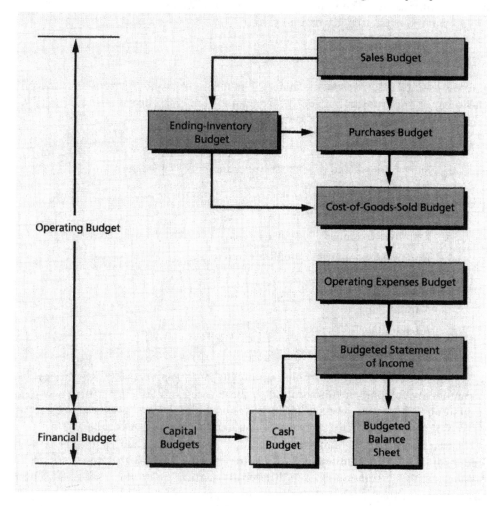

financial and operating decisions. For simplicity in this illustration, the planning horizon is only four months, April through July. In the past, sales have increased during this season. However, the company's collections have always lagged well behind its sales. As a result, the company has often found itself pressed to come up with the cash for purchases, employee wages, and other operating outlays. To help meet this cash squeeze, CHC has used short-term loans from local banks, paying them back when cash comes in. CHC plans to keep on using this system.

Exhibit 7-2 is the closing balance sheet for the fiscal year ending March 31, 20X1. Sales in March were $40,000. Monthly sales are forecasted as follows:

April	$50,000
May	$80,000
June	$60,000
July	$50,000
August	$40,000

Management expects future sales collections to follow past experience: customers pay 60% of the sales in cash and 40% on credit. All credit accounts are collected in the month following the sales. The $16,000 of accounts receivable on March 31 represents

Exhibit 7-2

The Cooking Hut Company

Balance Sheet March 31, 20X1

Assets		
Current assets		
Cash	$10,000	
Accounts receivable, net (.4 × March sales of $40,000)	16,000	
Merchandise inventory, $20,000 + 7 (.8 × April sales of $50,000)	48,000	
Unexpired insurance	1,800	$ 75,800
Plant assets		
Equipment, fixtures, and other	$37,000	
Accumulated depreciation	12,800	24,200
Total assets		$100,000

Liabilities and Owners' Equity		
Current liabilities		
Accounts payable (.5 × March purchases of $33,600)	$16,800	
Accrued wages and commissions payable ($1,250 + $3,000)	4,250	$ 21,050
Owners' equity		78,950
Total liabilities and owners' equity		$100,000

credit sales made in March (40% of $40,000). Uncollectible accounts are negligible and thus ignored. For simplicity's sake, we will ignore all local, state, and federal taxes for this illustration.

Because deliveries from suppliers and customer demands are uncertain, at the end of each month CHC wants to have on hand a basic inventory of items valued at $20,000 plus 80% of the expected cost of goods sold for the following month. The cost of merchandise sold averages 70% of sales. Therefore, the inventory on March 31 is $20,000 + .7(.8 × April sales of $50,000) = $20,000 + $28,000 = $48,000. The purchase terms available to CHC are net, 30 days. CHC pays for each month's purchases as follows: 50% during that month and 50% during the next month. Therefore, the accounts payable balance on March 31 is 50% of March's purchases, or $33,600 × .5 = $16,800.

CHC pays wages and commissions semimonthly, half a month after they are earned. They are divided into two portions: monthly fixed wages of $2,500 and commissions, equal to 15% of sales, which we will assume are uniform throughout each month. Therefore, the March 31 balance of accrued wages and commissions payable is (.5 × $2,500) + .5(.15 × $40,000) = $1,250 + $3,000 = $4,250. CHC will pay this $4,250 on April 15.

In addition to buying new fixtures for $3,000 cash in April, CHC's other monthly expenses are as follows.

Miscellaneous expenses	5% of sales, paid as incurred
Rent	$2,000, paid as incurred
Insurance	$200 expiration per month
Depreciation, including new fixtures	$500 per month

The company wants a minimum of $10,000 as a cash balance at the end of each month. To keep this simple, we will assume that CHC can borrow or repay loans in multiples of $1,000. Management plans to borrow no more cash than necessary and to

Photon Technology International, Inc., manufactures electro-optical instruments used for medical research and diagnostic procedures. Sales in 2000 were just over $7 million. Its products are state-of-the-art, but until the early 1990s, Photon did not have a formal budgeting procedure. Like many small, fast-growing companies, budgeting was not a priority. But as sales approached $5 million and the company found itself on the verge of financial failure, a budget became essential. Collection of sales from customers was slow, research and development outlays were high, and Photon was fast running out of cash.

Photon hired a professional financial manager who instituted a budget process that links cash flow, intensive high-technology research and development, customer training and education, and on-site product customization. Coordination of all of these factors is absolutely critical in this new, high-technology firm. This budget process develops three "what-if" scenarios: (1) a best-case budget where everything goes as hoped, (2) a worst-case budget that predicts just the opposite, and (3) a most-likely-case budget where each budget forecast (sales, sales collections, cost-driver activity, cost behavior, and so on) is examined and set at a realistic level. This budget process allows Photon to anticipate cash flow problems before they threaten the company's survival and to communicate critical resource needs within the company. Photon believes that implementing a formal budget process was a critical step in its transition from a start-up to a maturing company.

Source: Adapted from Charles L. Grant, "High-Tech Budgeting," *Management Accounting*, May 1991, pp. 30–31 and *Photon Technology International 2000 Annual Report.*

repay as promptly as possible. Assume that borrowing occurs at the beginning and repayment at the end of the months in question. Interest is paid, under the terms of this credit arrangement, when the related loan is repaid. The interest rate is 12% per year.

STEPS IN PREPARING THE MASTER BUDGET

Objective 2
Follow the principal steps in preparing a master budget.

The principal steps in preparing the master budget are

Basic Data

1. Using the data given, prepare the following detailed schedules for each of the months of the planning horizon:
   a. Sales budget
   b. Cash collections from customers
   c. Purchases budget
   d. Disbursements for purchases
   e. Operating expense budget
   f. Disbursements for operating expenses

Operating Budget

2. Using these schedules, prepare a budgeted income statement for the 4 months ending July 31, 20X1 (Exhibit 7-3).

Financial Budget

3. Using the data given and the supporting schedules, prepare the following forecasted financial statements:

   a. Capital budget
   b. Cash budget, including details of borrowings, repayments, and interest for each month of the planning horizon (Exhibit 7-4)
   c. Budgeted balance sheet as of July 31, 20X1 (Exhibit 7-5)

Exhibit 7-3

The Cooking Hut Company

Budgeted Income Statement for Four Months Ending July 31, 20X1

	Data		Source of Data
Sales		$240,000	Schedule a
Cost of goods sold		168,000	Schedule c
Gross margin		$ 72,000	
Operation expenses:			
Wages and commissions	$46,000		Schedule e
Rent	8,000		Schedule e
Miscellaneous	12,000		Schedule e
Insurance	800		Schedule e
Depreciation	2,000	68,800	Schedule e
Income from operations		$ 3,200	
Interest expense		440	Exhibit 7-4
Net income		$ 2,760	

Organizations with effective budget systems have specific guidelines for the steps and timing of budget preparation. Although the details differ, the guidelines invariably include the preceding steps. As we follow these steps to prepare CHC's master budget, be sure that you understand the source of each figure in each schedule and budget.

Exhibit 7-4

The Cooking Hut Company

Cash Budget for Four Months Ending July 31, 20X1

	April	May	June	July
Beginning cash balance	$ 10,000	$10,550	$ 10,980	$10,080
Minimum cash balance desired	10,000	10,000	10,000	10,000
Available cash balance (x)	$ 0	$ 550	$ 980	$ 80
Cash receipts and disbursements:				
Collections from customers (Schedule b*)	$ 46,000	$68,000	$ 68,000	$54,000
Payments for merchandise (Schedule d)	(42,700)	(48,300)	(40,600)	(32,900)
Payments for operating expenses (Schedule f)	(13,750)	(18,250)	(18,000)	(15,250)
Purchase of new fixtures (given)	(3,000)			
Net cash receipts and disbursements (y)	$(13,450)	$ 1,450	$ 9,400	$ 5,850
Excess (deficiency) of cash				
before financing ($x + y$)	$(13,450)	$ 2,000	$ 10,380	$ 5,930
Financing				
Borrowing (at beginning of month)	$ 14,000†			
Repayments (at end of month)	—	$(1,000)	$(10,000)	$ (3,000)
Interest (at 12% per year‡)	—	(20)	(300)	(120)
Total cash increase (decrease) from				
financing (z)	$ 14,000	$(1,020)	$(10,300)	$(3,120)
Ending cash balance (beginning balance $+ y + z$)	$ 10,550	$10,980	$ 10,080	$12,810

* Letters are keyed to the explanation in the text.
† Borrowing and repayment of principal are made in multiples of $1,000, at an interest rate of 12% per year.
‡ Interest computations: .12 × $1,000 × 2/12; .12 × $10,000 × 3/12; .12 × $3,000 × 4/12.

Exhibit 7-5

The Cooking Hut Company
Budgeted Balance Sheet July 31, 20X1

Assets		
Current assets		
Cash (Exhibit 7-4)	$ 12,810	
Accounts receivable, net (.4 × July sales of $50,000,		
Schedule a)	20,000	
Merchandise inventory (Schedule c)	42,400	
Unexpired insurance ($1,800 − $800)	1,000	$ 76,210
Plant assets		
Equipment, fixtures, and other ($37,000 + $3,000		
fixtures)	$ 40,000	
Accumulated depreciation ($12,800 + $2,000		
depreciation expense)	(14,800)	25,200
Total assets		$101,410

Liabilities and Owners' Equity		
Current liabilities		
Accounts payable (.5 × July purchases of		
$29,400, Schedule c)	$ 14,700	
Accrued wages and commissions payable		
(.5 × $10,000, Schedule e)	5,000	$ 19,700
Owners' equity ($78,950 + $2,760 net income)		81,710
Total liabilities and owners' equity		$101,410

Note: Beginning balances are used as a start for the computations of unexpired insurance, plant, and owners' equity.

STEP 1: PREPARING BASIC DATA

Step 1a: Sales Budget. The sales budget (Schedule a in the following table) is the starting point for budgeting for CHC because inventory levels, purchases, and operating expenses are geared to the expected level of sales. Accurate sales forecasting is essential to effective budgeting. (Sales forecasting is considered in a later section of this chapter.) March sales are included in Schedule a because they affect cash collections in April. Trace the final column in Schedule a to the first row of Exhibit 7-3. In nonprofit organizations, forecasts of revenue or some level of services are also the focal points for budgeting. Examples are patient revenues and government reimbursement expected by hospitals and donations expected by churches. If no revenues are generated, as in the case of municipal fire protection, a desired level of service is predetermined.

Step 1b: Cash Collections from Customers. It is easiest to prepare Schedule b, cash collections, at the same time that we prepare the sales budget. Cash collections from customers include the current month's cash sales plus the previous month's credit sales. We will use total collections in preparing the cash budget—see Exhibit 7-4.

	March	April	May	June	July	April–July Total
Schedule a: Sales Budget						
Credit sales, 40%	$16,000	$20,000	$32,000	$24,000	$20,000	
Plus cash sales, 60%	24,000	30,000	48,000	36,000	30,000	
Total sales	$40,000	$50,000	$80,000	$60,000	$50,000	$240,000

Schedule b: Cash Collections

Cash sales this month	$30,000	$48,000	$36,000	$30,000
Plus 100% of last month's credit sales	16,000	20,000	32,000	24,000
Total collections	$46,000	$68,000	$68,000	$54,000

Step 1c: Purchases Budget. After budgeting sales and cash collections, we prepare the purchases budget (Schedule c). The total merchandise needed will be the sum of the desired ending inventory plus the amount needed to fulfill budgeted sales demand. The total need will be partially met by the beginning inventory; the remainder must come from planned purchases. These purchases are computed as follows:

$$\text{budgeted purchases} = \text{desired ending inventory}$$
$$+ \text{ cost of goods sold} - \text{beginning inventory}$$

Trace the total purchases figure in the final column of Schedule c to the second row of Exhibit 7-3.

	March	April	May	June	July	April–July Total
Schedule c: Purchases Budget						
Desired ending inventory	$48,000*	$64,800	$ 53,600	$48,000	$42,400	
Plus cost of goods sold†	28,000	35,000	56,000	42,000	35,000	$168,000
Total needed	$76,000	$99,800	$109,600	$90,000	$77,400	
Less beginning inventory	42,400‡	48,000	64,800	53,600	48,000	
Purchases	$33,600	$51,800	$ 44,800	$36,400	$29,400	
Schedule d: Disbursements for Purchases						
50% of last month's purchases		$16,800	$ 25,900	$22,400	$18,200	
Plus 50% of this month's purchases		25,900	22,400	18,200	14,700	
Disbursements for purchases		$42,700	$ 48,300	$40,600	$32,900	

* $20,000 + (.8 × April cost of goods sold) = $20,000 + .8($35,000) = $48,000.
† .7 × March sales of $40,000 = $28,000; .7 × April sales of $50,000 = $35,000, and so on.
‡ $20,000 + (.8 × March cost of goods sold of $28,000) = $20,000 + $22,400 = $42,400.

Step 1d: Disbursements for Purchases. We next use the purchases budget to develop Schedule d, disbursements for purchases. In our example, disbursements include 50% of the current month's purchases and 50% of the previous month's purchases. We will use total disbursements in preparing the cash budget, Exhibit 7-4.

Step 1e: Operating Expense Budget. The budgeting of operating expenses depends on several factors. Month-to-month changes in sales volume and other cost-driver activities directly influence many operating expenses. Examples of expenses driven by sales volume include sales commissions and many delivery expenses. Other expenses, such as rent, insurance, depreciation, and salaries, are not influenced by sales within appropriate relevant ranges, and we regard them as fixed. Trace the total operating expenses in the final column of Schedule e, which summarizes these expenses, to the budgeted income statement, Exhibit 7-3.

	March	April	May	June	July	April–July Total
Schedule e: Operating Expense Budget						
Wages (fixed)	$2,500	$ 2,500	$ 2,500	$ 2,500	$ 2,500	
Commissions (15% of current month's sales)	6,000	7,500	12,000	9,000	7,500	
Total wages and commissions	$8,500	$10,000	$14,500	$11,500	$10,000	$46,000
Miscellaneous expenses (5% of current sales)		2,500	4,000	3,000	2,500	12,000
Rent (fixed)		2,000	2,000	2,000	2,000	8,000
Insurance (fixed)		200	200	200	200	800
Depreciation (fixed)		500	500	500	500	2,000
Total operating expenses		$15,200	$21,200	$17,200	$15,200	$68,800

Step 1f: Disbursements for Operating Expenses. Disbursements for operating expenses are based on the operating expense budget. Disbursements include 50% of last month's and this month's wages and commissions, and miscellaneous and rent expenses. We will use the total of these disbursements in preparing the cash budget, Exhibit 7-4.

	March	April	May	June	July	April–July Total
Schedule f: Disbursements for Operating Expenses						
Wages and commissions:						
50% of last month's expenses		$ 4,250	$ 5,000	$ 7,250	$ 5,750	
50% of this month's expenses		5,000	7,250	5,750	5,000	
Total wages and commissions		$ 9,250	$12,250	$13,000	$10,750	
Miscellaneous expenses		2,500	4,000	3,000	2,500	
Rent		2,000	2,000	2,000	2,000	
Total disbursements		$13,750	$18,250	$18,000	$15,250	

STEP 2: PREPARING THE OPERATING BUDGET

Steps 1a, 1c, and 1e provide enough information to construct a budgeted income statement from operations (Exhibit 7-3). The income statement will be complete after addition of the interest expense, which we can compute only after the cash budget has been prepared. Budgeted income from operations is often a benchmark for judging management performance.

STEP 3: PREPARATION OF FINANCIAL BUDGET

Objective 4
Prepare the financial budget.

The second major part of the master budget is the financial budget, which consists of the capital budget, cash budget, and ending balance sheet. This chapter focuses on the cash budget and the ending balance sheet. Chapter 11 discusses the capital budget. In our illustration, the $3,000 purchase of new fixtures would be included in the capital budget.

cash budget A statement of planned cash receipts and disbursements.

Step 3b: Cash Budget. The **cash budget** is a statement of planned cash receipts and disbursements. The cash budget is heavily affected by the level of operations summarized in the budgeted income statement. The cash budget has the following major sections, where the letters w, x, y, and z refer to the lines in Exhibit 7-4 that summarize the effects of that section:

- The available cash balance (x) equals the beginning cash balance less the minimum cash balance desired.
- Cash receipts and disbursements (y):

  1. Cash receipts depend on collections from customers' accounts receivable, cash sales, and on other operating cash income sources such as interest received on notes receivable. Trace total collections from Schedule b to Exhibit 7-4.

  2. Disbursements for purchases depend on the credit terms extended by suppliers and the bill-paying habits of the buyer. Trace payments for merchandise from Schedule d to Exhibit 7-4.

  3. Payroll depends on wage, salary, and commission terms and on payroll dates. Trace wages and commissions from Schedule f to Exhibit 7-4.

  4. Some costs and expenses depend on contractual terms for installment payments, mortgage payments, rents, leases, and miscellaneous items. Trace disbursements for operating expenses from Schedule f to Exhibit 7-4.

  5. Other disbursements include outlays for fixed assets, long-term investments, dividends, and the like. An example is the $3,000 expenditure for new fixtures.

- The cash needed from (or used for) financing (z) depend on the total available cash balance, x in Exhibit 7-4, and the net cash receipts and disbursements, y. If cash available plus net cash receipts less disbursements is negative, borrowing is necessary—Exhibit 7-4 shows that CHC will borrow $14,000 in April to cover the planned deficiency. If it is positive, loans may be repaid—$1,000, $10,000, and $3,000 are repaid in May, June, and July, respectively. The pertinent outlays for interest expenses are usually contained in this section of the cash budget. Trace the calculated interest expense to Exhibit 7-3, which then will be complete.

- The ending cash balance is the beginning cash balance + y + z. Financing, z, has either a positive (borrowing) or a negative (repayment) effect on the cash balance. The illustrative cash budget shows the pattern of short-term, "self-liquidating" financing. Seasonal peaks often result in heavy drains on cash—for merchandise purchases and operating expenses—before the company makes sales and collects cash from customers. The resulting loan is "self-liquidating"— that is, the company uses borrowed money to acquire merchandise for sale, and uses the proceeds from sales to repay the loan. This "working capital cycle" moves from cash to inventory to receivables and back to cash.

Cash budgets help management to avoid having unnecessary idle cash, on the one hand, and unnecessary cash deficiencies, on the other. A well-managed financing program keeps cash balances from becoming too large or too small.

Step 3: Budgeted Balance Sheet. The final step in preparing the master budget is to construct the budgeted balance sheet (Exhibit 7-5) that projects each balance sheet item in accordance with the business plan as expressed in the previous schedules. Specifically, the beginning balances at March 31 would be increased or decreased in light of the expected cash receipts and cash disbursements in Exhibit 7-4 and in light of the effects of noncash items appearing on the income statement in Exhibit 7-3. For example, unexpired insurance would decrease from its balance of $1,800 on March 31 to $1,000 on July 31, even though it is a noncash item.

When the complete master budget is formulated, management can consider all the major financial statements as a basis for changing the course of events. For example, the initial formulation of the financial statements may prompt management to try new sales strategies to generate more demand. Alternatively, management may explore the

The last decade has seen a flurry of entrepreneurial activities. Start-up companies in a variety of high-tech industries have mushroomed into multibillion dollar companies. Consider InfoSpace, Inc., as an example. Naveen Jain, chairman and chief strategist, founded InfoSpace in April 1996 after leaving Microsoft. Jain took InfoSpace public in December 1998. By March 2000 the market value of InfoSpace stock was $30 billion. Jain's vision for InfoSpace is grand: "When the history of the impending [information] revolution is written, one name will be credited for helping map its route, and powering its progress. InfoSpace."

How do start-up companies get started? An essential component in securing initial funding for a start-up is the development of a business plan. The federal government's Small Business Administration recommends a business plan with three sections:

1. **The Business**—Includes a description of the business, a marketing plan, an assessment of the competition, a listing of operating procedures, and a roster of personnel.

2. **Financial Data**—Includes the following items.

    Loan applications

    Capital equipment and supply list

    Balance sheet

    Break-even analysis

    Pro-forma income projections (profit and loss statements)
    >   Three-year summary
    >   Detail by month, first year
    >   Detail by quarters, second and third years
    >   Assumptions upon which projections were based

    Pro-forma cash flow

3. **Supporting Documents**—Includes a variety of legal documents and information about the principals involved, suppliers, customers, etc.

Financial data are an important part of a business plan, the centerpiece of which is the budget. Without a well-developed budget, companies such as InfoSpace would not be able to raise the capital needed to start and expand their businesses. The pro-forma income projections and pro-forma cash flow, essentially a budgeted income statement and budgeted cash flow statement, are essential to predicting the future prospects of any business. They are especially critical to assessing the prospects of a new company that has little history to analyze.

The importance of a budget to a start-up company was emphasized by Jim Rowan, former senior vice president of Sun America, Inc., who left to form a new company, EncrypTix. He raised $36 million in investment funding to spin EncrypTix off from Stamps.com. The company focuses on Internet delivery and storage of tickets, coupons, and vouchers. Rowan stated, "The key thing for a start-up is to develop a budget and put it like a stake in the ground, so you can measure against it. It's not a ceiling, it's not carved in stone, but you have to have something that's a benchmark."

Budgeting is not often the most exciting task for entrepreneurs. However, lack of a credible budget is one of the main reasons venture capitalists will refuse funding for start-up companies. Further, it is one of the main causes of failure of the companies themselves. Anyone wanting to be an entrepreneur would be well advised to study budgeting and learn how it can be a powerful tool both for managing the company and for promoting the company to potential investors.

Sources: Adapted from Small Business Administration, *The Business Plan: Roadmap to Success* (http://www.sba.gov/starting/indexbusplans.html), *InfoSpace 2000 Annual Report* (http://www.infospace.com/about/annual_report/html/home.htm), and K. Klein, "Budgeting Helps Secure Longevity," *Los Angeles Times* (Aug. 2, 2000), p. C6.

effects of various adjustments in the timing of receipts and disbursements. The large cash deficiency in April, for example, may lead to an emphasis on cash sales or an attempt to speed up collection of accounts receivable. In any event, the first draft of the master budget is rarely the final draft. As it is reworked, the budgeting process becomes an integral part of the management process itself—budgeting is planning and communicating.

How does the operating budget differ from the financial budget?

ANSWER

The operating budget focuses on the income statement, which is prepared using accrual accounting. It measures revenues and expenses. In contrast, the financial budget focuses primarily on cash flow. It measures the receipts and disbursements of cash. The operating budget is a better measure of overall performance, but the financial budget is essential to plan for cash needs. A lack of cash rather than poor operating performance often gets companies into trouble.

DIFFICULTIES OF SALES FORECASTING

Objective 5
Understand the difficulties of sales forecasting.

As you saw in the CHC example, the sales budget is the foundation of the entire master budget. The accuracy of estimated purchases budgets, production schedules, and costs depends on the detail and accuracy (in dollars, units, and mix) of the budgeted sales. At the Ritz-Carlton hotels, the process of developing the sales budget involves forecasting levels of room occupancy, group events, banquets, and other activities. Upper management initially sets the costs of these activities. Then, employee teams in each department provide ideas for improvements (cost reductions). Managers prepare monthly departmental budgets based on the annual master budget.

As we stated earlier, and as you might have noticed from Ritz-Carlton's budgeting practices, the sales budget depends entirely on sales forecasts. Although *sales budget* and *sales forecast* sound as if they might be the same thing, be aware that a forecast and a budget are not necessarily identical. A **sales forecast** is a prediction of sales under a given set of conditions. A **sales budget** is the result of decisions to create the conditions that will generate a desired level of sales. For example, you may have forecasts of sales at various levels of advertising. The forecast for the one level you decide to implement becomes the budget.

sales forecast A prediction of sales under a given set of conditions.

sales budget The result of decisions to create conditions that will generate a desired level of sales.

Sales forecasts are usually prepared under the direction of the top sales executive. Important factors considered by sales forecasters include the following.

1. *Past patterns of sales*: Past experience combined with detailed past sales by product line, geographical region, and type of customer can help predict future sales.

2. *Estimates made by the sales force*: A company's sales force is often the best source of information about the desires and plans of customers.

3. *General economic conditions*: Predictions for many economic indicators, such as gross domestic product and industrial production indexes (local and foreign), are published regularly. Knowledge of how sales relate to these indicators can aid sales forecasting.

4. *Competitors' actions*: Sales depend on the strength and actions of competitors. To forecast sales, a company should consider the likely strategies and reactions of competitors, such as changes in their prices, product quality, or services.

5. *Changes in the firm's prices*: Sales can be increased by decreasing prices and vice versa. A company should consider the effects of price changes on customer demand (see Chapter 5).

6. *Changes in product mix*: Changing the mix of products often can affect not only sales levels but also overall contribution margin. Identifying the most profitable products and devising methods to increase their sales is a key part of successful management.

7. *Market research studies*: Some companies hire market experts to gather information about market conditions and customer preferences. Such information is useful to managers making sales forecasts and product mix decisions.

8. *Advertising and sales promotion plans*: Advertising and other promotional costs affect sales levels. A sales forecast should be based on anticipated effects of promotional activities.

Sales forecasting usually combines various techniques. In addition to the opinions of the sales staff, statistical analysis of correlations between sales and economic indicators (prepared by economists and members of the market research staff) provide valuable help. The opinions of line management also heavily influence the final sales forecasts. Ultimately, no matter how many technical experts are used in forecasting, the sales budget is the responsibility of line management.

Sales forecasting is still somewhat mystical, but its procedures are becoming more formalized and are being reviewed more seriously because of the intensity of global competitive pressures. Although this book does not include a detailed discussion of the preparation of the sales budget, the importance of an accurate sales forecast cannot be overstressed.

Interestingly, governments and other nonprofit organizations also face a problem similar to sales forecasting. For example, the budget for city revenues may depend on a variety of factors, such as predicted property taxes, traffic fines, parking fees, license fees, and city income taxes. In turn, property taxes depend on the extent of new construction and, in most localities, general increases in real estate values. Thus, a municipal budget may require forecasting that is just as sophisticated as that required by a private firm.

GETTING EMPLOYEES TO ACCEPT THE BUDGET

Objective 6
Anticipate possible human relations problems caused by budgets.

No matter how accurate sales forecasts are, if budgets are to benefit an organization, they need the support of all the firm's employees. The attitude of top management will heavily influence lower-level workers' and managers' attitudes toward budgets. Even with the support of top management, however, budgets—and the managers who implement them—can run into opposition.

Managers often compare actual results with budgets in evaluating subordinates. Few individuals are immediately ecstatic about techniques used to check their performance. Lower-level managers sometimes regard budgets as embodiments of restrictive, negative top-management attitudes. Accountants reinforce this view if they use a budget only to point out managers' failings. Such negative attitudes are even greater when the budget's primary purpose is to limit spending. For example, budgets are generally unpopular in government agencies where their only use is to request and authorize funding. To avoid negative attitudes toward budgets, accountants and top management must demonstrate how budgets can help each manager and employee achieve better results. Only then will the budgets become a positive aid in motivating employees at all levels to work toward goals, set objectives, measure results accurately, and direct attention to the areas that need investigation.

Another serious human relations problem that can negate the benefits of budgeting arises if budgets stress one set of performance goals but employees and managers are rewarded for different performance measures. For example, a budget may concentrate on current costs of production, but managers and employees may be rewarded on quality of production (defect rate) and on timely delivery of products to customers (percent on time). These measures of performance could be in direct conflict.

The overriding importance of the human aspects of budgeting cannot be overemphasized. Too often, top management and accountants are overly concerned with the mechanics of budgets, ignoring the fact that the effectiveness of any budgeting system depends directly on whether the affected managers and employees understand and accept the budget. Budgets created with the active participation of all affected employees are generally more effective than budgets imposed on subordinates. This involvement is usually called **participative budgeting.**

participative budgeting
Budgets formulated with the active participation of all affected employees.

For example, Ritz-Carlton's budgeting system includes all hotel employees and is thus a participative system. In fact, employee "buy-in" to the budget is so important at Ritz-Carlton that self-directed employee teams at all levels of the company have the authority to change operations based on budgets as they see fit.

FINANCIAL PLANNING MODELS

Because a well-made budget considers all aspects of the company (the entire value chain), it serves as an effective model for decision making. For example, managers can use the master budget to predict how various decisions might affect the company in both the long run and the short run. Using the master budget in this way is a step-by-step process in which tentative plans are revised as managers exchange views on various aspects of expected activities.

Today, most large companies have developed **financial planning models,** mathematical models of the master budget that can react to any set of assumptions about sales, costs, product mix, and so on. For instance, Dow Chemical's model uses 140 separate, constantly revised cost inputs that are based on several different cost drivers.

financial planning models
Mathematical models of the master budget that can react to any set of assumptions about sales, costs, or product mix.

By mathematically describing the relationships among all the operating and financial activities covered in the master budget and among the other major internal and external factors that can affect the results of management decisions, financial planning models allow managers to assess the predicted impacts of various alternatives before final decisions are selected. For example, a manager might want to predict the consequences of changing the mix of products offered for sale to emphasize several products with the highest prospects for growth. A financial planning model would provide operational and financial budgets well into the future under alternative assumptions about the product mix, sales levels, production constraints, quality levels, scheduling, and so on. Most importantly, managers can get answers to "what if" questions, such as "What if sales are 10% below forecasts? What if material prices increase 8% instead of 4% as expected? What if the new union contract grants a 6% raise in consideration for productivity improvements?"

Financial planning models have shortened managers' reaction times dramatically. A revised plan for a large company that took many accountants many days to prepare by hand can be prepared in minutes. For example, Public Service Electric & Gas, a New Jersey utility company, can run its total master budget several times a day, if necessary.

Warning: The use of spreadsheet software on personal computers has put financial planning models within reach of even the smallest organizations. The ready access to powerful modeling, however, does not guarantee plausible or reliable results. Financial planning models are only as good as the assumptions and the inputs used to build and manipulate them—what computer specialists call GIGO (garbage in, garbage out). Nearly every chief financial officer has a horror story to tell about following bad advice from a faulty financial planning model.

8

FLEXIBLE BUDGETS AND VARIANCE ANALYSIS

The golden arches can even be found in Moscow. McDonald's restaurants are located in more than 120 countries.

www.prenhall.com/horngren

Learning Objectives

When you have finished studying this chapter, you should be able to

1. Distinguish between flexible budgets and master (static) budgets.

2. Use flexible-budget formulas to construct a flexible budget based on the volume of sales.

3. Prepare an activity-based flexible budget.

4. Understand the performance evaluation relationship between master (static) budgets and flexible budgets.

5. Compute flexible-budget variances and sales-activity variances.

6. Compute and interpret price and usage variances for inputs based on cost-driver activity.

7. Compute variable overhead spending and efficiency variances.

8. **Understand how management uses flexible budgets to evaluate the company's financial performance.**

A recent survey ranked McDonald's as the world's greatest brand. More than 1,600 new McDonald's restaurants were opened in 2000, most of them outside the United States. You can eat a Big Mac under the Golden Arches in more than 120 countries.

With revenues exceeding $14 billion and more than 28,000 restaurants, the challenge is to ensure that the taste of each Big Mac is the same. How does McDonald's maintain cost and quality control? How does it ensure that each of the 35 million customers it serves daily receives the same value? It uses standards, budgets, and variance analysis. For example, the standards for material are the same for hamburgers wherever they are sold—1 bun, 1 hamburger patty, 1 pickle slice, 1/8 tablespoon of dehydrated onion, 1/4 tablespoon mustard, and 1/2 ounce of ketchup. Material variances are figured for each of these ingredients by computing the amount actually used compared to what should have been used, given the number and types of sandwiches sold.

McDonald's managers budget sales for each hour during the day. Based on the sales budgeted, labor is scheduled. If sales are lower than budgeted, managers can control labor cost by sending some employees home early.

McDonald's also uses nonfinancial standards to help achieve its quality and service goals. For example, the standard time for a drive-through customer is 310 seconds, from pulling up to the menu board to driving away. Cooked meat that is not used in a sandwich within 30 minutes is destroyed. Once a sandwich is made and placed in the transfer bin, it must be sold within 10 minutes or it will be thrown away.

As is the case at McDonald's, managers and employees of any organization want to know how they are doing in meeting their goals. Upper-level managers also want to know how the organization is meeting its financial objectives. Knowing what went wrong and what went right should help managers plan and manage more effectively in future periods.

This chapter introduces flexible budgets, which are budgets designed to direct management to areas of actual financial performance that deserve attention. Managers can apply this same basic process to control other important areas of performance such as quality and service.

FLEXIBLE BUDGETS: BRIDGE BETWEEN STATIC BUDGETS AND ACTUAL RESULTS

STATIC BUDGETS

static budget Another name for a master budget.

Static budget is really just another name for master budget. All the master budgets discussed in Chapter 7 are static or inflexible, because even though they may be easily revised, these budgets assume fixed levels of activity. In other words, a master budget is prepared for only one level of a given type of activity. For example, consider a company using a traditional costing system with only one cost driver. The Dominion Company is a one-department firm in Toronto that manufactures and sells a wheeled, collapsible suitcase carrier that is popular with airline flight crews. Manufacture of this suitcase carrier requires several manual and machine operations. The product has some variations, but may be viewed for our purposes essentially as a single product bearing one selling price. Assume that the cost driver is sales volume (that is, units sold), and the projected level of activity (sales volume) is 9,000 units. All of the budget figures are then based on projected sales of 9,000 units.

All actual results could be compared with the original budgeted amounts, even though, for example, sales volume turned out to be only 7,000 units instead of the originally planned 9,000 units. The master (static) budget for June 20X1 included the condensed income statement shown in Exhibit 8-1, column 2. The actual results for June 20X1 are in column 1. Differences or variances between actual results and the master budget are in column 3. The master budget called for production and sales of 9,000 units, but only 7,000 units were actually produced and sold. There were no beginning or ending inventories, so the units made in June were sold in June.

master budget variance (static budget variance) The variance of actual results from the master (static) budget.

The performance report in Exhibit 8-1 compares the actual results with the master budget. Performance report is a generic term that usually means a comparison of actual results with some budget. A helpful performance report will include variances that direct management's attention to significant deviations from expected results, allowing management by exception. Recall that a variance is a deviation of an actual amount from the expected or budgeted amount. Exhibit 8-1 shows variances of actual results from the master budget; these are called **master (static) budget variances.** Actual revenues that exceed expected revenues result in favorable revenue variances. When actual revenues are below expected revenues, variances are unfavorable. Similarly, actual expenses that exceed budgeted expenses result in **unfavorable expense variances,** and actual expenses that are less than budgeted expenses, result in **favorable expense variances.** Each significant variance should cause a manager to ask, "Why?" By explaining why a variance occurs, managers

unfavorable expense variance A variance that occurs when actual expenses are more than budgeted expenses.

favorable expense variance A variance that occurs when actual expenses are less than budgeted expenses.

Exhibit 8-1

Dominion Company

Performance Report Using Master Budget for the Month Ended June 30, 20X1

	Actual (1)	Master Budget (2)	Master Budget Variances (3)
Units	7,000	9,000	2,000
Sales	$217,000	$279,000	$62,000 U
Variable expenses			
Variable manufacturing expenses	$151,270	$189,000	$37,730 F
Shipping expenses (selling)	5,000	5,400	400 F
Administrative expenses	2,000	1,800	200 U
Total variable expenses	$158,270	$196,200	$37,930 F
Contribution margin	$ 58,730	$ 82,800	$24,070 U
Fixed expenses			
Fixed manufacturing expenses	$ 37,300	$ 37,000	$ 300 U
Fixed selling and administrative expenses	33,000	33,000	—
Total fixed expenses	$ 70,300	$ 70,000	$ 300 U
Operating income (loss)	$(11,570)	$ 12,800	$24,370 U

U = Unfavorable expense variances occur when actual expenses are more than budgeted expenses.

F = Favorable expense variances occur when actual expenses are less than budgeted expenses

are forced to recognize changes that have affected revenues or costs and that might affect future decisions.

Suppose the president of Dominion Company asks you to explain why there was an operating loss of $11,570 when a profit of $12,800 was budgeted. Clearly, sales were $62,000 below expectations, but the favorable variances for the variable costs are misleading. Considering the lower-than-projected level of sales activity, was cost control really satisfactory? Would you really expect to pay $196,200 for variable expenses when only 7,000 units are produced? Of course not! Therefore, the comparison of actual results with a master budget is not very useful for management by exception.

FLEXIBLE BUDGETS

A more helpful benchmark for analysis is the flexible budget. A **flexible budget** (sometimes called variable budget) is a budget that adjusts for changes in sales volume and other cost-driver activities. The flexible budget is identical to the master budget in format, but managers may prepare it for any level of activity. So, when sales turn out to be 7,000 units instead of 9,000, managers can use the flexible budget to prepare a new budget based on this new cost-driver level. We can then see what the total variable expenses should be based on a sales level of 7,000 and compare this amount to the actual result. For performance evaluation, the flexible budget would be prepared at the actual levels of activity achieved. In contrast, the master budget is kept fixed or static to serve as the original benchmark for evaluating performance. It shows revenues and costs at only the originally planned levels of activity.

The flexible-budget approach says, "Give me any activity level you choose, and I'll provide a budget tailored to that particular level." Many companies routinely "flex" their budgets to help evaluate recent financial performance. For example, Ritz-Carlton managers evaluate monthly financial performance of all the company's hotels by comparing actual results to new, flexible budgets that are prepared for actual levels of activity.

flexible budget (variable budget) A budget that adjusts for changes in sales volume and other cost-driver activities.

Objective 1
Distinguish between flexible budgets and master (static) budgets.

Exhibit 8-2

Dominion Company
Flexible Budgets

	Flexible Budget Formula	Flexible Budgets for Various Levels of Sales/Production Activity		
Budget formula per unit				
Units		7,000	8,000	9,000
Sales	$ 31.00	$217,000	$248,000	$279,000
Variable costs/expense				
Variable manufacturing costs	$ 21.00	$147,000	$168,000	$189,000
Shipping expenses (selling)	.60	4,200	4,800	5,400
Administrative	.20	1,400	1,600	1,800
Total variable costs/expenses	$ 21.80	$152,600	$174,400	$196,200
Contribution margin	$ 9.20	$ 64,400	$ 73,600	$ 82,800
Budget formula per month				
Fixed costs				
Fixed manufacturing costs	$37,000	$ 37,000	$ 37,000	$ 37,000
Fixed selling and administrative costs	33,000	33,000	33,000	33,000
Total fixed costs	$70,000	$ 70,000	$ 70,000	$ 70,000
Operating income (loss)		$ (5,600)	$ 3,600	$ 12,800

FLEXIBLE-BUDGET FORMULAS

Objective 2
Use flexible-budget formulas to construct a flexible budget based on the volume of sales.

The flexible budget is based on assumptions of revenue and cost behavior (within the relevant range) with respect to appropriate cost drivers. The cost functions that you used in Chapter 2 and estimated in Chapter 3 can be used as flexible-budget formulas. The flexible budget incorporates effects on each cost and revenue caused by changes in activity. Exhibits 8-2 and 8-3 show Dominion Company's simple flexible budget, which has a single cost driver, units of output. Dominion Company's cost functions or flexible budget formulas are believed to be valid within the relevant range of 7,000 to 9,000 units. Be sure that you understand that each column of Exhibit 8-2 (7,000, 8,000, and 9,000 units, respectively) is prepared using the same flexible-budget formulas—and any activity level within

Exhibit 8-3

Dominion Company
Graph of Flexible Budget of Costs

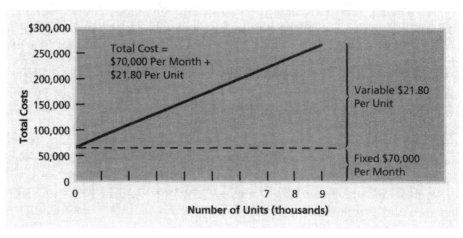

this range could be used, as shown in the graph in Exhibit 8-3. Note that fixed costs are expected to be constant across this range of activity.

ACTIVITY-BASED FLEXIBLE BUDGETS

The flexible budget for Dominion Company shown in Exhibit 8-2 is based on a single cost driver—units of product. For companies that use a traditional, volume-based costing system, this is an appropriate approach to flexible budgeting.

Objective 3
Prepare an activity-based flexible budget.

activity-based flexible budget   A budget based on budgeted costs for each activity and related cost driver.

Companies that have an activity-based costing system use a more detailed approach. An **activity-based flexible budget** is based on budgeted costs for each activity and related cost driver. Exhibit 8-4 shows an activity-based flexible budget for the Dominion Company. There are four activities: processing, setup, marketing, and administration. Within each activity, costs depend on an appropriate cost driver. Compare the traditional flexible budget (Exhibit 8-2) and the activity-based flexible budget (Exhibit 8-4). Note that the 8,000-unit columns in Exhibits 8-4 and 8-2 are the same, but at other volumes the costs diverge. The key difference is that some manufacturing costs that are fixed with respect to units are variable with respect to the cost-driver "setups." That is, the fixed manufacturing costs ($37,000) in Exhibit 8-2 include setup costs that are largely fixed with respect to "units produced" but that vary with respect to the "number of setups." An example is the cost of supplies used to set up the production run. Each time a setup is done, supplies are used. Therefore, the cost of supplies varies directly with the number of setups. However, no setup supplies are used during production, so there is little change in the cost of supplies over wide ranges of units produced. This basic difference is why the total budgeted costs differ using the two approaches— activity-based flexible budgets provide more accurate measures of cost behavior.

When should a company use activity-based flexible budgets? When a significant portion of its costs vary with cost drivers other than units of production. In our Dominion example, the $500 per setup is the only such cost. For the rest of this chapter we will ignore the fact that this cost varies with number of setups, and go back to assuming that Dominion's operations are simple enough that a traditional flexible budget with a single cost driver is appropriate.

EVALUATION OF FINANCIAL PERFORMANCE USING FLEXIBLE BUDGETS

Comparing the flexible budget to actual results accomplishes an important performance evaluation purpose. There are two reasons why actual results might differ from the master budget. One is that sales and other cost-driver activities were not the same as originally forecasted. The second is that revenues or variable costs per unit of activity and fixed costs per period were not as expected. Though these reasons may not be completely independent (for example, higher unit sales prices may have caused lower unit sales levels), it is useful to separate these effects because different people may be responsible for each and because different management actions may be indicated.

Objective 4
Understand the performance evaluation relationship between master (static) budgets and flexible budgets.

The intent of using the flexible budget for performance evaluation is to isolate unexpected effects on actual results that can be corrected if adverse or enhanced if beneficial. Because the flexible budget is prepared at the actual level of activity (in our example, sales volume), any variances between the flexible budget and actual results cannot be due to activity levels. They must be due to departures of actual costs or revenues from flexible-budget formula amounts—because of pricing or cost control. These variances between the flexible budget and actual results are called **flexible-budget variance.**

flexible-budget variances
The variances between the flexible budget and the actual results.

In contrast, any differences or variances between the master budget and the flexible budget are due to activity levels, not cost control. These latter differences between the master budget amounts and the amounts in the flexible budget are called **activity-level variances.** In other words, the original difference we saw between actual results and the original master budget, which we earlier could not fully explain, actually has two components: the sales-activity variance and the flexible-budget variance.

activity-level variances
The differences between the master budget amounts and the amounts in the flexible budget.

Exhibit 8-4

Dominion Company

Activity-Based Flexible Budget for the Month Ended June 30, 20X1

	BUDGET FORMULA	Units		
		7,000	8,000	9,000
Sales	$31.00	$217,000	$248,000	$279,000

ACTIVITY

Processing

		Cost Driver: Number of Machine Hours		
Cost-driver level		14,000	16,000	18,000
Variable costs	$10.50	$147,000	$168,000	$189,000
Fixed costs	$13,000	13,000	13,000	13,000
Total costs of processing activity		$160,000	$181,000	$202,000

Setup

		Cost Driver: Number of Setups		
Cost-driver level		21	24	27
Variable costs	$500	$ 10,500	$ 12,000	$ 13,500
Fixed costs	$12,000	12,000	12,000	12,000
Total costs of setup activity		$ 22,500	$ 24,000	$ 25,500

Marketing

		Cost Driver: Number of Orders		
Cost-driver level		350	400	450
Variable costs	$12.00	$ 4,200	$ 4,800	$ 5,400
Fixed costs	$15,000	15,000	15,000	15,000
Total costs of marketing activity		$ 19,200	$ 19,800	$ 20,400

Administration

		Cost Driver: Number of Units		
Cost-driver level		7,000	8,000	9,000
Variable costs	$.20	$ 1,400	$ 1,600	$ 1,800
Fixed costs	$18,000	18,000	18,000	18,000
Total costs of administration activity		$ 19,400	$ 19,600	$ 19,800

Total costs		$221,100	$244,400	$267,700
Operating income (loss)		$ (4,100)	$ 3,600	$ 11,300

Consider Exhibit 8-5. The flexible budget (column 3) taken from Exhibit 8-2 (and simplified) provides an explanatory bridge between the master budget (column 5) and the actual results (column 1). The variances for operating income are summarized at the bottom of Exhibit 8-5. Note that the sum of the activity-level variances (here sales-activity variances, because sales is the only activity used as a cost driver) and the flexible-budget variances equals the total of the master budget variances.

Exhibit 8-5

Dominion Company

Summary of Performance for the Month Ended June 30, 20X1

	Actual Results at Actual Activity Level* (1)	Flexible-Budget Variances† (2) = (1) − (3)	Flexible Budget for Actual Sales Activity‡ (3)	Sales-Activity Variances (4) = (3) − (5)	Master Budget (5)
Units	7,000	—	7,000	2,000 U	9,000
Sales	$217,000	—	$217,000	$62,000 U	$279,000
Variable costs	158,270	5,670 U	152,600	43,600 F	196,200
Contribution margin	$ 58,730	$5,670 U	$ 64,400	$18,400 U	$ 82,800
Fixed costs	70,300	300 U	70,000	—	70,000
Operating income	$(11,570)	$5,970 U	$ (5,600)	$18,400 U	$ 12,800

Total flexible-budget variances, $5,970 U

Total sales-activity variances, $18,400 U

Total master budget variances, $24,370 U

U = Unfavorable. F = Favorable.

* Figures are from Exhibit 8-1.

† Figures are shown in more detail in Exhibit 8-6.

‡ Figures are from the 7,000-unit column in Exhibit 8-2.

Consider a simple example of a company that plans to sell 1,000 units of a product for $2 per unit. Budgeted variable costs are $1 per unit, and budgeted operating income is $400. Suppose the company actually sells 800 units and makes an operating income of $200. Compute and interpret the master-budget variance, the sales-activity variance, and the flexible-budget variance.

ANSWER

The master budget variance is $400 − $200 = $200 U. The sales activity variance is the lost contribution margin on the 200 units of lost sales: $1.00 × 200 = $200. Therefore, the flexible budget variance is $0. The entire shortfall in operating income was caused by failing to meet the unit sales target of 1,000 units. The operation was efficient but not effective.

ISOLATING THE CAUSES OF VARIANCES

Managers use comparisons between actual results, master budgets, and flexible budgets to evaluate organizational performance. When evaluating performance, it is useful to distinguish between **effectiveness**—the degree to which a goal, objective, or target is met—and **efficiency**—the degree to which inputs are used in relation to a given level of outputs.

Performance may be effective, efficient, both, or neither. For example, Dominion Company set a master budget objective of manufacturing and selling 9,000 units. Only 7,000 units were actually made and sold, however. Performance, as measured by sales-activity variances, was ineffective because the sales objective was not met.

Was Dominion's performance efficient? Managers judge the degree of efficiency by comparing actual outputs achieved (7,000 units) with actual inputs (such as the costs of direct materials and direct labor). The less input used to produce a given output, the more efficient the operation. As indicated by the flexible-budget variances, Dominion was

effectiveness The degree to which a goal, objective, or target is met.

efficiency The degree to which inputs are used in relation to a given level of outputs.

inefficient because the actual cost of its inputs exceeded the cost expected for the actual level of output.

FLEXIBLE-BUDGET VARIANCES

Objective 5
Compute flexible-budget variances and sales-activity variances.

Recall that flexible-budget variances measure the *efficiency* of operations at the *actual* level of activity. The first three columns of Exhibit 8-5 compare the actual results with the flexible-budget amounts. The flexible-budget variances are the differences between columns 1 and 3, which total $5,970 unfavorable:

$$\text{total flexible-budget variance} = \text{total actual results} - \text{total flexible budget,}$$
$$\text{planned results}$$
$$= (-\$11{,}570) - (-\$5{,}600)$$
$$= -\$5{,}970, \text{ or } \$5{,}970 \text{ unfavorable}$$

The total flexible-budget variance arises from sales prices received and the variable and fixed costs incurred. Dominion Company had no difference between actual sales price and the flexible-budgeted sales price, so we must focus on the differences between actual costs and flexible-budgeted costs at the actual 7,000-unit level of activity. Without the flexible budget in column 3, we cannot separate the effects of differences in cost behavior from the effects of changes in sales activity. The flexible-budget variances indicate whether operations were efficient or not, and may form the basis for periodic performance evaluation. Operations managers are in the best position to explain flexible-budget variances.

Companies that use variances primarily to fix blame often find that managers resort to cheating and subversion to beat the system. Managers of operations usually have more information about those operations than higher-level managers. If that information is used against them, lower-level managers can be expected to withhold or misstate valuable information for their own self-protection. For example, one manufacturing firm actually reduced the next period's departmental budget by the amount of the department's unfavorable variances in the current period. If a division had a $50,000 expense budget and experienced a $2,000 unfavorable variance, the following period's budget would be set at $48,000. This system led managers to cheat and to falsify reports to avoid unfavorable variances. We can criticize departmental managers' ethics, but the system was as much at fault as the managers.

Exhibit 8-6 gives an expanded, line-by-line computation of variances for all master budget items at Dominion. Note how most of the costs that had seemingly favorable variances when a master budget was used as a basis for comparison (see Exhibit 8-1) have, in reality, unfavorable variances. Do not conclude automatically that favorable flexible-budget variances are good and unfavorable flexible-budget variances are bad. Instead, interpret all variances as signals that actual operations have not occurred exactly as anticipated when the flexible-budget formulas were set. Any cost that differs significantly from the flexible budget deserves an explanation. The last column of Exhibit 8-6 gives possible explanations for Dominion Company's variances.

SALES-ACTIVITY VARIANCES

sales-activity variances
Variances that measure how effective managers have been in meeting the planned sales objective, calculated as actual unit sales less master budget unit sales times the budgeted unit contribution margin.

Sales-activity variances measure how effective managers have been in meeting the planned sales objective. In Dominion Company, sales activity fell 2,000 units short of the planned level. The final three columns of Exhibit 8-5 clearly show how the sales-activity variances (totaling $18,400 U) are unaffected by any changes in unit prices or variable costs. Why? Because the same budgeted unit prices and variable costs are used in constructing both the flexible and master budgets. Therefore, all unit prices and variable costs are held constant in columns 3 through 5.

Exhibit 8-6

Dominion Company

Cost-Control Performance Report for the Month Ended June 30, 20X1

	Actual Costs Incurred	Flexible Budget*	Flexible-Budget Variances[†]	Explanation
Units	7,000	7,000	—	
Variable costs				
Direct material	$ 69,920	$ 70,000	$ 80 F	Lower prices but higher usage
Direct labor	61,500	56,000	5,500 U	Higher wage rates and higher usage
Indirect labor	9,100	11,900	2,800 F	Decreased setup time
Idle time	3,550	2,800	750 U	Excessive machine breakdowns
Cleanup time	2,500	2,100	400 U	Cleanup of spilled solvent
Supplies	4,700	4,200	500 U	Higher prices and higher usage
Variable manufacturing costs	$151,270	$147,000	$4,270 U	
Shipping	5,000	4,200	800 U	Use of air freight to meet delivery
Administration	2,000	1,400	600 U	Excessive copying and long-distance calls
Total variable costs	$158,270	$152,600	$5,670 U	
Fixed costs				
Factory supervision	$ 14,700	$ 14,400	$ 300 U	Salary increase
Factory rent	5,000	5,000	—	
Equipment depreciation	15,000	15,000	—	
Other fixed factory costs	2,600	2,600	—	
Fixed manufacturing costs	$ 37,300	$ 37,000	$ 300 U	
Fixed selling and administrative costs	33,000	33,000	—	
Total fixed costs	$ 70,300	$ 70,000	$ 300 U	
Total variable and fixed costs	$228,570	$222,600	$5,970 U	

* From 7,000-unit column of Exhibit 8-2.

[†] This is a line-by-line breakout of the variances in column 2 of Exhibit 8-5

The total of the sales-activity variances informs the manager that falling short of the sales target by 2,000 units caused operating income to be $18,400 lower than initially budgeted (a $5,600 loss instead of a $12,800 profit). In summary, the shortfall of sales by 2,000 units caused Dominion Company to incur a total sales activity variance of 2,000 units at a contribution margin of $9.20 per unit (from the first column of Exhibit 8-2):

total sales-activity variance = (actual sales units − master budgeted sales units)
   × budgeted contribution margin per unit

= (9,000 − 7,000) × $9.20

= $18,400 unfavorable

Who has responsibility for the sales-activity variance? Marketing managers usually have the primary responsibility for reaching the sales level specified in the static budget. Of course variations in sales may be attributable to many factors.[1] Nevertheless, marketing managers are typically in the best position to explain why sales activities attained differed from plans.

[1] For example, sales-activity variances can be subdivided into sales quantity, sales mix, market size, and market share variances This more advanced treatment of sales-activity variances is covered in Charles T Horngren, George Foster, and Srikant M Datar, Cost Accounting: A Managerial Emphasis (Upper Saddle River, N J: Prentice Hall, 2000), pp. 573–580 These sales-activity variances might result from changes in the product, changes in customer demand, effective advertising, and so on

SETTING STANDARDS

expected cost The cost most likely to be attained.

standard cost A carefully determined cost per unit that should be attained.

Expected costs or standard costs are the building blocks of a planning and control system. An **expected cost** is the cost that is most likely to be attained. A **standard cost** is a carefully developed cost per unit that should be attained. It is often synonymous with the expected cost, but some companies intentionally set standards above or below expected costs to create desired incentives.

What standard of expected performance should be used in flexible budgets? Should it be so strict that it is rarely, if ever, attained? Should it be attainable 50% of the time? 90%? 20%? Individuals who have worked a lifetime setting and evaluating standards for performance disagree, so there are no universal answers to this question.

perfection standards (ideal standards) Expressions of the most efficient performance possible under the best conceivable conditions, using existing specifications and equipment.

Perfection standards (also called ideal standards) are expressions of the most efficient performance possible under the best conceivable conditions, using existing specifications and equipment. No provision is made for waste, spoilage, machine breakdowns, and the like. Those who favor using perfection standards maintain that the resulting unfavorable variances will constantly remind personnel of the continuous need for improvement in all phases of operations. Though concern for continuous improvement is widespread, these standards are not widely used because they have an adverse effect on employee motivation. Employees tend to ignore unreasonable goals, especially if they would not share the gains from meeting imposed perfection standards. Organizations that apply the JIT philosophy (discussed in Chapter 1, p. 23) attempt to achieve continuous improvement from "the bottom up," not by prescribing what should be achieved via perfection standards.

currently attainable standards Levels of performance that can be achieved by realistic levels of effort.

Currently attainable standards are levels of performance that can be achieved by realistic levels of effort. Allowances are made for normal defectives, spoilage, waste, and nonproductive time. There are at least two popular interpretations of the meaning of currently attainable standards. The first interpretation has standards set just tightly enough that employees regard their attainment as highly probable if normal effort and diligence are exercised. That is, variances should be random and negligible. Hence, the standards are predictions of what will likely occur, anticipating some inefficiencies. Managers accept the standards as being reasonable goals. The major reasons for "reasonable" standards, then, are

1. The resulting standards serve multiple purposes. For example, the same cost can be used for financial budgeting, inventory valuation, and budgeting departmental performance. In contrast, perfection standards cannot be used for inventory valuation or financial budgeting, because the costs are known to be inaccurate.

2. Reasonable standards have a desirable motivational impact on employees, especially when combined with incentives for continuous improvement. The standard represents reasonable future performance, not fanciful goals. Therefore, unfavorable variances direct attention to performance that is not meeting reasonable expectations.

A second interpretation of currently attainable standards is that standards are set tightly. That is, employees regard their fulfillment as possible, though unlikely. Standards can be achieved only by very efficient operations. Variances tend to be unfavorable; nevertheless, employees accept the standards as being tough but not unreasonable goals. Is it possible to achieve continuous improvement using currently attainable standards? Yes, but expectations must reflect improved productivity and must be tied to incentive systems that reward continuous improvement.

TRADE-OFFS AMONG VARIANCES

Because the operations of organizations are linked, the level of performance in one area of operations will affect performance in other areas. Nearly any combination of effects is

The use of standard costs and variance analysis came under attack during the last two decades of the twentieth century. Critics maintained that comparing actual costs to predetermined standards is a static approach that does not work well in today's dynamic, fast-paced, just-in-time environment. However, companies continue to use standards and to measure performance against them. Surveys in five different countries have shown that between 65% and 86% of manufacturing companies use standard costs, with the high level of 86% being applied in the United States. Companies have apparently adapted the approach to fit their modern environments.

To apply standards in a dynamic environment, how should managers measure and report variances? First, standards should be regularly evaluated. If a company is in a state of continuous improvement, standards must be constantly revised. Second, standards and variances should measure key strategic variables. The concept of setting a benchmark, comparing actual results to the benchmark, and identifying causes for any differences is universal. It can be applied to many types of measures, such as production quantity or quality, as well as to costs. Finally, variances should not lead to affixing blame. Standards are plans, and things do not always go according to plan—often with no one being at fault.

One company that has adapted standard costs to meets its particular needs is the Brass Products Division (BPD) at Parker Hannifin Corporation. The BPD uses standard costs and variances to pinpoint problem areas that need attention if the division is to meet its goal of continuous improvement. Among the changes that have increased the value of the standard cost information are more timely product cost information, variances computed at more detailed levels, and regular meetings held to help employees understand their impact on the variances.

The BPD also created three new variances: (1) standard run quantity variance—examines the effect of actual compared to optimal batch size for production runs; (2) material substitution variance—compares material costs to the costs of alternative materials; and (3) method variance—measures costs using actual machines compared to costs using alternative machines. All three variances use the concept of setting a standard and comparing actual results to the standard, but they do not apply the traditional standard cost variance formulas.

It was premature to declare standard costs dead. They are alive and well in many companies. However, there are fewer and fewer environments where traditional variance analysis is useful, and more and more environments where managers and accountants must adapt the standard cost concept to fit the particular needs of a company.

Sources: Adapted from D. Johnsen and P. Sopariwala, "Standard Costing Is Alive and Well at Parker Brass," *Management Accounting Quarterly*, Winter 2000, pp. 12–20; C. B. Cheatham and L. R. Cheatham, "Redesigning Cost Systems: Is Standard Costing Obsolete?", *Accounting Horizons*, December 1996, pp. 23–31; and C. Horngren, G. Foster, and S. Datar, *Cost Accounting: A Managerial Emphasis* (Upper Saddle River, N.J.: Prentice Hall, 2000), p. 226.

possible: Improvements in one area could lead to improvements in others and vice versa. Likewise, substandard performance in one area may be balanced by superior performance in others. For example, a service organization may generate favorable labor variances by hiring less-skilled and thus lower-paid customer representatives, but this favorable variance may lead to unfavorable customer satisfaction and future unfavorable sales-activity variances. In another situation, a manufacturer may experience unfavorable materials variances by purchasing higher-quality materials at a higher than planned price, but this variance may be more than offset by the favorable variances caused by less waste, fewer inspections, and higher-quality products.

Because of the many interdependencies among activities, an "unfavorable" or "favorable" label should not lead the manager to jump to conclusions. By themselves, such labels merely raise questions and provide clues to the causes of performance. They are attention directors, not problem solvers. Furthermore, the cause of variances might be faulty expectations rather than the execution of plans by managers. One of the first questions a manager should consider when explaining a large variance is whether expectations were valid.

WHEN TO INVESTIGATE VARIANCES

When should variances be investigated? Managers recognize that, even if everything operates as planned, variances are unlikely to be exactly zero. They predict a range of "normal" variances. This range is usually based on economic analysis of how big a variance must be before investigation could be worth the effort. For some critical items, any deviation may prompt a follow-up. For most items, a minimum dollar or percentage deviation from budget may be necessary before managers expect investigations to be worthwhile. For example, a 4% variance in a $1 million material cost may deserve more attention than a 20% variance in a $10,000 repair cost. Because knowing exactly when to investigate is difficult, many organizations have developed such rules of thumb as "Investigate all variances exceeding $5,000 or 25% of expected cost, whichever is lower."

COMPARISONS WITH PRIOR PERIOD'S RESULTS

Some organizations compare the most recent budget period's actual results with last year's results for the same period rather than use flexible budget benchmarks. For example, an organization might compare June 20X2's actual results to June 20X1's actual results. In general these comparisons are not as useful for evaluating the performance of an organization as comparisons of actual outcomes with planned results for the same period. Why? Because many changes probably have occurred in the environment and in the organization. Such changes make a comparison across years invalid. Very few organizations and environments are so stable that the only difference between now and a year ago is merely the passage of time. Even comparisons with last month's actual results may not be as useful as comparisons with flexible budgets. Comparisons over time may be useful for analyzing trends in such key variables as sales volume, market share, and product mix, but they do not help answer questions such as "Why did we have a loss of $11,570 in June, when we expected a profit of $12,800?"

SUMMARY PROBLEM FOR YOUR REVIEW

PROBLEM

Refer to the data contained in Exhibits 8-1 and 8-2. Suppose actual production and sales were 8,500 units instead of 7,000 units; actual variable costs were $188,800; and actual fixed costs were $71,200. The selling price remained at $31 per unit.

Required

1. Compute the master budget variance. What does this tell you about the efficiency of operations? The effectiveness of operations?
2. Compute the sales-activity variance. Is the performance of the marketing function the sole explanation for this variance? Why?
3. Using a flexible budget at the actual activity level, compute the budgeted contribution margin, budgeted operating income, and flexible-budget variance. What do you learn from this variance?

SOLUTION

1.

$$\text{actual operating income} = (8,500 \times \$31) - \$188,800 - \$71,200 = \$3,500$$

$$\text{master budget operating income} = \$12,800 \text{ (from Exhibit 8-1)}$$

$$\text{master budget variance} = \$12,800 - \$3,500 = \$9,300 \text{ U}$$

Three factors affect the master budget variance: sales activity, efficiency, and price changes. There is no way to tell from the master budget variance alone how much of the $9,300 U was caused by each of these factors.

2.

$$\text{sales-activity variance} = \text{budgeted unit contribution margin} \times \text{difference between the}$$
$$\text{master budget unit sales and the actual unit sales}$$
$$= \$9.20 \text{ per unit CM} \times (9{,}000 - 8{,}500)$$
$$= \$4{,}600 \text{ U}$$

This variance is labeled as a sales-activity variance because it quantifies the impact on operating income of the deviation from an original sales target while holding price and efficiency factors constant. This is a measure of the effectiveness of the operations—Dominion was ineffective in meeting its sales objective. Of course, the failure to reach target sales may be traceable to several causes beyond the control of marketing personnel, including material shortages, factory breakdowns, and so on.

3. The budget formulas in Exhibit 8-2 are the basis for the following answers.

$$\text{flexible-budget contribution margin} = \$9.20 \times 8{,}500 = \$78{,}200$$
$$\text{flexible-budget operating income} = \$78{,}200 - \$70{,}000 \text{ fixed costs} = \$8{,}200$$
$$\text{actual operating income} = \$3{,}500 \text{ (from requirement 1)}$$
$$\text{flexible-budget variance} = \$8{,}200 - \$3{,}500 = \$4{,}700 \text{ U}$$

The flexible-budget variance shows that the company spent $4,700 more to produce and sell the 8,500 units than it should have if operations had been efficient and unit sales prices had not changed. Note that this variance plus the $4,600 U sales-activity variance total to the $9,300 U master budget variance.

FLEXIBLE-BUDGET VARIANCES IN DETAIL

The rest of this chapter probes the flexible budget variance in detail. The emphasis is on subdividing labor, material, and overhead cost variances into their component parts. Note that in companies where direct-labor costs are small in relation to total costs (that is, in highly automated companies) direct-labor costs may be treated as an overhead-cost item. Such companies do not compute separate labor standards, budgets, or variances.

VARIANCES FROM MATERIAL AND LABOR STANDARDS

Consider Dominion Company's $10 standard cost of direct materials and $8 standard cost of direct labor. These standards per unit are derived from two components: a standard quantity of an input and a standard price for the input.

	Standards		
	Standard Inputs Expected per Unit of Output	*Standard Price Expected per Unit of Input*	*Standard Cost Expected per Unit of Output*
Direct material	5 pounds	$2/pound	$10
Direct labor	1/2 hour	16/hour	8

Once standards are set and actual results are observed, we can measure variances from the flexible budget. To show how the analysis of variances can be pursued more fully, we will reconsider Dominion's direct-material and direct-labor costs, as shown in Exhibit 8-6, and assume that the following actually occurred for the production of 7,000 units of output:

- Direct material: Dominion purchased and used 36,800 pounds of material at an actual unit price of $1.90 for a total actual cost of $69,920.
- Direct labor: Dominion used 3,750 hours of labor at an actual hourly price (rate) of $16.40, for a total cost of $61,500.

Flexible budget variances for direct material and direct labor are $80 F and $5,500 U, respectively:

	(1) **Actual** **Costs**	**(2)** **Flexible** **Budget**	**(3)** **Flexible-** **Budget** **Variance**
Direct material	$69,920	$70,000	$ 80 F
Direct labor	61,500	56,000	5,500 U

The flexible-budget totals [column (2)] for direct materials and direct labor are the amounts that would have been spent with expected efficiency. They are often labeled total standard costs allowed, computed as follows:

$$\text{flexible budget or total standard cost allowed} = \frac{\text{units of good output achieved}}{} \times \frac{\text{input allowed per unit of output}}{} \times \frac{\text{standard unit price of input}}{}$$

$$\text{standard direct-materials cost allowed} = 7{,}000 \text{ units} \times 5 \text{ pounds} \times \$2.00 \text{ per pound} = \$70{,}000$$

$$\text{standard direct-labor cost allowed} = 7{,}000 \text{ units} \times 1/2 \text{ hour} \times \$16.00 \text{ per hour} = \$56{,}000$$

Objective 6
Compute and interpret price and usage variances for inputs based on cost-driver activity.

Before reading on, note particularly that the flexible-budget amounts (that is, the standard costs allowed) are tied to an initial question: What was the output achieved? Always ask yourself: What was the good output? Then proceed with your computations of the total standard cost allowed for the good output achieved.

PRICE AND USAGE VARIANCES

price variance The difference between actual input prices and expected input prices multiplied by the actual quantity of inputs used.

usage variance (quantity variance, efficiency variance) The difference between the quantity of inputs actually used and the quantity of inputs that should have been used to achieve the actual quantity of output multiplied by the expected price of the input.

Flexible-budget variances [column (3) in the table above] measure the relative efficiency with which Dominion produced its 7,000 units. We can examine this efficiency by analyzing whether Dominion (1) used more or less of the resource than planned for the actual level of output achieved and (2) paid more or less than planned for each unit of the resources used. We measure these two components by computing price and usage variances, which subdivide each flexible-budget variance into the following two parts:

1. **Price variance**—difference between actual input prices and standard input prices multiplied by the actual quantity of inputs used.
2. **Usage variance**—difference between the quantity of inputs actually used and the quantity of inputs that should have been used to achieve the actual quantity of output multiplied by the expected price of the input (also called a **quantity variance** or **efficiency variance**).

The objective of these variance calculations is to hold either price or usage constant so that the effect of the other can be isolated. When calculating the price variance, you hold use of inputs constant at the actual level of usage. When calculating the usage variance, you hold price constant at the standard price. For Dominion Company the price variances are

Direct-material price variance = (actual price − standard price) × actual quantity
$$= (\$1.90 - \$2.00) \text{ per pound} \times 36{,}800 \text{ pounds}$$
$$= \$3{,}680 \text{ favorable}$$

Direct-labor price variance = (actual price − standard price) × actual quantity
$$= (\$16.40 - \$16.00) \text{ per hour} \times 3{,}750 \text{ hours}$$
$$= \$1{,}500 \text{ unfavorable}$$

The usage variances are

Direct-material usage variance = (actual quantity used − standard quantity allowed) × standard price
$$= [36{,}800 - (7{,}000 \times 5)] \text{ pounds} \times \$2.00 \text{ per pound}$$
$$= (36{,}800 - 35{,}000) \times \$2$$
$$= \$3{,}600 \text{ unfavorable}$$

Direct-labor usage variance = (actual quantity used − standard quantity allowed) × standard price
$$= [3{,}750 - (7{,}000 \times 1/2)] \text{ hours} \times \$16 \text{ per hour}$$
$$= (3{,}750 - 3{,}500) \times \$16$$
$$= \$4{,}000 \text{ unfavorable}$$

To determine whether a variance is favorable or unfavorable, use logic rather than memorizing a formula. A price variance is favorable if the actual price is less than the standard. A usage variance is favorable if the actual quantity used is less than the standard quantity allowed. The opposite relationships imply unfavorable variances.

Note that the sum of the direct-labor price and usage variances equals the direct-labor flexible-budget variance. Furthermore, the sum of the direct-material price and usage variances equals the total direct-material flexible-budget variance.

Direct-materials flexible-budget variance = $3,680 favorable + $3,600 unfavorable
$$= \$80 \text{ favorable}$$

Direct-labor flexible-budget variance = $1,500 unfavorable + $4,000 unfavorable
$$= \$5{,}500 \text{ unfavorable}$$

INTERPRETATION OF PRICE AND USAGE VARIANCES

When feasible, managers try to separate the variances that are subject to their direct influence from those that are not. The usual approach is to separate price factors from usage factors. Price factors often are less subject to immediate control than are usage factors, principally because of external forces, such as general economic conditions, that can influence prices. Even when price factors are regarded as being outside management control, isolating them helps to focus on the efficient usage of inputs. For example, the commodity prices of wheat, oats, corn, and rice may be outside the control of General Mills.

By separating price variances from usage variances, the breakfast-cereal maker can focus on whether grain was used efficiently.

Price and usage variances are helpful because they provide feedback to those responsible for inputs. These variances should not be the only information used for decision making, control, or evaluation, however. Exclusive focus on material price variances by purchasing agents or buyers, for example, can work against an organization's JIT and total quality management goals. A buyer may be motivated to earn favorable material price variances by buying in large quantities and by buying low-quality material. The result could then be excessive inventory-handling and opportunity costs and increased manufacturing defects owing to faulty material. Similarly, exclusive focus on labor price and usage variances could motivate supervisors to use lower-skilled workers or to rush workers through critical tasks, both of which could impair quality of products and services.

Variances themselves do not show why the budgeted operating income was or was not achieved. They raise questions, provide clues, and direct attention, however. For instance, one possible explanation for Dominion's set of variances is that a manager might have made a trade-off—the manager might have purchased at a favorable price some materials that were substandard quality, saving $3,680 (the materials price variance). Excessive waste might have nearly offset this savings, as indicated by the $3,600 unfavorable material usage variance and net flexible-budget variance of $80 favorable. The material waste also might have caused at least part of the excess use of direct labor. Suppose more than $80 of the $4,000 unfavorable direct-labor usage variance was caused by reworking units with defective materials. Then the manager's trade-off was not successful. The cost inefficiencies caused by using substandard materials exceeded the savings from the favorable price.

Exhibit 8-7 shows the price and usage variance computations for labor graphically. The standard cost (or flexible budget) is the standard quantity multiplied by the standard price—the rectangle shaded light blue. The price variance is the difference between the unit prices, actual and standard, multiplied by actual quantity used—the rectangle shaded dark blue. The usage variance is the standard price multiplied by the difference between the actual quantity used and the standard quantity allowed for the good output achieved—the rectangle shaded gray. (Note that for clarity the graph portrays only unfavorable variances.)

Exhibit 8-7

Graphical Representation of Price and Usage Variances for Labor

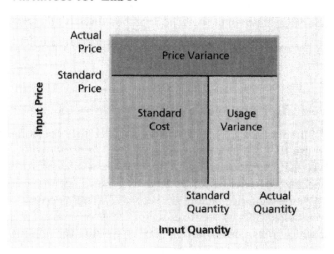

Consider a production plant that is supposed to produce 50 units per hour and work 8 hours each day. On March 23 the plant produced 325 units. Because of machine breakdowns, the plant operated for only 7.5 hours that day. Using the same conceptual framework as used for separating usage and price variances, determine how much of the 75 unit shortfall in production was caused by working only 7.5 hours and how much was caused by inefficiencies during the hours of actual operation.

ANSWER

Normal production would be 8 × 50 = 400 units per day. If the only difference from plan was the loss of 1/2 hour of productive time, production would have been 7.5 × 50 = 375 units. Therefore, 25 units of shortfall were caused by the machine breakdowns. The other 375 – 325 = 50 units were caused by producing fewer than 50 units per hour. The actual rate of production was 325 ÷ 7.5 = 43.3 units per hour, 6.7 units fewer than budgeted.

EFFECTS OF INVENTORIES

Analysis of Dominion Company was simplified because (1) there were no finished goods inventories—any units produced were sold in the same period—and (2) there was no direct-material inventory—the materials were purchased and used in the same period.

What if there are finished goods inventories and production does not equal sales? The sales-activity variance then is the difference between the static budget and the flexible budget for the number of units sold. In contrast, the flexible-budget cost variances compare actual costs with flexible-budgeted costs for the number of units produced.

What if there are direct materials inventories? Generally managers want quick feedback and want variances to be identified as early as is practical. In the case of the price of direct materials, that time is when the materials are purchased rather than when they are used, which may be much later. Therefore, the material price variance is usually based on the quantity purchased, measured at the time of purchase. The material usage variance remains based on the quantity used. Suppose Dominion Company purchased 40,000 pounds of material (rather than the 36,800 pounds used) at $1.90 per pound. The material price variance would be (actual price − standard price) × material purchased = ($1.90 − $2.00) per pound × 40,000 pounds = $4,000 favorable. The mateial usage variance would remain at $3,600 unfavorable because it is based on the material used.

CAPITAL
BUDGETING

Skiers do not often realize the
planning and investment that goes into
preparing the slopes. Managers at
Deer Valley Lodge, a ski resort in
Utah's Wasatch Mountains and one
of the hosts of the 2002 Winter
Olympics, understand this fully. Much
effort goes into their capital budgeting
decisions—decisions that affect the
fun, comfort, and safety of their guests.

www.prenhall.com/horngren

Learning Objectives

When you have finished studying this chapter, you should be able to

1. Describe capital budgeting decisions and use the net-present-value (NPV) method to make such decisions.

2. Evaluate projects using sensitivity analysis.

3. Calculate the NPV difference between two projects using both the total project and differential approaches.

4. Identify relevant cash flows for NPV analyses.

5. Compute the after-tax net present values of projects.

6. Explain the after-tax effect on cash of disposing of assets.

7. Compute the impact of inflation on a capital-budgeting project.

8. Use the payback model and the accounting rate-of-return model and compare them with the NPV model.

9. Reconcile the conflict between using an NPV model for making a decision and using accounting income for evaluating the related performance.

10. **Understand how companies make long-term capital investment decisions and how such decisions can affect the companies' financial results for years to come.**

Capital investment is probably the last thing you would think of while schussing down the snow-covered slopes of the Rockies—unless you happen to be the manager of a ski resort. A resort guest might see slopes, chairlifts, and a nice warm lodge, while a resort manager will see millions of dollars worth of investments.

Consider Deer Valley Lodge, a posh ski resort in the Wasatch Mountains of Utah. Deer Valley has a strong customer orientation—what Director of Finance Jim Madsen calls "the Deer Valley difference." From valets who help with skis to gourmet meals in the lodges, Deer Valley is a first-class resort. When facilities become too crowded, the resort limits sales of lift tickets to keep lift lines from getting too long. After crowding forced Deer Valley officials to close ticket sales offices early several times in 1994–1995, managers started thinking it was time to expand.

Deer Valley keeps a 10-year plan for capital expansion. Recent plans included five new lifts that will expand operations into neighboring Empire Canyon, a day lodge, and a new parking facility. By continually measuring crowding, using measures such as waiting time for lifts and length of lines at restaurants and cafeterias, Deer Valley managers decide when the next capital expansion phase is needed.

One capital expansion phase will be needed just before Deer Valley hosts the Olympic Winter Games in 2002. Deer Valley will feature slalom and freestyle skiing, with slalom competition on a ski run called Know You Don't, moguls on Champion, and aerial events on White Owl. Just as athletes hone their skills to compete in these events, Deer Valley managers must improve their facilities through additional capital investments.

CAPITAL BUDGETING FOR PROGRAMS OR PROJECTS

capital budgeting The long-term planning for making and financing investments that affect financial results over more than just the next year.

Ski resorts such as Deer Valley are not the only companies that face decisions about capital investment and expansion. At some time, every company needs to decide where and how to spend its money on major projects that will affect company financial results for years to come. This chapter concentrates on the planning and controlling decisions for programs or projects that affect financial results over more than just the next year. Such decisions require investments of large amounts of resources (capital) that are often called capital outlays. The term **capital budgeting** describes the long-term planning for making and financing such outlays.

Capital budgeting has three phases: (1) identifying potential investments, (2) choosing which investments to make (which includes gathering data to aid the decision), and (3) follow-up monitoring, or "postaudit," of the investments. Accountants usually are not involved in the first phase, but they play important roles in phases 2 and 3.

Why are accountants involved in capital budgeting decisions? They function primarily as information specialists. As you know, one of the purposes of a cost management system is to provide cost measurements for strategic decisions such as major capital-budgeting decisions.

Accountants will gather and interpret as much information as possible to help managers make such decisions. To help organize what could be pages and pages worth of information, accountants rely on capital-budgeting models. Let's take a look at how some of these models work.

DISCOUNTED-CASH-FLOW MODELS

discounted-cash-flow (DCF) models A type of capital-budgeting model that focuses on cash inflows and outflows while taking into account the time value of money.

The most widely used capital-budgeting models are **discounted-cash-flow (DCF) models.** These models focus on a project's cash inflows and outflows while taking into account time value of money. They are based on the old adage that a bird in the hand is worth two in the bush—that a dollar in the hand today is worth more than a dollar to be received (or spent) five years from today. This adage applies because the use of money has a cost (interest), just as the use of a building or an automobile may have a cost (rent). More than 85% of the large industrial firms in the United States use a DCF model.

MAJOR ASPECTS OF DCF

As the name suggests, DCF models focus on expected cash inflows and outflows rather than on net income. Companies invest cash today in order to receive cash in future periods. DCF models compare the value of today's *cash outflows* with the value of the future *cash inflows*.

DCF methods are based on the theory of compound interest which you should be familiar with from your course in financial accounting. For those of you whose knowledge of compound interest and time value of money is a little rusty, be sure to read Appendix B, pages B1–B8. Do not try to learn about the DCF methods until you are able to use Tables 1 (p. B7) and 2 (p. B8) in Appendix B.

To illustrate how DCF models work, we will use the following example throughout the rest of this section: A buildings and grounds manager at the University of Minnesota is contemplating the purchase of some lawn maintenance equipment that is expected to increase efficiency and produce cash-operating savings of $2,000 per year. The useful life of the equipment is four years, after which it will have a net disposal value of zero. The equipment will cost $6,075 now, and the minimum desired rate of return is 10% per year.

NET PRESENT VALUE (NPV)

We will focus on the most popular version of DCF, the **net-present-value (NPV) method.** The NPV method computes the present value of all expected future cash flows using a minimum desired rate of return. The minimum desired rate of return depends on the risk of a proposed project—the higher the risk, the higher the rate. Based on the cost of capital—what the firm pays to acquire more capital—this minimum rate is also called the **required rate of return, hurdle rate,** or **discount rate.** Using this required rate, managers determine the sum of the present values of all expected cash flows from the project. If this sum is positive, the project is desirable. If the sum is negative, the project is undesirable. Why? A positive NPV means that accepting the project will increase the value of the firm because the present value of the project's cash inflows exceeds the present value of its cash outflows. (An NPV of zero means that the present value of the inflows equals the present value of the outflows, and the project will exactly break even.) When choosing among several investments, managers should pick the one with the greatest net present value.

net-present-value (NPV) method A discounted-cash-flow approach to capital budgeting that computes the present value of all expected future cash flows using a minimum desired rate of return.

required rate of return (hurdle rate, discount rate) The minimum desired rate of return, based on the firm's cost of capital.

APPLYING THE NPV METHOD

To apply the NPV method, you can use the following three steps, which are shown in Exhibit 11-1.

Objective 1
Describe capital budgeting decisions and use the net-present-value (NPV) method to make such decisions.

1. *Prepare a diagram of relevant expected cash inflows and outflows:* The right-hand side of Exhibit 11-1 shows how these cash flows are sketched. Outflows are in parentheses. Be sure to include the outflow at time zero, the date of acquisition. You do not have to use a sketch, but sketches do help you to see costs and cost relationships.

2. *Find the present value of each expected cash inflow or outflow:* Examine Table 1 in Appendix B on page B7. Find the present-value (PV) factor for each year's cash flow from the correct row and column of the table. Multiply each expected cash inflow or outflow by the appropriate present-value factor. For example, the $2,000 cash savings that will occur two years hence is worth $2,000 × .8264 = $1,653 today.

3. *Sum the individual present values:* The sum is the project's NPV. Accept a project whose NPV is positive, and reject a project whose NPV is negative.

The value today (at time zero) of the four $2,000 cash inflows is $6,340. The manager pays only $6,075 to obtain these cash inflows. Thus, the net present value is $6,340 − $6,075 = $265, so the investment is desirable.

Exhibit 11-1

Net-Present-Value Method

Original investment, $6,075. Useful life, four years. Annual cash inflow from operations, $2,000. Minimum desired rate of return, 10%. Cash outflows are in parentheses; cash inflows are not. Total present values are rounded to the nearest dollar.

	Present Value of $1, Discounted at 10%	Total Present Value	Sketch of Cash Flows at End of Year				
			0	1	2	3	4

Approach 1: Discounting Each Year's Cash Inflow Separately*

Cash flows

Annual savings	.9091	$1,818		$2,000			
	.8264	1,653			$2,000		
	.7513	1,503				$2,000	
	.6830	1,366					$2,000
Present value of future inflows		$6,340					
Initial outlay	1.0000	(6,075)	$(6,075)				
Net present value		$ 265					

Approach 2: Using Annuity Table†

Annual savings	3.1699	$6,340		$2,000	$2,000	$2,000	$2,000
Initial outlay	1.0000	(6,075)	$(6,075)				
Net present value		$ 265					

*Present values from Table 1, Appendix B, page B7.
†Present values of annuity from Table 2, Appendix B, page B8. (Incidentally, calculators or computers may give slightly different answers than tables because of rounding differences.)

CHOICE OF THE CORRECT TABLE

Exhibit 11-1 also shows another way to calculate the NPV, shown here as approach 2. The basic steps are the same as for approach 1. The only difference is that approach 2 uses Table 2 in Appendix B (see page B8) instead of Table 1. Table 2 is an annuity table that provides a shortcut to reduce hand calculations. It gives discount factors for computing the present value of a *series* of equal cash flows at equal intervals. Because the four cash flows in our example are all equal, you can use Table 2 to make one present-value computation instead of using Table 1 to make four individual computations. Table 2 merely sums up the pertinent present-value factors of Table 1. Therefore the annuity factor for four years at 10% is[1]

$$.9091 + .8264 + .7513 + .6830 = 3.1698$$

Beware of using the wrong table. You should use Table 1 for discounting individual amounts, Table 2 for a series of equal amounts. Of course, Table 1 is the basis for Table 2, and it can be used for all present-value calculations.

You can avoid Tables 1 and 2 entirely by using the present-value function on a hand-held calculator or the present-value function on a computer spreadsheet program. However, we encourage you to use the tables when learning the NPV method. Using the tables will let you better understand the process of present-value computation. Once you are comfortable with the method, you can take advantage of the speed and convenience of calculators and computers.

 To confirm your understanding of Tables 1 and 2, compute the following using a discount rate of 8%.

1. Present value of $1,000 to be received in 5 years.
2. Present value of $1,000 to be received at the end of each year for 5 years.
3. Present value of $1,000 to be received at the end of years 3, 4, and 5.

ANSWERS

The solution to 1 requires the factor from row 5, 8% column of Table 1:
$1,000 × .6806 = $680.60.

The solution to 2 requires the factor from row 5, 8% column of Table 2:
$1,000 × 3 9927 = $3,9927.00.

The solution to 3 can be done in several ways. Two of them are
Use only Table 2: $1,000 × (3.9927 − 1.7833) = $2,209.40
Use Tables 1 and 2: $1,000 × 2.5771 × .8573 = $2,209.35

These two solutions differ by a $.05 rounding error.

EFFECT OF MINIMUM RATE

The minimum desired rate of return can have a large effect on NPVs. The higher the minimum desired rate of return, the lower the present value of each future cash inflow. Why? Because the higher the rate of return, the more it costs you to wait for the cash rather than having it available to invest today. Thus, higher required rates lead to lower project NPVs. For example, at a rate of 16%, the NPV of the project in Exhibit 11-1 would be −$479 (that is, $2,000 × 2.7982 = $5,596, which is $479 less than the required investment

---

[1] *Rounding error causes a 0001 difference between the Table 2 factor and the summation of Table 1 factors.*

of $6,075), instead of the +$265 computed with a 10% rate. (Present-value factor 2.7982 is taken from Table 2 in Appendix B on page B8.) When the desired rate of return is 16% rather than 10%, the project is undesirable at a price of $6,075.

Assumptions of the NPV Model

We have to make two major assumptions to use the NPV model. First, we assume a world of certainty. That is, we act as if the predicted cash inflows and outflows are certain to occur at the times specified. Second, we assume perfect capital markets. That is, if we need to have extra cash at any time, we can borrow or lend money at the same interest rate. This rate is our minimum desired rate of return. If these assumptions are met, no model could possibly be better than the NPV model.

Unfortunately, the real world has neither certainty nor perfect capital markets. Nevertheless, the NPV model is usually preferred to other models because the assumptions of most other models are even less realistic. The NPV model is not perfect, but it generally meets our cost-benefit criterion. That is, the benefit of better decisions based on NPV is greater than the cost of applying it. More sophisticated models often do not improve decisions enough to be worth their cost.

Depreciation and NPV

NPV calculations do not include deductions for depreciation. Why not? Because NPV is based on inflows and outflows of cash and not on the accounting concepts of revenues and expenses.[2] Depreciation is not a cash flow. It is a way of allocating the cost of a long-lived asset (which was usually paid for in cash upon purchase) to different periods. Because the cash outflow for the cost of the asset has already been recorded and accounted for, deducting depreciation from future cash flows would be like counting this cost twice—once at purchase and again over the asset's life.

Review of Decision Rules

Be sure that you understand why the NPV method works, not just how to apply it. The decision maker in our example cannot directly compare an immediate outflow of $6,075 with a series of future inflows of $2,000 each because of the time value of money. The NPV model aids comparison by expressing all amounts in today's monetary units (such as dollars, francs, marks, or yen) at time zero. The required rate of return measures the cost of using money. At a rate of 12%, the comparison would be

Outflow in today's dollars	$(6,075)
Inflow equivalent in today's dollars @ 12%	6,075
Net present value	$ 0

Therefore, at a required rate of return of 12%, the decision maker is indifferent between having $6,075 now or having a stream of four annual inflows of $2,000 each. If

---

[2] *Throughout this chapter, our examples often assume that cash inflows are equivalent to revenues and that cash outflows are equivalent to expenses (except for depreciation). Of course, if the revenues and expenses are accounted for on the accrual basis of accounting, there will be leads and lags of cash inflows and cash outflows that a precise DCF model must recognize For example, a $10,000 sale on credit may be recorded as revenue in one period, but the related cash inflow would not be recognized in a DCF model until collected, which may be in a second period. Such refinements are not made in this chapter.*

the interest rate were 16%, the decision maker would find the project unattractive because the net present value would be a negative $479, as shown in the following graph.

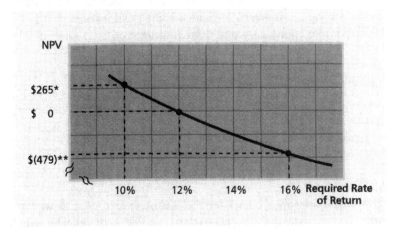

*($2,000 × 3.1699) − $6,075 = $265
**($2,000 × 2.7982) − $6,075 = $(479)

At 10%, the NPV is a positive $265, so the project is desirable. At all rates below 12%, the NPV is positive. At all rates above 12%, the NPV is negative.

SENSITIVITY ANALYSIS AND RISK ASSESSMENT IN DCF MODELS

Because the future is uncertain, actual cash inflows may differ from what was expected or predicted. To examine this uncertainty, managers often use sensitivity analysis, which shows the financial consequences that would occur if actual cash inflows and outflows differ from those expected. It can answer such what-if? questions as: What will happen to my NPV if my predictions of useful life or cash flows change? The best way to understand sensitivity analysis is to see it in action, so let's take a look at an example.

Objective 2
Evaluate projects using sensitivity analysis.

Suppose that a manager knows that the actual cash inflows in Exhibit 11-1 could fall below the predicted level of $2,000. How far below $2,000 must the annual cash inflow drop before the NPV becomes negative? The cash inflow at the point where NPV = 0 is the "break-even" cash flow:

$$NPV = 0$$
$$(3.1699 \times \text{cash flow}) - \$6,075 = 0$$
$$\text{cash flow} = \$6,075 \div 3.1699$$
$$= \$1,916$$

If the annual cash inflow is less than $1,916, the NPV is negative, and the project should be rejected. Therefore annual cash inflows can drop only $2,000 − $1,916 = $84, or 4.2%, before the manager would change the decision.

Managers like sensitivity analysis because it can give them immediate answers about possible future events. It also shows managers how risky a given project might be by showing how sensitive the decision is to changes in predictions. The more sensitive to change a project is (the more NPV changes as cash flows change), the riskier it is. Of course, sensitivity analysis can become complicated very quickly, and doing all of the calculations by hand can be tricky and tedious. Fortunately, there is a good deal of sensitivity analysis software available that lets managers and accountants sit back while computers do all the work.

THE NPV COMPARISON OF TWO PROJECTS

So far we have seen how to use the NPV method to evaluate a single given project. In practice, managers very rarely look at one project or option at a time. Instead, managers need to compare several options to see which is the best or most profitable. We will now see how to use NPV to compare two or more alternatives.

TOTAL PROJECT VERSUS DIFFERENTIAL APPROACH

Objective 3
Calculate the NPV difference between two projects using both the total project and differential approaches.

total project approach A method for comparing alternatives that computes the total impact on cash flows for each alternative and then converts these total cash flows to their present values.

differential approach A method for comparing alternatives that computes the differences in cash flows between alternatives and then converts these differences in cash flows to their present values.

Two common methods for comparing alternatives are (1) the total project approach and (2) the differential approach.

The **total project approach** computes the total impact on cash flows for each alternative and then converts these total cash flows to their present values. It is the most popular approach and can be used for any number of alternatives. The alternative with the largest NPV of total cash flows is best.

The **differential approach** computes the differences in cash flows between alternatives and then converts these differences to their present values. This method cannot be used to compare more than two alternatives. Often the two alternatives being compared are (1) take on a project and (2) do nothing.

Let's compare the differential and total project approaches. Suppose a company owns a packaging machine that it purchased three years ago for $56,000. The machine has a remaining useful life of five years but will require a major overhaul at the end of two more years at a cost of $10,000. Its disposal value now is $20,000. Its predicted disposal value in five years is $8,000, assuming that the $10,000 major overhaul will be done on schedule. The predicted cash-operating costs of this machine are $40,000 annually. A sales representative has offered a substitute machine for $51,000, or for $31,000 plus the old machine. The new machine will reduce annual cash-operating costs by $10,000, will not require any overhauls, will have a useful life of five years, and will have a disposal value of $3,000. If the minimum desired rate of return is 14%, what should the company do to minimize long-run costs? (Try to solve this problem yourself before examining the solution that follows.)

Regardless of the approach used, perhaps the hardest part of making capital-budgeting decisions is predicting the relevant cash flows. Seeing which events will cause money to flow either in or out can be very tricky, especially when there are many sources of cash flows. However, you cannot compare alternatives if you do not know their costs, so the first step for either the total project or differential approach is to arrange the relevant cash flows by project. Exhibit 11-2 shows how the cash flows for each alternative are sketched. The next step depends on the approach used.

Total Project Approach: Determine the net present value of the cash flows for each individual project. Choose the project with the largest positive net present value (i.e., the largest benefit) or smallest negative net present value (i.e., the smallest cost).

Differential Approach: Compute the differential cash flows. In other words, subtract the cash flows for project B from the cash flows for project A for each year. Remember that cash inflows are positive numbers, while cash outflows are negative. Next, calculate the present value of the differential cash flows. If this present value is positive, choose project A; if it is negative, choose project B.

Exhibit 11-2 illustrates both the total project approach and the differential approach. Note that both methods produce the same answer. As a result, these methods can be used interchangeably, as long as there are only two alternatives under consideration. Because our example had only two alternatives, we could use either method. If our example had more than two alternatives, our only choice would be to use the total project approach.

Exhibit 11-2
Total Project versus Differential Approach to Net Present Value

	Present Value Discount Factor, at 14%	Total Present Value	Sketch of After-Tax Cash Flows at End of Year					
			0	1	2	3	4	5
I. Total Project Approach								
A. Replace								
Recurring cash operating costs, using an annuity table*	3.4331	$ (102,993)		($30,000)	($30,000)	($30,000)	($30,000)	($30,000)
Disposal value, end of year 5	.5194	1,558						$3,000
Initial required investment	1.0000	(31,000)	($31,000)					
Present value of net cash outflows		$ (132,435)						
B. Keep								
Recurring cash operating costs, using an annuity table*	3.4331	$ (137,324)		($40,000)	($40,000)	($40,000)	($40,000)	($40,000)
Overhaul, end of year 2	.7695	(7,695)			$(10,000)			
Disposal value, end of year 5	.5194	4,155						$8,000
Present value of net cash outflows		$ (140,864)						
Difference in favor of replacement		$ 8,429						
II. Differential Approach								
A – B. Analysis confined to differences								
Recurring cash operating savings, using an annuity table*	3.4331	$ 34,331		$10,000	$10,000	$10,000	$10,000	$10,000
Overhaul avoided, end of year 2	.7695	7,695			$10,000			
Difference in disposal values, end of year 5	.5194	(2,597)						$(5,000)
Incremental initial investment	1.0000	(31,000)	($31,000)					
Net present value of replacement		$ 8,429						

*Table 2, Appendix B.

443

RELEVANT CASH FLOWS FOR NPV

Objective 4
Identify relevant cash flows for NPV analyses.

As we said earlier, predicting cash flows is the hardest part of capital budgeting. When you array the relevant cash flows, be sure to consider four types of inflows and outflows: (1) initial cash inflows and outflows at time zero, (2) investments in receivables and inventories, (3) future disposal values, and (4) operating cash flows.

Initial Cash Inflows and Outflows at Time Zero. These cash flows include both outflows for the purchases and installation of equipment and other items required by the new project, and either inflows or outflows from disposal of any items that are replaced. In Exhibit 11-2 the $20,000 received from selling the old machine was offset against the $51,000 purchase price of the new machine, resulting in a net cash outflow of $31,000. If the old machine could not be sold, any cost incurred to dismantle and discard it would have been added to the purchase price of the new machine.

Investments in Receivables and Inventories. Investments in receivables and inventories are initial cash outflows just like investments in plant and equipment. In the NPV model, the initial outlays are entered in the sketch of cash flows at time zero. However, receivables and inventories usually differ from plant and equipment at the end of the useful life of the project. Investment in plant and equipment is usually used up during the life of the project, leaving little, if any, salvage value. In contrast, the entire original investments in receivables and inventories are usually recouped when the project ends. Therefore all initial investments are typically regarded as outflows at time zero, and their terminal disposal values, if any, are regarded as inflows at the end of the project's useful life.

The example in Exhibit 11-2 required no additional investment in inventory or receivables. However, the expansion of a retail store, for example, entails an additional investment in a building and fixtures plus inventories. Such investments would be shown in the format of Exhibit 11-2 as follows:

	Sketch of Cash Flows			
End of year	0	1	2 . . . 19	20
Investment in building and fixtures	(10)			1
Investment in working capital (inventories)	(6)			6

As the table shows, the residual value of the building and fixtures might be small. However, the entire investment in inventories would ordinarily be recouped when the company terminates the venture.

The difference between the initial outlay for working capital (mostly receivables and inventories) and the present value of its recovery is the present value of the cost of using working capital in the project.

Future Disposal Values. Assets other than receivables and inventories may have relevant disposal values. The disposal value at the end of a project is an increase in the cash inflow in the year of disposal. Errors in forecasting terminal disposal values are usually not crucial because the present value is usually small.

Operating Cash Flows. The major purpose of most investments is to affect operating cash inflows and outflows. Many of these effects are difficult to measure, and three points deserve special mention.

First, using relevant-cost analysis, the only relevant cash flows are those that will differ among alternatives. Often fixed overhead will be the same under all the available alternatives. If so, it can be safely ignored. In practice, it is not easy to identify exactly which costs will differ among alternatives.

Recent surveys have shown that nearly all large companies use discounted-cash-flow (DCF) methods for their capital-budgeting decisions. This is true in most of the developed countries in the world, not just the United States. But even as DCF is becoming dominant, it is being criticized by some for leading to overly cautious investment decisions in information technology (IT). The critics maintain that the benefits of IT investments are difficult to quantify and such investments lead to unforeseen opportunities. By ignoring some of the potential benefits and opportunities, companies pass up desirable IT investments.

Recently, two ways to rectify this situation have been suggested. Both use the basic tenets of DCF analysis but add degrees of sophistication to help identify and value all the benefits of IT investments: (1) use of activity-based costing (ABC) to better define and quantify the benefits of IT investments and (2) use of options pricing models to recognize the value of future options that result from IT investments.

Using ABC to better assess the benefits of an IT investment is simply a refinement in how to measure the cash flows for a DCF model. Scott Gamster of Grant Thornton's Performance Management Practice suggests that capital budgeting analyses of IT investments often look primarily at the direct costs and benefits and ignore many of the savings in indirect costs. Because an ABC system focuses on indirect costs, it can help identify other cost impacts of new IT systems. The attention to activities lets managers better assess the various impacts on a new IT system. For example, an enterprise resource planning (ERP) system will transform much of the work in many of a company's activities. Examining each activity in light of the potential implementation of an ERP will help managers assess the full impact of the new system.

The other suggestion is to use options pricing theory for valuing IT investments. This is a refinement of DCF, not an alternative to it. It was applied to the decision on timing of the deployment of point-of-sale-debit services by the Yankee 24 shared electronic banking network in New England. It explicitly recognizes the future opportunities created by a current investment decision, and it uses the complete range of possible outcomes to determine a potential investment's value. It is not our purpose to describe options pricing models; we leave that to the finance textbooks. However, the essence of the models is the impact of the possible future options on the value of a current investment decision. For example, investment today may eliminate the option of making a similar investment in six months when more information is available. Or investment today may create an infrastructure that will allow additional investments in the future that would not be otherwise possible. Limiting or expanding future options by today's investment decision can certainly affect the desirability of the investment.

Criticisms of DCF models for IT investments should lead to refinements of DCF, not rejection of it. Of course, if refinements are not used, managers must use judgment regarding subjective impacts of the investment that are not measured in the DCF analysis.

Sources: Adapted from S. Gamster, "Using Activity Based Management to Justify ERP Implementations," *Journal of Cost Management*, September/October 1999, pp. 24–33; M. Benaroch and R. J. Kauffman, "A Case for Using Real Options Pricing Analysis to Evaluate Information Technology Project Investments," *Information Systems Research*, March 1999, pp. 70–76; and G. C. Arnold and P. D. Aatzopoulos, "The Theory-Practice Gap in Capital Budgeting: Evidence from the United Kingdom," *Journal of Business Finance and Accounting*, June/July 2000, pp. 603–626.

Second, as mentioned earlier, depreciation and book values should be ignored. The cost of assets is recognized by the initial outlay, not by depreciation as computed under accrual accounting.

Third, a reduction in a cash outflow is treated the same as a cash inflow. Both signify increases in value.

CASH FLOWS FOR INVESTMENTS IN TECHNOLOGY

Many capital-budgeting decisions compare undertaking a possible investment with doing nothing. One such decision is investment in a highly automated production system to replace a traditional system. Cash flows predicted for the automated system should be compared with those predicted for continuation of the present system into the future. The latter are not necessarily the cash flows currently being experienced. Why? Because the competitive environment is changing. If others invest in automated systems, failure to invest may cause a decline in sales and an uncompetitive cost structure. The future without an automated system might be a continual decline in cash flows.

Suppose a company has a $10,000 net cash inflow this year using a traditional system. Investing in an automated system will increase the net cash inflow to $12,000. Failure to invest will cause net cash inflows to fall to $8,000. The benefit from the investment is a cash inflow of $12,000 − $8,000 = $4,000, not $12,000 − $10,000 = $2,000.

SUMMARY PROBLEM FOR YOUR REVIEW

PROBLEM

Review the problem and solution shown in Exhibit 11-2, page 443. Conduct a sensitivity analysis as indicated below. Consider each requirement as independent of other requirements.

1. Compute the NPV if the minimum desired rate of return were 20%.
2. Compute the NPV if predicted cash operating costs were $35,000 instead of $30,000, using the 14% discount rate.
3. By how much may the cash operating savings fall short of the $30,000 predicted before the NPV of the project reaches zero, using the original discount rate of 14%?

SOLUTION

1. Either the total project approach or the differential approach could be used. The differential approach would show:

	Total Present Value
Recurring cash operating savings, using an annuity table (Table 2, p. B8): 2.9906 × $10,000 =	$29,906
Overhaul avoided: .6944 × $10,000 =	6,944
Difference in disposal values:	
.4019 × $5,000 =	(2,010)
Incremental initial investment	(31,000)
NPV of replacement	$ 3,840

2.		Total Present Value
	NPV value in Exhibit 11-2	$ 8,429
	Present value of additional $5,000 annual operating costs	
	3.4331 × $5,000	(17,166)
	New NPV	$(8,737)

With $5,000 less in annual savings, the new machine has a negative NPV and therefore is not desirable.

3. Le X = annual cash operating savings and find the value of X that NPV = 0. Then

$$0 = 3.4331(X) + \$7,695 - \$2,597 - \$31,000$$
$$3.4331X = \$25,902$$
$$X = \$7,545$$

(Note that the $7,695, $2,597, and $31,000 are at the bottom of Exhibit 11-2.)

If the annual savings fall from $10,000 to $7,545, a decrease of $2,455 or almost 25%, the NPV will hit zero.

An alternative way to obtain the same answer would be to divide the NPV of $8,429 (see bottom of Exhibit 11-2) by 3.4331, obtaining $2,455, the amount of the annual difference in savings that will eliminate the $8,429 of NPV.

INCOME TAXES AND CAPITAL BUDGETING

We must consider another type of cash flow when making capital-budgeting decisions: income taxes. Income taxes paid by companies are cash outflows. Their basic role in capital budgeting does not differ from that of any other cash outflow. However taxes tend to narrow the cash differences between projects. For example, if the cash savings from operations of one project over another were $1 million, a 40% tax rate would shrink the savings to $600,000. Why? Because $400,000 (40% × $1 million) of the savings would have to be paid in taxes.

Corporations in the United States must pay both federal income taxes and state income taxes. Federal taxes are based on income, with tax rates rising as income rises. The current federal tax rate on ordinary corporate taxable income below $50,000 is 15%. Rates then increase until companies with taxable income over $335,000 pay between 34% and 38% on additional income. State tax rates vary widely from state to state. Therefore, the total tax rate a company has to pay, federal rates plus state rates, also varies widely.

In capital budgeting, the relevant tax rate is the **marginal income tax rate,** that is, the tax rate paid on additional amounts of pretax income. Suppose a corporation pays income taxes of 15% on the first $50,000 of pretax income and 30% on pretax income over $50,000. What is the company's *marginal income tax rate* when it has $75,000 of pretax income? The marginal rate is 30%, because the company will pay 30% of any additional income in taxes. In contrast, the company's *average income tax rate* is only 20% (i.e., 15% × $50,000 + 30% × $25,000 = $15,000 of taxes on $75,000 of pretax income). When we assess tax effects of capital-budgeting decisions, we will always use the marginal tax rate because that is the rate applied to the additional cash flows generated by a proposed project.

EFFECTS OF DEPRECIATION DEDUCTIONS

Organizations that pay income taxes generally keep two sets of books—one for reporting to the public and one for reporting to the tax authorities. In the United States, this practice is not illegal or immoral—in fact, it is necessary. Tax reporting must follow detailed rules designed to achieve certain social goals. These rules do not usually lead to financial statements that best measure an organization's financial results and position, so it is more informative to financial statement users if a separate set of rules is used for financial reporting. In this chapter, we are concerned with measuring cash payments for taxes. Therefore we focus on the tax reporting rules, not those for public financial reporting.

One item that often differs between tax reporting and public reporting is depreciation. Recall that depreciation spreads the cost of an asset over its useful life. Income tax laws and regulations generally permit the cost to be spread over depreciable lives that are shorter than the assets' useful lives. In addition, U.S. tax authorities allow **accelerated depreciation,** which charges a larger proportion of an asset's cost to the earlier years and less to later years. In contrast, an asset's depreciation for public reporting purposes is usually the same each year, called straight-line depreciation. For example, a $10,000 asset depreciated over a 5-year useful life would result in *straight-line depreciation* of $10,000 ÷ 5 = $2,000 each year but *accelerated depreciation* of more than $2,000 per year in the early years and less than $2,000 in the later years.

Exhibit 11-3 shows the interrelationship of income before taxes, income taxes, and depreciation for Martin's Printing. Assume that the company has a single fixed asset, a

Objective 5
Compute the after-tax net present values of projects.

marginal income tax rate
The tax rate paid on additional amounts of pretax income.

accelerated depreciation
A pattern of depreciation that charges a larger proportion of an asset's cost to the earlier years and less to later years.

Exhibit 11-3

Martin's Printing

Basic Analysis of Income Statement, Income Taxes, and Cash Flows

	Traditional Annual Income Statement	
(S)	Sales	$130,000
(E)	Less: Expenses, excluding depreciation	$ 70,000
(D)	Depreciation (straight-line)	25,000
	Total expenses	$ 95,000
	Income before taxes	$ 35,000
(T)	Income taxes @ 40%	14,000
(I)	Net income	$ 21,000
	Total after-tax effect on cash is	
	either S − E − T = $130,000 − $70,000 − $14,000 = $46,000	
	or I + D = $21,000 + $25,000 = $46,000	

	Analysis of the Same Facts for Capital Budgeting	
	Cash effects of operations:	
(S − E)	Cash inflow from operations: $130,000 − $70,000	$ 60,000
	Income tax outflow @ 40%	24,000
	After-tax inflow from operations	
	(excluding depreciation)	$ 36,000
	Cash effects of depreciation:	
(D)	Straight-line depreciation:	
	$125,000 ÷ 5 = $25,000	
	Income tax savings @ 40%	10,000
	Total after-tax effect on cash	$ 46,000

recovery period The number of years over which an asset is depreciated for tax purposes.

printing press, that it purchased for $125,000 cash. The press has a 5-year **recovery period,** which is the number of years over which an asset is depreciated for tax purposes. Using the press produces annual sales revenue of $130,000 and expenses (excluding depreciation) of $70,000. The purchase cost of the press is tax deductible in the form of yearly depreciation.

Depreciating a fixed asset such as the press creates future tax deductions. In this case, these deductions will total the full purchase price of $125,000. The present value of this deduction depends directly on its specific yearly effects on future income tax payments. Therefore the recovery period, the depreciation method selected, the tax rates, and the discount rate all affect the present value.

Exhibit 11-4 analyzes the Martin's Printing data for capital budgeting, assuming that the company uses straight-line depreciation for tax purposes. The net present value is $40,821 for the investment in this asset.

The $125,000 investment really buys two streams of cash: (1) net inflows from operations plus (2) savings of income tax outflows (which have the same effect in capital budgeting as do additions to cash inflows) because the company can deduct depreciation in computing taxable income. The choice of depreciation method will not affect the cash inflows from operations. But different depreciation methods will affect the cash outflows for income taxes. That is, a straight-line method will produce one present value of tax savings, and an accelerated method will produce a different present value.

TAX DEDUCTIONS, CASH EFFECTS, AND TIMING

Note that the net cash effects of operations in Exhibit 11-4 are computed by multiplying the pretax amounts by one minus the tax rate, or 1 − .40 = .60. The total effect is the cash

Exhibit 11-4

Impact of Income Taxes on Capital-Budgeting Analysis

Assume: original cost of equipment, $125,000; 5-year life; zero terminal disposal value; pretax annual cash inflow from operations, $60,000; income tax rate, 40%; required after-tax rate of return, 12%. All items are in dollars except discount factors. The after-tax cash flows are from Exhibit 11-3.

	12% Discount Factors, from Appropriate Tables	Total Present Value at 12%	Sketch of After-Tax Cash Flows at End of Year					
			0	1	2	3	4	5
Cash effects of operations, excluding depreciation, $60,000 × (1 − .4)	3.6048	$129,773		36,000	36,000	36,000	36,000	36,000
Cash effects of straight-line depreciation: savings of income taxes, $25,000 × .4	3.6048	36,048		10,000	10,000	10,000	10,000	10,000
Total after-tax effect on cash		165,821						
Investment	1.0000	(125,000)	(125,000)					
Net present value of the investment		$ 40,821						

flow itself less the tax effect. Each additional $1 of sales also adds $.40 of taxes, leaving a net cash inflow of $.60. Each additional $1 of cash expense reduces taxes by $.40, leaving a net cash outflow of $.60. Thus, the after-tax effect of the $130,000 − $70,000 = $60,000 net cash inflow from operations is $130,000 × .6 − $70,000 × .6 = ($130,000 − $70,000) × .6 = $60,000 × .6 = $36,000.

In contrast, the after-tax effects of the *noncash* expenses (depreciation) are computed by multiplying the tax deduction of $25,000 by the tax rate itself, or $25,000 × .40 = $10,000. Note that this is a cash inflow because it is a decrease in the tax payment. The total cash effect of a noncash expense is only the tax-savings effect.

Throughout the illustrations in this chapter, we assume that all income tax flows occur at the same time as the related pretax cash flows. For example, we assume that both the net $60,000 pretax cash inflow and the related $24,000 tax payment occurred in year 1 and that no part of the tax payment was delayed until year 2. We also assume that the companies in question are profitable. That is, the companies will have enough taxable income from all sources to use all income tax benefits in the situations described.

Accelerated Depreciation

Governments frequently allow accelerated depreciation to encourage investments in long-lived assets. To see why accelerated depreciation is attractive to investors, reconsider the facts in Exhibit 11-4. Suppose, as is the case in some countries, that the entire initial investment can be written off immediately for income tax reporting. We see that net present value will rise from $40,821 to $54,773.

	Present Values	
	As in Exhibit 11-4	Complete Write-Off Immediately
Cash effects of operations	$129,773	$ 129,773
Cash effects of depreciation	36,048	50,000*
Total after-tax effect on cash	165,821	179,773
Investment	(125,000)	(125,000)
Net present value	$ 40,821	$ 54,773

*Assumes that the tax effect occurs simultaneously with the investment at time zero: $125,000 × .40 = $50,000.

In summary, the earlier you can take the depreciation, the greater the present value of the income tax savings. The total tax savings will be the same regardless of the depreciation method. In the example, the tax savings from the depreciation deduction is either .40 × $125,000 = $50,000 immediately or .40 × $25,000 = $10,000 per year for five years, a total of $50,000. However, the time value of money makes the immediate savings worth more than future savings. The mottoes in income tax planning are "When there is a legal choice, take the deduction sooner rather than later," and "Recognize taxable income later rather than sooner."

Managers have an obligation to stockholders to minimize and delay taxes to the extent permitted by law. For example, astute managers use accelerated depreciation instead of straight-line depreciation whenever the law permits its use. This is called tax avoidance. Careful tax planning can have large financial payoffs. In contrast, managers must not engage in tax evasion, which is illegally reducing taxes by recording fictitious deductions or failing to report income. Managers who *avoid* taxes get bonuses; those who *evade* taxes often land in jail.

Exhibit 11-5

Examples of Assets in Modified Accelerated Cost Recovery System (MACRS) Classes

3-year	Special tools for several specific industries; tractor units for over-the-road.
5-year	Automobiles; trucks; research equipment; computers; machinery and equipment in selected industries.
7-year	Office furniture; railroad tracks; machinery and equipment in a majority of industries.
10-year	Water transportation equipment; machinery and equipment in selected industries.
15-year	Most land improvements; machinery and equipment in selected industries.
20-year	Farm buildings; electricity generation and distribution equipment.
27.5-year	Residential rental property.
31.5-year	Nonresidential real property.

MODIFIED ACCELERATED COST RECOVERY SYSTEM (MACRS)

Under U.S. income tax laws, companies depreciate most assets using the Modified Accelerated Cost Recovery System (MACRS). This system specifies a recovery period and an accelerated depreciation schedule for all types of assets. Each asset is placed in one of the eight classes shown in Exhibit 11-5.

Exhibit 11-6 presents MACRS depreciation schedules for recovery periods of 3, 5, 7, and 10 years. Note that each schedule extends one year beyond the recovery period because MACRS assumes one half-year of depreciation in the first year and one half-year in the final year. Thus, a 3-year MACRS depreciation schedule has one half-year of depreciation in years 1 and 4 and a full year of depreciation in years 2 and 3. We can apply MACRS depreciation to the example in Exhibit 11-4 as follows, assuming that the printing press that was purchased is a 5-year MACRS asset.

Year	Tax Rate (1)	PV Factor @12% (2)	Depreciation (3)	Present Value of Tax Savings (1) × (2) × (3)
1	.40	0.8929	$125,000 × .2000 = $25,000	$ 8,929
2	.40	0.7972	125,000 × .3200 = 40,000	12,755
3	.40	0.7118	125,000 × .1920 = 24,000	6,833
4	.40	0.6355	125,000 × .1152 = 14,400	3,660
5	.40	0.5674	125,000 × .1152 = 14,400	3,268
6	.40	0.5066	125,000 × .0576 = 7,200	1,459
				$36,904

How much did Martin's Printing gain by using MACRS instead of straight-line depreciation? The $36,904 present value of tax savings is $856 higher with MACRS than the $36,048 achieved with straight-line depreciation (see Exhibit 11-4 on p. 449).

PRESENT VALUE OF MACRS DEPRECIATION

In capital-budgeting decisions managers often want to know the present value of the tax savings from depreciation. Exhibit 11-7 provides present values for $1 to be depreciated over MACRS schedules for 3-, 5-, 7-, and 10-year recovery periods for a variety of interest

Exhibit 11-6
Selected MACRS Depreciation Schedules

Tax Year	3-Year Property	5-Year Property	7-Year Property	10-Year Property
1	33.33%	20.00%	14.29%	10.00%
2	44.45	32.00	24.49	18.00
3	14.81	19.20	17.49	14.40
4	7.41	11.52	12.49	11.52
5		11.52	8.93	9.22
6		5.76	8.92	7.37
7			8.93	6.55
8			4.46	6.55
9				6.56
10				6.55
11				3.28

rates. For example, consider a company with a 3-year asset and 10% minimum desired rate of return. The present value of $1 of MACRS depreciation is:

Year	Depreciation* (1)	PV Factor @10% (2)	PV of Depreciation (1) × (2)
1	$0.3333	0.9091	$0.3030
2	0.4445	0.8264	0.3673
3	0.1481	0.7513	0.1113
4	0.0741	0.6830	0.0506
Total Depreciation	1.0000		
Present Value of $1 depreciation, shown in Exhibit 11-7			$0.8322

*From the 3-Year Property column of Exhibit 11-6.

Exhibit 11-7
Present Value of $1 of MACRS Depreciation

Discount Rate	3-year	5-year	7-year	10-year
3%	0.9439	0.9215	0.9002	0.8698
4%	0.9264	0.8975	0.8704	0.8324
5%	0.9095	0.8746	0.8422	0.7975
6%	0.8931	0.8526	0.8155	0.7649
7%	0.8772	0.8315	0.7902	0.7344
8%	0.8617	0.8113	0.7661	0.7059
9%	0.8468	0.7919	0.7432	0.6792
10%	0.8322	0.7733	0.7214	0.6541
12%	0.8044	0.7381	0.6810	0.6084
14%	0.7782	0.7055	0.6441	0.5678
15%	0.7657	0.6902	0.6270	0.5492
16%	0.7535	0.6753	0.6106	0.5317
18%	0.7300	0.6473	0.5798	0.4993
20%	0.7079	0.6211	0.5517	0.4702
22%	0.6868	0.5968	0.5257	0.4439
24%	0.6669	0.5740	0.5019	0.4201
25%	0.6573	0.5631	0.4906	0.4090
26%	0.6479	0.5526	0.4798	0.3985
28%	0.6299	0.5327	0.4594	0.3787
30%	0.6128	0.5139	0.4404	0.3606
40%	0.5381	0.4352	0.3632	0.2896

You can find the present value of tax savings in three steps:

1. Find the factor from Exhibit 11-7 for the appropriate recovery period and required rate of return.
2. Multiply the factor by the tax rate to find the tax savings per dollar of investment.
3. Multiply the result by the amount of the investment to find the total tax savings.

Consider our investment of $125,000 in equipment with a 5-year MACRS recovery period. A 12% after-tax required rate of return and a 40% tax rate produce a tax savings with a present value of .7381 × .40 × $125,000 = $36,905. This differs from the $36,904 calculated earlier by a $1 rounding error.

Why do managers like accelerated depreciation for tax purposes? Consider an investment of $100,000 in an asset with a 10-year economic life and a 10-year MACRS recovery period. The asset has no salvage value at the end of ten years. The tax rate is 40%, and the required rate of return is 10%. What is the present value of the depreciation tax savings using straight-line depreciation? What is the present value of the depreciation tax savings using MACRS depreciation? Which depreciation method is most beneficial to the company?

ANSWERS

Straight-line depreciation = $10,000 per year, so tax savings is .40 × $10,000 = $4,000 per year. Thus, the present value of the tax savings is $4,000 × 6.1446 = $24,578.40.

The present value of MACRS depreciation is .6541 × .40 × $100,000 = $26,164.00. Although the total tax savings is $40,000 regardless of the depreciation method, the MACRS accelerated depreciation schedule creates a greater present value by $26,164.00 − $24,578.40 = $1,585.60.

GAINS OR LOSSES ON DISPOSAL

The disposal of equipment for cash can also affect income taxes. Suppose Martin's Printing sells its $125,000 press at the end of year 3 after taking three years of straight-line depreciation. If Martin's Printing sells it for its book value, $125,000 − (3 × $25,000) = $50,000, there is no tax effect. If Martin's Printing receives more than $50,000, there is a gain and an additional tax payment. If the company receives less than $50,000 there is a loss and a tax savings. The following table shows the effects on cash flow for sales prices of $70,000 and $20,000:

Objective 6
Explain the after-tax effect on cash of disposing of assets.

(a)	Cash proceeds of sale	$70,000	$ 20,000
	Book value: [$125,000 − 3 ($25,000)]	50,000	50,000
	Gain (loss)	$20,000	$(30,000)
	Effect on income taxes at 40%:		
(b)	Tax saving, an inflow effect: .40 × loss		$ 12,000
(c)	Tax paid, an outflow: .40 × gain	$(8,000)	
	Net cash inflow from sale:		
	(a) plus (b)		$ 32,000
	(a) minus (c)	$62,000	

SUMMARY PROBLEM FOR YOUR REVIEW

PROBLEM

Consider the investment opportunity in Exhibit 11-4, page 449: original cost of equipment, $125,000; 5-year economic life; zero terminal salvage value; pretax annual cash inflow from operations, $60,000; income tax rate, 40%; required after-tax rate of return,

12%. Assume the equipment is a 5-year MACRS asset for tax purposes. The net present value (NPV) is

	Present Values (PV)
Cash effects of operations,*	
$60,000 \times (1 - .40) \times 3.6048$	$129,773
Cash effects of depreciation on income tax savings using MACRS,	
$125,000 \times .40 \times .7381^\dagger$	36,905
Total after-tax effect on cash	$166,678
Investment	125,000
Net present value	$ 41,678

*See Exhibit 11-4, page 449, for details.
†Factor .7381 is from Exhibit 11-7, page 452

Consider each requirement independently. Compute the NPV of the investment for each.

Required

1. Suppose the equipment was expected to be sold for $20,000 cash immediately after the end of year 5.

2. Ignore the assumption in requirement 1. Return to the original data. Suppose the economic life of the equipment was 8 years, not 5 years. But, MACRS cost recovery over 5 years is still allowed for tax purposes.

SOLUTION

1. Net present value as given		$41,678
Cash proceeds of sale	$ 20,000	
Book value	0	
Gain	$ 20,000	
Income taxes at 40%	8,000	
Total after-tax effect on cash	$ 12,000	
PV of $12,000 to be received in		
5 years at 12%, $12,000 \times .5674$		6,809
NPV of investment		$48,487
2. Net present value as given		$41,678
Add the present value of $36,000 per year for 8 years		
Discount factor of 4.9676 \times $36,000 =	$178,834	
Deduct the present value of $36,000 per year for 5 years	129,773	
Increase in present value		49,061
Net present value		$90,739

The investment would be very attractive. Note especially that the recovery period for tax purposes and the economic useful life of the asset need not be equal. The tax law specifies lives (or recovery periods) for various types of depreciable assets. The economic useful life of the asset does not affect the tax life. Thus, a longer useful life for an asset increases operating cash flows without decreasing the present value of the tax savings.

CONFUSION ABOUT DEPRECIATION

The meanings of *depreciation* and *book value* are widely misunderstood. Let's review their role in decisions. Suppose a bank is considering the replacement of some old copying equipment with a book value of $30,000, an expected terminal disposal value of zero, a current disposal value of $12,000, and a remaining useful life of three years. For

Exhibit 11-8
Perspective on Book Value and Depreciation

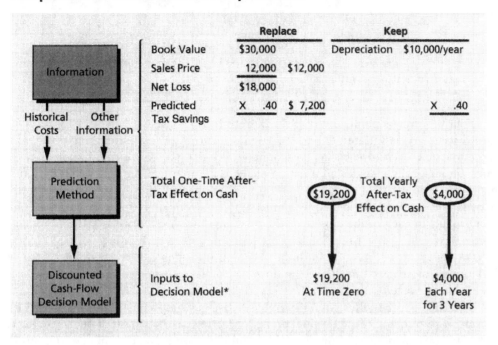

		Replace		Keep	
Book Value		$30,000		Depreciation	$10,000/year
Sales Price		12,000	$12,000		
Net Loss		$18,000			
Predicted Tax Savings		X .40	$ 7,200		X .40
Total One-Time After-Tax Effect on Cash			$19,200	Total Yearly After-Tax Effect on Cash	$4,000
Inputs to Decision Model*			$19,200 At Time Zero		$4,000 Each Year for 3 Years

(Left-hand flow chart: Information ← Historical Costs, Other Information → Prediction Method → Discounted Cash-Flow Decision Model)

*There will, of course, be other related inputs to this decision model—for example, the cost of the new equipment and the differences in future annual cash flows from operations.

simplicity, assume that the bank will take straight-line depreciation of $10,000 yearly. The tax rate is 40%.

These data should be examined in perspective, as Exhibit 11-8 indicates. In particular, note that the inputs to the decision model are the predicted income tax effects on cash. Book values and depreciation may be necessary for making predictions. By themselves, however, they are not inputs to DCF decision models.

CAPITAL BUDGETING AND INFLATION

In addition to taxes, capital-budgeting decision makers should consider the effects of inflation on their cash-flow predictions. **Inflation** is the decline in the general purchasing power of the monetary unit. For example, a dollar today will buy only half as much as it did in the early 1980s. At a 5% annual inflation rate, average prices rise more than 60% over 10 years. In countries such as Brazil and Argentina, triple-digit annual inflation rates (that is, average prices more than doubling each year) have been commonplace and have significantly affected business decisions. If significant inflation is expected over the life of a project, it should be specifically and consistently analyzed in a capital-budgeting model.

inflation The decline in the general purchasing power of the monetary unit.

Objective 7
Compute the impact of inflation on a capital-budgeting project.

WATCH FOR CONSISTENCY

The key to appropriate consideration of inflation in capital budgeting is consistent treatment of the minimum desired rate of return and the predicted cash inflows and outflows. We can achieve such consistency by including an element for inflation in both the minimum desired rate of return and in the cash-flow predictions.

Many firms base their minimum desired rate of return on market interest rates, also called **nominal rates,** that include an inflation element. For example, consider three possible components of a 12% nominal rate.

nominal rate Quoted market interest rate that includes an inflation element.

(a)	Risk-free element—the "pure" rate of interest	3%
(b)	Business-risk element—the "risk" premium that is demanded for taking larger risks	5
(a) + (b)	Often called the "real rate"	8%
(c)	Inflation element—the premium demanded because of expected deterioration of the general purchasing power of the monetary unit	4
(a) + (b) + (c)	Often called the "nominal rate"	12%

Four percentage points out of the 12% return compensate an investor for receiving future payments in inflated dollars, that is, in dollars with less purchasing power than those invested. Therefore, basing the minimum desired rate of return on quoted market rates automatically includes an inflation element in the rate. Companies that base their minimum desired rate of return on market rates should also adjust their cash-flow predictions for anticipated inflation. For example, suppose a company expects to sell 1,000 units of a product in each of the next two years. Assume this year's price is $50, and inflation causes next year's price to be $52.50. This year's predicted cash inflow is 1,000 × $50 = $50,000 and next year's inflation-adjusted cash inflow is 1,000 × $52.50 = $52,500. Inflation-adjusted cash flows are the inflows and outflows expected after adjusting prices to reflect anticipated inflation.

Consider another illustration: purchase cost of equipment, $200,000; useful life, 5 years; zero terminal salvage value; pretax operating cash savings per year, $83,333 (in 20X0 dollars); income tax rate, 40%. For simplicity, we assume ordinary straight-line depreciation of $200,000 ÷ 5 = $40,000 per year. The after-tax minimum desired rate, based on quoted market rates, is 25%. It includes an inflation factor of 10%.

Exhibit 11-9 displays correct and incorrect ways to analyze the effects of inflation. The key words are *internal consistency*. The correct analysis (1) uses a minimum desired rate that includes an element attributable to inflation and (2) explicitly adjusts the predicted operating cash flows for the effects of inflation. Note that the correct analysis favors the purchase of the equipment, but the incorrect analysis does not.

The incorrect analysis in Exhibit 11-9 is inherently inconsistent. The predicted cash inflows exclude adjustments for inflation. Instead, they are stated in 20X0 dollars. However, the discount rate includes an element attributable to inflation. Such an analytical flaw may induce an unwise refusal to purchase.

ROLE OF DEPRECIATION

The correct analysis in Exhibit 11-9 shows that the tax effects of depreciation are not adjusted for inflation. Why? Because U.S. income tax laws permit a depreciation deduction based on the original dollars invested, nothing more.

Critics of income tax laws emphasize that capital investment is discouraged by not allowing the adjusting of depreciation deductions for inflationary effects. For instance, the net present value in Exhibit 11-9 would be larger if depreciation were not confined to the $40,000 amount per year. The latter generates a $16,000 saving in 20X1 dollars, then $16,000 in 20X2 dollars, and so forth. Defenders of existing U.S. tax laws assert that capital investment is encouraged in many other ways. The most prominent example is provision for accelerated depreciation over lives that are much shorter than the economic lives of the assets.

IMPROVEMENT OF PREDICTIONS WITH FEEDBACK

The ability to forecast and cope with changing prices is a valuable management skill, especially when inflation is significant. Auditing and feedback should help evaluate management's predictive skills.

Exhibit 11-9
Inflation and Capital Budgeting

Description	At 25%		Sketch of Relevant Cash Flows (at End of Year)					
	PV Factor	Present Value	0	1	2	3	4	5
Correct Analysis (Be sure the discount rate includes an element attributable to inflation and adjust the predicted cash flows for inflationary effects.)								
Cash operating inflows:								
Pretax inflow in 20X0 dollars $83,333								
Income tax effect at 40% 33,333								
After-tax effect on cash $50,000								
	.8000	$ 44,000		$55,000*				
	.6400	38,720			$60,500			
	.5120	34,074				$66,550		
	.4096	29,985					$73,205	
	.3277	26,388						$80,526
Subtotal		$173,167						
Annual depreciation $200,000 ÷ 5 = $40,000								
Cash effect of depreciation Savings in income taxes @ 40% = $40,000 × .40 = $16,000	2.6893	43,029		$16,000†	$16,000	$16,000	$16,000	$16,000
Investment in equipment	1.0000	(200,000)	($200,000)					
Net present value		$ 16,196						
Incorrect Analysis (A common error is to include an inflation element in the discount rate as above, but not adjust the predicted cash inflows.)								
Cash operating inflows after taxes	2.6893	$134,465		$50,000	$50,000	$50,000	$50,000	$50,000
Tax effect of depreciation	2.6893	43,029		16,000	16,000	16,000	16,000	16,000
Investment in equipment	1.0000	(200,000)	($200,000)					
Net present value		$ 22,506						

*Each year is adjusted for anticipated inflation: $50,000 × 1.10. $50,000 × 1.10², $50,000 × 1.10³, and so on.

†Inflation will not affect the annual savings in income taxes from depreciation. Why? Because the income tax deduction must be based on original cost of the asset in 20X0 dollars.

The adjustment of the operating cash flows in Exhibit 11-9 uses a *general-price-level* rate of 10%. However, where feasible, managers should use *specific* rates or tailor-made predictions for price changes in materials, labor, and other items. These predictions may have different percentage changes from year to year.

SUMMARY PROBLEMS FOR YOUR REVIEW

PROBLEM

Examine the correct analysis in Exhibit 11-9, page 457. Suppose the cash-operating inflows persisted for an extra year. Compute the present value of the inflow for the sixth year. Ignore depreciation.

SOLUTION

The cash operating inflow would be $50,000 \times 1.10^6$, or $80,526 \times 1.10$, or $88,579$. Its present value would be $88,579 \times .2621$, the factor from Table 1 of Appendix B (period 6 row, 25% column), or $23,217.

PROBLEM

Examine the MACRS depreciation schedule near the middle of page 452. Assume an anticipated inflation rate of 7%. How would you change the present values of depreciation to accommodate the inflation rate?

SOLUTION

The computations on page 452 would not change. Inflation does not affect the tax effects of depreciation. U.S. income tax laws permit a deduction based on the original dollars invested, nothing more.

OTHER MODELS FOR ANALYZING LONG-RANGE DECISIONS

Objective 8
Use the payback model and the accounting rate-of-return model and compare them with the NPV model.

Although more and more companies are using DCF models to make their capital-budgeting decisions, there are still other models in use. All of these models are simpler than NPV, but they are also less useful. However, many companies still use these lesser models, which can provide some interesting supplemental information to DCF models. We will examine the payback and accounting-rate-of-return models.

PAYBACK MODEL

payback time (payback period)
The time it will take to recoup, in the form of cash inflows from operations, the initial dollars invested in a project.

Payback time or **payback period** is the time it will take to recoup, in the form of cash inflows from operations, the initial dollars invested in a project. Assume that $12,000 is spent for a machine with an estimated useful life of 8 years. Annual savings of $4,000 in cash outflows are expected from operations. Depreciation is ignored. The payback period is three years, calculated as follows.

$$\text{payback time} = \frac{\text{initial incremental amount invested}}{\text{equal annual incremental cash inflow from operations}}$$

$$P = \frac{I}{O} = \frac{\$12,000}{\$4,000} = 3 \text{ years}$$

This formula for payback time can be used only when there are equal annual cash inflows from operations. When annual cash inflows are not equal, we must add up each year's net cash flows until the initial investment is recouped. Assume the following cash flow pattern:

End of Year	0	1	2	3
Investment	($31,000)			
Cash inflows		$10,000	$20,000	$10,000

The calculation of the payback period is

Year	Initial Investment	Net Cash Inflows Each Year	Net Cash Inflows Accumulated
0	$31,000	—	—
1	—	$10,000	$10,000
2	—	20,000	30,000
2.1	—	1,000	31,000

In this case, the payback time is slightly beyond the second year. Interpolation within the third year reveals that an additional .1 years is needed to recoup the final $1,000, making the payback period 2.1 years:

$$2 \text{ years} + \left(\frac{\$1,000}{\$10,000} \times 1 \text{ year} \right) = 2.1 \text{ years}$$

A major weakness of the payback model is that it does not measure profitability, which is a primary goal of businesses. The payback model merely measures how quickly investment dollars may be recouped. However, a project with a shorter payback time is not necessarily preferable to one with a longer payback time. After all, a company can recoup its entire investment immediately by not investing.

Sometimes managers use the payback period as a rough estimate of the riskiness of a project. Suppose a company faces rapid technological changes. Cash flows beyond the first few years may be extremely uncertain. In such a situation, projects that recoup their investment quickly may be less risky than those that require a longer wait until the cash starts flowing in.

ACCOUNTING RATE-OF-RETURN MODEL

The **accounting rate-of-return (ARR) model** expresses a project's return as the increase in expected average annual operating income divided by the initial required investment.

accounting rate-of-return (ARR) = $\dfrac{\text{increase in expected average annual operating income}}{\text{initial required investment}}$

$= \dfrac{O - D}{I} = \dfrac{\begin{array}{c}\text{average annual incremental cash inflow from operations} \\ - \text{ incremental average annual depreciation}\end{array}}{\text{initial required investment}}$

accounting rate-of-return (ARR) model A non-DCF capital-budgeting model expressed as the increase in expected average annual operating income divided by the initial required investment.

Its computations dovetail most closely with conventional accounting models of calculating income and required investment, and they show the effect of an investment on an organization's financial statements.

To see how ARR works, assume the same facts as in Exhibit 11-1: Investment is $6,075, useful life is four years, estimated disposal value is zero, and expected annual cash inflow from operations is $2,000. Annual depreciation would be $6,075 ÷ 4 = $1,518.75, rounded to $1,519. Substitute these values in the accounting rate-of-return equation:

$$\text{ARR} = \frac{\$2,000 - \$1,519}{\$6,075} = 7.9\%$$

Some companies use the "average" investment (often assumed for equipment as being the average book value over the useful life) instead of original investment in the denominator. Therefore, the denominator[3] becomes $6,075 ÷ 2 = $3,037.50:

$$\text{ARR} = \frac{\$2,000 - \$1,519}{\$3,037.50} = 15.8\%$$

The accounting rate-of-return model is based on the familiar financial statements prepared under accrual accounting. Unlike the payback model, the accounting model at least has profitability as an objective. Nevertheless, it has a major drawback. The accounting model ignores the time value of money. Expected future dollars are erroneously regarded as equal to present dollars. DCF models explicitly allow for the force of interest and the timing of cash flows. In contrast, the accounting model is based on annual averages. It uses concepts of investment and income that were originally designed for the quite different purpose of accounting for periodic income and financial position.

13

JOB-COSTING SYSTEMS

13 JOB-COSTING SYSTEMS

Dell Computer Corporation's
workers assemble computers based
on individual customer specifications.
The assembly activity is a key part of
the production process.

www.prenhall.com/horngren

Learning Objectives

When you have finished studying this chapter, you should be able to

1. Distinguish between job-order costing and process costing.

2. Prepare summary journal entries for the typical transactions of a job-costing system.

3. Compute budgeted factory-overhead rates and factory overhead applied to production.

4. Use appropriate cost drivers for overhead application.

5. Identify the meaning and purpose of normalized overhead rates.

6. Use an activity-based-costing system in a job-order environment.

7. Show how job costing is used in service organizations.

8. **Understand how a job-order-costing system tracks the flow of costs to products.**

Dell Computer Corporation is the world's leading direct marketer of made-to-order computer systems. Dell does not manufacture computer components (e.g., circuit boards, hard drives), but instead assembles them into computers on a made-to-order basis.

Dell pioneered the "direct business model"—selling directly to end users instead of using a network of dealers, which avoids the dealer markup and gives Dell a competitive price advantage. Customers can design their own computer systems to specifications they desire, choosing from among a full complement of options. Before ordering, customers can receive advice and price quotes for a wide variety of computer configurations.

Once an order is taken, it is assembled in a manufacturing work cell called a mod. There is a separate mod for each of Dell's "lines of business" (Dimension Desktop PCs, OptiPlex Desktops for networked environments, Latitude and Inspiron Notebooks, PowerEdge and PowerApp network servers, and Precision workstation products). Management considers rapid response to customer orders a key to gaining and maintaining a competitive edge.

Orders at Dell can be taken over the phone or placed over the Internet. In fact, about 50% of Dell's revenues are derived from the company's Internet site, www.dell.com, with daily revenues in excess of $40 million and weekly "hits" of over 3,000,000. Customers may review, configure, and price systems within Dell's entire product line. Web sites also offer personalized system-support pages and technical services. "The Internet was tailor-made for Dell," said Michael Dell, chairman and chief executive officer. "Customers of all kinds prefer direct. They like the immediacy, convenience, savings and personal touches the Internet-direct customer experience provides." Because each computer is built to customer specifications, each order is considered a separate job for costing purposes.

Why would managers at Dell and other companies need to know product cost? Accountants compute product costs for both decision-making and financial-reporting purposes. They supply product costs to managers for evaluating pricing policy and product lines. For example, Chrysler managers need to know the cost of each kind of auto being produced to set prices, to determine marketing and production strategies for various models, and to evaluate production operations. At the same time, product costs appear as cost of goods sold in income statements and as finished-goods inventory values in balance sheets. Although it would be possible to have two product-costing systems, one for management decision making and one for financial reporting, seldom do the benefits of using two completely separate systems exceed the costs. Therefore, both decision-making and financial-reporting needs influence the design of product-costing systems.

In this chapter, we focus on one type of product-costing system—the job-order-costing system. We look at the elements of such systems and how they track the flow of costs. This system focuses on costs involved in the production of goods and services (i.e., on the production phase of the value chain). Costs of activities in the other phases of the value chain (R&D, design, distribution, marketing, and customer service) are period costs, not product costs, and they are expensed immediately and excluded from the costs of product for inventory valuation and other external reporting purposes. Because this chapter draws heavily on terminology and concepts explained in Chapters 4 and 12, you might want to review those chapters before reading further.

DISTINCTION BETWEEN JOB COSTING AND PROCESS COSTING

Objective 1
Distinguish between job-order costing and process costing.

job-order costing (job costing) The method of allocating costs to products that are readily identified by individual units or batches, each of which requires varying degrees of attention and skill.

process costing The method of allocating costs to products by averaging costs over large numbers of nearly identical products.

The two most common systems of product costing are job-order costing and process costing. **Job-order costing** (or simply **job costing**) allocates costs to products that are readily identified by individual units or batches, each of which requires varying degrees of attention and skill. Industries that commonly use job-order methods include construction, printing, aircraft, furniture, special-purpose machinery, and any manufacture of tailor-made or unique goods.

Process costing averages costs over large numbers of nearly identical products. It is most often found in such industries as chemicals, oil, plastics, rubber, lumber, food processing, glass, mining, cement, and meatpacking. These industries involve mass production of like units, that usually pass in continuous fashion through a series of uniform production steps called operations or processes.

The distinction between the job-cost and the process-cost methods centers largely on how product costing is accomplished. Job costing applies costs to specific jobs, which may consist of either a single physical unit (such as a custom sofa) or a few like units (such as a dozen tables) in a distinct batch or job lot. In contrast, process costing deals with great masses of like units and broad averages of unit costs.

The most important point is that product costing is an averaging process. The unit cost used for inventory purposes is the result of taking some accumulated cost (e.g., the sum of production-related activity costs) of production and dividing it by some measure of production. The basic distinction between job-order costing and process costing is the breadth of the denominator: In job-order costing, the denominator is small (e.g., one painting, 100 advertising circulars, or one special packaging machine);

however, in process costing, the denominator is large (e.g., thousands of pounds, gallons, or board feet).

Job costing and process costing are extremes along a continuum of potential costing systems. Each company designs its own accounting system to fit its underlying production activities. Some companies use hybrid costing systems, which are blends of ideas from both job costing and process costing. Chapter 14 describes process costing.

ILLUSTRATION OF JOB COSTING

Job costing is best learned by example. But first we examine the basic records used in a job-cost system. The centerpiece of a job-costing system is the **job-cost record** (also called a **job-cost sheet** or **job order**), shown in Exhibit 13-1. All costs for a particular product,

job-cost record (job-cost sheet, job order) A document that shows all costs for a particular product, service, or batch of products.

Exhibit 13-1

Completed Job-Cost Record and Sample Source Documents

```
                Job Cost Record: _____Machining_____ Department

Date Started _____1/7/20X2_____     Job No. _____963_____
Date Completed _____1/14/20X2_____       Units Completed ___12___

Cost                 Date      Ref.   Quantity        Amount      Summary
Direct Materials:
6" Bars              1/7/20X2  N41     24              120.00
Casings              1/9/20X2  K56     12              340.00      460.00
Direct Labor:
Drill                1/8/20X2  7Z4     7.0             105.00*
                     1/9/20X2  7Z5     5.5             82.50
Grind                1/13/20X2 9Z2     4.0             80.00       267.50
Factory Overhead:
Applied              1/14/20X2         9.0 Mach. Hrs.  180.00      180.00

Total Cost                                                        907.50

Unit Cost                                                         75.625
```

```
Direct Materials Requisition: No. _N41_
Job No. _____   Date _1/7/20X2_
Department _____Machining_____

| Descript | Quantity | Unit Cost | Amount |
| 6" Bars  | 24       | 5.00      | 120.00 |

Authorization ____J. Hays____
```

```
Time Ticket: No. _____7Z4_____
Employee No. _____464-89-7265_____
Department _____Machining_____
Date _____1/8/20X2_____

| Start | End   | Hours | Rate  | Amount | Job |
| 8:00  | 11:30 | 3.5   | 15.00 | 52.50  | 963 |
| 12:30 | 4:00  | 3.5   | 15.00 | 52.50  | 963 |
| 4:00  | 5:00  | 1.0   | 15.00 | 15.00  | 571 |

Totals          8.0           120.00

Supervisor ____M. Butler____
```

* Note that 7 of the 8 hours and $105 of the $120 in time ticket 7Z4 belong to job no. 963.

service, or batch of products are recorded on the job-cost record. A file of job-cost records for partially completed jobs provides supporting details for the Work-in-Process Inventory account, often simply called Work in Process (WIP). A file of completed job-cost records comprises the Finished-Goods Inventory account.

As Exhibit 13-1 shows, the job-cost record summarizes information contained on source documents such as materials requisitions and labor time tickets. **Materials requisitions** are records of materials used in particular jobs. **Labor time tickets** (or **time cards**) record the time a particular direct laborer spends on each job.

Today job-cost records and source documents are likely to be computer files, not paper records. In fact, with on-line data entry, bar coding, and optical scanning, much of the information needed for such records enters the computer without ever being written on paper. Nevertheless, whether records are on paper or in computer files, the accounting system must collect and maintain the same basic information.

As each job begins, its own job-cost record is created. As units are worked on, entries are made on the job-cost record. Three classes of costs are accumulated on the job-cost record as units pass through the departments: Materials requisitions are the source of direct-material costs, time tickets provide direct-labor costs, and budgeted overhead rates (a separate rate for each overhead cost pool) are used to apply factory overhead to products. (The computation of these budgeted rates will be described later in this chapter.)

materials requisitions
Records of materials issued to particular jobs.

labor time tickets (time cards) The record of the time a particular direct laborer spends on each job.

BASIC RECORDS OF ENRIQUEZ MACHINE PARTS COMPANY

To illustrate the functioning of a job-order-costing system, we will use the records and journal entries of the Enriquez Machine Parts Company. On December 31, 20X1, the firm had the following inventories.

Direct materials (12 types)	$110,000
Work in process	—
Finished goods (unsold units from two jobs)	12,000

The following is a summary of pertinent transactions for the year 20X2:

	Machining	Assembly	Total
1. Direct materials purchased on account	—	—	$1,900,000
2. Direct materials requisitioned for manufacturing	$1,000,000	$890,000	1,890,000
3. Direct-labor costs incurred	200,000	190,000	390,000
4a. Factory overhead incurred	290,000	102,000	392,000
4b. Factory overhead applied	280,000*	95,000	375,000
5. Cost of goods completed and transferred to finished-good inventory	—	—	2,500,000
6a. Sales on account	—	—	4,000,000
6b. Cost of goods sold	—	—	2,480,000

* We explain the nature of factory overhead applied later in this chapter

Exhibit 13-2

Job-Order Costing, General Flow of Costs (Thousands)

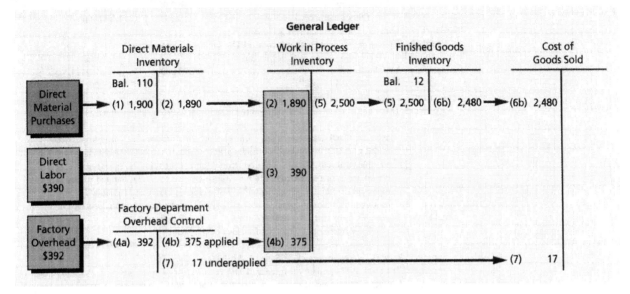

Exhibit 13-2 is an overview of the general flow of costs through the Enriquez Machine Parts Company's job-order-costing system.[1] The exhibit summarizes the effects of transactions on the key manufacturing accounts in the firm's books. As you proceed through the detailed explanation of transactions, keep checking each explanation against the overview in Exhibit 13-2.

EXPLANATION OF TRANSACTIONS

The following transaction-by-transaction summary analysis will explain how product costing is achieved. Entries are usually made as transactions occur. However, to obtain a sweeping overview, our illustration uses a summary for the entire year 20X2.

Objective 2
Prepare summary journal entries for the typical transactions of a job-costing system.

1. Transaction: Direct materials purchased, $1,900,000.
    Analysis: The asset Direct-Materials Inventory is increased The liability
       Accounts Payable is increased
    Journal Entry: Direct-Materials Inventory 1,900,000
          Accounts Payable 1,900,000

---

[1] *Exhibit 13-2 and the following explanation of transactions assume knowledge of basic accounting procedures. We will use the T-account format for a company's accounts. Entries on the left of the "T" are debits and those on the right are credits. Asset T-accounts, such as the inventory accounts, show increases on the left (debit) side and decreases on the right (credit) side of the "T":*

Inventory	
Beginning Balance	Decreases
Increases	
Ending Balance	

Transactions affecting the accounts are recorded as journal entries. Debit (left side) entries are shown flush with the left margin, and credit (right side) entries are indented, and often an explanation is included For example, a $10,000 transfer from Direct Materials Inventory to WIP (Work in Process) Inventory would be shown as follows:

WIP Inventory 10,000
   Direct Materials Inventory 10,000
   To increase WIP Inventory and decrease Direct
   Materials Inventory by $10,000

2.   Transaction: Direct materials requisitioned, $1,890,000.
      Analysis: The asset Work in Process (WIP) Inventory is increased The asset
                Direct-Materials Inventory is decreased
      Journal Entry: WIP Inventory   1,890,000
                        Direct-Materials Inventory   1,890,000

3   Transaction: Direct-labor cost incurred, $390,000
      Analysis: The asset WIP Inventory is increased. The liability Accrued Payroll
                is increased.
      Journal Entry: WIP Inventory   390,000
                        Accrued Payroll   390,000

4a.   Transaction: Factory overhead incurred, $392,000
      Analysis: These actual costs are first charged to departmental overhead accounts, which may be
                regarded as assets until their amounts are later "cleared" or transferred to other
                accounts. Each department has detailed overhead accounts such as indirect labor,
                utilities, repairs, depreciation, insurance, and property taxes These details support a
                summary Factory Department Overhead Control account. The managers are responsi-
                ble for regulating these costs, item by item. As these costs are charged to the depart-
                ments, the other accounts affected will be assorted assets and liabilities Examples
                include cash, accounts payable, accrued payables, and accumulated depreciation.
      Journal Entry: Factory Department Overhead Control   392,000
                        Cash, Accounts Payable, and various other balance
                        sheet accounts   392,000

4b   Transaction: Factory overhead applied, $95,000 + $280,000 = $375,000
      Analysis: The asset WIP Inventory is increased The asset Factory Department
                Overhead Control is decreased (A fuller explanation occurs
                later in this chapter.)
      Journal Entry: WIP Inventory   375,000
                        Factory Department Overhead
                        Control   375,000

5.   Transaction: Cost of goods completed, $2,500,000.
      Analysis: The asset Finished Goods Inventory is increased The asset
                WIP Inventory is decreased
      Journal Entry: Finished Goods Inventory   2,500,000
                        WIP Inventory   2,500,000

6a   Transaction: Sales on account, $4,000,000.
      Analysis: The asset Accounts Receivable is increased. The
                revenue account Sales is increased
      Journal Entry: Accounts Receivable   4,000,000
                        Sales   4,000,00

6b   Transaction: Cost of goods sold, $2,480,000.
      Analysis: The expense Cost of Goods Sold is increased. The asset
                   Finished Goods Inventory is decreased.
      Journal Entry: Cost of Goods Sold   2,480,000
                        Finished Goods Inventory   2,480,000

Confirm your understanding of product costing in a job-order environment by indi-
cating the transactions that occurred for each of the following journal entries. Which
of these transactions records actual costs versus cost estimates?

    1   WIP Inventory   XXX
            Accrued Payroll   XXX
    2   WIP Inventory   XXX
            Factory Department Overhead Control   XXX
    3   Cost of Goods Sold   XXX
            Finished Goods   XXX

ANSWER

The first entry records the actual cost of direct labor that is traced to the specific order being
costed. The second entry is made when the order is completed to record the application of factory overhead. This is an estimate of the costs of indirect resources used to complete the order.
The last entry records the cost of goods sold when the order is shipped. This cost is a mix of
actual costs (direct material and direct labor) and estimated costs (applied factory overhead).

SUMMARY OF TRANSACTIONS

Review Exhibit 13-2. It summarizes the Enriquez transactions for the year, focusing on the inventory accounts. WIP Inventory receives central attention. The costs of direct material used, direct labor, and factory overhead applied to product are brought into WIP. In turn, the costs of completed goods are transferred from WIP to Finished Goods. As goods are sold, their costs become expense in the form of Cost of Goods Sold. The year-end accounting for the $17,000 of underapplied overhead is explained later.

ACCOUNTING FOR FACTORY OVERHEAD

In the Enriquez Machine Parts Company example, factory overhead of $375,000 was applied to the WIP account. This section describes how to determine the amount of applied factory overhead.

HOW FACTORY OVERHEAD IS APPLIED TO PRODUCTS

Managers need to know product costs in order to make ongoing decisions such as which products to emphasize and which to deemphasize and product pricing. Ideally, all costs, including overhead, are known when these decisions must be made. Unfortunately, actual overhead costs are not available when managers need them. For this reason, budgeted (predetermined) overhead rates are used to apply overhead to jobs as they are completed.

The size of overhead costs in many manufacturing companies is large enough to motivate companies to search for ways to convert them into direct costs. Dell Computer Corporation has increased the accuracy of its product cost information by converting some of its factory-overhead costs from indirect to direct costs. How was this done? By dedicating assembly labor and factory equipment to specific product lines. Work cells (mods) do the assembly and software loading for specific product lines. This makes it easier to trace equipment costs to products. Nevertheless, significant overhead costs remain to be allocated.

BUDGETED OVERHEAD APPLICATION RATES

The following steps summarize how to account for factory overhead:

1. Select one or more cost drivers to serve as a base for applying overhead costs. Examples include direct-labor hours, direct-labor costs, machine hours, and production setups. The cost driver should be an activity that is the common denominator for systematically relating a cost or a group of costs, such as machinery cost, set-up costs, or energy cost, with products. The cost driver(s) should be the best available measure of the cause-and-effect relationships between overhead costs and production volume.

2. Prepare a factory-overhead budget for the planning period, ordinarily a year. The two key items are (1) budgeted overhead and (2) budgeted volume of the cost driver. There will be a set of budgeted overhead costs and an associated budgeted cost-driver level for each overhead cost pool. In businesses with simple production systems, there may be just one set.

3. Compute the **budgeted factory-overhead rate**(s) by dividing the budgeted total overhead for each cost pool by the budgeted cost-driver level.

4. Obtain actual cost-driver data (such as machine hours) as jobs are produced.

5. Apply the budgeted overhead to the jobs by multiplying the budgeted rate(s) times the actual cost-driver data.

6. At the end of the year, account for any differences between the amount of overhead actually incurred and overhead applied to products.

budgeted factory-overhead rate The budgeted total overhead for each cost pool divided by the budgeted cost-driver level.

ILLUSTRATION OF OVERHEAD APPLICATION

Now that you know the steps in accounting for factory overhead in a job-costing system, we can examine how they work in a real example. Consider the Enriquez illustration again.

This manufacturing-overhead budget has been prepared for the coming year, 20X3:

	Machining	Assembly
Indirect labor	$ 75,600	$ 36,800
Supplies	8,400	2,400
Utilities	20,000	7,000
Repairs	10,000	3,000
Factory rent	10,000	6,800
Supervision	42,600	35,400
Depreciation on equipment	104,000	9,400
Insurance, property taxes, etc.	7,200	2,400
Total	$277,800	$103,200

As products are worked on, Enriquez applies the factory overhead to the jobs. A budgeted overhead rate is used, computed as follows:

$$\text{budgeted overhead application rate} = \frac{\text{total budgeted factory overhead}}{\substack{\text{total budgeted amount of cost driver} \\ \text{(such as direct-labor costs or machine hours)}}}$$

Suppose machine hours are chosen as the only cost driver in the Machining Department, and direct-labor cost is chosen in the Assembly Department. The overhead rates are as follows.

	Year 20X3	
	Machining	*Assembly*
Budgeted manufacturing overhead	$277,800	$103,200
Budgeted machine hours	69,450	
Budgeted direct-labor cost		$206,400
Budgeted overhead rate, per machine hour: $277,800 ÷ 69,450 =	$4	
Budgeted overhead rate, per direct-labor dollar: $103,200 ÷ $206,400 =		50%

Note that the overhead rates are budgeted; they are estimates. These rates are then used to apply overhead based on actual events. That is, the total overhead applied in our illustration is the result of multiplying actual machine hours or labor cost by the budgeted overhead rates:

Machining: actual machine hours of 70,000 × $4 =	$280,000
Assembly: actual direct-labor cost of $190,000 × .50 =	95,000
Total factory overhead applied	$ 375,200

The summary journal entry for the application (entry 4b) is

4b. WIP Inventory	375,000	
Factory Department Overhead Control		375,000

In 1999, Milwaukee-based Harley-Davidson, the motorcycle manufacturer, captured the number one market position from Honda for the first time in three decades. Harley-Davidson (2000 sales of $2.9 billion) is the only major U.S.-based motorcycle producer. One of the keys to the company's return to competitiveness was the adoption of a just-in-time (JIT) philosophy. It is not unusual for a company to discover that a change in an important component of operations requires a corresponding change in the company's accounting system. The main focus of the accounting system was direct labor, which not only made up a part of product cost itself, but also functioned as an all-purpose base for allocating overhead. However, direct labor was only 10% of total product cost. It certainly did not generate a majority of overhead costs. As Harley-Davidson's production process had changed, the accounting system had remained static.

The first point that became apparent with the JIT system was that detailed information on direct-labor costs was not useful to managers. It was costly to have each direct laborer record the time spent on each product or part and then enter the information from these time cards into the accounting system. For example, if each of 500 direct laborers works on 20 products per day, the system must record 10,000 entries per day, which is 200,000 entries per month. The time spent by direct laborers to record the time, by clerks to enter the data into the system, and by accountants to check the data's accuracy is enormous—and all to produce product cost information that was used for financial reporting but was useless to managers.

The JIT system forced manufacturing managers to focus on satisfying customers and minimizing non-value-added activities. Gradually, accountants began to focus on the same objectives. Accounting's customers were the managers who used the accounting information, and effort put into activities that did not help managers was deemed counterproductive (non-value-added). Therefore, eliminating the costly, time-consuming recording of detailed labor costs became a priority. Direct labor was eliminated as a direct cost, and consequently it could not be used for overhead allocation. After considering process hours, flow-through time, material value, and individual cost per unit as possible cost drivers for allocating overhead, the company selected process hours. Direct labor and overhead were combined to form conversion costs, which were applied to products on the basis of total process hours. This did not result in costs significantly different from the old system, but the new system was much simpler and less costly. Only direct material was traced directly to the product. Conversion costs were applied at completion of production based on a simple measure of process time.

Accounting systems should generate benefits greater than their costs. More sophisticated systems are not necessarily better systems. Harley-Davidson's main objective in changing its accounting system was simplification—eliminating unnecessary tasks and streamlining others. These changes resulted in a revitalized accounting system.

Sources: Adapted from W. T. Turk, "Management Accounting Revitalized: The Harley-Davidson Experience," in B. J., Brinker, ed., *Emerging Practices in Cost Management* (Boston: Warren, Gorham & Lamont, 1990), pp.155–166; K. Barron, "Hog Wild," *Forbes*, May 15, 2000.

CHOICE OF COST DRIVERS

As we have noted several times in this text, no one cost driver is right for all situations. The accountant's goal is to find the driver that best links cause and effect. In the Enriquez Machining Department, use of machines causes most overhead cost, for example, depreciation and repairs. Therefore, machine hours is the cost driver and the appropriate base for applying overhead costs. Thus, Enriquez must keep track of the machine hours used for each job, creating an added data collection cost. That is, direct-materials costs, direct-labor costs, and machine hours must be accumulated for each job.

In contrast, direct labor is the principal cost driver in the Enriquez Assembly Department because parts are assembled by hand. The workers are paid equal hourly rates. Therefore, all that is needed is to apply the 50% overhead rate to the cost of direct

Objective 4
Use appropriate cost drivers for overhead application.

labor already entered on the job-cost records. No separate job records of the labor hours have to be kept. If the hourly labor rates differ greatly for individuals performing identical tasks, the hours of labor, rather than the dollars spent for labor, might be used as a base. Otherwise, a $9-per-hour worker would cause more overhead applied than an $8-per-hour worker, even though the same time would probably be taken and the same facilities used by each employee for the same work.

Sometimes direct-labor cost is the best overhead cost driver even if wage rates vary within a department. For example, higher-skilled labor may use more costly equipment and have more indirect labor support. Moreover, many factory-overhead costs include costly labor fringe benefits such as pensions and payroll taxes. The latter are often more closely driven by direct-labor cost than by direct-labor hours.

If a department identifies more than one cost driver for overhead costs, these costs ideally should be put into as many cost pools as there are cost drivers. In practice, such a system is too costly for many organizations. Instead, these organizations select a few cost drivers (often only one) to serve as a basis for allocating overhead costs. The 80-20 rule can be used in these situations. In many cases, 80% of total overhead cost can be accounted for with just a few drivers (20% of all the drivers identified). For example, a company may identify 10 separate overhead pools with 10 different drivers. Often, approximately 80% of the total cost can be applied with only two drivers.

The selected cost drivers should be the ones that cause most of the overhead costs. For example, suppose machine hours cause 70% of the overhead costs in a particular department, number of component parts causes 20%, and five assorted cost drivers cause the other 10%. Instead of using seven cost pools allocated on the basis of the seven cost drivers, most managers would use one cost driver—machine hours—to allocate all overhead costs. Others would assign all cost to two cost pools, one allocated on the basis of machine hours and one on the basis of number of component parts.

No matter which cost drivers are chosen, the overhead rates are applied day after day throughout the year to cost the various jobs worked on by each department. All overhead is applied to all jobs worked on during the year on the appropriate basis of machine hours or direct-labor costs of each job. Suppose management predictions coincide exactly with actual amounts (an extremely unlikely situation). Then the total overhead applied to the year's jobs via these budgeted rates would be equal to the total overhead costs actually incurred.

Consider Dell Computer Corporation. As we said earlier, Dell has converted many of its overhead costs into direct costs. However, two important costs that cannot be directly traced (i.e., indirect costs) are facilities and engineering. Facilities cost includes occupancy costs such as depreciation on the factory, insurance, and taxes. These costs are allocated using the cost driver "square footage used by each line of business (assembly line)." Product and process engineering activities are part of the design phase of the company's value chain and the associated costs incurred are significant. These costs are allocated to lines of business using a "complexity" cost driver (e.g., number of distinct parts in the mother board). Server computer products, for example, require much more engineering time and effort due to the complexity of the product compared to laptops or PCs, so this would be reflected in a greater number of distinct parts in the mother board. Thus, server products receive a much greater allocation of engineering costs than laptops or PCs.

PROBLEMS OF OVERHEAD APPLICATION

Objective 5
Identify the meaning and purpose of normalized overhead rates.

NORMALIZED OVERHEAD RATES

Basically, our illustration has demonstrated the normal costing approach. Why the term *normal*? Because an annual average overhead rate is used consistently throughout the year for product costing, without altering it from day to day and from month to month.

The resultant "normal" product costs include an average or normalized chunk of overhead. As actual overhead costs are incurred by departments from month to month, they are charged to the departments. Hence, we shall label the system a **normal costing system.** The cost of the manufactured product is composed of actual direct material, actual direct labor, and normal applied overhead.

During the year and at year-end, the actual overhead amount incurred will rarely equal the amount applied. This variance between incurred and applied cost can be analyzed. The most common—and important—contributor to these variances is operating at a different level of volume than the level used as a denominator in calculating the budgeted overhead rate (for instance, using 100,000 budgeted direct-labor-hours as the denominator and then actually working only 80,000 hours). Other frequent contributory causes include poor forecasting, inefficient use of overhead items, price changes in individual overhead items, erratic behavior of individual overhead items (e.g., repairs made only during slack time), and calendar variations (e.g., 20 workdays in one month, 22 in the next).

All these peculiarities of overhead are mingled in an annual overhead pool. Thus, an annual rate is budgeted and used regardless of the month-to-month peculiarities of specific overhead costs. Such an approach is more defensible than, say, applying the actual overhead for each month. Why? Because a normal product cost is more useful for decisions, and more representative for inventory-costing purposes, than an "actual" product cost that is distorted by month-to-month fluctuations in production volume and by the erratic behavior of many overhead costs. For example, the employees of a gypsum plant using an "actual" product cost system had the privilege of buying company-made items "at cost." Employees joked about the benefits of buying "at cost" during high-volume months, when unit costs were lower because volume was higher, as shown in the following table.

normal costing system
The cost system in which overhead is applied on an average or normalized basis, in order to get representative or normal inventory valuations.

	Actual Overhead			Direct-Labor Hours	Actual Overhead Application Rate* per Direct-Labor Hour
	Variable	Fixed	Total		
Peak-volume month	$60,000	$40,000	$100,000	100,000	$1.00
Low-volume month	30,000	40,000	70,000	50,000	1.40

* Divide total overhead by direct-labor hours Note that the presence of fixed overhead causes the fluctuation in unit overhead costs from $1.00 to $1.40 The variable component is $.60 an hour in both months, but the fixed component is $.40 in the peak-volume month ($40,000 ÷ 100,000) and $.80 in the low-volume month ($40,000 ÷ 50,000).

The overall system we have just described is sometimes called an actual costing system because every effort is made to trace the actual costs, as incurred, to the physical units benefited.

DISPOSITION OF UNDERAPPLIED OR OVERAPPLIED OVERHEAD

Our Enriquez illustration contained the following data:

Transaction	
4a. Factory overhead incurred	$392,000
4b. Factory overhead applied	375,000
Underapplied factory overhead	$ 17,000

Total costs of $392,000 must eventually be charged to expense in some way. The $375,000 will become part of the Cost of Goods Sold expense when the products to which it is applied are sold. The remaining $17,000 must also become expense by some method.

When budgeted rates are used, the difference between incurred and applied overhead is typically allowed to accumulate during the year. When the amount applied to product exceeds the amount incurred by the departments, the difference is called **overapplied overhead.** When the amount applied is less than incurred, the difference is called **underapplied overhead.** At year-end, the difference ($17,000 underapplied in our illustration) is disposed of through either a write-off or through proration.

IMMEDIATE WRITE-OFF

Under the immediate write-off method, the $17,000 is regarded as a reduction in current income by adding the underapplied overhead to the cost of goods sold. The same logic is followed for overapplied overhead except that the result would be a decrease in cost of goods sold.

The theory underlying the direct write-off is that most of the goods worked on have been sold, and a more elaborate method of disposition is not worth the extra trouble. Another justification is that the extra overhead costs represented by underapplied overhead do not qualify as part of ending inventory costs because they do not represent assets. They should be written off because they largely represent inefficiency or the underutilization of available facilities in the current period.

The immediate write-off eliminates the $17,000 difference with a simple journal entry, labeled as transaction 7 in Exhibit 13-2.

```
7. Cost of Goods Sold (or a separate
      charge against revenue) ........................    17,000
         Factory Department Overhead Control .........           17,000
      To close ending underapplied overhead directly to Cost of
      Goods Sold.
```

Because of its simplicity, the immediate write-off method is most commonly used.

PRORATION AMONG INVENTORIES

Another method prorates over- or underapplied overhead among WIP, Finished Goods, and Cost of Goods Sold. To **prorate** underapplied overhead means to assign it in proportion to the sizes of the ending account balances. Theoretically, if the objective is to obtain as accurate a cost allocation as possible, all the overhead costs of the individual jobs worked on should be recomputed, using the actual, rather than the budgeted, rates. This approach is rarely feasible, so a practical attack is to prorate on the basis of the ending balances in each of three accounts (WIP, $155,000; Finished Goods, $32,000; and Cost of Goods Sold, $2,480,000).

	(1) Unadjusted Balance, End of 20X2*	(2) Proration of Underapplied Overhead	(3) Adjusted Balance, End of 20X2
WIP	$ 155,000	155/2,667 × 17,000 = $ 988	$ 155,988
Finished Goods	32,000	32/2,667 × 17,000 = 204	32,204
Cost of Goods Sold	2,480,000	2,480/2,667 × 17,000 = 15,808	2,495,808
Total	$2,667,000	$17,000	$2,684,000

* See Exhibit 13-2 for details.

The journal entry for the proration follows:

```
WIP   . . . . . . . .  . . . . . . . . . .  . .  . . . . . . .  . . . . . . . . .      988
Finished Goods   . .  . . . . . . . . . . . . .  . . . . . . . . . . . .  . . .        204
Cost of Goods Sold   . . . . . . . . . . . .  .  . . . . . .  . . . . . .   15,808
      Factory Department Overhead Control   . . .  . . . . . . . .              17,000
To prorate ending underapplied overhead among
      three accounts.
```

The amounts prorated to inventories here are not significant. In actual practice, prorating is done only when inventory valuations would be materially affected.

THE USE OF VARIABLE AND FIXED APPLICATION RATES

As we have seen, overhead application is the most troublesome aspect of product costing. The presence of fixed costs is a major reason for the costing difficulties. Most companies have made no distinction between variable- and fixed-cost behavior in the design of their accounting systems. For instance, the Machining Department at Enriquez Machine Parts Company developed the following rate:

$$\text{budgeted overhead application rate} = \frac{\text{budgeted total overhead}}{\text{budgeted machine hours}}$$

$$= \frac{\$277,800}{69,450} = \$4 \text{ per machine hour}$$

Some companies, though, do distinguish between variable overhead and fixed overhead for product costing as well as for control purposes. If the Machining Department at Enriquez had made this distinction, then rent, supervision, depreciation, and insurance would have been considered the fixed portion of the total manufacturing overhead, and two rates would have been developed:

$$\text{budgeted variable-overhead application rate} = \frac{\text{budgeted total variable overhead}}{\text{budgeted machine hours}}$$

$$= \frac{\$114,000}{69,450}$$

$$= \$1.64 \text{ per machine hour}$$

$$\text{budgeted fixed-overhead application rate} = \frac{\text{budgeted total fixed overhead}}{\text{budgeted machine hours}}$$

$$= \frac{\$163,800}{69,450}$$

$$= \$2.36 \text{ per machine hour}$$

Such rates can be used for product costing. Distinctions between variable- and fixed-overhead incurrence can also be made for control purposes.

ACTIVITY-BASED COSTING/MANAGEMENT IN A JOB-COSTING ENVIRONMENT

Regardless of the nature of the company's production system, there will always be resources that are shared among different products. The costs of these resources are part of overhead and must be accounted for in the company's cost accounting system. In many cases, the magnitude of overhead is large enough to justify investing in a costing system that provides accurate cost information. Whether this cost information is being used for inventory reporting, to cost jobs, or for cost planning and control, most often the benefits of more accurate costs exceed the costs of installing and maintaining the cost system. As we have seen, activity-based costing usually increases costing accuracy because it focuses on the cause-and-effect relationships between work performed (activities) and the consumption of resources (costs).

ILLUSTRATION OF ACTIVITY-BASED COSTING IN A JOB-ORDER ENVIRONMENT

Objective 6
Use an activity-based-costing system in a job-order environment.

We illustrate an activity-based-costing (ABC) system in a job-order environment by again considering Dell Computer Corporation. What motivated Dell to adopt activity-based costing? Company managers cite two reasons: (1) the aggressive cost reduction targets set by top management and (2) the need to understand product-line profitability. As is the case with any business, understanding profitability means understanding the cost structure of the entire business. One of the key advantages of an ABC system is its focus on understanding how work (activity) is related to the consumption of resources (costs). So, an ABC system was a logical choice for Dell. And, of course, once Dell's managers improved their understanding of the company's cost structure, cost reduction through activity-based management was much easier.

Like most companies that implement ABC, Dell began developing its ABC system by focusing on the most critical (core) processes across the value chain. These were the design and production processes. After the initial system was in place, the remaining phases of the value chain were added. Exhibit 13-3 shows the functions (or core

Exhibit 13-3

Dell Computer Corporation's Value Chain and ABC System

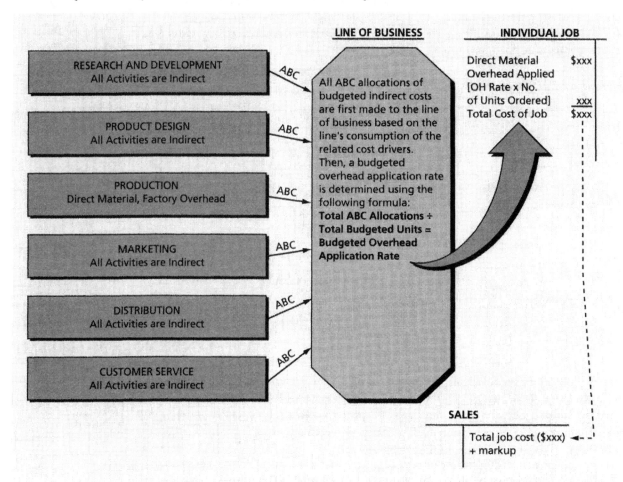

processes) that add value to the company's products and how the costs of these functions are assigned to an individual job under the current ABC system.

To understand product-line profitability, Dell managers identified key activities for the research and development, product design, production, distribution, marketing, and customer service phases. Then, they used appropriate cost drivers to allocate activity costs to the produced product lines. While each of the phases shown in Exhibit 13-3 is important, we will focus on the product design and production phases. Product design is one of Dell's most important value-adding functions. The role of design is providing a defect-free computer product that is easy to manufacture and reliable to the customer. Engineering costs (primarily salaries and CAD equipment depreciation) account for most of the design costs. These costs are indirect and thus must be allocated to product lines using a cost driver.

The production costs include direct materials and factory overhead. Factory overhead consists of six activity centers and related cost pools: receiving, preparation, assembly, testing, packaging, and shipping. Facility costs (plant depreciation, insurance, taxes) are considered part of the production function and are allocated to each activity center based on the square feet occupied by the center.

At Dell the total annual budgeted indirect cost allocated to a product line is divided by the total budgeted units produced to find a budgeted overhead rate. This rate, which is adjusted periodically to reflect changes in the budget, is used to cost individual jobs.

Dell is now breaking down the costs in each activity center into value added and non-value added. Non-value-added costs are targeted for cost reduction programs. An example of a non-value-added activity is the preparation activity in the production function.

Refer to Exhibit 13-3. One of the primary purposes of an ABC system is to increase the accuracy of product costs so that managers have a high level of confidence in cost-based decisions. Assume that Dell's managers determine prices for computers by adding a markup to the cost computed in Exhibit 13-3. For example, if the computed total job cost is $1,200, a markup sufficient to "cover" all unallocated costs and provide a reasonable profit is added. Using the table below, determine whether the percentage markup under the ABC system is higher or lower than under the 1993 system. Which system produces a higher confidence level that the price for a computer is adequate to cover all costs and provide a reasonable profit? Why?

| | ABC or Unallocated | |
Value Chain Function	1993 Costing System	ABC Costing System
Research and Development	Unallocated	ABC
Design	Unallocated	ABC
Production	Traditional Allocation	ABC
Marketing	Unallocated	ABC
Distribution	Unallocated	ABC
Customer Service	Unallocated	ABC

ANSWER

In 1993, the markup on cost was based on only the cost of production. Thus, the markup was high so that all the unallocated costs would be covered and a reasonable profit would result. Managers had a low level of confidence in this cost system The ABC system provided improved estimates of all value chain costs. The size of the markup was low, and the confidence level in the costs provided was high.

PRODUCT COSTING IN SERVICE AND NONPROFIT ORGANIZATIONS

Objective 7
Show how job costing is used in service organizations.

This chapter has concentrated on how to apply costs to manufactured products. However, the job-costing approach is used in nonmanufacturing situations too. For example, universities have research "projects," airlines have repair and overhaul "jobs," and public accountants have audit "engagements." In such situations, the focus shifts from the costs of products to the costs of services.

In nonprofit organizations, the "product" is usually not called a "job order." Instead, it may be called a program or a class of service. A "program" is an identifiable group of activities that frequently produces outputs in the form of services rather than goods. Examples include a safety program, an education program, and a family counseling program. Costs or revenues may be traced to individual hospital patients, individual social welfare cases, and individual university research projects. However, departments often work simultaneously on many programs, so the "job-order" costing challenge is to "apply" the various department costs to the various programs. Only then can managers make wiser decisions regarding the allocation of limited resources among competing programs.

In service industries—such as repairing, consulting, legal, and accounting services—each customer order is a different job with a special account or order number. Sometimes only costs are traced directly to the job, sometimes only revenue is traced, and sometimes both. For example, automobile repair shops typically have a repair order for each car worked on, with space for allocating materials and labor costs. Customers are permitted to see only a copy showing the retail prices of the materials, parts, and labor billed to their orders. If the repair manager wants cost data, a system may be designed so that the "actual" parts and labor costs of each order are traced to a duplicate copy of the repair order. That is why you often see auto mechanics "punching in" and "punching out" their starting and stopping times on "time tickets" as each new order is worked on.

BUDGETS AND CONTROL OF ENGAGEMENTS

In many service organizations and some manufacturing operations, job orders are used not only for product costing, but also for planning and control purposes. For example, a public accounting firm might have a condensed budget for 20X2 as follows:

Revenue	$10,000,000	100%
Direct labor (for professional hours charged to engagements)	2,500,000	25%
Contribution to overhead and operating income	$ 7,500,000	75%
Overhead (all other costs)	6,500,000	65%
Operating income	$ 1,000,000	10%

In this illustration:

$$\text{budgeted overhead rate} = \frac{\text{budgeted overhead}}{\text{budgeted direct labor}}$$

$$= \frac{\$6,500,000}{\$2,500,000} = 260\%$$

As each engagement is budgeted, the partner in charge of the audit predicts the expected number of necessary direct-professional hours. Direct-professional hours are those worked by partners, managers, and subordinate auditors to complete the engagement. The budgeted direct-labor cost is the pertinent hourly labor costs multiplied by the budgeted hours. Partners' time is charged to the engagement at much higher rates than subordinates' time.

How is overhead applied? Accounting firms usually use either direct-labor cost or direct-labor hours as the cost driver for overhead application. In our example, the firm uses direct-labor cost. Such a practice implies that partners require proportionately more overhead support for each of their hours charged.

The budgeted total cost of an engagement is the direct-labor cost plus applied overhead (260% of direct-labor cost in this illustration) plus any other direct costs.

The engagement partner uses a budget for a specific audit that includes detailed scope and steps. For instance, the budget for auditing cash or receivables would specify the exact work to be done, the number of hours, and the necessary hours of partner time, manager time, and subordinate time. The partner monitors progress by comparing the hours logged to date with the original budget and with the estimated hours remaining on the engagement. Obviously, if a fixed audit fee has been quoted, the profitability of an engagement depends on whether the audit can be accomplished within the budgeted time limits.

ACCURACY OF COSTS OF ENGAGEMENTS

Suppose the accounting firm has costs on an auditing engagement as follows:

Direct-professional labor	$ 50,000
Applied overhead, 260% of $50,000	130,000
Total costs excluding travel costs	$180,000
Travel costs	14,000
Total costs of engagement	$194,000

Two direct costs, professional labor and travel costs, are traced to the jobs. But only direct-professional labor is a cost driver for overhead. (Note that costs reimbursed by the client—such as travel costs—do not add to overhead costs and should not be subject to any markups in the setting of fees.)

Managers of service firms, such as auditing and consulting firms, frequently use either the budgeted or "actual" costs of engagements as guides to pricing and to allocating effort among particular services or customers. Hence, the accuracy of costs of various engagements may affect decisions.

ACTIVITY-BASED COSTING IN SERVICE AND NONPROFIT ENVIRONMENTS

Our accounting firm example described a widely used, relatively simple job-costing system. Only two direct-cost items (direct-professional labor and travel costs) are used, and only a single overhead application rate is used.

In recent years, to obtain more accurate costs, many professional service firms have refined their data processing systems and adopted activity-based costing. Computers help accumulate information that is far more detailed than was feasible a few years ago. As noted in earlier chapters, firms that use activity-based costing generally shift cost classifications from overhead to direct costs. Using our previously assumed numbers for direct labor ($50,000) and travel ($14,000), we recast the costs of our audit engagement as follows:

Direct-professional labor	$ 50,000
Direct-support labor, such as secretarial costs	10,000
Fringe benefits for all direct labor*	24,000
Telephone calls	1,000
Photocopying	2,000
Computer time	7,000
Total direct costs	94,000
Applied overhead†	103,400
Total costs excluding travel costs	197,400
Travel costs	14,000
Total costs of engagement	$211,400

* 40% assumed rate multiplied by ($50,000 + $10,000) = $24,000.
† 110% assumed rate multiplied by total direct costs of $94,000 = $103,400.

In an ABC system, costs such as direct-support labor, telephone calls, photocopying, and computer time are applied by directly measuring their usage on each engagement. The remaining costs to be allocated are assigned to cost pools based on their cause. The cost driver for other overhead is total direct costs.

The more detailed approach of activity-based costing will nearly always produce total costs that differ from the total costs in the general approach shown earlier: $211,400 compared with $194,000. Of course, any positive or negative difference is attributable to having more types of costs traced directly to the engagement.

EFFECTS OF CLASSIFICATIONS ON OVERHEAD RATES

The activity-based-costing approach also has a lower overhead application rate, assumed at 110% of total direct costs instead of the 260% of direct labor used in the first example, for two reasons. First, there are fewer overhead costs because more costs are traced directly. Second, the application base is broader including all direct costs rather than only direct labor.

Even with activity-based costing, some firms may prefer to continue to apply their overhead based on direct-labor costs rather than total direct costs. Why? Because the partners believe that overhead is dominantly affected by the amount of direct-labor costs rather than other direct costs such as telephone calls. But at least the activity-based-costing firm has made an explicit decision that direct-labor costs is the best cost driver.

Whether the overhead cost driver should be total direct costs, direct-professional labor costs or hours, or some other cost driver is a knotty problem for many firms, including most professional service firms. Ideally, activity analysis should uncover the principal cost drivers, and those cost drivers should all be used for overhead application. In practice, only one or two cost drivers are usually used.

16

Basic Accounting: Concepts, Techniques, & Conventions

BASIC ACCOUNTING: CONCEPTS, TECHNIQUES, & CONVENTIONS

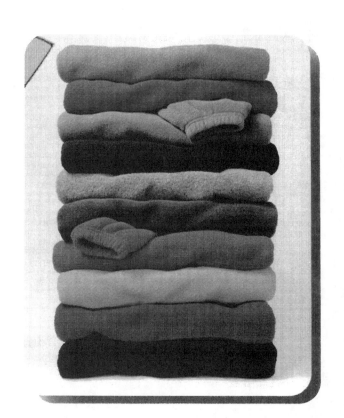

Lands' End is a mail-order retailer of clothing and other items. The company's accounting system gives financial results for each product line. For example, managers can determine the profitability of Polartec Pullovers, shown here.

www.prenhall.com/horngren

Learning Objectives

When you have finished studying this chapter, you should be able to

1. Read and interpret the basic financial statements.

2. Analyze typical business transactions using the balance sheet equation.

3. Distinguish between the accrual basis of accounting and the cash basis of accounting.

4. Relate the measurement of expenses to the expiration of assets.

5. Explain the nature of dividends and retained income.

6. Select relevant items from a set of data and assemble them into a balance sheet, an income statement, and a statement of retained income.

7. Distinguish between the reporting of corporate owner's equity and the reporting of owner's equity for partnerships and sole proprietorships.

8. Identify how the measurement conventions of recognition, matching and cost recovery, and stable monetary unit affect financial reporting.

9. **Understand how managers and investors can learn about the financial position and prospects of an organization from its financial statements.**

Chances are you or someone you know is one of the 8 million customers of Lands' End, the Wisconsin-based mail-order company. Most people who order from Lands' End are concerned about the company's prices, quality, and customer service. Lands' End managers are also concerned about these factors, and they take pride in their high ratings for customer satisfaction. Just as important to Lands' End's managers is whether the company is making a profit. How can the company's managers see how much profit Lands' End is making? The same way you can—by reading the company's financial statements.

Financial statements are generated by a company's financial accounting system. Lands' End has a financial accounting system that not only generates financial statements but also provides additional information about the company's financial success. And most important to managers, it also provides detailed information about the financial results of each product. As Don Hughes, Lands' End's Vice President of Finance, says, "We record all the activities [of Lands' End] in the financial statements. We make decisions primarily from the financial information about individual products."

Suppose you want to buy Lands' End stock instead of its clothes. Then you, too, would be interested in the company's financial statements. You would want to know the company's financial position and prospects to judge whether it is wise to invest in Lands' End stock. The company's financial statements can be a great help in making this judgment, but only if you know a bit about accounting.

Accounting is the language of business. Its special vocabulary conveys the financial story of organizations. To understand corporate annual reports, you must learn this language—the words and ideas used by accountants and other managers when discussing financial matters.[1]

This chapter explores the essence of profit-making activities and how accountants portray them in financial statements. The more technical topics are left for the chapter appendices. As you examine what accountants do, you will also learn many of the relevant concepts and conventions of accounting. Although the focus will be on profit-seeking organizations, the main ideas also apply to nonprofit organizations.

THE NEED FOR ACCOUNTING

Most people think of accountants as scorekeepers who determine how much money a business is making. In fact, all kinds of organizations—government agencies, nonprofit organizations, and others—rely on accounting to gauge their progress.

Managers, investors, and other interest groups often want the answers to two important questions about an organization: How well did the organization perform for a given period? Where does the organization stand at a given point? Accountants answer these questions with three major financial statements: an income statement, a statement of cash flows, and a balance sheet. This chapter discusses the income statement and balance sheet. The next chapter introduces the statement of cash flows.

transaction Any event that affects the financial position of an organization and requires recording.

To prepare data for the financial statements, accountants record an organization's transactions. A **transaction** is any event that affects the financial position of an organization and requires recording. Many concepts, conventions, and rules determine what events are to be recorded as accounting transactions and how their financial impact is measured. As you learn about those transactions, you will also learn about financial statements, which are summarized reports of accounting transactions.

FINANCIAL STATEMENTS

Objective 1
Read and interpret the basic financial statements.

An efficient way to learn about accounting is to study a specific illustration. Suppose King Hardware Company began business as a **corporation**—a business organized as a separate legal entity and owned by its stockholders—on March 1. An opening balance sheet follows:

corporation A business organized as a separate legal entity and owned by its stockholders.

King Hardware
Balance Sheet (Statement of Financial Position)
As of March 1, 20X1

Assets		Equities	
Cash	$100,000	Paid-in capital	$100,000

---

[1]The aim of this section of the book (Chapters 16–19) is to provide a brief overview of financial accounting For expanded coverage, see Introduction to Financial Accounting, Charles T. Horngren, Gary L Sundem, and John A Elliott (Upper Saddle River, N J : Prentice Hall, 2002)

The **balance sheet** (also called **statement of financial position** or **statement of financial condition**) is a snapshot of the financial status of an organization at an instant of time. It has two sections—assets and equities. **Assets** are economic resources that are expected to benefit future activities. **Equities** are the claims against, or interests in, the assets.

You can think of the balance sheet as an equation:

$$\text{assets} = \text{equities}$$

The equities side of this equation is often divided into two parts:

$$\text{assets} = \text{liabilities} + \text{owners' equity}$$

Liabilities are the entity's economic obligations to nonowners. **Owners' equity** is the excess of the assets over the liabilities. Because the owners of a corporation are its stockholders, the owners' equity of a corporation is called **stockholders' equity.** In turn, the stockholders' equity is composed of the ownership claim arising from funds paid-in by the owners **(paid-in capital),** plus the ownership claim arising from reinvestment of previous profits **(retained income** or **retained earnings):**

$$\text{assets} = \text{liabilities} + \text{stockholders' equity}$$
$$= \text{liabilities} + (\text{paid-in capital} + \text{retained earnings})$$

Consider a summary of King Hardware's transactions in March:

1. Initial investment by owners, $100,000 cash.
2. Acquisition of inventory for $75,000 cash.
3. Acquisition of inventory for $35,000 on open account. A purchase on open account allows the buyer to pay cash some time after the date of sale, often in 30 days. Amounts owed to vendors for purchases on open accounts are usually called **accounts payable,** liabilities of the purchasing entity.
4. Merchandise carried in inventory at a cost of $100,000 was sold on open account for $120,000. The amounts due from customers for sales on open accounts are called **accounts receivable,** assets of the selling entity.
5. Cash collections of accounts receivable, $30,000.
6. Cash payments of accounts payable, $10,000.
7. On March 1, King Hardware paid $3,000 cash for store rent for March, April, and May. Rent is $1,000 per month, payable quarterly in advance, beginning March 1.

We can analyze the foregoing transactions using the balance sheet equation, as shown in Exhibit 16-1. Note that most of these are summarized transactions. For example, all the sales did not occur at once, nor did all purchases of inventory, collections from customers, or disbursements to suppliers. Many repetitive transactions occur in practice, and accountants use specialized data collection techniques to measure the effects of the transactions on the organization.

Transaction 1, the initial investment by owners, increases assets and increases equities. That is, cash increases and so does paid-in capital—the claim arising from the owners' total initial investment in the corporation.

Transactions 2 and 3, the purchases of inventory, are exchanges of one asset for another. Neither total assets nor claims on those assets changes.

Transaction 4 is the sale of $100,000 of inventory for $120,000. Two things happened simultaneously: A new asset, Accounts Receivable, is acquired (4a) in exchange for the giving up of Inventory (4b), and the retained earnings portion of Stockholders' Equity is increased by the amount of the asset received ($120,000) and decreased by the amount of the asset given up ($100,000). The $20,000 net increase in retained earnings represents stockholders' claims arising from the profitable sale.

balance sheet (statement of financial position, statement of financial condition) A snapshot of the financial status of an organization at an instant of time.

assets Economic resources that are expected to benefit future activities.

equities The claims against, or interests in, an organization's assets.

liabilities The entity's economic obligations to nonowners.

owners' equity The excess of the assets over the liabilities.

stockholders' equity The owners' equity of a corporation.

paid-in capital The ownership claim arising from funds paid-in by the owners.

retained income (retained earnings) The ownership claim arising from the reinvestment of previous profits.

accounts payable Amounts owed to vendors for purchases on open accounts.

accounts receivable Amounts due from customers for sales on open account.

Objective 2
Analyze typical business transactions using the balance sheet equation.

Exhibit 16-1

King Hardware Co.

Analysis of Transactions (in Dollars) for March 20X1

		Assets					Equities		
Transactions	Cash	+	Accounts Receivable	+	Inventory	+	Prepaid Rent	= Liabilities + Accounts Payable	+ Paid-in Capital	+ Stockholders' Equity Retained Income
1. Initial investment	+100,000								+100,000	
2. Acquire inventory for cash	− 75,000				+ 75,000					
3. Acquire inventory for credit					+ 35,000			+35,000		
4a. Sales on credit			+120,000							+120,000 (revenue)
4b. Cost of inventory sold					−100,000					−100,000 (expense)
5. Collect from customers	+ 30,000		− 30,000							
6. Pay accounts of suppliers	− 10,000							−10,000		
7a. Pay rent in advance	− 3,000						+3,000			
7b. Recognize expiration of rental services							−1,000			− 1,000 (expense)
Balance, 3/31/X1	+ 42,000		+ 90,000		+ 10,000		+2,000	+25,000	+100,000	+ 19,000

144,000 = 144,000

Transaction 5, cash collection of accounts receivable, is another example of an event that has no impact on stockholders' equity. Collections are merely the transformation of one asset (Accounts Receivable) into another (Cash).

Transaction 6, cash payment of accounts payable, also does not affect stockholders' equity—it affects assets and liabilities only. In general, collections from customers and payments to suppliers have no direct impact on stockholders' equity.

Transaction 7, the cash disbursement for rent, is made to acquire the right to use store facilities for the next three months. On March 1, the $3,000 measured the future benefit from these services, so the asset Prepaid Rent was created (7a). Prepaid rent is an asset even though you cannot see or touch it as you can such assets as cash or inventory. Assets also include legal rights to future services such as the use of facilities.

Transaction 7b recognizes that one-third of the rental services has expired during March, so the asset is reduced and stockholders' equity is also reduced by $1,000. This means that $1,000 of the asset Prepaid Rent has been "used up" (or has flowed out of the entity) in the conduct of operations during March, so stockholders no longer have a claim on this $1,000.

The balance sheet for King Hardware at the end of March follows.

King Hardware Co.
Balance Sheet as of March 31, 20X1

Assets		Liabilities and Stockholders' Equity		
Cash	$ 42,000	Liabilities: accounts payable		$ 25,000
Accounts receivable	90,000	Stockholders' equity		
Inventory	10,000	Paid-in capital	$100,000	
Prepaid rent	2,000	Retained income	19,000	119,000
Total	$144,000	Total		$144,000

REVENUES AND EXPENSES

Let's review transaction 4 in more detail. Recall that this transaction has two phases, (a) and (b). Transaction 4a illustrates the recognition of revenue. **Revenues** are increases in ownership claims arising from the delivery of goods or services. To be recognized (i.e., formally recorded in the accounting records as revenue during the current period), revenue must ordinarily meet two tests. First, revenues must be *earned*. That is, the goods must be delivered or services must be fully rendered to customers. Second, revenues must be *realized*. That is, the seller must be reasonably sure of receiving the resources promised in exchange for the goods or services. For example, if the seller does not receive cash directly, the collectibility of the account receivable must be reasonably assured.

Transaction 4b illustrates the incurrence of an expense. **Expenses** are decreases in ownership claims arising from delivering goods or services or using up assets.

Transactions 4a and 4b also illustrate the fundamental meaning of **profits** or **earnings** or **income,** which is the excess of revenues over expenses. As the Retained Income column in Exhibit 16-1 shows, increases in revenues also increase stockholders' equity. In contrast, increases in expenses decrease stockholders' equity.

RELATIONSHIP OF BALANCE SHEET AND INCOME STATEMENT

A company's **income statement** summarizes its revenues and expenses. It measures the performance of an organization by matching its accomplishments (revenue from customers, which is usually called *sales*)[2] and its efforts (*cost of goods sold* and other

revenue Increases in ownership claims arising from the delivery of goods or services.

expenses Decreases in ownership claims arising from delivering goods or services or using up assets.

profits (earnings, income) The excess of revenues over expenses.

income statement A statement that summarizes a company's revenues and expenses. It measures the performance of an organization by matching its accomplishments (revenue from customers, which is usually called sales) and its efforts (cost of goods sold and other expenses).

---

[2] *Income statements for British companies use "turnover" instead of "sales." Other countries' financial statements use the same basic approach as U S statements, but terminology and specific measurement rules may differ.*

expenses). Recall that the balance sheet shows the organization's financial position at an instant of time. In contrast, the income statement measures performance for a *span of time,* whether it be a month, a quarter, or longer.

The King Hardware income statement for the month of March follows:

King Hardware Co.
Income Statement for the
Month Ended March 31, 20X1

Sales (revenue)		$120,000
Expenses		
Cost of goods sold	$100,000	
Rent	1,000	
Total expenses		101,000
Net income		$ 19,000

The income statement is the major link between balance sheets:

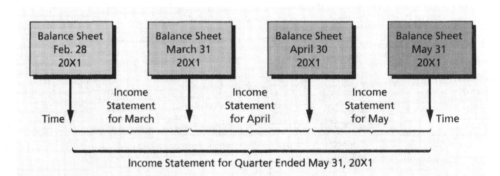

Examine the changes in retained income in Exhibit 16-1. The revenues and expenses during March explain why retained earnings changed from $0 at the beginning of the month to $19,000 at the end of the month. The income statement measures financial performance during the month, while the balance sheet measures financial position at the end of the month.

account Each item in a financial statement.

Each item in a financial statement is an **account.** Expense accounts are basically negative elements of the stockholders' equity account. Similarly, the sales (revenue) account is a positive element of stockholders' equity.

Real income statements and balance sheets use the same formats as those for King Hardware, though they usually contain more details. Consider Microsoft, the world's largest software company. A simplified version of its balance sheet follows (in millions):

Microsoft Corporation
Balance Sheet June 30, 2000

Assets:		Liabilities and Stockholders' Equity	
Cash	$23,798	Liabilities	$ 9,753
Accounts receivable	3,250	Stockholders' equity:	
Other assets	23,394	Paid-in capital	22,516
		Retained earnings	18,173
Total assets	$50,442	Total liabilities & stockholders' equity	$50,442

Microsoft's condensed income statement shows that retained earnings increased by $9,421 million because of profitable operations in 2000 (in millions):

Microsoft Corporation
Income Statement for the
Year Ended June 30, 2000

Sales	$22,956
Expenses	13,535
Net income	$ 9,421

THE ANALYTICAL POWER OF THE BALANCE SHEET EQUATION

The balance sheet equation can highlight the link between the income statement and balance sheet. Indeed, the entire accounting system is based on the simple balance sheet equation

$$\text{assets (A)} = \text{liabilities (L)} + \text{stockholders' equity (SE)} \qquad (1)$$

SE equals the original ownership claim plus the increase in ownership claim because of profitable operations. That is, SE equals the claim arising from paid-in capital plus the claim arising from retained income. Therefore,

$$A = L + \text{paid-in capital} + \text{retained income} \qquad (2)$$

Then, because retained income equals revenue minus expenses (see Exhibit 16-1)

$$A = L + \text{paid-in capital} + \text{revenue} - \text{expenses} \qquad (3)$$

Revenue and expense accounts are nothing more than subdivisions of stockholders' equity—temporary stockholders' equity accounts. They summarize the sales and expenses, so that management can easily see the reasons for the increases and decreases in stockholders' equity in the course of ordinary operations. In this way, managers can make comparisons, set standards or goals, and exercise better control.

Notice in Exhibit 16-1 that, for each transaction, the equation is *always* in balance. If the items affected are confined to one side of the equation, you will find that the total amount added is equal to the total amount subtracted on that side. If the items affected are on both sides, then equal amounts are simultaneously added or subtracted on each side.

Consider the relationship between the balance sheet and the income statement. Suppose a company has no transactions with its owners during 20X1. That is, paid-in capital remains unchanged and retained earnings increases by the entire amount of the net income. During 20X1 the company's net income is $100,000. At the beginning of the year, the company's balance sheet equation was:

Assets = Liabilities + Stockholders' Equity
$500,000 = $200,000 + $300,000

What do you know about the balance sheet equation at the end of 20X1?
   ANSWER
The one thing that we know for sure is that Stockholders' Equity at the end of 20X1 must be $300,000 + $100,000 = $400,000 because retained income increased by $100,000 and paid-in capital was unchanged. Also, assets minus liabilities must also be $400,000, compared with $300,000 at the beginning of the year. We don't know whether assets increased by $100,000, or liabilities decreased by $100,000, or there is some combination of increase in assets and decrease in liabilities equaling $100,000, but we know that the difference must increase by $100,000 to keep the balance sheet equation in balance.

The striking feature of the balance sheet equation is its universal applicability. No transaction has ever been conceived, no matter how simple or complex, that cannot be analyzed via the equation. The top technical partners in the world's largest professional accounting firms, when confronted with the most intricate transactions of multinational companies, will inevitably discuss and think about their analyses in terms of the balance sheet equation.

ACCRUAL BASIS AND CASH BASIS

Objective 3
Distinguish between the accrual basis of accounting and the cash basis of accounting.

accrual basis A process of accounting that recognizes the impact of transactions on the financial statements in the time periods when revenues and expenses occur instead of when cash is received or disbursed.

cash basis A process of accounting where revenue and expense recognition would occur when cash is received and disbursed.

Measurements of income and financial position use the accrual basis of accounting. The **accrual basis** recognizes the impact of transactions on the financial statements in the periods when revenues and expenses occur instead of when the company receives or pays cash. That is, we record revenue as it is earned, and we record expenses as they are incurred—not necessarily when cash changes hands.

Transaction 4a in Exhibit 16-1, page 640, shows an example of the accrual basis. King Hardware recognizes revenue when it makes sales on credit, not when it receives cash. Similarly, transactions 4b and 7b (for cost of goods sold and rent) show that King Hardware records expenses as it expends efforts or uses services to obtain the revenue (regardless of when it disburses cash). Therefore, measurements of noncash resources and obligations directly affect income. The accrual basis is the principal conceptual framework for relating accomplishments (revenues) with efforts (expenses).

More than 95% of all business is conducted on a credit basis; cash receipts and disbursements are not the critical transactions for the recognition of revenue and expense. Thus, the accrual basis evolved in response to a desire for a more complete, and therefore more accurate, report of the financial impact of various events.

If King Hardware used the **cash basis** of accounting instead of the accrual basis, revenue and expense recognition would occur when the company received and disbursed cash. In March, King Hardware would show $30,000 of revenue, the amount of cash collected from customers. Similarly, cost of goods sold would be the $10,000 cash payment for the purchase of inventory, and rent expense would be $3,000 (the cash disbursed for rent) rather than the $1,000 rent applicable to March. A cash measurement of net income or net loss is obviously ridiculous in this case, and it could mislead those unacquainted with the fundamentals of accounting.

Ponder the rent example. Under the cash basis, March must bear expenses for the entire quarter's rent of $3,000, merely because cash outflows occurred then. In contrast, the accrual basis measures performance more sharply by allocating the rental expenses to the operations of each of the three months that benefited from the use of the facilities. In this way, the economic performance of each month will be comparable. Most accountants maintain that it is nonsense to say that March's rent expense was $3,000 and April's and May's was zero.

The major deficiency of the cash basis of accounting is that it is incomplete. It fails to match efforts and accomplishments (expenses and revenues) in a manner that properly measures economic performance and financial position. Moreover, it omits key assets (such as accounts receivable and prepaid rent) and key liabilities (such as accounts payable) from balance sheets.

NONPROFIT ORGANIZATIONS

The examples in this chapter focus on profit-seeking organizations, but nonprofit organizations also use balance sheets and income statements. For example, hospitals and universities have income statements, although they are called "statements of revenue and expense." The "bottom line" is frequently called "excess of revenue over expense" rather than "net income."

The basic concepts of assets, liabilities, revenues, and expenses apply to all organizations, whether they be utilities, symphony orchestras, private, public, American, Asian, and so forth. However, some nonprofit organizations have been slow to adopt several ideas that are widespread in progressive companies. For example, many government organizations still use the cash basis of accounting. The lack of accrual-based financial statements has hampered the evaluation of the performance of such organizations.

ADJUSTMENTS TO THE ACCOUNTS

To measure income under the accrual basis, accountants use adjustments at the end of each reporting period. **Adjustments** record *implicit transactions,* in contrast to the *explicit transactions* that trigger nearly all day-to-day routine entries.

Earlier, we defined a *transaction* as any economic event that should be recorded by the accountant. Note that this definition is not confined to market transactions, which are actual exchanges of goods and services between the entity and another party. For instance, the losses of assets from fire or theft are also transactions even though no market exchange occurs.

Entries for explicit transactions such as credit sales, credit purchases, cash received on account, and cash disbursed on account are supported by explicit evidence, usually in the form of **source documents** (e.g., sales slips, purchase invoices, and employee time records). In contrast, companies prepare adjustments for implicit transactions, such as unpaid wages, prepaid rent, interest owed, and the like, from special schedules or memorandums that recognize events (such as the passage of time) that are temporarily ignored in day-to-day recording procedures. Adjustments refine the accountant's accuracy and provide a more complete measure of efforts, accomplishments, and financial position. They are an essential part of accrual accounting. Companies generally make adjustments when the financial statements are about to be prepared.

We classify the principal adjustments into four types:

I. Expiration of Unexpired Costs
II. Recognition (Earning) of Unearned Revenues
III. Accrual of Unrecorded Expenses
IV. Accrual of Unrecorded Revenues

adjustments Recording of implicit transactions, in contrast to the explicit transactions that trigger nearly all day-to-day routine entries.

source documents Explicit evidence of any transactions that occur in the entity's operation, for example, sales slips and purchase invoices.

ADJUSTMENT TYPE I: EXPIRATION OF UNEXPIRED COSTS

Assets frequently expire because of the passage of time. We illustrated this first type of adjustment in Exhibit 16-1 by recognizing the rent expense in transaction 7b.

Assets may be viewed as bundles of economic services awaiting future use. You can think of assets, other than cash and receivables, as prepaid or stored costs that are carried forward to future periods rather than immediately charged as expenses:

Objective 4
Relate the measurement of expenses to the expiration of assets.

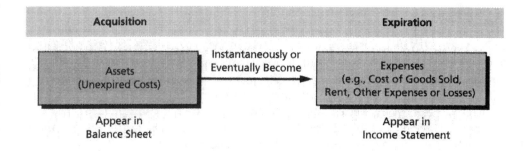

unexpired cost Any asset that ordinarily becomes an expense in future periods, for example, inventory and prepaid rent.

Expenses are used-up assets. An **unexpired cost** is any asset that ordinarily becomes an expense in future periods. Examples in our King Hardware Co. illustration are inventory and prepaid rent. Other examples are equipment and various prepaid expenses such as prepaid insurance and prepaid property taxes. When costs expire, accountants often say they are *written off* to expenses.

The analysis of the inventory and rent transactions in Exhibit 16-1 maintains this distinction of acquisition and expiration. The unexpired costs of inventory and prepaid rent are assets until they are used up, at which time they become expenses.

TIMING OF ASSET EXPIRATION

Sometimes companies acquire and use services almost instantaneously. Examples are advertising services, interest services (the cost of money, which is a service), miscellaneous supplies, and sales salaries and commissions. Conceptually, these costs should, at least momentarily, be viewed as assets on acquisition before being written off as expenses. For example, suppose an eighth transaction in Exhibit 16-1 was newspaper advertising acquired for $1,000 cash. The transaction might be analyzed in two phases:

	Assets			=	Liabilities	+	Stockholders' Equity	
Transaction	Cash	+ Other Assets	+ Unexpired Advertising	=			Paid-in Capital	+ Retained Income
8a. Acquire advertising services	−1,000		+1,000	=				
8b. Use advertising services			−1,000	=				−1,000 (expense)

However, companies often use services so quickly after acquiring them that accountants do not bother recording an asset such as Unexpired Advertising for them. Instead, they take a shortcut:

Transaction	Cash	+ Other Assets	= Liabilities	+ Paid-in Capital	+ Retained Income
8	−1,000		=		−1,000 (expense)

Making the entry in two steps instead of one is cumbersome from a practical bookkeeping viewpoint. But our purpose is not to teach you to be efficient bookkeepers. We want you to develop an orderly way of thinking about what managers do. Managers acquire goods and services, not expenses per se. These goods and services become expenses as managers use them to obtain revenue.

When does an asset expire and become an expense? Sometimes this question is hard to answer. For example, some accountants prefer to record research and development costs as assets (listed on balance sheets as "Deferred Research and Development Costs") and write them off (charge as an expense) in some systematic manner over a period of years. Why? Because they maintain that money spent for research and development creates future benefits and thus qualifies as an asset. But the regulators of financial accounting in the United States have ruled that such costs have vague future benefits that are difficult to measure reliably. Thus, companies must write off research costs as expenses immediately. In the United States, you will not find research costs listed as assets in balance sheets. Outside the United States, however, many countries, such as Japan and France, allow research and development to be recorded as an asset.

DEPRECIATION

To keep the expense-adjustment illustration simple, until now we have deliberately ignored the accounting for long-lived assets such as equipment. Equipment is really a bundle of future services that will have a limited useful life. Accountants usually (1) predict the length of the useful life, (2) predict the ultimate **residual value** (the predicted sales value of a long-lived asset at the end of its useful life), and (3) allocate the cost of the equipment to the years of its useful life in some systematic way. This process, called the recording of depreciation expense, applies to physical assets such as buildings, equipment, furniture, and fixtures owned by the entity. (Land is not subject to depreciation.)

residual value The predicted sales value of a long-lived asset at the end of its useful life.

The most popular depreciation method for financial reporting is the *straight-line method,* which depreciates an asset by the same amount each year. Suppose King Hardware Co. had acquired some store equipment for $14,000 on March 1. The predicted life of the equipment is 10 years, and the estimated residual value is $2,000:

$$\text{straight-line depreciation per year} = \frac{\text{original cost} - \text{estimated residual value}}{\text{years of useful life}}$$

$$= \frac{\$14,000 - \$2,000}{10}$$

$$= \$1,200 \text{ per year, or } \$100 \text{ per month}$$

We discuss depreciation in more detail in subsequent chapters. But the essence of the general concept of expense should be clear by now. The purchase and use of a good or service (e.g., inventories, rent, or equipment) ordinarily consists of two basic steps: (1) the acquisition of the asset (transactions 2, 3, and 7a) and (2) the expiration of the asset as an expense (transactions 4b and 7b). When an asset expires, both the value of the asset and owners' equity are decreased.

SUMMARY PROBLEM FOR YOUR REVIEW

PROBLEM

The King Hardware Co. transactions for March were analyzed in Exhibit 16-1, page 640. The balance sheet showed the following balances as of March 31, 20X1:

	Assets	Equities
Cash	$ 42,000	
Accounts receivable	90,000	
Inventory	10,000	
Prepaid rent	2,000	
Accounts payable		$ 25,000
Paid-in capital		100,000
Retained income		19,000
	$144,000	$144,000

The following is a summary of the transactions that occurred during the next month, April:

1. Cash collections of accounts receivable, $88,000.
2. Cash payments of accounts payable, $24,000.

3. Acquisitions of inventory on open account, $80,000.

4. Merchandise carried in inventory at a cost of $70,000 was sold on open account for $85,000.

5. Adjustment for recognition of rent expense for April.

Required Using the accrual basis of accounting, prepare an analysis of transactions, employing the equation approach demonstrated in Exhibit 16-1.

SOLUTION

The answer is in the top half of Exhibit 16-2. We will explain the bottom half of the exhibit in the following sections.

ADJUSTMENT TYPE II: RECOGNITION (EARNING) OF UNEARNED REVENUES

Consider the following transaction for King Hardware:

6. Some customers paid $3,000 in advance for merchandise that they ordered but that King did not expect to deliver until mid-May.

unearned revenue (deferred revenue)
Collections from customers received and recorded before they are earned

See transaction 6 in Exhibit 16-2. We call this $3,000 collected from customers and recorded before it was earned **unearned revenue** or **deferred revenue.** It is a liability because the retailer is obligated to deliver the goods ordered or to refund the money if the goods are not delivered. Some companies call this account *advances from customers* or *customer deposits,* but it is an unearned revenue account no matter what its label. That is, it is revenue collected in advance that has not yet been earned. Advance collections of rent and magazine subscriptions are other examples.

Sometimes it is easier to see how accountants analyze transactions by visualizing the financial positions of both parties to a contract. For instance, consider the rent transaction of March 1. Compare the financial impact on King Hardware Co. with the impact on the landlord who received the rental payment:

	Owner of Property (Landlord, Lessor)			King Hardware Co. (Tenant, Lessee)			
	A =	L	+ SE	A	=	L +	SE
	Cash	Unearned Rent Revenue	Rent Revenue	Cash	Prepaid Rent		Rent Expense
(a) Explicit transaction (advance payment of three months' rent)	+3,000 =	+3,000		−3,000	+3,000	=	
(b) March adjustment (for one month's rent)	=	−1,000	+1,000		−1,000	=	−1,000
(c) April adjustment (for one month's rent)	=	−1,000	+1,000		−1,000	=	−1,000
(d) May adjustment (for one month's rent)	=	−1,000	+1,000		−1,000	=	−1,000

You are already familiar with the King Hardware analysis. The $1,000 monthly entries for King Hardware are examples of the first type of adjustments, the expiration of unexpired costs.

Now study the transactions from the viewpoint of the owner of the rental property. The first transaction recognizes unearned revenue, which is a liability because the lessor is

Exhibit 16-2

King Hardware Co.

Analysis of Transactions (in Dollars) for April 20X1

| | | | **Assets** | | | | | **Equities** | | | | |
| | | | | | | | | **Liabilities** | | | **Stockholders' Equity** | |
Transaction	Cash +	Accounts Receivable +	Inventory +	Prepaid Rent	=	Accounts Payable +	Accrued Wages Payable +	Unearned Sales Revenue* +	Paid-in Capital +	Retained Income
Bal. 3/31/X1	+42,000	+90,000	+10,000	+2,000	=	+25,000			+100,000	+19,000
1.	+88,000	−88,000			=					
2.	−24,000				=	−24,000				
3.			+80,000		=	+80,000				
4a.		+85,000			=					+ 85,000 (revenue)
4b.			−70,000		=					− 70,000 (expense)
5.				−1,000	=					− 1,000 (expense)
6.	+ 3,000				=			+3,000*		
7.	− 6,000				=					− 6,000 (expense)
8.					=		+600			− 600 (expense)
9.	−18,000				=					−18,000 (dividend)
4/30/X1	+85,000	+87,000	+20,000	+1,000	=	+81,000	+600	+3,000	+100,000	+ 8,400
	193,000				=		193,000			

*Some accountants would call this account "Customer Deposits," "Advances from Customers," "Deferred Sales Revenue," or "Unrealized Sales Revenue."

obligated to deliver the rental services (or to refund the money if the services are not delivered).

As you can see from the table on p. 648, adjustments for the expiration of unexpired costs (Type I) and for the realization of unearned revenues (Type II) are really mirror images of each other. If one party to a contract has a prepaid expense, the other has unearned revenue. A similar analysis could be conducted for, say, a three-year fire insurance policy or a three-year magazine subscription. The buyer recognizes a prepaid expense (asset) and uses adjustments to spread the initial cost to expense over the life of the services. In turn, the seller, such as a magazine publisher, must initially recognize its liability, unearned subscription revenue. The *unearned* revenue is then recognized as *earned* revenue when the company delivers magazines throughout the life of the subscription.

You have now seen how two types of adjustments might occur: (1) expiration of unexpired costs and (2) recognition (earning) of unearned revenues. Next we consider the third type of adjustment: accrual of unrecorded expenses.

ADJUSTMENT TYPE III: ACCRUAL OF UNRECORDED EXPENSES

accrue To accumulate a receivable or payable during a given period even though no explicit transaction occurs.

Accrue means to accumulate a receivable or payable during a given period even though no explicit transaction occurs. Examples of accruals are the wages of employees for partial payroll periods and the interest on borrowed money before the interest payment date. The receivables or payables grow as the clock ticks or as some services are continuously acquired and used, so they are said to accrue (accumulate).

Computerized accounting systems can make weekly, daily, or even "real-time" recordings in the accounts for many accruals. However, such frequent entries are often costly and unnecessary. Usually, adjustments are made to bring each expense (and corresponding liability) account up to date just before the formal financial statements are prepared.

ACCOUNTING FOR PAYMENT OF WAGES

Consider the following two transactions relating to wages paid by King Hardware to its employees:

7. Total wages of $6,000 (which were ignored for simplicity in March) were paid on four Fridays in April. King Hardware recognizes these payments for employee services by increasing Wages Expense and decreasing Cash.

8. King Hardware incurred wages of $600 near the end of April, but it did not pay the employees until after April 30. Accordingly, the accountant increased Wages Expense and increased a liability, Accrued Wages Payable.

Most companies pay their employees at predetermined times. Here is a sample calendar for April:

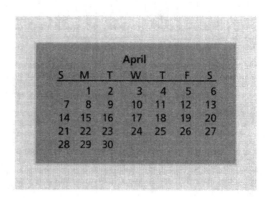

King Hardware pays its employees each Friday for services rendered during that week. For example, wages paid on April 26 are compensation for the week ended April 26. The cumulative total wages paid on the Fridays during April were $6,000. King Hardware accounts for wages expense using the shortcut procedure described earlier for goods and services that are routinely consumed in the period of their purchase. Transaction 7 in Exhibit 16-2 (and summarized below) shows King Hardware's entry for April's wages through April 26:

	Assets (A) = Liabilities (L) + Stockholders' Equity (SE)		
	Cash		Wages Expense
7. Routine entry for explicit transactions	−6,000 =		−6,000

ACCOUNTING FOR ACCRUAL OF WAGES

King Hardware's wages are $300 per day. At the end of April, in addition to the $6,000 already paid, King Hardware owes $600 for employee services rendered during the last two days of April. King Hardware will not pay the employees for these services until the next regular weekly payday, May 3, so an accrual is necessary. Periodic adjustments ensure that the financial statements adhere to accrual accounting. King Hardware accomplishes this with entry 8:

	A	=	L	+	SE
			Accrued Wages Payable		Wages Expense
8. Adjustment for implicit transaction, the accrual of unrecorded wages		=	+600		−600

Conceptually, we could divide entries 7 and 8 into the asset acquisition-asset expiration sequence, but companies seldom use this two-step sequence in practice for expenses that represent services that are purchased and used in the same accounting period.

Accrued expenses arise when payment *follows* the rendering of services; prepaid expenses arise when payment *precedes* the services. Other examples of accrued expenses include sales commissions, property taxes, income taxes, and interest on borrowed money. Interest is rent paid for the use of money, just as rent is paid for the use of buildings or automobiles. The interest accumulates (accrues) as time unfolds, regardless of when the actual cash for interest is paid.

ADJUSTMENT TYPE IV: ACCRUAL OF UNRECORDED REVENUES

The final type of adjustment, the realization of revenues that have been earned but not yet recorded as such in the accounts, is not illustrated in Exhibit 16-2. It is the mirror image of the accrual of unrecorded expenses. Suppose Security State Bank lends cash to King Hardware Co. on a 3-month promissory note for $50,000 with interest at 1% per month payable at maturity. The following tabulation shows the mirror-image effect of the adjustment for interest at the end of the first month (.01 × $50,000 = $500):

	Security State Bank (Lender)				King Hardware Co. (Borrower)			
A	=	L	+	SE	A	=	L	+	SE
Accrued Interest Receivable	=			Interest Revenue			Accrued Interest Payable		Interest Expense
+500	=			+500		=	+500		−500

Consider the four types of accrual adjustments. Prepare a 2 × 2 matrix with the first column labeled Expense and the second column labeled Revenue. Label the first row "Payment precedes recognition of expense or revenue" and the second row "Recognition of expense or revenue precedes payment." Fill in each of the four cells of the matrix with the type of accrual adjustment represented in that cell and give one example of that type of adjustment.

ANSWER

See Exhibit 16-3.

DIVIDENDS AND RETAINED INCOME

Objective 5
Explain the nature of dividends and retained income.

Exhibit 16-2 shows how revenues increase and expenses decrease the retained income portion of stockholders' equity. Transaction 9 shows another type of transaction that affects retained income—payment of dividends:

9. Cash dividends declared by the board of directors and disbursed to stockholders on April 29 equaled $18,000.

DIVIDENDS ARE NOT EXPENSES

dividends Distributions of assets to stockholders that reduce retained income.

Dividends are distributions of assets to stockholders that reduce retained income. (Cash dividends are distributions of cash rather than some other asset.) Dividends are not expenses like rent and wages. Companies do not deduct them from revenues when measuring income because dividends do not relate directly to the generation of sales or the conduct of operations.

Exhibit 16-3

Four Major Types of Accounting Adjustments Before Preparation of Financial Statements

	Expense		Revenue
Payment Precedes Recognition of Expense or Revenue	I	Expiration of unexpired costs. *Illustration:* The write-off of prepaid rent as rent expense (Exhibit 16-2, entry 5)	II Recognition (earning) of unearned revenues. *Illustration:* The mirror image of Type I, whereby the landlord recognizes rent revenue and decreases unearned rent revenue (rent collected in advance)
Recognition of Expense or Revenue Precedes Payment	III	Accrual of unrecorded expenses. *Illustration:* Wage expense for wages earned by employees but not yet paid (Exhibit 16-2, entry 8)	IV Accrual of unrecorded revenues. *Illustration:* Interest revenue earned but not yet collected by a financial institution

Profitable operations create the ability to pay dividends. Retained income increases as profits accumulate and decreases as dividends occur.

You can think of the entire right-hand side of the balance sheet equation as claims against the total assets. The liabilities are the claims of creditors. The stockholders' equity represents the claims of owners arising out of their initial investment (paid-in capital) and subsequent profitable operations (retained income). As a company grows, the retained income account can soar enormously if the company does not pay dividends. Retained income is frequently the largest stockholders' equity account. For example, General Electric had retained income of $57,749 million in 2000 compared to paid-in capital of only $669 million.

RETAINED INCOME IS NOT CASH

Although retained income is a result of profitable operations, it is not a pot of cash awaiting distribution to stockholders. Consider the following illustration:

Step 1. Assume an opening balance sheet of

Cash	$100	Paid-in capital	$100

Step 2. Purchase inventory for $50 cash. The balance sheet now reads

Cash	$ 50	Paid-in capital	$100
Inventory	50		
	$100		

Steps 1 and 2 demonstrate a fundamental point. Ownership equity (paid-in capital, here) is an undivided claim against the total assets (in the aggregate). For example, half the shareholders do not have a specific claim on cash, and the other half do not have a specific claim on inventory. Instead, all the shareholders have an undivided claim against (or, if you prefer, an undivided interest in) all the assets.

Step 3. Now sell the inventory for $80, which produces a retained income of $80 − $50 = $30:

Cash	$130	Paid-in capital	$100
		Retained income	30
		Total equities	$130

At this stage, the retained income might be related to a $30 increase in cash. But the $30 in retained income connotes only a general claim against total assets. This may be clarified by the transaction that follows.

Step 4. Purchase equipment and inventory, in the amounts of $70 and $50, respectively. Now cash is $130 − $70 − $50 = $10:

Cash	$ 10	Paid-in capital	$100
Inventory	50	Retained income	30
Equipment	70		
Total assets	$130	Total equities	$130

To what assets is the $30 in retained income related? Is it linked to Cash, to Inventory, or to Equipment? The answer is, to all three. This example helps to explain the nature of the Retained Income account. It is a claim, not a pot of gold. You cannot buy a loaf of bread with retained income. Retained income (and also paid-in capital) is a general claim against, or undivided interest in, total assets, not a specific claim against cash or against any other particular asset. Do not confuse the assets themselves with the claims against the assets.

NATURE OF DIVIDENDS

As stated earlier, dividends are distributions of assets that reduce ownership claims. The cash assets that companies disburse typically arise from profitable operations. Thus, dividends or withdrawals are often spoken of as "distributions of profits" or "distributions of retained income." Dividends are often erroneously described as being "paid out of retained income." In reality, cash dividends are distributions of assets that liquidate a portion of the ownership claim. The distribution is made possible by profitable operations.

The amount of cash dividends declared by the board of directors of a company depends on many factors, the least important of which is usually the balance in retained income. Although profitable operations are generally essential, the company's cash position and future needs for cash to pay debts or to purchase additional assets also influences its dividend policy. In addition, many companies are committed to a stable dividend policy or to a policy that ties dividends to fluctuations in net income. Under a stable policy, a company may pay dividends consistently even if it encounters a few years of little or no net income.

PREPARING FINANCIAL STATEMENTS

Objective 6
Select relevant items from a set of data and assemble them into a balance sheet, an income statement, and a statement of retained income.

You can use the balance sheet equation to prepare a company's financial statement. King Hardware's April financial statements are based on the information in Exhibit 16-2. The income statement and balance sheet, shown in Exhibits 16-4 and 16-5, are similar to those illustrated earlier. A third financial statement, the Statement of Retained Earnings, is shown in Exhibit 16-6. It is a formal presentation of the items affecting retained earnings during April. It starts with the beginning balance, adds net income for the period, and deducts cash dividends, to arrive at the ending balance. Frequently, this statement is tacked on to the bottom of an income statement. If so, the result is a combined statement of income and statement of retained income.

Exhibit 16-4

King Hardware Company
Balance Sheet as of April 30, 20X1

Assets		Liabilities and Stockholders' Equity		
Cash	$ 85,000	Liabilities		
Accounts receivable	87,000	Accounts payable	$ 81,000	
Inventory	20,000	Accrued wages payable	600	
Prepaid rent	1,000	Unearned sales revenue	3,000	$ 84,600
		Stockholders' equity		
		Paid-in capital	$100,000	
		Retained income	8,400	108,400
Total assets	$193,000	Total equities		$193,000

Exhibit 16-5

King Hardware Company

Income Statement for the Month Ended
April 30, 20X1

Sales		$85,000
Cost of goods sold		70,000
Gross profit		$15,000
Operating expenses		
Rent	$1,000	
Wages	6,600	7,600
Net income		$ 7,400

Exhibit 16-6

King Hardware Company

Statement of Retained Income for the
Month Ended April 30, 20X1

Retained income, March 31, 20X1	$19,000
Net income for April	7,400
Total	$26,400
Dividends	18,000
Retained income, April 30, 20X1	$ 8,400

Accountants call the income statement in Exhibit 16-5 a "multiple-step" statement because it includes a subtotal for gross profit. *Gross profit* (sometimes called *gross margin*) is the excess of sales over the cost of the inventory that was sold. A "single step" statement would merely list all the expenses, including cost of goods sold, and deduct the total from sales.

UNDERSTANDING CORPORATE ANNUAL REPORTS: BASIC FINANCIAL STATEMENTS

Lawrence J. Ellison, Chairman and CEO of Oracle, expounds on the "software that powers the Internet." In 2000 Oracle used its own application software, Oracle E-Business Suite, to put every aspect of its business on the Internet.

www.prenhall.com/horngren

Learning Objectives

When you have finished studying this chapter, you should be able to

1. Identify and explain the main types of assets in the balance sheet of a corporation.

2. Identify and explain the main types of liabilities in the balance sheet of a corporation.

3. Identify and explain the main elements of the stockholders' equity section of the balance sheet of a corporation.

4. Identify and explain the principal elements in the income statement of a corporation.

5. Identify and explain the elements in the statement of retained earnings.

6. Identify activities that affect cash, and classify them as operating, investing, or financing activities.

7. Interpret a statement of cash flows that uses the direct method.

8. Understand the reconciliation of net income to net cash provided by operations.

9. Explain the role of depreciation in the statement of cash flows.

10. **Understand how investors and managers use balance sheets, income statements, and cash flow statements to aid their decision making.**

Not many companies seek the permission of the CIA when naming products. Yet that's precisely what System Development Laboratories did back in 1977 when it created a new type of database. Called the "Oracle," this new relational database structure would soon prove to be the world's most popular form. For the company, now called Oracle Corporation, it was a huge financial success. Revenues for its most recent fiscal year-end topped $10 billion for software sales worldwide.

Of course, sales revenue is important to Oracle's management team. But for every sale generated, the company must either collect cash or record an accounts receivable from the customer. It must then collect the receivable so that the company has adequate cash to continue its operations. Managing accounts receivable and collecting cash is a key activity for Oracle. The faster it can collect the cash, the more use of it the company will have. But good accounts receivable management also plays other vital roles for the company. For example, at quarter-end and year-end, Oracle must report its financial results to the investment community. Recording sales revenue in the right time period is essential if the matching principle is to be followed for sales and expenses on the income statement. There is a balance sheet effect, too. The cash and receivables associated with sales revenue show up as current assets, and if not properly recorded, will distort Oracle's financial position.

Of course, sales revenue, cash, and receivables aren't the only items of interest for Oracle. The company reports information about assets such as investments and software development costs. It reports liabilities related to debt and unearned revenues on its financial statements. It lists stockholders' equity positions with their changes, and it shows the cash flows surrounding operating, investing, and financing activities.

Investors use all this information to make stock purchase decisions. Thus, Oracle's financial reports affect the price of its stock. As Oracle grew in the late 1990s, most of the reports were good, and stock purchased for $10 per share in 1996 could be sold for more than $150 in 2000. For Oracle, whose very company name means "source of wisdom," issuing timely and accurate financial statements is smart business.

This chapter focuses on what investors and other decision makers can learn from financial statements such as those of Oracle. It extends the discussion of balance sheets and income statements from the preceding chapter and introduces another major financial statement, the statement of cash flows.

Accounting is commonly misunderstood as being a precise discipline that produces exact measurements of a company's financial position and performance. As a result, many individuals regard accountants as little more than mechanical tabulators who grind out financial reports after processing an imposing amount of detail in accordance with stringent predetermined rules. Although accountants do take methodical steps with masses of data, their rules of measurement allow room for judgment. Managers and accountants who exercise this judgment have more influence on financial reporting than is commonly believed. To understand financial statements fully, you must recognize the judgments that go into their construction.

CLASSIFIED BALANCE SHEET

Objective 1
Identify and explain the main types of assets in the balance sheet of a corporation.

Exhibit 17-1 shows the 1999 and 2000 classified balance sheets for Nike, Inc., maker of athletic footwear and other leisure wear. They classify assets and equities into five main sections: current assets, noncurrent assets, current liabilities, noncurrent liabilities, and shareholders' equity. Be sure to locate each of these items in the exhibit when you read the description of the item in the following pages.

CURRENT ASSETS

current assets Cash and all other assets that are reasonably expected to be converted to cash or sold or consumed within one year or during the normal operating cycle, if longer than a year.

Current assets include cash and all other assets that are reasonably expected to be converted to cash or sold or consumed within one year or during the normal operating cycle, if longer than a year. An **operating cycle** is the time span during which a company spends cash to acquire goods and services that it uses to produce the organization's output, which in turn it sells to customers, who in turn pay for their purchases with cash. Consider a retail business. The following diagram illustrates its operating cycle (figures are hypothetical):

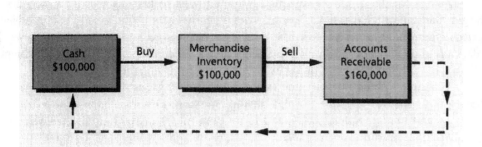

operating cycle The time span during which a company spends cash to acquire goods and services that it uses to produce the organization's output, which it in turn sells to customers, who in turn pay for their purchases with cash.

Exhibit 17-1

Nike, Inc.

Balance Sheet (in millions)

	May 31	
	1999	*2000*
ASSETS		
Current assets		
Cash and equivalents	$ 198.1	$ 254.3
Accounts receivable, less allowance for		
doubtful accounts of 73.2 and 65.4	1,540.1	1,567.2
Inventories	1,170.6	1,446.0
Prepaid expenses	219.6	215.2
Other current assets	136.5	113.7
Total current assets	3,264.9	3,596.4
Noncurrent assets		
Property, plant, and equipment		
At cost	2,001.3	2,393.8
Less: accumulated depreciation	735.5	810.4
Net property, plant, and equipment	1,265.8	1,583.4
Intangible assets and goodwill	426.6	410.9
Other assets	290.4	266.2
Total noncurrent assets	1,982.8	2,260.5
Total assets	$5,247.7	$5,856.9
LIABILITIES AND SHAREHOLDERS' EQUITY		
Current liabilities		
Notes payable	$ 419.1	$ 924.2
Accounts payable	473.6	543.8
Accrued liabilities	553.2	621.9
Current portion of long-term debt	1.0	50.1
Total current liabilities	1,446.9	2,140.0
Noncurrent liabilities		
Long-term debt	386.1	470.3
Deferred income taxes and		
other liabilities	79.8	110.3
Total noncurrent liabilities	465.9	580.6
Total liabilities	1,912.8	2,720.6
Shareholders' equity		
Redeemable preferred stock	0.3	0.3
Common stock at stated value	2.9	2.8
Capital in excess of stated value	334.1	369.0
Retained earnings	3,066.5	2,887.0
Other	(68.9)	(122.8)
Total shareholders' equity	3,334.9	3,136.3
Total liabilities and shareholders' equity	$5,247.7	$5,856.9

The box for Accounts Receivable (amounts owed to the business by customers) is larger than the other two boxes because the objective of a business is to sell goods at a price higher than acquisition cost. The total amount of profit a firm earns during a particular period depends on how much its selling prices exceed its costs of producing or purchasing the products and additional expenses incurred during the period.

Accountants sometimes assume that an operating cycle is one year. But some businesses have several operating cycles during one year. Others—such as the distillery, tobacco, and lumber industries—need more than one year to complete a single cycle. Nevertheless, accountants regard inventories in such industries as current assets. Similarly, they classify installment accounts and notes receivable as current assets, even though they may not be fully collected within one year.

As Exhibit 17-1 shows, current assets fall into several broad categories, such as cash and cash equivalents, accounts receivable, inventories, prepaid expenses, and other current assets. Cash consists of bank deposits in checking accounts plus money on hand. **Cash equivalents** are short-term investments that a company can easily convert into cash with little delay. Examples include money market funds and Treasury bills. They represent an investment of excess cash not needed immediately. The balance sheet usually shows these securities at cost or market price, whichever is lower. The market price is disclosed parenthetically if it is above cost. In 2000, Nike had $254.3 million in cash and cash equivalents.

Accounts receivable is the total amount owed to the company by its customers. Because some customers ultimately will not pay their bill, the total is reduced by an allowance or provision for doubtful accounts (i.e., possible "bad debts"). The difference represents the net amount that the company will probably collect. At the end of the 2000 fiscal year,[1] Nike had gross accounts receivable of $1,632.6 million, but after deducting $65.4 million for doubtful accounts, the company expects to collect $1,567.2 million from its accounts receivable.

Inventories consist of merchandise, finished products of manufacturers, goods in the process of being manufactured, and raw materials. Accountants state inventories at their cost or market price (defined as replacement cost), whichever is lower. Cost of manufactured products normally includes raw material cost plus the costs of converting it into a finished product (direct labor and manufacturing overhead). Nike's 2000 inventories stood at $1,446.0 million.

Prepaid expenses are advance payments to suppliers. They are usually unimportant in relation to other assets. Examples are prepayment of rent and insurance premiums for coverage over the coming operating cycle. They belong in current assets because, if they were not present, more cash would be needed to conduct current operations. In 2000, Nike shows $215.2 million of prepaid expenses, which is less than 6% of total current assets.

Other current assets are miscellaneous current assets that do not fit into the listed categories. They might include notes receivable and short-term investments that are not cash equivalents. For Nike, such assets amounted to $113.7 million in 2000.

NONCURRENT ASSETS: PROPERTY, PLANT, AND EQUIPMENT

Property, plant, and equipment are examples of **fixed assets** or **tangible assets**—physical items that a person can see and touch. Companies usually provide details about property, plant, and equipment in a footnote to the financial statements, such as the one for Nike shown in Exhibit 17-2. Footnotes are an integral part of financial statements. They contain explanations for the summary figures that appear in the statements.

Companies typically show *land* as a separate item and carry it indefinitely at its original cost.

cash equivalents Short-term investments that a company can easily convert into cash with little delay.

fixed assets (tangible assets) Physical items that a person can see and touch, such as property, plant, and equipment.

---

[1] *A fiscal year is defined as the year established for accounting purposes for the preparation of annual reports. Nike's fiscal year is June 1 through May 31*

Exhibit 17-2

Nike, Inc.

Footnote 3 to the 2000 Financial Statements

	Note 3. Property, Plant, and Equipment (millions)	
	1999	2000
Land	$ 99.6	$ 180.6
Buildings	374.2	503.4
Machinery and equipment	923.3	981.9
Leasehold improvements	273.4	279.6
Construction-in-progress	330.8	448.3
	2,001.3	2,393.8
Less: accumulated depreciation	735.5	810.4
Net property, plant, and equipment	$1,265.8	$1,583.4

They also initially record *buildings* and *machinery and equipment* at cost: the invoice amount, plus freight and installation, less cash discounts. However, buildings, machinery, and equipment gradually decline in value through depreciation (see Chapter 16, page 647). The major difficulties of measurement center on the choice of depreciation method—that is, the allocation of the original cost to the particular periods or products that benefit from the use of the assets. Remember that depreciation only means allocating the original cost of plant and equipment, not valuing them in the ordinary sense of the term. Balance sheets typically do not show replacement cost, resale value, or the price changes since acquisition. The balance sheet amount is simply the original cost less the *accumulated depreciation,* which is the sum of all depreciation taken to date on the asset.

The amount of depreciation charged as expense each year depends on three factors:

1. The depreciable amount (the difference between the total acquisition cost and the estimated residual value). The residual value is the amount a company expects to receive when selling the asset at the end of its economic life.

2. The estimate of the asset's useful life. This estimate is influenced by estimates of physical wear and tear, technological change, and economic obsolescence. Thus, the useful life is usually less than the physical life.

3. The depreciation method. There are three general methods of depreciation: straight line, accelerated, and units of production. The straight-line method allocates the same cost to each year of an asset's useful life. Accelerated methods allocate more of the cost to the early years and less to the later years.[2] The units-of-production method allocates cost based on the amount of production rather than the passage of time.

Which method is best? It depends on the firm's goals, the asset involved, and the type of financial statement being prepared. The straight-line method is most popular. More than 90% of all firms use it for at least some assets when preparing financial statements for reporting to the public. In contrast, most U.S. firms use accelerated depreciation when preparing financial statements for tax reporting to the IRS.

Suppose a business spends $42,000 to buy equipment with an estimated useful life of four years and an estimated residual value of $2,000. Using the straight-line method of depreciation, the annual depreciation expense in each of the four years would be

---

[2] *Methods of accelerated depreciation are described in Chapter 11 However, knowledge of accelerated depreciation methods is not necessary for understanding this chapter.*

Exhibit 17-3

Straight-line Depreciation

(figures assumed)

	Balances at End of Year			
	1	*2*	*3*	*4*
Plant and equipment (at original acquisition cost)	$42,000	$42,000	$42,000	$42,000
Less: accumulated depreciation (the portion of original cost that has already been charged to operations as depreciation expense)	10,000	20,000	30,000	40,000
Net book value (the portion of original cost not yet charged as expense)	$32,000	$22,000	$12,000	$ 2,000

$$\frac{\text{original cost} - \text{estimated residual value}}{\text{years of useful life}}$$

$$= \frac{(\$42,000 - \$2,000)}{4}$$

$$= \$10,000 \text{ per year}$$

Exhibit 17-3 shows how the asset would be displayed in the balance sheet. In Exhibits 17-1 and 17-2, the original cost of fixed assets on Nike's 2000 balance sheet is $2,393.8 million. There is accumulated depreciation of $810.4 million, the portion of the original cost of the asset that was previously charged as depreciation expense, so the net property, plant, and equipment at May 31, 2000 is $2,393.8 million − $810.4 million = $1,583.4 million.

Depreciation is the part of an asset that has been used up. It is gone. It is not a pool of cash set aside to replace the asset. If a company decides to accumulate specific cash to replace assets, such cash should be specifically labeled as a cash fund for replacement and expansion. Holiday Inns, Inc., has used such a fund, calling it a capital construction fund. Such funds are quite rare because most companies can earn better returns by investing any available cash in ordinary operations rather than in special funds. Typically, companies use or acquire cash for the replacement and expansion of plant assets only as specific needs arise.

Leasehold improvements are investments made by a lessee (tenant) in items such as painting, decorating, fixtures, and air-conditioning equipment that cannot be removed from the premises when a lease expires. The costs of leasehold improvements are written off in the same manner as depreciation, but their periodic write-off is called amortization.

Construction in progress is shown separately from other assets because the assets are not yet ready for use. It represents assets that will be part of buildings or machinery and equipment when completed.

We do not illustrate natural resources, such as mineral deposits, but they are typically grouped with plant assets. Companies write off their original cost in the form of depletion as they use the resources. For example, a coal mine may cost $10 million and originally contain an estimated 5 million tons. The depletion rate would be $2 per ton. If 500,000 tons were mined during the first year, depletion would be $1 million for that year. If 300,000 tons were mined the second year, depletion would be $600,000. Such depletion charges would continue until the entire $10 million has been charged as depletion expense.

Long-term investments are also noncurrent assets. They include long-term holdings of securities of other firms. We discuss the accounting for such investments in Chapter 18. Nike does not have any long-term investments, unless they are combined with other small, miscellaneous noncurrent assets in the $113.7 million of other assets shown in Exhibit 17-1.

INTANGIBLE ASSETS

Tangible assets such as cash or equipment can be physically observed. In contrast, **intangible assets** are a class of long-lived assets that are not physical in nature. They are rights to expected future benefits deriving from their acquisition and continued possession. Examples are goodwill, franchises, patents, trademarks, and copyrights. In Exhibit 17-1, Nike shows intangible assets and goodwill of $410.9 million at May 31, 2000.

Goodwill, which we will discuss in more detail in the next chapter, is the excess of the cost of an acquired company over the sum of the fair market values of its identifiable individual assets less its liabilities. For example, Nike acquired Cole Haan for $95 million. It could assign only $13 million to various identifiable assets such as receivables, plant, and patents less liabilities assumed by Nike; it recorded the remainder, $82 million, as goodwill.

The accounting for goodwill illustrates how an exchange transaction is a basic concept of accounting. After all, many owners could obtain a premium price if they sold their companies. But such goodwill is never recorded. Only the goodwill arising from an actual acquisition should be shown as an asset on the purchaser's records.

For shareholder-reporting purposes, between 1970 and 2001 companies had to amortize (depreciate) goodwill, generally in a straight-line manner, over the periods benefited. In the United States, the longest allowed amortization period was 40 years. Nike is amortizing its $82 million of goodwill from the Cole Haan purchase at the rate of $82,000,000 \div 40 = $2,050,000 per year.

Based on a ruling in 2001, goodwill is no longer amortized. Instead, it remains on a company's books until it is determined that its value is impaired. The 2001 decision reversed a position that had stood for more than 30 years. Before 1970, the amortization of goodwill was not mandatory in the United States. But in 1970, the regulators ruled that the values of all intangible assets eventually disappear, thus making amortization mandatory. Now we have come full circle. However, even though amortization is not mandatory, an impairment test must be applied annually to assure that the goodwill has kept its value.

Companies in many countries also regard research and development costs as assets. They assume that companies incur research costs to purchase an asset that would benefit future operations and thus amortize research costs over the years of expected benefit, usually three to six years. In the United States, however, the FASB has banned deferral and required write-off of these costs as incurred. The FASB admits that research and development costs may generate many long-term benefits, but the general high degree of uncertainty about the extent and measurement of future benefits has led to conservative accounting in the form of immediate write-off.

LIABILITIES

Assets are, of course, only part of the picture of any organization's financial health. Its liabilities, both current and noncurrent, are equally important.

Current liabilities are an organization's debts that fall due within the coming year or within the normal operating cycle if longer than a year. Turn again to Exhibit 17-1 on page 681. Notes payable are short-term debts backed by formal promissory notes held by a bank or business creditors. Accounts payable are amounts owed to suppliers who extended credit for purchases on open account. Accrued liabilities or accrued expenses payable are recognized for wages, salaries, interest, and similar items. The accountant recognizes expenses as they occur—regardless of when they are paid for in cash. Income taxes payable is a special accrued expense of enough magnitude to warrant a separate classification. The current portion of long-term debt shows the payments due within the next year on bonds and other long-term debt.

Some companies also list unearned revenue, also called deferred revenue. Such revenue occurs when a company receives cash before delivering the related goods or

intangible assets Long-lived assets that are not physical in nature. Examples are goodwill, franchises, patents, trademarks, and copyrights.

goodwill The excess of the cost of an acquired company over the sum of the fair market values of its identifiable individual assets less its liabilities.

current liabilities An organization's debts that fall due within the coming year or within the normal operating cycle if longer than a year.

Objective 2
Identify and explain the main types of liabilities in the balance sheet of a corporation.

services. For example, *Newsweek* magazine has such an account because it is obligated to send magazines to subscribers with prepaid subscriptions. Nike had no unearned revenue in 2000, but it did have current liabilities totaling $2,140.0 million.

noncurrent liabilities (long-term liabilities) An organization's debts that fall due beyond one year.

Noncurrent liabilities, also called **long-term liabilities,** are an organization's debts that fall due beyond one year. Exhibit 17-1 shows Nike's noncurrent liabilities for 2000 as $580.6 million, making its total liabilities $2,720.6 million. Nike has two noncurrent liabilities, long-term debt (which we will discuss in more depth in a moment) and deferred income taxes. The latter rather technical and controversial item arises because the financial statements used for reporting to shareholders differ legitimately from those used for reporting to the income tax authorities. Appendix 17 provides more details about deferred taxes.

Exhibit 17-4 is a footnote from the financial statements that provides details about Nike's long-term debts. Note especially the next to last line in this exhibit, "Less: current maturities." This item refers to payments due in the next year. Nike subtracts the $50.1 million noted on this line from long-term debt because the company has already included it in current liabilities. Nike shows the remaining $470.3 million as "Long-term debt" in Exhibit 17-1. Long-term debt may be secured or unsecured. Secured debt provides debtholders with first claim on specified assets. Mortgage bonds are an example of secured debt. If the company is unable to meet its regular obligations on the bonds, it may sell the specified assets and use the proceeds to pay off the firm's obligations to its bondholders, in which case secured debt holders have first claim.

debentures Formal certificates of indebtedness that are accompanied by a promise to pay interest at a specified annual rate.

Unsecured debt consists of **debentures** (i.e., bonds, notes, or loans), which are formal certificates of indebtedness that are accompanied by a promise to pay interest at a specified annual rate. Unsecured debt holders are general creditors who have a general claim against total assets rather than a specific claim against particular assets. Most of Nike's long-term debt is unsecured. Holders of **subordinated** bonds or debentures are junior to the other creditors in exercising claims against assets.

subordinated A creditor claim that is junior to the other creditors in exercising claims against assets.

Consider the following simplified example. Suppose a corporation is liquidated. **Liquidation** means converting assets to cash and using the cash to pay off outside claims. The company had a single asset, a building, that it sold for $120,000 cash:

liquidation Converting assets to cash and using the cash to pay off outside claims.

Assets		Liabilities and Stockholders' Equity	
Cash	$120,000	Accounts payable	$ 60,000
		First-mortgage bonds payable	80,000
		Subordinated debentures payable	40,000
		Total liabilities	$180,000
		Stockholders' equity (negative)	(60,000)
Total assets	$120,000	Total liabilities and stockholders' equity	$120,000

The company would pay the mortgage (secured) bondholders in full ($80,000). It would pay trade creditors, such as suppliers, the remaining $40,000 for their $60,000 claim ($.67 on the dollar). Other claimants would get nothing. If the debentures were unsubordinated, the $40,000 of cash remaining after paying $80,000 to the mortgage holders would be used to settle the $100,000 claims of the unsecured creditors as follows:

To trade creditors	6/10 × $40,000 = $24,000
To debenture holders	4/10 × $40,000 = 16,000
Total cash distributed	$40,000

Exhibit 17-4

Nike, Inc.

Footnote 5 to the 2000 Financial Statements

	May 31	
Note 5. Long-Term Debt (millions)	*1999*	*2000*
6.375% Medium term notes, payable December 1, 2003	$199.5	$199.6
4.3% Japanese yen notes, payable June 26, 2011	84.6	98.2
2.6% Japanese yen loans, payable November 20, 2020	—	84.2
2.0% Japanese yen loans, payable November 20, 2020	—	37.4
6.51% Medium term notes, payable June 16, 2000	50.0	50.0
6.69% Medium term notes, payable June 17, 2002	50.0	50.0
Other	3.0	1.0
	387.1	520.4
Less: Current maturities	1.0	50.1
Total	$386.0	$ 470.3

To increase the appeal of their bonds, many companies issue debt that is convertible into common stock. Convertibility allows bondholders to participate in a company's success without the risk of holding common stock. Suppose a company issues convertible bonds for $1,000 when the stock price is $22, with a provision that each bond can be converted into 40 common shares. If the stock price increases by 50% to $33 a share, the bondholder could exchange the $1,000 bond for 40 shares worth 40 × $33 = $1,320. If the stock price falls (or does not increase beyond $25 a share), the bondholder can keep the bond and receive $1,000 at maturity.

STOCKHOLDERS' EQUITY

The final element of a balance sheet is stockholders' equity (also called shareholders' equity or owners' equity or capital or net worth), the total residual interest in the business. As noted in Chapter 16, it is the excess of total assets over total liabilities. The main elements of stockholders' equity arise from two sources: (1) contributed or paid-in capital, and (2) retained income.

Paid-in capital typically comes from owners who invest in the business in exchange for stock certificates, which are issued as evidence of stockholder rights. There are two major classes of capital stock: common stock and preferred stock. Some companies have several categories of each, all with a variety of different attributes.

All corporations have **common stock.** Such stock has no predetermined rate of dividends and is the last to obtain a share in the assets when the corporation is dissolved. Common shares usually have voting power to elect the board of directors of the corporation. Common stock is usually the riskiest investment in a corporation, being unattractive in dire times but attractive in prosperous times because, unlike other stocks, there is no limit to the stockholder's potential participation in earnings.

Exhibit 17-1 shows that Nike has a small amount of preferred stock, in addition to common stock. About 40% of the major companies in the United States issue **preferred stock.** It typically has some priority over other shares regarding dividends or the distribution of assets on liquidation. For example, Nike pays an annual preferred stock dividend of $.10 per share, or $30,000 in total. Nike must pay these dividends in full before it pays dividends to any other classes of stock. Preferred shareholders in Nike, as in most companies with preferred stock, do not have voting privileges regarding the management of the corporation.

Stock frequently has a designated **par** or **legal** or **stated value** that is printed on the face of the certificate. For preferred stock (and bonds), par is a basis for designating the amount

common stock Stock that has no predetermined rate of dividends and is the last to obtain a share in the assets when the corporation is dissolved. It usually has voting power to elect the board of directors of the corporation.

preferred stock Stock that typically has some priority over other shares regarding dividends or the distribution of assets upon liquidation.

par value (legal value, stated value) The value that is printed on the face of the certificate.

of dividends or interest. Many preferred stocks have $100 par values. That is, a 9%, $100-par preferred stock would carry a $9 annual dividend. Most bonds have par values of $1,000. Thus, an 8% bond usually means that the investor is entitled to annual interest of $80.

In contrast, par value has no practical importance for common stock. Historically, the par amount of common stock specified the maximum legal liability of the stockholder in case the corporation could not pay its debts. (Shareholders typically have **limited liability,** which means that a company's creditors cannot seek payment from stockholders as individuals if the corporation itself cannot pay its debts.) Currently, companies set par at a nominal amount (e.g., $1) in relation to the market value of the stock on issuance (e.g., $70). It is generally illegal for a corporation to sell an original issue of its common stock below par.

Capital in excess of stated value is the excess received over the stated, par, or legal value of the shares issued. Common shares are almost always issued at a price substantially greater than par. Suppose all outstanding common shares of Nike had been issued for cash. The cumulative balance sheet effect at May 31, 2000, would be

limited liability Creditors cannot seek payment from shareholders as individuals if the corporation itself cannot pay its debts.

Cash	$371,800,000	Common stock, at stated value	$ 2,800,000
		Capital in excess of stated value	369,000,000
		Total paid-in capital	$371,800,000

Retained earnings, also called retained income, is the increase in stockholders' equity caused by profitable operations (see Chapter 16). Retained earnings is the dominant item of stockholders' equity for most companies. For instance, as of May 31, 2000, Nike had common stockholders' equity of $3,136.3 million of which $2,887.0 million was retained earnings.

treasury stock A corporation's own stock that has been issued and subsequently repurchased by the company and is being held for a specific purpose.

Many companies have **treasury stock,** which is a corporation's own stock that the company issued and subsequently repurchased and is holding for a specific purpose. Such repurchase is a decrease in ownership claims. It should therefore appear on a balance sheet as a deduction from total stockholders' equity. The stock is not retired; it is only held temporarily "in the treasury" to be distributed later, possibly as a part of an employee stock purchase plan or as an executive bonus or for use in acquiring another company. A company does not pay cash dividends on shares held in the treasury. Companies distribute dividends only to the outstanding shares (those in the hands of stockholders). Nike had no treasury stock in 2000. In contrast, McDonald's Corporation had more than $8 billion of treasury stock:

Shareholders' equity before deducting treasury stock	$17,315,500,000
Treasury stock	(8,111,100,000)
Total shareholders' equity	$ 9,204,400,000

SUMMARY PROBLEMS FOR YOUR REVIEW

PROBLEM

"The book value of plant assets is the amount that would be spent today for their replacement." Do you agree? Explain.

SOLUTION

Net book value of the plant assets is the result of deducting accumulated depreciation from original cost. This process does not attempt to capture all the technological and economic events that may affect replacement value. Consequently, there is little likelihood that net book value will approximate replacement cost.

PROBLEM

On December 31, 20X1, a magazine publishing company receives $150,000 in cash for three-year subscriptions. It regards this sum as unearned revenue. Show the balances in that account at December 31, 20X2, 20X3, and 20X4. How much revenue would be earned in each of those three years?

SOLUTION

The balance in unearned revenue would decline at the rate of $50,000 yearly. The company would recognize $50,000 as earned revenue in each of the three years.

	December 31			
	20X1	*20X2*	*20X3*	*20X4*
Unearned revenue	$150,000	$100,000	$50,000	$0

INCOME STATEMENT

Most investors are vitally concerned about a company's ability to produce long-run earnings and dividends. In this regard, income statements are more important than balance sheets. Income statements show revenue first; this represents the total sales value of products delivered and services rendered to customers. Then they list expenses, which are deducted to get net income.

Objective 4
Identify and explain the principal elements in the income statement of a corporation.

USE OF SUBTOTALS

An income statement can take one of two major forms: single step or multiple step. A single-step statement merely lists all expenses without drawing subtotals, whereas a multiple-step statement contains one or more subtotals. Subtotals highlight significant relationships.

Exhibit 17-5 illustrates the two most common subtotals: gross profit and income from operations (also called operating income or operating profit). Gross profit or gross margin is sales less cost of goods sold. It measures the size of the margin above merchandise costs and is an important statistic for many managers and analysts. Operating income (or loss) summarizes the results of the basic operating activities of the company. Income statements often group depreciation expense, selling expenses, and administrative expenses as "operating expenses" and deduct them from the gross profit to obtain operating income. (Of course, cost of goods sold is also an operating expense. Why? Because it is also deducted from sales revenue to obtain "operating income.") In 2000, Nike had a gross profit of $3,591.3 million and operating income of $984.9 million.

To interpret a company's financial statements, it is important to identify whether a particular account is an asset, liability, stockholders' equity, revenue, or expense account. Identify the type of account for each of the following accounts: accounts receivable, accounts payable, investments in marketable securities, depreciation, paid-in capital, cost of goods sold, income taxes, income taxes payable, bank loans, common stock, and inventories.

ANSWER

Asset accounts are accounts receivable, investments in marketable securities, and inventories. Liability accounts are accounts payable and bank loans. Stockholders' equity accounts are paid-in capital and common stock. No revenue accounts are listed. Expense accounts are depreciation, cost of goods sold, and income taxes.

Exhibit 17-5

Nike, Inc.

Statement of Income (millions except per share data)

	Year Ended May 31	
	1999	2000
Revenues	$8,776.9	$8,995.1
Cost of sales	5,493.5	5,403.8
Gross profit	$3,283.4	$3,591.3
Selling and administrative expenses	2,426.6	2,606.4
Income from operations	$ 856.8	$ 984.9
Other expense (income)		
Interest expense	$ 44.1	$ 45.0
Other income/expense, net	66.6	20.7
Total other expense	$ 110.7	$65.7
Income before income taxes	$ 746.1	$ 919.2
Income taxes	294.7	340.1
Net income	$ 451.4	$ 579.1
Earnings per share*	$1.59	$2.10

*Computation of earnings per share:

	1999	2000
Net income	$451,400,000	$579,100,000
Divided by average common shares outstanding	283,300,000	275,700,000
Earnings per share	$1.59	$2.10

OPERATING AND FINANCIAL MANAGEMENT

Operating income is a popular subtotal because of the often made distinction between operating management and financial management. Operating management focuses on the major day-to-day activities that generate sales revenue. In contrast, financial management focuses on where to get cash and how to use cash for the benefit of the organization. That is, financial management attempts to answer such questions as: How much cash should be held in checking accounts? Should we pay a dividend? Should we borrow or issue common stock? The best managers are superb at both operating management and financial management. However, many managers are better operating managers than financial managers, or vice versa.

Because financial rather than operating decisions affect interest income and expense, they often appear as separate items after operating income. This approach facilitates comparisons of operating income between years and between companies. Some companies make heavy use of debt, which causes high interest expense, whereas other companies incur little debt and interest expense. Other nonoperating items might include gains or losses from foreign exchange transactions or from disposals of fixed assets.

INCOME, EARNINGS, AND PROFITS

Although this book tends to use the term *income* most often, you will also see the terms *earnings* and *profits* used as synonyms. Other names for the income statement include *statement of earnings, statement of profit and loss,* and *P&L statement*. Most companies still use net income on their income statements, but the term *earnings* is becoming increasingly popular because it has a preferable image. Nike's 2000 net income was $579.1 million.

Exhibit 17-6

Nike, Inc.

Statement of Retained Earnings for the Year
Ended May 31, 2000 (millions of dollars)

Retained earnings, May 31, 1999	$3,066.5
Net income (Exhibit 17-5)	579.1
Total	3,645.6
Deduct: dividends on common stock	131.5
Repurchase of common stock	627.1
Retained earnings, May 31, 2000	$2,887.0

The term **net income** is the popular "bottom line"—the residual after deducting all expenses including income taxes. The term *net* is seldom used for any subtotals that precede the calculation of net income. Instead, the subtotals are called *income*. Thus, the appropriate term is *operating income* or *income from operations,* not *net operating income.*

Income taxes are often a prominent expense and are not merely listed with operating expenses. Instead, income statements usually deduct income taxes as a separate item immediately before net income, as in Exhibit 17-5.

Income statements conclude with disclosure of **earnings per share.** Exhibit 17-5 illustrates this as the net income divided by the average number of common shares outstanding during the year. Nike earned $2.10 per share in 2000.

net income The popular "bottom line"—the residual after deducting from revenues all expenses, including income taxes.

earnings per share Net income divided by the average number of common shares outstanding during the year.

STATEMENT OF RETAINED EARNINGS

To explain the changes in retained earnings, companies frequently include a separate financial statement, the **statement of retained earnings** (also called **statement of retained income**). This may also be one part of a larger statement, the statement of changes in stockholders' equity. As Exhibit 17-6 demonstrates, the major reasons for changes in retained earnings are dividends and net income. Net income increases retained earnings, and losses and dividends reduce retained earnings. Note especially that dividends are not expenses; they are not deductions in computing net income, as explained in Chapter 16 on page 652.

Objective 5
Identify and explain elements in the statement of retained earnings.

statement of retained earnings (statement of retained income) A financial statement that analyzes changes in the retained earnings or retained income account for a given period.

SUMMARY PROBLEM FOR YOUR REVIEW

PROBLEM

Companies sometimes combine the income statement and statement of retained earnings into a single statement. Prepare a combined income statement and statement of retained earnings from the following data. Use a multiple-step format for the income statement.

Cost of goods sold	$420,000
Net sales	750,000
Income taxes	80,000
Beginning retained earnings	440,000
Dividends	30,000
Interest expense	20,000
Selling and administrative expenses	110,000

SOLUTION

Statement of Income and Retained Earnings	
Net sales	$750,000
Cost of goods sold	420,000
Gross margin	330,000
Selling and administrative expenses	110,000
Operating income	220,000
Interest expense	20,000
Income before income taxes	200,000
Income taxes	80,000
Net income	120,000
Beginning retained earnings	440,000
Dividends	(30,000)
Ending retained earnings	$530,000

STATEMENT OF CASH FLOWS

statement of cash flows A statement that reports the cash receipts and cash payments of an organization during a particular period.

Until recently, many decision makers focused primarily on the income statement and the balance sheet. However, an increasing number of decision makers are now carefully examining another important statement, the statement of cash flows. A **statement of cash flows** reports the cash receipts and cash payments of an organization during a particular period. The statement has the following purposes:

1. It shows the relationship of net income to changes in cash balances. Cash balances can decline despite positive net income and vice versa.

2. It reports past cash flows as an aid to
   a. Predicting future cash flows
   b. Evaluating management's generation and use of cash
   c. Determining a company's ability to pay interest and dividends, and to pay debts when they are due

3. It reveals commitments to assets that may restrict or expand future courses of action.

BASIC CONCEPTS

Recall that balance sheets show the status of an entity at a day in time. In contrast, statements of cash flows, income statements, and statements of retained income cover periods. They provide the explanations of why the balance sheet items have changed. The accompanying diagram depicts this linkage:

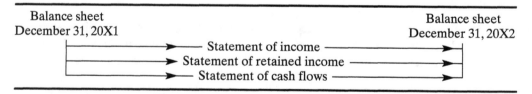

In particular, the statement of cash flows explains where cash came from during a period and where it was spent.

The statement of cash flows explains changes in cash and cash equivalents, both of which can quickly be used to meet obligations. Cash equivalents, as noted earlier in this chapter, are highly liquid short-term investments that a company can easily convert into cash with little delay. Hereafter, when we refer to cash, we mean both cash and cash equivalents.

TYPICAL ACTIVITIES AFFECTING CASH

The fundamental approach to the statement of cash flows is simple: (1) List the activities that increased cash (i.e., cash inflows) and those that decreased cash (cash outflows), and (2) place each cash inflow and outflow into one of three categories according to the type of activity that caused it: operating activities, investing activities, and financing activities.

The following activities are those found most often in statements of cash flows:

Objective 6
Identify activities that affect cash, and classify them as operating, investing, or financing activities.

Operating Activities

Cash Inflows	*Cash Outflows*
Collections from customers	Cash payments to suppliers
Interest and dividends collected	Cash payments to employees
Other operating receipts	Interest paid
	Taxes paid
	Other operating cash payments

Investing Activities

Cash Inflows	*Cash Outflows*
Sale of property, plant, and equipment	Purchase of property, plant, and equipment
Sale of securities that are not cash equivalents	Purchase of securities that are not cash equivalents
Receipt of loan repayments	Making loans

Financing Activities

Cash Inflows	*Cash Outflows*
Borrowing cash from creditors	Repayment of amounts borrowed
Issuing equity securities	Repurchase of equity shares (including the purchase of treasury stock)
	Payment of dividends

As the lists of activities indicate, **cash flows from operating activities** are generally the effects of transactions that affect the income statement (e.g., sales and wages). Investing activities include (1) lending and collecting on loans and (2) acquiring and selling long-term assets. Financing activities include obtaining resources from creditors and owners and providing them with returns of their investments and owners with returns on their investments in the form of cash dividends.

Perhaps the most troublesome classifications are the receipts and payments of interest and the receipts of dividends. After all, these items are associated with investment and financing activities. After much debate, the FASB decided to include these items with cash flows from operating activities. Why? Mainly because they affect the computation of income. In contrast, payments of cash dividends are financing activities because they do not affect income.

cash flows from operating activities The section in the statement of cash flows that lists the cash-flow effects of transactions that affect the income statement.

FOCUS OF A STATEMENT OF CASH FLOWS

To see the basic ideas underlying the statement of cash flows, consider the Balmer Company. Exhibit 17-7 shows the company's condensed balance sheets and income statement.

Because the statement of cash flows explains the causes for the change in cash, the first step is to compute the amount of the change (which represents the net effect to be explained):

Cash, December 31, 20X1	$25,000
Cash, December 31, 20X2	16,000
Net decrease in cash	$ 9,000

Exhibit 17-7

Balmer Company

Statement of Income for the Year Ended
December 31, 20X2 (in thousands)

Sales		$200
Costs and expenses		
Cost of goods sold	$100	
Wages and salaries	36	
Depreciation	17	
Interest	4	
Total costs and expenses		157
Income before income taxes		43
Income taxes		20
Net income		$ 23

Balmer Company

Balance Sheet as of December 31 (in thousands)

Assets	20X2	20X1	Increase (Decrease)	Liabilities and Stockholders' Equity	20X2	20X1	Increase (Decrease)
Current assets				Current liabilities			
Cash	$ 16	$ 25	$ (9)	Accounts payable	$ 74	$ 6	$ 68
Accounts receivable	45	25	20	Wages and salaries			
Inventory	100	60	40	payable	25	4	21
Total current assets	161	110	51	Total current liabilities	99	10	89
Fixed assets, gross	581	330	251	Long-term debt	125	5	120
Less accum. depreciation	(101)	(110)	9	Stockholders' equity	417	315	102
Net fixed assets	480	220	260	Total liabilities and			
Total assets	$641	$330	$311	stockholders' equity	$641	$330	$311

Exhibit 17-8 illustrates a statement of cash flows with this information shown at the bottom. The statement adds the beginning cash balance to the net change to compute the ending cash balance. Another common practice is to place the beginning cash balance at the top of the statement and the ending cash balance at the bottom. However, there is no requirement that the statement of cash flows explicitly show the beginning and ending cash balances. Showing only the net change is sufficient.

When business expansion occurs, as in this case, and where there is a strong cash position at the outset, cash often declines. Why? Because growing companies usually need cash for investment in various business assets required for expansion, including investment in accounts receivable and inventories.

The statement in Exhibit 17-8 gives a direct picture of where cash came from and where it went. In this instance, the excess of cash outflows over cash inflows reduced cash by $9,000. Without the statement of cash flows, the readers of the annual report would have to conduct their own analyses of the beginning and ending balance sheets, the income statement, and the statement of retained income to get a grasp of the impact of financial management decisions.

Most important, this illustration demonstrates how a firm may simultaneously (1) have a significant amount of net income, as computed by accountants on the accrual basis, and yet (2) have a decline in cash that could become severe. Indeed, many growing businesses are desperate for cash even though reported net income zooms upward.

Exhibit 17-8

Balmer Company

Statement of Cash Flows for the Year Ended December 31, 20X2 (in thousands)

Cash Flows from Operating Activities		
Cash collections from customers		$180
Cash payments		
To suppliers	$72	
To employees	15	
For interest	4	
For taxes	20	
Total cash payments		(111)
Net cash provided by operating activities		$ 69

Cash Flows from Investing Activities		
Purchases of fixed assets	$(287)	
Proceeds from sale of fixed assets	10	
Net cash used in investing activities		(277)

Cash Flows from Financing Activities		
Proceeds from issue of long-term debt	$120	
Proceeds from issue of common stock	98	
Dividends paid	(19)	
Net cash provided by financing activities		199
Net decrease in cash		$ (9)
Cash, December 31, 20X1		25
Cash, December 31, 20X2		$ 16

18

MORE ON UNDERSTANDING CORPORATE ANNUAL REPORTS

If General Motors (GM) had to rely on customers to pay cash for an auto like this one, it would not sell many cars. So GM created a subsidiary company, General Motors Acceptance Corporation (GMAC), to help customers finance the purchase of GM cars. Because of GMAC, General Motors sells more automobiles and earns profits from the interest paid by borrowers. The financial results of GM and GMAC are consolidated into one set of financial statements.

www.prenhall.com/horngren

PART TWO: ANALYSIS OF FINANCIAL STATEMENTS

For financial statements to be useful, managers and investors need to be able to analyze and interpret the statements. Careful analysis of financial statements can help decision makers evaluate an organization's past performance and predict its future performance. Such evaluations help managers, investors, and others make intelligent, informed financial decisions. We use the 1999 and 2000 financial statements of Microsoft Corporation in Exhibits 18-4 and 18-5 to focus on financial statement analysis.

Exhibit 18-4
Microsoft Corporation
Balance Sheet (millions)

	June 30			
	1999		2000	
Assets				
Current assets				
Cash and short-term investments	$17,236		$23,798	
Accounts receivable	2,245		3,250	
Other	752		1,552	
Total current assets		$20,233		$28,600
Long-term assets*				
Property, plant and equipment, net		1,611		1,903
Equity and other investments		14,372		17,726
Other assets		940		2,213
Total assets		$37,156		$50,442
Liabilities and Stockholders' Equity				
Current liabilities				
Accounts payable	$ 874		$ 1,083	
Income taxes payable	1,607		583	
Accrued compensation	396		557	
Unearned revenue	4,239		4,816	
Other	1,602		2,714	
Total current liabilities		$ 8,718		$ 9,753
Stockholders' equity				
Convertible preferred stock	$ 980		$ 0	
Paid-in capital	13,844		22,516	
Retained earnings	13,614		18,173	
Total shareholders' equity		28,438		40,689
Total liabilities and shareholders' equity		$37,156		$50,442

* This caption is frequently omitted. Instead, the long-term assets are merely listed as separate items following the current assets.

Decisions based on comparisons of financial statements span a wide range. For example, investors use them to decide whether to buy, sell, or hold common stock. Managers and the financial community (such as bank officers and stockholders) use them as clues to help evaluate the operating and financial outlook for an organization. Budgets or pro forma statements—carefully formulated expressions of predicted results, including a schedule of the amounts and timing of cash repayments—are helpful to extenders of credit, who want assurance of being paid in full and on time. For example, a set of budgeted financial statements is one of the first things a banker will request from an entrepreneur proposing a new business. Even well established companies usually need to provide pro forma statements to assure creditors that the company will pay back the amounts borrowed.

COMPONENT PERCENTAGES

component percentages
Analysis and presentation of financial statements in percentage form to aid comparability, frequently used when companies differ in size.

common-size statements
Financial statements expressed in component percentages.

When comparing companies that differ in size, analysts often apply percentage relationships, called **component percentages,** to income statements and balance sheets (see Exhibit 18-6). We call the resulting statements **common-size statements.** For example, it is difficult to compare Microsoft's $28,600 billion of current assets with the $13.1 million of Interlinq, a smaller software company. It's much easier to compare Microsoft's 57% current asset percentage (shown in Exhibit 18-6) with Interlinq's $13.1 million ÷ $21.8 million = 60%.

Income statement percentages are usually based on sales = 100%. Microsoft seems reasonably profitable, but such percentages would have more meaning when compared

Exhibit 18-5

Microsoft Corporation Statement of Income
(millions except earnings per share)

	For the Year Ended June 30			
	1999		2000	
Net revenues		$19,747		$22,956
Cost of revenues*		2,814		3,002
Gross profit		16,933		19,954
Operating expenses:				
General and administrative	$ 689		$1,009	
Research and development	2,970		3,775	
Sales and marketing	3,231		4,141	
Other expenses	115	7,005	92	9,017
Operating income		9,928		10,937
Other income (expense)†		1,963		3,338
Income before income taxes		11,891		14,275
Provision for income taxes		4,106		4,854
Net income		7,785		9,421
Preferred stock dividends		28		0
Net income available for common shareholders		$ 7,757		$9,421
Earnings per share‡		$ 1.54		$ 1.81

* Also called cost of goods sold.
† Primarily investment revenue.
‡ Microsoft pays no dividends. Publicly held companies must show earnings per share on the face of the income statement, but it is not necessary to show dividends per share. Average shares outstanding for computation of EPS are approximately 5,028 million in 1999 and 5,188 million in 2000.

Exhibit 18-6

Microsoft Corporation

Common-Size Statements (millions except percentages)

Statement of Income	For the Year Ended June 30			
	1999		2000	
Net revenues	$19,747*	100%	$22,956	100%
Cost of revenues	2,814	14	3,002	13
Gross profit (or gross margin)	$16,933	86%	$19,954	87%
General and administrative	$ 689	4%	$ 1,009	4%
Research and development	2,970	15	3,775	16
Sales and marketing	3,231	16	4,141	18
Other	115	1	92	1
Operating expenses	$ 7,005	36%	$ 9,017	39%
Operating income	$ 9,928	50%	$10,937	48%
Other income (expense)	1,963	10	3,338	14
Income before income taxes	$11,891	60%	$14,275	62%
Provision for income taxes	4,106	21	4,854	21
Net income	$ 7,785	39%	$ 9,421	41%
Balance Sheet				
Current assets	$20,233	55%	$28,600	57%
Plant, property, and equipment, net	1,611	4	1,903	4
Other assets	15,312	41	19,939	39
Total assets	$37,156	100%	$50,442	100%
Current liabilities	$ 8,716	23%	$ 9,753	19%
Long-term liabilities	0	0	0	0
Stockholders' equity	28,438	77	40,689	81
Total equities	$37,156	100%	$50,442	100%

* Note the use of dollar signs in columns of numbers. Frequently, they are used at the top and bottom only and not for every subtotal. Their use by companies depends on the preference of management.

with the budgeted performance for the current year (not shown here). Both the gross margin rate and net income percentage seem outstanding. However, averages for these items vary greatly by industry. Comparison with other similar firms or industry averages is necessary to interpret the rates fully. Changes between one year and the next can also reveal important information. Microsoft's net income rose from 39% to 41% of sales, primarily because of an increase in other income. Net income rose despite an increase in operating expenses (from 36% to 39% of sales).

Balance sheet percentages are usually based on total assets = 100%. Note in Exhibit 18-6 that Microsoft's current assets and stockholders' equity increased, while current liabilities decreased.

Corporate annual reports to the public must contain a section that is usually labeled *management's discussion and analysis*. This section concentrates on explaining the major changes in the income statement, changes in liquidity and capital resources, and the impact of inflation. The focus is on a comparison of one year with the next. For example, Microsoft's annual report had several pages of detailed discussions, including

> The Company's revenue growth rate was 28% in fiscal 1998, 29% in fiscal 1999, and 16% in fiscal 2000. Revenue growth in fiscal 2000 was driven by strong licensing of the Microsoft suite of products including Microsoft Windows NT® Workstation, Windows 2000 Professional, Windows NT Server, Windows 2000 Server,

Microsoft Office 2000, and SQL Server 7.0. . . . Cost of revenue as a percent of revenue was 16.1% in 1998, 14.3% in 1999, and 13.1% in 2000. Cost of revenue in fiscal 2000 reflected lower costs associated with WebTV Networks' operations, partially offset by the growth in hardware peripherals costs. . . . Investment income increased primarily as a result of a larger investment portfolio generated by cash from operations in 1998, 1999, and 2000, coupled with realized gains from the sale of securities in 1999 and 2000.
. . . The Company's cash and short-term investment portfolio totaled $23.80 billion at June 30, 2000. The portfolio consists primarily of fixed-income securities, diversified among industries and individual issuers. . . . Management believes existing cash and short-term investments together with funds generated from operations will be sufficient to meet operating requirements. . . . Microsoft has not paid cash dividends on its common stock.

USES OF RATIOS

Objective 4
Explain and use a variety of popular financial ratios.

In addition to or instead of budgets and common-size statements, investors and creditors often use ratios computed from published financial statements. Exhibit 18-7 shows how some typical ratios are computed. Many more ratios could be computed. For example, Standard & Poor's Corporation sells a COMPUSTAT service which, via computer, can provide financial and statistical information for more than 16,000 companies. The information includes 332 financial statement items on an annual basis and 128 items on a quarterly basis, plus limited footnote information. Exhibit 18-7 contains only the most popular ratios.

COMPARISONS

time-series comparisons Comparison of a company's financial ratios with its own historical ratios.

Evaluation of a financial ratio requires a comparison. There are three main types of comparisons: (1) with a company's own historical ratios (called **time-series comparisons**), (2) with general rules of thumb or **benchmarks,** and (3) with ratios of other companies or with industry averages for the same period (called **cross-sectional comparisons**).

Consider first time-series comparisons. Much can be learned by examining the trend of a company's ratios. This is why annual reports typically contain a table of comparative statistics for 5 or 10 years. For example, consider the trends in three of Microsoft's profitability ratios.

benchmarks General rules of thumb specifying appropriate levels for financial ratios.

cross-sectional comparisons Comparisons of a company's financial ratios with ratios of other companies or with industry averages for the same period.

	1996	1997	1998	1999	2000
Return on sales	24.3%	28.9%	29.4%	39.4%	41.0%
Return on stockholders' equity	35.6%	39.1%	32.8%	34.6%	27.3%
Earnings per share	$.46	$.72	$.92	$1.54	$1.81

Note that return on sales increased significantly in 1999 and return on stockholders' equity had increases in both 1997 and 1998 before a large decrease in 2000. Earnings per share has increased substantially each year.

The second type of comparison uses broad rules of thumb as benchmarks. For instance, the most quoted benchmark is a current ratio of 2 to 1. Others are described in *Key Business Ratios* by Dun & Bradstreet, a financial services firm. For example,

Total debt to equity. In general, total liabilities shouldn't exceed net worth [equity] (100%) since in such cases creditors have more at stake than owners.

Exhibit 18-7
Some Typical Financial Ratios

Typical Name of Ratio	Numerator	Denominator	Appropriate Microsoft Numbers Applied to June 30 of Year	
			1999	*2000*
Short-term ratios				
Current ratio	Current assets	Current liabilities	20,233 ÷ 8,718 = 2.3	28,600 ÷ 9,753 = 2.9
Average collection period in days	Average accounts receivable[†] × 365	Sales on account	[1/2(2,245 + 1,460) × 365] ÷ 19,747 = 34 days*	[1/2(3,250 + 2,245) × 365] ÷ 22,956 = 44 days
Debt-to-equity ratio				
Total debt to equity	Total liabilities	Stockholders' equity	8,718 − 28,438 = 30.7%	9,753 ÷ 40,689 = 24.0%
Profitability ratios				
Gross profit rate or percentage	Gross profit or gross margin	Sales	16,933 ÷ 19,747 = 85.7%	19,954 ÷ 22,956 = 86.9%
Return on sales	Net income	Sales	7,785 ÷ 19,747 = 39.4%	9,421 ÷ 22,956 = 41.0%
Return on stockholders' equity	Net income	Average stockholders' equity[†]	7,785 ÷ 1/2(28,438 + 16,627) = 34.6%	9,421 ÷ 1/2(40,689 + 28,438) = 27.3%
Earnings per share	Net income less dividends on preferred stock, if any	Average common shares outstanding	7,757 ÷ 5,028 = $1.54	9,421 ÷ 5,188 = $1.81
Price earnings	Market price per share of common stock[‡]	Earnings per share	77 ÷ 1.54 = 50.0	62 ÷ 1.81 = 34.3
Dividend ratios				
Dividend yield	Dividends per common share	Market price per common share[‡]	0 ÷ 77 = 0.0%	0 ÷ 62 = 0.0%
Dividend payout	Dividends per common share	Earnings per share	0 ÷ 1.54 = 0.0%	0 ÷ 1.81 = 0.0%

* This may be easier to see as follows:
Average receivables = 1/2 (2,245 + 1,460) = 1,852.5
Average receivables as a percentage of annual sales = 1,852.5 ÷ 19,747 = 9.38%
Average collection period = 9.38% × 365 days = 34 days
[†] Relevant 1998 amounts: accounts receivable, $1,460 million; stockholders' equity, $16,627 million.
[‡] Market price: June 30, 1999, $77; June 30, 2000, $62.

Return on equity. *Generally, a relationship of at least 10 percent is regarded as a desirable objective.*

Obviously, such benchmarks are only general guides. More specific analyses come from the third type of comparisons, examining ratios of similar companies or industry averages. Dun & Bradstreet informs its subscribers of the creditworthiness of thousands of individual companies. In addition, the firm regularly compiles many ratios of the companies it monitors. Each ratio in Exhibit 18-7 can be compared with industry statistics. For example, some of the Dun & Bradstreet ratios for 411 prepackaged software companies showed:

	Current Ratio	Collection Period	Total Debt to Equity	Return on Sales	Return on Stockholders' Equity
	(Times)	*(Days)*	*(Percent)*	*(Percent)*	*(Percent)*
649 companies					
Upper quartile*	4.5	39	25.0	12.6	45.0
Median	2.4	72	51.5	6.1	16.9
Lower quartile	1.4	103	126.0	0.6	2.4
Microsoft†	2.9	44	24.0	41.0	27.3

* The individual ratios are ranked from best to worst. The middle figure is the median. The figure ranked halfway between the median and the best is the upper quartile. Similarly, the figure ranked halfway between the median and the worst is the lower quartile.

† Ratios are from Exhibit 18-7. Please consult that exhibit for an explanation of the components of each ratio.

Our illustration focuses on one company and one or two years. This is sufficient as a start, but analysts also examine other firms in the industry, industry averages, and a series of years to get a better perspective. Above all, recognize that a ratio by itself is of limited use. There must be a standard for comparison—a history, a similar entity, an industry average, a benchmark, or a budget.

DISCUSSION OF SPECIFIC RATIOS

Consider again the ratios in Exhibit 18-7. Shown first is the current ratio, a widely used statistic. Other things being equal, the higher the current ratio, the more assurance the creditor has about being paid in full and on time. Microsoft's current ratio of 2.9 has improved from 2.3 and is above the industry median of 2.4.

Microsoft's average collection period of 44 days places Microsoft just below the upper quartile of prepackaged software firms, according to Dun & Bradstreet industry data. A lengthening collection period might indicate increasing acceptance of poor credit risks or less energetic collection efforts.

Note how the average collection period depends on sales on account. The computation in Exhibit 18-7 assumes that all sales are credit sales. However, if we relax our assumption, the 44-day period would rise markedly. For example, if half the sales were for cash, the average collection period for accounts receivable would change from 44 to 87 days:

$$\frac{\frac{1}{2}\,(3{,}250 + 2{,}245) \times 365}{\frac{1}{2}\,(22{,}956)} = 87 \text{ days}$$

The third column of the Dun & Bradstreet tabulation shows the total debt-to-equity ratio. Both creditors and shareholders watch this ratio to judge the degree of risk of insolvency and stability of profits. Typically, companies with heavy debt in relation to ownership capital are in greater danger of suffering net losses or even bankruptcy when business conditions sour. Why? Because revenues and many expenses decline, but interest expenses and maturity dates do not change. Microsoft's ratio of 24.0% is well below the median for the industry; it reflects low levels of risk or uncertainty concerning the company's ability to pay its debts on time.

Investors find profitability ratios especially helpful. Examine the gross profit rate and the return on sales. Microsoft's gross profit rate increased from 85.7% in 1999 to 86.9% in 2000, and its return on sales increased from 39.4% to 41.0%. These are both measures of *operating success.* Dun & Bradstreet does not report gross profit rates, but Microsoft's return on sales is high enough to rank high in the top quartile of prepackaged software companies.

More important to shareholders is the rate of return on their invested capital, a measure of overall accomplishment. Microsoft's 2000 rate of 27.3% is down from the 34.6% of 1999, but it is well above the industry median of 16.9%.

The final four ratios in Exhibit 18-7 are based on earnings and dividends. The first, earnings per share of common stock (EPS), is the most popular of all ratios. This is the only ratio that is required as part of the body of financial statements of publicly held companies in the United States. Companies must present the EPS on the face of the income statement. Most companies calculate it as in Exhibit 18-7: net income less dividends on preferred stock divided by average common shares outstanding. For companies holding securities that can be exchanged for or converted to common shares, EPS calculations are more complex. Such computations are beyond the scope of this discussion.

The computation of three other ratios is shown in Exhibit 18-7: price earnings, dividend yield, and dividend payout. These ratios are especially useful to investors in the common stock of the company. Because Microsoft pays no dividends, the last two ratios are both zero.

OPERATING PERFORMANCE RATIOS

In addition to the more focused ratios just cited, businesspeople often look at the rate of return on invested capital as an important measure of overall accomplishment:

$$\text{rate of return on investment} = \frac{\text{income}}{\text{invested capital}} \qquad (1)$$

On the surface, this measure is straightforward, but its ingredients may differ according to the purpose it is to serve. What is invested capital, the denominator of the ratio? What income figure is appropriate?

The measurement of operating performance (how profitably assets are employed) should not be influenced by the management's financial decisions (i.e., how assets are obtained). The best measure of operating performance is pretax operating rate of return on average total assets:

$$\text{pretax operating rate of return on average total assets} = \frac{\text{operating income}}{\text{average total assets}} \qquad (2)$$

For Microsoft, this ratio is $10,937 ÷ $43,799 = 25.0%

The right-hand side of equation 2 consists, in turn, of two important ratios:

$$\frac{\text{operating income}}{\text{average total assets}} = \frac{\text{operating income}}{\text{sales}} \times \frac{\text{sales}}{\text{average total assets}} \qquad (3)$$

The right-hand terms in equation 3 are often called the *operating income percentage on sales* and *total asset turnover,* respectively. Therefore, Microsoft's operating performance can be expressed as :

$$\begin{array}{c} \text{pretax operating rate} \\ \text{of return on average total assets} \end{array} = \begin{array}{c} \text{operating income} \\ \text{percentage on sales} \end{array} \times \begin{array}{c} \text{total asset} \\ \text{turnover} \end{array}$$

$$= \frac{10{,}937}{\$22{,}956} \times \frac{\$22{,}956}{\frac{1}{2}(\$50{,}442 + \$37{,}156)} \quad (4)$$

$$= 47.64\% \times .5241 = 25.0\%$$

When analysts use ratios to evaluate operating performance, they usually exclude extraordinary items. Such items are not expected to recur, and therefore they should not be included in measures of normal performance.

A scrutiny of equation 4 shows that there are two basic factors in profit making: operating margin percentages and turnover. An improvement in either will, by itself, increase the rate of return on total assets.

Which is better, an investment in Wal Mart or one in Saks, Incorporated, operators of Saks Fifth Avenue? How might one use financial ratios to better understand the different ways that Wal-Mart and Saks create value for investors? Would you expect Wal-Mart and Saks to have different pretax operating rate of return on average total assets? Would you expect them to have different operating income percentage on sales and total asset turnover?

ANSWERS

Investors have many different alternative investments. If either Wal-Mart or Saks offered lower returns to investors, they would not find many people willing to invest. (This assumes that the riskiness of investing in the two companies is about the same.) However, even if the two companies seek the same total return on assets, they pursue this return quite differently. Wal-Mart has a high total asset turnover and a low operating income percentage on sales, while Saks has the opposite (dollar amounts are in millions):

Wal-Mart: Operating income percentage on sales = $8,309 ÷ $165,013 = 5.0%
               Total asset turnover = $165,013 ÷ ½ ($70,349 + $49,996) = 2.74
               Return on assets = 5.0% × 2.74 = 13.7%

    Saks: Operating income percentage on sales = $510.3 ÷ $6,423.8 = 7.9%
               Total asset turnover = $6,423.8 ÷ ½ ($5,099 + $5,189) = 1.75
               Return on assets = 7.9% × 1.75 = 9.8%

The year 2000 was better for Wal-Mart than for Saks as judged by their return on assets. Saks has the higher return or sales, but Wal-Mart had the higher total asset turnover.

EFFICIENT MARKETS AND INVESTOR DECISIONS

efficient capital market A market in which market prices fully reflect all information available to the public.

How investors use accounting information depends on whether they believe stock markets are "efficient." An **efficient capital market** is one in which market prices "fully reflect" all information available to the public. Therefore, searching for "underpriced" securities in such a market would be fruitless unless an investor has information that is not generally available. If the real-world markets are indeed efficient, a relatively inactive portfolio approach would be an appropriate investment strategy for most investors. The hallmarks of the approach are risk control, high diversification, and low turnover of securities. The role of accounting information would mainly be in identifying the different degrees of risk among various stocks so that investors can maintain desired levels of risk and diversification.

Research has shown that financial ratios and other data such as reported earnings help predict such economic phenomena as financial failure or earnings growth. Furthermore, analysts use many ratios simultaneously rather than one at a time for such predictions. Above all, the research shows that accounting reports are only one source of information and that in the aggregate the market is not fooled by companies that choose the least-conservative accounting policies. In sum, the market as a whole generally sees through any attempts by companies to gain favor through the choice of accounting policies that tend to boost immediate income. Thus, there is evidence that the stock markets may indeed be "efficient," at least in their reflection of most accounting data.[3]

Objective 5
Identify the major implications that efficient stock markets have for accounting.

Suppose you are the chief executive officer of a company with reported earnings of $4 per share and a stock price of $40. You are contemplating changing your method of depreciation for investor-reporting purposes from accelerated to straight-line. Your competitors use straight-line. You think your company's stock price unjustifiably suffers in comparison with other companies in the same industry.

If straight-line depreciation is adopted, your company's reported earnings will be $5 instead of $4 per share. Would the stock price rise accordingly from $40 to $50? No, the research on these issues indicates that the stock price would remain at $40 (all other things equal).

Many managers share the chief executive's beliefs illustrated in the preceding example. They essentially adhere to an extremely narrow view of the role of an income statement. Such a "bottom-line" mentality is slowly, surely, and sensibly falling into disrepute. At the risk of unfair exaggeration, the view is summarized as

1. The income statement is the sole (or at least the primary) source of information about a company.
2. Lenders and shareholders invest in a company because of its reported earnings. For instance, the higher the reported earnings per share, the higher the stock price, and the easier it is to raise capital.

Basically, these arguments assume that investors can be misled by how companies measure reported earnings. But there is considerable evidence that securities markets are not fooled with respect to accounting changes that are devoid of economic substance (i.e., have no effect on cash flows). Why? Because the change generally reveals no new information, so no significant change in stock price is likely.

Remember that the market is efficient only with respect to publicly available information. Therefore, accounting issues that deal with the disclosure of new information are more important than those that simply change the format for reporting already available data.

Be aware also that accounting statements are not the only source of financial information about companies. Some alternative sources are the following: company press releases (e.g., capital expenditure announcements); trade association publications (e.g., reports with industry statistics); brokerage house analyses (e.g., company or industry studies); and government economic reports (e.g., gross national product and unemployment figures). If accounting reports are to be useful, they must have some advantage over alternative sources in disclosing new information. Financial statement information may be more directly related to the item of interest, and it may be more reliable, less costly, or more timely than information from alternative sources.

The research described previously concentrates on the effects of accounting on investors in the aggregate. Individual investors vary in how they analyze financial

---

[3] *Several "anomalies" prevent unqualified endorsement of stock market efficiency. Recent research shows that accounting data may be combined to yield information that is not reflected in stock prices. Nevertheless, the evidence that stock prices efficiently reflect basic accounting data is quite strong.*

statements. One by one, individual users must either incur the costs of conducting careful analyses or delegate that chore to professional analysts. In any event, intelligent analysis cannot be accomplished without an understanding of the assumptions and limitations of financial statements including the presence of various alternative accounting methods.

SUMMARY PROBLEM FOR YOUR REVIEW

PROBLEM

Examine Exhibits 18-4 and 18-5, pages 737–738. Assume some new data in place of certain old data for the June 30, 2000, balance sheet (in millions):

	Old Data	New Data
Accounts receivable	$ 3,250	$ 3,500
Total current assets	28,600	31,200
Paid-in capital	22,516	27,000
Total stockholders' equity	40,689	45,000

Compute the following ratios applicable to June 30, 2000, or to the fiscal year 2000, as appropriate: current ratio, average collection period, and return on stockholders' equity. Compare this new set of ratios with the old set of ratios. Are the new ratios more desirable? Explain.

SOLUTION

All the ratios would be affected.

$$\text{current ratio} = \frac{\text{current assets}}{\text{current liabilities}}$$

$$= \frac{\$31,200}{\$ 9,753} = 3.2 \text{ instead of } 2.9$$

$$\text{average collection period} = \frac{\text{average accounts receivable}}{\text{sales on account}} \times 365$$

$$= \frac{\frac{1}{2}(\$3,500 + \$2,245) \times 365}{\$22,956}$$

$$= \frac{\$2,872.5 \times 365}{\$22,956} = 46 \text{ days instead of } 44 \text{ days}$$

$$\text{return on stockholders' equity} = \frac{\text{net income}}{\text{average stockholders' equity}}$$

$$= \frac{\$9,421}{\frac{1}{2}(\$45,000 + \$28,438)}$$

$$= 25.7\% \text{ instead of } 27.3\%$$

The new set of ratios has good news and bad news. The good news is that the company would appear to be slightly more liquid (a current ratio of 3.2 instead of 2.9). The bad news is that the average collection period and the rate of return on stockholders' equity are less attractive.

Highlights to Remember: Part Two

Explain and use a variety of popular financial ratios.   Financial ratios aid the intelligent analysis of financial statements. To compare companies that differ in size, analysts use component percentages. They also prepare a variety of ratios and compare them with the company's own historical ratios, with general benchmarks, and with ratios of other companies or industry averages. They use short-term ratios, debt-to-equity ratios, profitability ratios, and dividend ratios. An especially important ratio for assessing operating performance is the rate of return on invested capital.

Identify the major implications that efficient stock markets have for accounting. Financial statements are only one source of information used by investors. Evidence indicates that stock prices fully reflect most publicly available information, including accounting numbers. The format of the information apparently does not fool investors. Therefore, accounting regulators should focus on disclosure issues, not format.

Understand how financial analysts use ratios and other analysis techniques to interpret the consolidated financial statements of a company.   Financial analysts and other investment advisors use financial statements to assess the prospects for companies that they consider for investment. They use the various ratios and other techniques shown in this chapter, together with other information, for the investment decisions.

B

FUNDAMENTALS OF COMPOUND INTEREST AND THE USE OF PRESENT-VALUE TABLES

NATURE OF INTEREST

Interest is the cost of using money. It is the rental charge for cash, just as rental charges are often made for the use of automobiles or boats.

Interest does not always entail an outlay of cash. The concept of interest applies to ownership funds as well as to borrowed funds. The reason why interest must be considered on *all* funds in use, regardless of their source, is that the selection of one alternative necessarily commits funds that could otherwise be invested in some other opportunity. The measure of the interest in such cases is the return foregone by rejecting the alternative use. For instance, a wholly owned home or business asset is not cost free. The funds so invested could alternatively be invested in government bonds or in some other venture. The measure of this opportunity cost depends on what alternative incomes are available.

Newspapers often contain advertisements of financial institutions citing interest rates that are "compounded." This appendix explains compound interest, including the use of present-value tables.

Simple interest is calculated by multiplying an interest rate by an unchanging principal amount. In contrast, *compound interest* is calculated by multiplying an interest rate by a principal amount that is increased each interest period by the previously accumulated (unpaid) interest. The accumulated interest is added to the principal to become the principal for the new period. For example, suppose you deposited $10,000 in a financial institution that promised to pay 10% interest per annum. You then let the amount accumulate for three years before withdrawing the full balance of the deposit. The *simple-interest* deposit would accumulate to $13,000 at the end of three years:

	Principal	Simple Interest	Balance, End of Year
Year 1	$10,000	$10,000 × 0.10 = $1,000	$11,000
Year 2	10,000	10,000 × 0.10 = 1,000	12,000
Year 3	10,000	10,000 × 0.10 = 1,000	13,000

Compound interest provides interest on interest. That is, the principal changes from period to period. The deposit would accumulate to $10,000 \times (1.10)^3 = \$10,000 \times 1.331 = \$13,310$:

	Principal	Compound Interest	Balance, End of Year
Year 1	$10,000	$10,000 × 0.10 = $1,000	$11,000
Year 2	11,000	11,000 × 0.10 = 1,100	12,100
Year 3	12,100	12,100 × 0.10 = 1,210	13,310

The "force" of compound interest can be staggering. For example, the same deposit would accumulate as follows:

	At End of		
	10 Years	*20 Years*	*40 Years*
Simple interest			
$10,000 + 10 ($1,000) =	$20,000		
10,000 + 20 ($1,000) =		$30,000	
10,000 + 40 ($1,000) =			$ 50,000
Compound interest			
$10,000 \times (1.10)^{10} = \$10,000 \times 2.5937 =$	$25,937		
$10,000 \times (1.10)^{20} = \$10,000 \times 6.7275 =$		$67,275	
$10,000 \times (1.10)^{40} = \$10,000 \times 45.2593 =$			$452,593

Hand calculations of compound interest quickly become burdensome. Therefore compound interest tables have been constructed to ease computations. (Indeed, many hand-held calculators contain programs that provide speedy answers.) Hundreds of tables are available, but we will use only the two most useful for capital budgeting.[1]

TABLE 1: PRESENT VALUE OF $1

How shall we express a future cash inflow or outflow in terms of its equivalent today (at time zero)? Table 1 provides factors that give the present value of a single, lump-sum cash flow to be received or paid at the end of a future period.[2]

Suppose you invest $1.00 today. It will grow to $1.06 in one year at six percent interest; that is, $1 \times 1.06 = \$1.06$. At the end of the second year its value is $(\$1 \times 1.06) \times 1.06 = \$1 \times (1.06)^2 = \$1.124$, and at the end of the third year it is $\$1 \times (1.06)^3 = 1.191$. In general, $1.00 grows to $(1 + i)^n$ in n years at i percent interest.

To determine *the present value*, you reverse this accumulation process. If $1.00 is to be received in one year, it is worth $1 \div 1.06 = \$0.9434$ today at an interest rate of 6%. Suppose you invest $0.9434 today. In one year you will have $0.9434 \times 1.06 = \$1.00$. Thus $0.9434 is the *present value* of $1.00 a year hence at 6%. If the dollar will be received in two years, its present value is $\$1.00 \div (1.06)^2 = \$0.8900$. The general formula for the present value (PV) of an amount S to be received or paid in n periods at an interest rate of i% per period is

$$PV = \frac{S}{(1 + i)^n}$$

Table 1 on page B7 gives factors for the present value of $1.00 at various interest rates over several different periods. Present values are also called *discounted* values, and the process of finding the present value is *discounting*. You can think of this as discounting

---

[1] *For additional tables, see R. Vichas,* Handbook of Financial Mathematics, Formulas and Tables *(Upper Saddle River, NJ: Prentice Hall, 1979).*

[2] *The factors are rounded to four decimal places. The examples in this text use these rounded factors. If you use tables with different rounding, or if you use a calculator or personal computer, your answers may differ from those given because of a small rounding error.*

(decreasing) the value of a future cash inflow or outflow. Why is the value discounted? Because the cash is to be received or paid in the future, not today.

Assume that a prominent city is issuing a 3-year non-interest-bearing note payable that promises to pay a lump sum of $1,000 exactly three years from now. You desire a rate of return of exactly 6%, compounded annually. How much would you be willing to pay now for the 3-year note? The situation is sketched as follows:

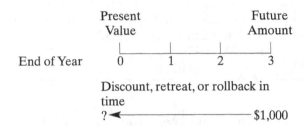

The factor in the period 3 row and 6% column of Table 1 is 0.8396. The present value of the $1,000 payment is $1,000 × 0.8396 = $839.60. You would be willing to pay $839.60 for the $1,000 to be received in three years.

Suppose interest is compounded semiannually rather than annually. How much would you be willing to pay? The three years become six interest payment periods. The rate per period is half the annual rate, or 6% ÷ 2 = 3%. The factor in the period 6 row and 3% column of Table 1 is 0.8375. You would be willing to pay $1,000 × 0.8375 or only $837.50 rather than $839.60.

As a further check on your understanding, review the earlier example of compound interest. Suppose the financial institution promised to pay $13,310 at the end of three years. How much would you be willing to deposit at time zero if you desired a 10% rate of return compounded annually? Using Table 1, the period 3 row and the 10% column show a factor of 0.7513. Multiply this factor by the future amount:

$$PV = 0.7513 \times \$13,310 = \$10,000$$

A diagram of this computation follows:

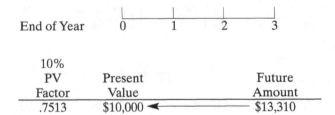

Pause for a moment. Use Table 1 to obtain the present values of

1. $1,700, at 20%, at the end of 20 years
2. $8,300, at 10%, at the end of 12 years
3. $8,000, at 4%, at the end of 4 years

Answers:

1. $1,700 (0.0261) = $44.37
2. $8,300 (0.3186) = $2,644.38
3. $8,000 (0.8548) = $6,838.40

TABLE 2: PRESENT VALUE OF AN ORDINARY ANNUITY OF $1

An ordinary annuity is a series of equal cash flows to take place at the end of successive periods of equal length. Its present value is denoted PV_A. Assume that you buy a note from a municipality that promises to pay $1,000 at the end of *each* of three years. How much should you be willing to pay if you desire a rate of return of 6%, compounded annually?

You could solve this problem using Table 1. First, find the present value of each payment, and then add the present values as in Exhibit B-1. You would be willing to pay $943.40 for the first payment, $890.00 for the second, and $839.60 for the third, a total of $2,673.00.

Since each cash payment is $1,000 with equal 1-year periods between them, the note is an ordinary annuity. Table 2 provides a shortcut method. The present value in Exhibit B-1 can be expressed as

$$PV_A = \$1,000 \times \frac{1}{1.06} + \$1,000 \times \frac{1}{(1.06)^2} + \$1,000 \times \frac{1}{(1.06)^3}$$

$$= \$1,000 \left[\frac{1}{1.06} + \frac{1}{(1.06)^2} + \frac{1}{(1.06)^3} \right]$$

The three terms in brackets are the first three numbers from the 6% column of Table 1, and their sum is in the third row of the 6% column of Table 2: .9434 + .8900 + .8396 = 2.6730. Instead of calculating three present values and adding them, you can simply multiply the PV factor from Table 2 by the cash payment: 2.6730 × $1,000 = $2,673.

This shortcut is especially valuable if the cash payments or receipts extend over many periods. Consider an annual cash payment of $1,000 for 20 years at 6%. The present value, calculated from Table 2, is $1,000 × 11.4699 = $11,469.90. To use Table 1 for this calculation, you would perform 20 multiplications and then add the twenty products.

The factors in Table 2 can be calculated using the following general formula:

$$PV_A = \frac{1}{i} \left[1 - \frac{1}{(1 + i)^n} \right]$$

Applied to our illustration:

$$PV_A = \frac{1}{.06} \left[1 - \frac{1}{(1.06)^3} \right] = \frac{1}{.06}(1 - .8396) = \frac{.1604}{.06} = 2.6730$$

Use Table 2 to obtain the present values of the following ordinary annuities:

1. $1,600 at 20% for 20 years
2. $8,300 at 10% for 12 years
3. $8,000 at 4% for 4 years

Exhibt B-1

Payment	End of Year Table One Factor	0 Present Value	1	2	3
1	$\frac{1}{1.06} = .9434$	$ 943.40	$1,000		
2	$\frac{1}{(1.06)^2} = .8900$	890.00		1,000	
3	$\frac{1}{(1.06)^3} = .8396$	839.60			$1,000
Total		$2,673.00			

Answers:

1. $1,600 (4.8696) = $7,791.36
2. $8,300 (6.8137) = $56,553.71
3. $8,000 (3.6299) = $29,039.20

In particular, note that the higher interest rate, the lower the present value.

Table I
Present Value of $1

$$PV = \frac{1}{(1+i)^n}$$

Periods	3%	4%	5%	6%	7%	8%	10%	12%	14%	16%	18%	20%	22%	24%	25%	26%	28%	30%	40%
1	.9709	.9615	.9524	.9434	.9346	.9259	.9091	.8929	.8772	.8621	.8475	.8333	.8197	.8065	.8000	.7937	.7813	.7692	.7143
2	.9426	.9246	.9070	.8900	.8734	.8573	.8264	.7972	.7695	.7432	.7182	.6944	.6719	.6504	.6400	.6299	.6104	.5917	.5102
3	.9151	.8890	.8638	.8396	.8163	.7938	.7513	.7118	.6750	.6407	.6086	.5787	.5507	.5245	.5120	.4999	.4768	.4552	.3644
4	.8885	.8548	.8227	.7921	.7629	.7350	.6830	.6355	.5921	.5523	.5158	.4823	.4514	.4230	.4096	.3968	.3725	.3501	.2603
5	.8626	.8219	.7835	.7473	.7130	.6806	.6209	.5674	.5194	.4761	.4371	.4019	.3700	.3411	.3277	.3149	.2910	.2693	.1859
6	.8375	.7903	.7462	.7050	.6663	.6302	.5645	.5066	.4556	.4104	.3704	.3349	.3033	.2751	.2621	.2499	.2274	.2072	.1328
7	.8131	.7599	.7107	.6651	.6227	.5835	.5132	.4523	.3996	.3538	.3139	.2791	.2486	.2218	.2097	.1983	.1776	.1594	.0949
8	.7894	.7307	.6768	.6274	.5820	.5403	.4665	.4039	.3506	.3050	.2660	.2326	.2038	.1789	.1678	.1574	.1388	.1226	.0678
9	.7664	.7026	.6446	.5919	.5439	.5002	.4241	.3606	.3075	.2630	.2255	.1938	.1670	.1443	.1342	.1249	.1084	.0943	.0484
10	.7441	.6756	.6139	.5584	.5083	.4632	.3855	.3220	.2697	.2267	.1911	.1615	.1369	.1164	.1074	.0992	.0847	.0725	.0346
11	.7224	.6496	.5847	.5268	.4751	.4289	.3505	.2875	.2366	.1954	.1619	.1346	.1122	.0938	.0859	.0787	.0662	.0558	.0247
12	.7014	.6246	.5568	.4970	.4440	.3971	.3186	.2567	.2076	.1685	.1372	.1122	.0920	.0757	.0687	.0625	.0517	.0429	.0176
13	.6810	.6006	.5303	.4688	.4150	.3677	.2897	.2292	.1821	.1452	.1163	.0935	.0754	.0610	.0550	.0496	.0404	.0330	.0126
14	.6611	.5775	.5051	.4423	.3878	.3405	.2633	.2046	.1597	.1252	.0985	.0779	.0618	.0492	.0440	.0393	.0316	.0254	.0090
15	.6419	.5553	.4810	.4173	.3624	.3152	.2394	.1827	.1401	.1079	.0835	.0649	.0507	.0397	.0352	.0312	.0247	.0195	.0064
16	.6232	.5339	.4581	.3936	.3387	.2919	.2176	.1631	.1229	.0930	.0708	.0541	.0415	.0320	.0281	.0248	.0193	.0150	.0046
17	.6050	.5134	.4363	.3714	.3166	.2703	.1978	.1456	.1078	.0802	.0600	.0451	.0340	.0258	.0225	.0197	.0150	.0116	.0033
18	.5874	.4936	.4155	.3503	.2959	.2502	.1799	.1300	.0946	.0691	.0508	.0376	.0279	.0208	.0180	.0156	.0118	.0089	.0023
19	.5703	.4746	.3957	.3305	.2765	.2317	.1635	.1161	.0829	.0596	.0431	.0313	.0229	.0168	.0144	.0124	.0092	.0068	.0017
20	.5537	.4564	.3769	.3118	.2584	.2145	.1486	.1037	.0728	.0514	.0365	.0261	.0187	.0135	.0115	.0098	.0072	.0053	.0012
21	.5375	.4388	.3589	.2942	.2415	.1987	.1351	.0926	.0638	.0443	.0309	.0217	.0154	.0109	.0092	.0078	.0056	.0040	.0009
22	.5219	.4220	.3418	.2775	.2257	.1839	.1228	.0826	.0560	.0382	.0262	.0181	.0126	.0088	.0074	.0062	.0044	.0031	.0006
23	.5067	.4057	.3256	.2618	.2109	.1703	.1117	.0738	.0491	.0329	.0222	.0151	.0103	.0071	.0059	.0049	.0034	.0024	.0004
24	.4919	.3901	.3101	.2470	.1971	.1577	.1015	.0659	.0431	.0284	.0188	.0126	.0085	.0057	.0047	.0039	.0027	.0018	.0003
25	.4776	.3751	.2953	.2330	.1842	.1460	.0923	.0588	.0378	.0245	.0160	.0105	.0069	.0046	.0038	.0031	.0021	.0014	.0002
26	.4637	.3607	.2812	.2198	.1722	.1352	.0839	.0525	.0331	.0211	.0135	.0087	.0057	.0037	.0030	.0025	.0016	.0011	.0002
27	.4502	.3468	.2678	.2074	.1609	.1252	.0763	.0469	.0291	.0182	.0115	.0073	.0047	.0030	.0024	.0019	.0013	.0008	.0001
28	.4371	.3335	.2551	.1956	.1504	.1159	.0693	.0419	.0255	.0157	.0097	.0061	.0038	.0024	.0019	.0015	.0010	.0006	.0001
29	.4243	.3207	.2429	.1846	.1406	.1073	.0630	.0374	.0224	.0135	.0082	.0051	.0031	.0020	.0015	.0012	.0008	.0005	.0001
30	.4120	.3083	.2314	.1741	.1314	.0994	.0573	.0334	.0196	.0116	.0070	.0042	.0026	.0016	.0012	.0010	.0006	.0004	.0000
40	.3066	.2083	.1420	.0972	.0668	.0460	.0221	.0107	.0053	.0026	.0013	.0007	.0004	.0002	.0001	.0001	.0001	.0000	.0000

Table 2
Present Value of Ordinary Annuity of $1

$$PV_A = \frac{1}{i}\left[1 - \frac{1}{(1+i)^n}\right]$$

Periods	3%	4%	5%	6%	7%	8%	10%	12%	14%	16%	18%	20%	22%	24%	25%	26%	28%	30%	40%
1	.9709	.9615	.9524	.9434	.9346	.9259	.9091	.8929	.8772	.8621	.8475	.8333	.8197	.8065	.8000	.7937	.7813	.7692	.7143
2	1.9135	1.8861	1.8594	1.8334	1.8080	1.7833	1.7355	1.6901	1.6467	1.6052	1.5656	1.5278	1.4915	1.4568	1.4400	1.4235	1.3916	1.3609	1.2245
3	2.8286	2.7751	2.7232	2.6730	2.6243	2.5771	2.4869	2.4018	2.3216	2.2459	2.1743	2.1065	2.0422	1.9813	1.9520	1.9234	1.8684	1.8161	1.5889
4	3.7171	3.6299	3.5460	3.4651	3.3872	3.3121	3.1699	3.0373	2.9137	2.7982	2.6901	2.5887	2.4936	2.4043	2.3616	2.3202	2.2410	2.1662	1.8492
5	4.5797	4.4518	4.3295	4.2124	4.1002	3.9927	3.7908	3.6048	3.4331	3.2743	3.1272	2.9906	2.8636	2.7454	2.6893	2.6351	2.5320	2.4356	2.0352
6	5.4172	5.2421	5.0757	4.9173	4.7665	4.6229	4.3553	4.1114	3.8887	3.6847	3.4976	3.3255	3.1669	3.0205	2.9514	2.8850	2.7594	2.6427	2.1680
7	6.2303	6.0021	5.7864	5.5824	5.3893	5.2064	4.8684	4.5638	4.2883	4.0386	3.8115	3.6046	3.4155	3.2423	3.1611	3.0833	2.9370	2.8021	2.2628
8	7.0197	6.7327	6.4632	6.2098	5.9713	5.7466	5.3349	4.9676	4.6389	4.3436	4.0776	3.8372	3.6193	3.4212	3.3289	3.2407	3.0758	2.9247	2.3306
9	7.7861	7.4353	7.1078	6.8017	6.5152	6.2469	5.7590	5.3282	4.9464	4.6065	4.3030	4.0310	3.7863	3.5655	3.4631	3.3657	3.1842	3.0190	2.3790
10	8.5302	8.1109	7.7217	7.3601	7.0236	6.7101	6.1446	5.6502	5.2161	4.8332	4.4941	4.1925	3.9232	3.6819	3.5705	3.4648	3.2689	3.0915	2.4136
11	9.2526	8.7605	8.3064	7.8869	7.4987	7.1390	6.4951	5.9377	5.4527	5.0286	4.6560	4.3271	4.0354	3.7757	3.6564	3.5435	3.3351	3.1473	2.4383
12	9.9540	9.3851	8.8633	8.3838	7.9427	7.5361	6.8137	6.1944	5.6603	5.1971	4.7932	4.4392	4.1274	3.8514	3.7251	3.6059	3.3868	3.1903	2.4559
13	10.6350	9.9856	9.3936	8.8527	8.3577	7.9038	7.1034	6.4235	5.8424	5.3423	4.9095	4.5327	4.2028	3.9124	3.7801	3.6555	3.4272	3.2233	2.4685
14	11.2961	10.5631	9.8986	9.2950	8.7455	8.2442	7.3667	6.6282	6.0021	5.4675	5.0081	4.6106	4.2646	3.9616	3.8241	3.6949	3.4587	3.2487	2.4775
15	11.9379	11.1184	10.3797	9.7122	9.1079	8.5595	7.6061	6.8109	6.1422	5.5755	5.0916	4.6755	4.3152	4.0013	3.8593	3.7261	3.4834	3.2682	2.4839
16	12.5611	11.6523	10.8378	10.1059	9.4466	8.8514	7.8237	6.9740	6.2651	5.6685	5.1624	4.7296	4.3567	4.0333	3.8874	3.7509	3.5026	3.2832	2.4885
17	13.1661	12.1657	11.2741	10.4773	9.7632	9.1216	8.0216	7.1196	6.3729	5.7487	5.2223	4.7746	4.3908	4.0591	3.9099	3.7705	3.5177	3.2948	2.4918
18	13.7535	12.6593	11.6896	10.8276	10.0591	9.3719	8.2014	7.2497	6.4674	5.8178	5.2732	4.8122	4.4187	4.0799	3.9279	3.7861	3.5294	3.3037	2.4941
19	14.3238	13.1339	12.0853	11.1581	10.3356	9.6036	8.3649	7.3658	6.5504	5.8775	5.3162	4.8435	4.4415	4.0967	3.9424	3.7985	3.5386	3.3105	2.4958
20	14.8775	13.5903	12.4622	11.4699	10.5940	9.8181	8.5136	7.4694	6.6231	5.9288	5.3527	4.8696	4.4603	4.1103	3.9539	3.8083	3.5458	3.3158	2.4970
21	15.4150	14.0292	12.8212	11.7641	10.8355	10.0168	8.6487	7.5620	6.6870	5.9731	5.3837	4.8913	4.4756	4.1212	3.9631	3.8161	3.5514	3.3198	2.4979
22	15.9369	14.4511	13.1630	12.0416	11.0612	10.2007	8.7715	7.6446	6.7429	6.0113	5.4099	4.9094	4.4882	4.1300	3.9705	3.8223	3.5558	3.3230	2.4985
23	16.4436	14.8568	13.4886	12.3034	11.2722	10.3711	8.8832	7.7184	6.7921	6.0442	5.4321	4.9245	4.4985	4.1371	3.9764	3.8273	3.5592	3.3254	2.4989
24	16.9355	15.2470	13.7986	12.5504	11.4693	10.5288	8.9847	7.7843	6.8351	6.0726	5.4509	4.9371	4.5070	4.1428	3.9811	3.8312	3.5619	3.3272	2.4992
25	17.4131	15.6221	14.0939	12.7834	11.6536	10.6748	9.0770	7.8431	6.8729	6.0971	5.4669	4.9476	4.5139	4.1474	3.9849	3.8342	3.5640	3.3286	2.4994
26	17.8768	15.9828	14.3752	13.0032	11.8258	10.8100	9.1609	7.8957	6.9061	6.1182	5.4804	4.9563	4.5196	4.1511	3.9879	3.8367	3.5656	3.3297	2.4996
27	18.3270	16.3296	14.6430	13.2105	11.9867	10.9352	9.2372	7.9426	6.9352	6.1364	5.4919	4.9636	4.5243	4.1542	3.9903	3.8387	3.5669	3.3305	2.4997
28	18.7641	16.6631	14.8981	13.4062	12.1371	11.0511	9.3066	7.9844	6.9607	6.1520	5.5016	4.9697	4.5281	4.1566	3.9923	3.8402	3.5679	3.3312	2.4998
29	19.1885	16.9837	15.1411	13.5907	12.2777	11.1584	9.3696	8.0218	6.9830	6.1656	5.5098	4.9747	4.5312	4.1585	3.9938	3.8414	3.5687	3.3317	2.4999
30	19.6004	17.2920	15.3725	13.7648	12.4090	11.2578	9.4269	8.0552	7.0027	6.1772	5.5168	4.9789	4.5338	4.1601	3.9950	3.8424	3.5693	3.3321	2.4999
40	23.1148	19.7928	17.1591	15.0463	13.3317	11.9246	9.7791	8.2438	7.1050	6.2335	5.5482	4.9966	4.5439	4.1659	3.9995	3.8458	3.5712	3.3332	2.5000